American Arabesque

America and the Long 19th Century

GENERAL EDITORS
David Kazanjian, Elizabeth McHenry, and Priscilla Wald

Black Frankenstein: The Making of an American Metaphor
Elizabeth Young

*Neither Fugitive nor Free: Atlantic Slavery, Freedom Suits,
and the Legal Culture of Travel*
Edlie L. Wong

*Shadowing the White Man's Burden: U.S. Imperialism
and the Problem of the Color Line*
Gretchen Murphy

Bodies of Reform: The Rhetoric of Character in Gilded Age America
James B. Salazar

*Empire's Proxy: American Literature and U.S. Imperialism
in the Philippines*
Meg Wesling

Sites Unseen: Architecture, Race, and American Literature
William A. Gleason

*Racial Innocence: Performing American Childhood
from Slavery to Civil Rights*
Robin Bernstein

*American Arabesque: Arabs, Islam, and the
19th-Century Imaginary*
Jacob Rama Berman

American Arabesque

Arabs, Islam, and the
19th-Century Imaginary

Jacob Rama Berman

NEW YORK UNIVERSITY PRESS

New York and London

NEW YORK UNIVERSITY PRESS
New York and London
www.nyupress.org

LIBRARY OF CONGRESS CATALOGING-IN-PUBLICATION DATA

Berman, Jacob Rama.
American arabesque : Arabs, Islam, and the 19th-century imaginary /
Jacob Rama Berman.
p. cm. — (America and the long 19th century)
Includes bibliographical references and index.
ISBN-13: 978-0-8147-8950-6 (cloth : acid-free paper)
ISBN-10: 0-8147-8950-1 (cloth : acid-free paper)
ISBN-13: 978-0-8147-4518-2 (pbk. : acid-free paper)
ISBN-10: 0-8147-4518-0 (pbk. : acid-free paper)
[etc.]
1. American literature—19th century—History and
criticism.   2. Arabs in literature.   3. National characteristics,
American, in literature.   4. Islam in literature.   5. Arabs—Race
identity.   6. National characteristics, American—History—19th
century.   I. Title.
PS217.A72B47   2012
810.9'3529927—dc23

2011043495

References to Internet websites (URLs) were accurate at the time of
writing. Neither the author nor New York University Press is responsible
for URLs that may have expired or changed since the manuscript was
prepared.

New York University Press books are printed on acid-free paper,
and their binding materials are chosen for strength and durability.
We strive to use environmentally responsible suppliers and materials
to the greatest extent possible in publishing our books.

Manufactured in the United States of America
c 10 9 8 7 6 5 4 3 2 1
p 10 9 8 7 6 5 4 3 2 1

THE
AMERICAN
LITERATURES
INITIATIVE

A book in the American Literatures Initiative (ALI), a collaborative
publishing project of NYU Press, Fordham University Press, Rutgers
University Press, Temple University Press, and the University of Virginia
Press. The Initiative is supported by The Andrew W. Mellon Foundation.
For more information, please visit www.americanliteratures.org.

To الشباب
and their Arab Spring

Contents

Preface

Roadside Attraction

Every January 10, the desert city of Quartzite, Arizona, holds a festival in honor of the "Syrian" camel driver Hi Jolly. Often cited as the first Arab to make his permanent residence in America, Hi Jolly arrived in the United States in 1856 as part of Jefferson Davis's Fort Tejon Camel Corp experiment. The story of the Camel Corps is a story of fascinating failure. Davis sought to provide a reliable long-distance supply system for the dispersed forts on the frontier and commissioned forty or so camels to be shipped to the American Southwest from the Levant for that purpose. The camels performed well, but the outbreak of the Civil War made their job obsolete. Most of the dromedaries were dispersed in the desert. Eventually they entered into the myth of the American West spawning numerous folk tales and ghost stories. Reportedly the camels were last sighted as late as 1946. A man named Hadji Ali was among the camel drivers who accompanied the beasts of burden from the Levant. When the camels were released, Ali remained in the Arizona territory, occupying a number of colorful jobs before his death in 1902. A pyramidal monument marks Ali's gravesite in Quartzite's pioneer cemetery (figure 1). Atop the tomb is a bronze camel.

The Hi Jolly Memorial is significant not because it marks the burial site of the "first Arab" to live in America but rather because it demonstrates the role of translation in creating American images of the Arab, in creating American arabesques. The plaque adjacent to Ali's tomb explains that because the soldiers whom the "Syrian" was tasked with training in the ways of the camel could not pronounce "Hadji Ali," they changed it to "Hi Jolly." Hadji Ali signifies, to a speaker of Arabic, a devout man who has made a pilgrimage to Mecca in accordance with religious duty. Hi Jolly, to an English speaker, is a somewhat ridiculous name that evokes laughter even as it speaks to the incongruity of a Levantine camel driver trying to

Figure 1. Hi Jolly Memorial, Quartzite, Arizona. Photograph by Jacob Rama Berman.

make his fortune on the nineteenth-century American frontier. Both significations, in their own cultural context, are appropriate nominations for the man behind the name. But between the two there is a cultural gap, one that can only be bridged by attention to the multiple linguistic registers the name evokes.

The name Hadji Ali is Arab. The name Hi Jolly is an arabesque—an imitation of the original that translates its meaning into a new cultural context. American arabesques emerge from the contact between Americans and Arab culture. *American Arabesque* traces the influence of this contact on the literary formation of nineteenth-century American identity. It is my argument that in the nineteenth century, Arabo-Islamic figures were woven into the very fabric of American culture. To dismiss the presence of referents such as Sherezade, Mecca, Alhambra, and the Sahara in contemporary America as kitsch or as mere adornment is to ignore the deep influence Arab culture has had and continues to have on the American imaginary, both national and personal.

The plaque relating the details of Hadji Ali's American name change also relays the tantalizing piece of information that the camel driver had a Greek name, reading "His Greek (?) name was Philip Tedro." The bracketed question mark embedded in the official history of Hi Jolly speaks volumes about the vernacular slippages of his identity. Was this putative first Arab resident in America actually a Greek man born in Smyrna who then converted to Islam and took the Hajj (thus acquiring the nickname "Hadji")? Research on Philip Tedro reveals several sources devoted to the man's Greek ancestry. These sources claim Hi Jolly as a pioneer Greek American. When later in life Ali/Jolly/Tedro married a woman from Tucson, he insisted on his Greek ethnicity (perhaps in order to avoid racist marriage restrictions). Yet his daughters were purportedly raised as Muslims. Other men in the group of Levantine camel drivers brought over in 1856 are alternately identified as Arabs, Turks, and Greeks in historical accounts. What would it mean if Hadji Ali was not an Arab from Syria but rather a mixed Greek-Syrian who took an Arab name?

Hadji Ali's multiplicity of names gesture toward the profound cultural multiplicity of the nineteenth-century Levantine context from which he hails. The competing claims about Hi Jolly's origin and legacy demonstrate that European, Turkish, and Arab culture are often blended in nineteenth-century American representations of the Orient. On the whole, whether a person is marked as a Turk, an Arab, an Oriental, a Syrian, or a Muslim has much more to do with an American context than it has to do with the actual cultural or ethnic background of the subject. The mystery surrounding Ali/Tedro indexes larger questions about the American imaginary and the place Arab and Islamic culture hold in it. What does it mean exactly to be Arab? For my purposes, what does it mean to be called an Arab in nineteenth-century America? How and when was being Arab different from being a Turk, a Syrian, a Jew, or an Oriental in American nomenclature? What are the stakes when these delineations are made?

Acknowledgments

The inspiration for this book is the time I have spent in North Africa, the Arabian Peninsula, and the Near East. The people I met in these places, the stories I heard, and the things I have learned and unlearned about Arabo-Islamic culture motivated me to take a closer look at its representation in American literature. I had long felt that the narrative about Orientalist aesthetics dominating the conversation in the American academy told only part of the story. It took actual and prolonged first-hand contact with the Arabo-Islamic world to open my eyes and ears to the other parts.

This book has many translators, men, women, and organizations that have helped me turn ideas into words on the page. To Elsie Michie I owe a debt beyond my capacity to describe. The ultimate fruition of this book would be inconceivable without her patient engagement with both its ideas and its writing style. At every turn and with every read, Elsie has made this book better. I also owe a tremendous debt to my close friend, the indefatigable Matthew Sandler. Matt's perspicacity, referential capacity, and sympathetic intelligence made this project a pleasure to share and were integral to its final improvements. I have received particularly illuminating commentary on sections of this book from Wail Hassan, Courtney Thorssen, Lauren Coats, Akram Khater, and Hester Blum. The engagement of these particular scholars is especially gratifying because of the immense respect I have for their own work in both American Studies and Arab American Studies. Lily Balloffet has been an invaluable resource for me as well, and this book has benefited incalculably from her historical knowledge, perceptive eye, and sensitive ear.

I thank Ivy Wilson for lending his considerable talents to *American Arabesque* in a number of ways both material and spiritual. I benefited a great deal from an invitation Ivy extended to me to present at a Nineteenth-Century American Literature conference he organized in the spring of 2008 at Notre Dame University. I received generous input on my project that weekend from Dana Nelson, Chris Castiglia, Rodrigo Lazlo, David Luis-Brown, Glenn Hendler, and Chris Freeburg. This is also where I met David Kazanjian, who had the faith in the book that eventually led to my connection with NYU Press. The staff at NYU Press has made the experience of publishing my first book a pleasure from start to finish. To Eric Zinner and Ciara McLaughlin I extend my personal appreciation for your warmth and professionalism. I also would like to give a heartfelt thank you to the series editors, Priscilla Wald, Elizabeth McHenry, and David Kazanjian. My pride in the work I have produced is augmented by the superior quality of the scholarship these three editors have produced individually.

This book would not be possible without the institutional guidance, support, and training I have received over the years. From my time at the University of Chicago, I want to thank Gerald Graff, William Veeder, J. M. Coetzee, and Robert von Hallberg in particular for helping me hone the craft of research. I took a class with Bill Brown in the spring of 1996 that opened my eyes to the wonderful complications of nineteenth-century American literature, and for that, I thank him as well. At the University of California, Santa Barbara, I learned what it meant to be a professional scholar and teacher from the examples of Maurizia Boscagli, Giles Gunn, Chris Newfield, Aranya Fradenburg, and Dwight Reynolds. Maurizia's intellectual honesty and scholarly rigor still drives me to do better and think smarter. Giles always asked me the right questions, the ones that made me puzzle through my arguments from a different vantage point. Chris's enviable talent of distilling complex phenomena and sophisticated analysis into straightforward language has taught me a great deal about what good writing looks like. Aranya nurtured my propensity to make counterintuitive connections, and she encouraged me to take risks, for which I am forever grateful. I would also like to thank Rita Raley and Stephanie LeManager, both of whom gave me timely writing advice when they easily and justifiably could have demurred. Dwight is everything you could ever hope for in an intellectual interlocutor—incisive, knowledgeable, and demanding. He is also the most inspiring language teacher I have ever had. The classic Arabic poems you made me memorize, Dwight, have unlocked countless smiles and doors for me. I thank Magda Campo, Sandra Campbell, and Dwight for setting me on the path to speaking, reading, and writing Arabic. The job of a language teacher demands patience and passion. These three have an enormous supply of both. I would also like to thank the teachers and the staff at the Yemen Language

Center in Sana'a, Yemen, and at ALIF in Fez, Morocco. My experience in both Yemen and Morocco was immeasurably improved by the graciousness, hospitality, and kindness of the people who work at these two language centers. The English Department at Louisiana State University has provided me with all the intellectual camaraderie I could have ever hoped for. I am especially thankful for the various forms of support extended by J. Gerald Kennedy and Rick Moreland. Jerry's expertise in all things Poe is an invaluable resource, but even more importantly, for me, he has always been open to entertaining a different perspective on subjects in which he is the expert.

The book never would have been completed without the financial and temporal support provided by fellowships. During my time at graduate school in California, I received multiple Foreign Language and Area Studies Fellowships from the U.S. government. Without the FLAS awards, I would not have been able to travel to the Arab world for study and research. These stints abroad changed the very fabric of my project and helped me develop the language skills necessary to write the kind of book I believe in. The University of California also generously supported my project while I was in graduate school, in the form of several research fellowships and a President's Dissertation Year Fellowship. The funding and teaching releases I was afforded as a result of this support allowed me to spend essential time with the archives at the Huntington Library in Pasadena, California. I would like to thank the staff at the Huntington Library for their attention and assistance. The Office of Research and Development at Louisiana State University has provided welcome financial support for this project in the form of a generous year-long research travel fellowship and two summer research stipends. These awards allowed me to give sedulous attention to archives at the Library of Congress in Washington, D.C., at the New York Public Library's main branch, at the American Antiquarian Society in Worcester, Massachusetts, and at the Schomburg Center for Research in Black Culture. I would also like to thank the staffs at these libraries for their help, as well as their patience.

There have been many who have shaped this book in more informal ways. Dan Binkiewicz, Vaughn Montgomery, Adam Durflinger, Magaly Carranza, Teddy Macker, Laura Macker, Ryan Goodspeed, Aysha Hidayatullah, Aaron Tapper, Layla Lyne-Winkler, Jason Loverti, Chris Holmes, Rand Dotson, Todd Hedge, Sherri Folk, Hannah Shaw, and Ken Shaw have all, at one time or another, given me a reason to write something that matters. If I ever wondered why I was writing the book, I almost always thought of one of them. Finally, I thank Richard and Elizabeth Berman, my parents. This book is full of words, but I still don't possess the ones that express how much I love you. I am grateful to the end for your steadfast belief in me.

An early version of chapter 1 appeared in the journal *American Literature*, and an early version of chapter 3 appeared in the journal *ESC: English Studies in Canada.*

Introduction

Guest Figures

In nineteenth-century American discourse, the term *Arab* is often figurative. *Arab* could and did indicate an intermediary position between foreigner and citizen, black and white, primitive and civilized. Literate black slaves on the Southern plantation, American Indians on the western frontier, and new immigrants in the urban slum were all, at one time or another, referred to as Arabs. The discursive creation of these figurative Arabs speaks to the shifting racial parameters of American citizenship, as well as to American writers' propensity to use foreign references to redefine those parameters. Figurative Arabs thus acted as cross-cultural references that destabilized the very terms of identification by which American national discourse distinguished the United States as a historically and spatially unique entity. *American Arabesque* provides an account of why these figurative Arabs of American literature were created and how they influenced definitions of national belonging. The mutability of the term *Arab* reveals American racial categories fluctuating in response to crises of national identity, such as slavery, westward expansion, and immigration. But tracking the figure of the Arab also demonstrates that the category of American citizenship was shaped by transnational phenomena such as Barbary captivity, Near Eastern travel, and Orientalist romance.

Of course, not all Arabs in nineteenth-century American discourse are figurative. By the end of the century, the first wave of "Arab" immigration touched American shores. These migrants, predominantly Christians from the Mount Lebanon area, inherited an American narrative on the Arabo-Islamic world that predated their physical presence in the country. How these migrants, and other groups such as African American Muslims, reconciled their own sense of Arab and/or Islamic identity with this Orientalist narrative to create minority claims to American citizenship is the other half of the story *American Arabesque* tells. In my analysis of the recurring image of the Arab in American literature, I demonstrate that figures of the Arab not only were used to create fantasies of national unity, but they also generate alternative visions of American belonging.

Let me begin by stretching out the theoretical canvas that puts this book's methodological intervention in perspective. Edward Said's general premise in his landmark study *Orientalism* is that the West creates the Orient as an object of self-contemplation. But as Said himself points out in his final collection of printed essays, *Humanism and Democratic Criticism*, the book *Orientalism* fails to fully account for the manifold question of agency: the agency of the Western critic, the agency of the Eastern artist, the agency of humanists both receiving and resisting the tradition they inherit.[1] As a result, the Orient of the imagination still too often replaces the concrete Arab world and real Arabic words of thinkers such as Ibn Khaldun, Ibn Battutah, Ibn Arabi, and Ali Ahmed Sa'id (Adonis) as a source of literary inquiry. Constructing a critique of Western identity politics that incorporates the writings of the Arab world is integral to answering the elusive question of agency, as well as the lingering question of what the Orient represents and how the Orient as a concept shapes modern subjectivity. This step toward intercultural dialectic is essential if the literary study of the Orient in the Western academy is going to produce critical interventions that do more than detail co-option, misrepresentation, and the discursive practices of hegemony.

Albert Hourani's *Arabic Thought in the Liberal Age, 1798–1939* is an account of how various prominent nineteenth-century Arab intellectuals encountered, wrestled with, and transformed the terms of Western modernity to fit an Arab, Islamic, and/or Arabo-Islamic worldview. It provides, in many ways, the other half of the story Said tells about the West creating a fantasy Orient. Men such as the al-Azhar sheikh Rifa'a al-Tahtawi were active, if largely ignored, participants in modernity and formative influences on how its terms were interpreted in relation to Arab, Islamic, and Arabo-Islamic identity. Sent by Muhammad Ali to Paris in 1826, al-Tahtawi returned five years later and eventually published an account of his impressions of French society in 1834. He also undertook a massive program of translating French scientific, cultural, and philosophical works into Arabic. Al-Tahtawi introduced "modern" terms such as *patriotism* into Arab political consciousness and Arabic vernacular by creating conversations between French Enlightenment thinkers such as Montesquieu and classic Arab philosophers of the state such as Ibn Khaldun. The progressive and nationalist strains of Arab thought that found expression in al-Tahtawi's political philosophy were taken up by artists and intellectuals of a later generation often referred to as the Arab Renaissance, or *al Nahdah* (النهضة).

Al-Tahtawi's views of the state were enacted on a literal, territorial level by the monarch he served, Egypt's great nineteenth-century modernizer Muhammad Ali. Though Ali's military, political, educational, social, and technical reforms were more successful and sweeping than those of other mid-nineteenth-century Arab statesman, they were part and parcel of a period in which "Arabic-speaking peoples were drawn, in different ways, into the new world order which sprang from the technical and industrial revolutions" of Europe and America.[2] This period, marked by prominent debates about reform and the compatibility of European liberalism with Islamic law as well as Arab cultural identity, is what Hourani refers to as the "liberal age." Men such as al-Tahtawi provide a vocabulary for Arabo-Islamic encounters with the West. It is not enough, I believe, to read Arab writers and American writers side by side; they must be made to converse. Placing the writings of al-Tahtawi in the context of his contemporary Edgar Allan Poe or the nation-state-building practices of Muhammad Ali in the context of Andrew Jackson's policy of Indian removal does more than ground the fantasy Orient of nineteenth-century American literature in lived experience. This contrapuntal approach creates an opportunity to reformulate the parameters of American Studies.

Recent critical interventions such as those compiled by Amy Kaplan and Donald Pease in *Cultures of United States Imperialism,* or those explored by Wai Chee Dimock and Lawrence Buell in *Shades of the Planet,* have emphasized the importance of recognizing alternative origin narratives in the formation of American national culture. These origin narratives, the argument goes, challenge a view of America as bounded by the physical parameters of the United States.[3] My own emphasis on images of the Arab and references to Islam troubles conceptions of American culture as formed by Judeo-Christian genealogies and European lineages.[4] By looking at American culture through the lens of the Arabic language and American history through the filter of Arabo-Islamic history I aim to destabilize the nation's founding narratives of identity and reconceptualize their message from a different vantage point.[5] Acknowledging the presence of the Arab embedded within icons of American identity formation erodes superficial dichotomies such as East and West, revealing the strata of cultural interpenetration that undergird exceptionalist national fantasies.

"We are bound together because we inhabit the *political* space of the nation," explains Lauren Berlant, "which is not just juridical (*jus soli*), genetic (*jus sanguinis*), linguistic, or experiential, but some tangled cluster of these."[6] Berlant calls this space of American group identification the "National Symbolic" and argues that it aims to link affect to political life through the production of national fantasy. National fantasy creates "citizens" by connecting narratives of national identity to "more local and personal forms of identification."[7] National fantasy, in other words, can counteract the alienating element of national identification, the fact that it requires self-ablation, by binding national narratives to personal narratives. Critics such as Berlant and Dana D. Nelson have demonstrated the double movement of national fantasy and its legal counterpart, national citizenship. American citizenship disembodies the material individual in order to embody virtually the abstract notion of the nation in images, sites, and narratives that can then be reabsorbed as personalized expressions of group identity. These abstractions mediate the national symbolic through fantasy. That is, these abstractions remove racial, ethnic, religious, and cultural difference to create a national identity. But, as critics such as David Kazanjian have argued, erasures of difference are often recursive in that they simultaneously work to inscribe a normative (white, Christian, European) particularity into the putatively universal national identity.

The dialectic between amelioration and alienation played out through national fantasy resonates with the etymology of the word for translation in Arabic, *tarjamah* (ترْخمة). "*Tarjamah*, therefore, carries connotations of alienated speech that has the flavor of falsehood, damnation, and death," Wail Hassan explains, "but also possibilities of survival, narration, and understanding."[8] *American Arabesque* does more than suggest that American citizenship is a form of translation. It argues that aesthetic abstractions of material Arab culture limn the affinities between representing Arabs and creating American citizens. What if key national fantasies turn on the translation of Arabo-Islamic referents into American cultural property? What if references to the Arab world are integral to the mediation between citizen and nation? What if one of the basic discursive articulations connecting, as well as dividing, the American citizen and his or her foreign "other" is representations of the Arab? What can nineteenth-century American literature reveal to us about the continuing use of the image of the Arab to unify the "political space" of the American nation? What affect do images of the Arab conjure, and how is that affect related to the creation of American identity?

Questions such as these treat literature as a significant mediator of national fantasy. The aesthetics literature promotes are a window into both the effort to unite the individual citizen to the dominant values of the national culture and the effort to challenge and reconstitute those values. Nineteenth-century American writers who traded in Orientalism, regardless of their personal politics or individual relationship to structures of power, produced an archive of imagery that attests to the American public's taste for representations of Arabs and Islam: their taste for the arabesque. *American Arabesque* examines this taste for the Arab not only to provide evidence of literature's capacity to normalize imperialist, colonialist, and racist values but also to exercise the critic's right to deconstruct and reconstruct those values from multiple and often historically occluded perspectives. In this sense, the literary critic engages in forms of translation and retranslation, asserting his or her agency in relation to an archive that has many voices, as well as many silences.

Wai Chee Dimock, in her book *Through Other Continents*, demonstrates how the scope of American Studies is broadened when American literature is read comparatively and across "deep time."[9] I would suggest that while these comparative approaches reveal cultural connections worth exploring, they also divulge the misappropriations that more often than not define American literary representations of ostensibly foreign cultures. I am interested in fleshing out cultural continua lurking within American representations of the Arab, but I acknowledge that cultural exchange is characterized by definitional co-option and seizure as much as it is by reciprocity and mutuality. When a word is borrowed, it is often never returned or, more likely, returned in a radically altered condition. To fully appreciate the stakes in the act of borrowing, it is necessary to understand the context out of which something was taken. The "possibilities for survival, narration, and understanding" emerge when the image of the Arab in American literature is reconnected with the cultural contexts from which it was wrested. The goal is not to salvage the pure products of any language or culture but rather to watch them as they go wild.

Approaches to literary and linguistic exchange such as Dimock's "deep time" or Homi Bhabha's "hybridity" celebrate cross-cultural miscegenation, misinterpretation, and misappropriation as signs of a triumphant multiculturalism and evidence of practices of marginal resistance to master narratives of the nation. The often unabashed embrace of the contaminated products of cultural translation, however, is usefully balanced against other, more conservative views of cultural identity. These other voices point to the epistemic violence the Moroccan critic Abdelfattah Kilito argues is the condition of all translation. In his book *Thou Shalt Not Speak My Tongue*, Kilito discusses the Arabic notion of *adab* (أدب), which refers to both "good manners" and "literature." After cultivating sensitivity for *adab*'s range of meaning, Kilito points his reader to the expression "we are all guests of language." Kilito uses the idea of the guest and its intertwining senses in Arabic of chivalric and literary civility to make a stunning admission: "one day I realized I dislike having foreigners speak my language."¹⁰ It is not only that a history of colonialism and cultural hegemony in North Africa has revealed Western Orientalists to be rude guests. It is not only the humiliating reversal whereby Arab writers in the era of Ibn Khaldun could expect everyone else to learn Arabic in order to be considered literate, but Arabs in the contemporary world are compelled to learn other languages in order to be considered literate.¹¹ In hearing Arabic on the tongue of foreigners, Kilito is struck with the fear that he may lose his language to foreigners, that he may be robbed of his cultural identity. Kilito's book addresses a history of translation that is not one of cultural exchange but rather of warfare. The stakes in translation, then, are high—the extinction of that which makes Arabs unique (Arabic) or, at the very least, the occupation of the Arabic language by foreigners. Kilito reminds us that language, like physical space, can be the victim of colonialism.

By focusing on both American and Arab literary traditions, I mark the epistemic violence that is the source of Kilito's anxiety and cultivate an appreciation for the original meanings of Arabic terms. But origins, of course, are disappearing points, and words are always undergoing definitional transformations. In this sense, Arab phrases, words, and terms borrowed by American writers are not properly any culture's property. Tracking a word's transformation over time and/or space is the point, as well as a path that connects cultural traditions that are too often separated by prejudices of discipline, ideology, or language. The result is a study that uses the dynamics of translation to interpret the national fantasies that

American literature perpetuates and to highlight the stakes inherent in forming national identities through figurative representation.

The Persian scholar Abd al-Qahir al-Jurjani, in his eleventh-century treatise on rhetoric, *Asrar al-Balagha* (اسرار البلاغة; *The Secrets of Eloquence*), introduces Arabic's first qualitative classification of figurative language (مجاز/*majaaz*).[12] Differentiating simile from metaphor and several types of metaphoric comparison from one another, al-Jurjani stresses the importance of context, both linguistic and nonlinguistic, to understanding the expressive power of a word. Al-Jurjani distinguished himself from his predecessors in the field by creating a method that focuses not on what a figure *is* but rather on what a figure *does* to create various modes of meaning.[13] *Majaaz*, al-Jurjani argues, occurs when a word references something other than what it was coined to mean. This second, or nonliteral, meaning arises out of a perceptual connection that the reader/listener recognizes between the two denotations of the word. The most sophisticated *majaaz* allow words to mean two different things at the same time. Literary tropes, in other words, involve a temporary transfer of meaning, or what al-Jurjani refers to as a "borrowing." A person's delight in these borrowings increases proportionally to the difference between the two objects brought together. Discussing a form of abstract comparison known as *tamtheel* (تمثيل), al-Jurjani suggests that figurative language brings "a harmony to the unharmonious as if shortening the distance between East and West, making opposites agree, and uniting life and death, fire and water."[14]

A brief introduction to Islamic literary hermeneutics contextualizes al-Jurjani's approach to figurative language. The practice of Islamic literary hermeneutics grows out of the need to understand ambiguous Qur'anic passages known as *mutashaabih* (متشابه), a term derived from the root شبه, suggesting similarity. The difficulty with interpreting *mutashaabih* is not only that they lend themselves to more than one similar meaning. It is also that, as some Islamic scholars argue, the literal sense of these passages is not the same as their real message.[15] The possibility, as well as the danger, of interpreting *mutashaabih* verses is referenced in the Qur'an:

> He sent down to you this scripture, containing straightforward verses—which constitute the essence of the scripture—as well as multiple-meaning or allegorical verses (*mutashaabih*). Those who harbor doubts in their hearts will pursue the multiple-meaning verses to create confusion, and to extricate a certain meaning. None knows the true meaning thereof except

GOD and those well founded in knowledge. They say, "We believe in this—
all of it comes from our Lord." Only those who possess intelligence will
take heed. (3:7)[16]

Understood by some Islamic scholars as an implicit invitation to decipher
mutashaabih, the passage gave impetus to the practice of *taa'weel* (تأويل),
or figurative interpretation. *Taa'weel* is the act of bringing a word back to
its origin or archetype in order to reveal a verse's "true" meaning.[17] In a
treatise that extends Islamic hermeneutic principles to pre-Islamic Arab
poetry and literature in general, al-Jurjani argues that interpreting figurative language reveals the secret affinities in the world and synthesizes
apparent opposites. This aesthetic observation has an essential religious
connotation for al-Jurjani. *Majaaz* exercises Arabic language's sacred
power. Figurative language, in al-Jurjani's assessment, is a vehicle of revelation that confirms the Islamic creed of unity.

Al-Jurjani wrote in a historical moment when debates over figurative
language and the legitimacy of the exegetical method known as *taa'weel*
divided Islamic intellectuals into groups roughly associated with Rationalism on the one hand and Traditionalism on the other.[18] The Aristotelian-
influenced speculative tendencies of the Rationalists opened sacred scripture to nonliteral interpretation and contrasted with the literalist bent of
the Traditionalists. One need not understand the fine points of difference
between the *mutakallimun* and the *muhaddithun*, or between Mut'azillite
epistemology and Ash'arite theology, to recognize why debates between
Rationalists and Traditionalists often devolved into the question of divine
anthropomorphism.[19] A majority of Qur'anic verses are categorized as
muhkam (مُحْكَم), meaning firm or strong, that is, clear in meaning. But
of the approximately two hundred verses considered *mutashaabih*, many
attribute hands, eyes, ears, or a face to Allah. If God is indeed distinct
from that which he created and is inimitable, as the Qur'an repeatedly
states, and if the Qur'an is the revealed word of God, then how are the
Qur'anic metaphors that give Allah human attributes to be interpreted?[20]
Are these metaphors meant to be interpreted literally as truth (حقيقة/*haqe-
eqa*) or figuratively (*majaaz*)?[21]

Rather than placing figurative language in opposition to truth, al-
Jurjani creates a system that divides meaning into what is intellectually
verifiable and what is an imaginative conceit: *ma'ani 'aqiliyya* (rational
meaning) and *ma'ani takhiliyya* (imaginative meaning). By categorizing
majaaz in relation to literal meaning rather than in opposition to truth,

al-Jurjani presents figurative language not as inappropriate or false but as uttered with the purpose of making a comparison.[22] Taking al-Jurjani as an impetus, *American Arabesque* uses figurative language not only to examine the relationships between Arab and American culture and secular and sacred discourses on identity but also to probe how the literary imaginary structures the real material experiences of concrete individuals. In this sense, I approach American arabesques as a form of *poesis*, figurative constructions that create new subjectivities and subject experiences of the world by creating new words, images, and perceptions.

In the past thirty years of scholarship on Western literature's relationship to the East, the displacing power of figurative language has received far more attention than has its capacity to create connections. Beginning with *Orientalism*, there has been an emphasis in postcolonial criticism on analyzing how Western representations of the East replace the material Orient in favor of an Oriental imaginary that has far more to say about Western fantasies of difference than any reality of the East. Western representations of the East that work to incorporate Oriental cultural references and even Oriental languages into the idioms of democratic, progressive, and modern identity have only recently begun to receive the attention of scholars.[23] In the field of American Studies, Timothy Marr's *The Cultural Roots of American Islamicism* makes the convincing argument that "Americans have long pressed orientalist images of Islam into domestic service as a means to globalize the authority of the cultural power of the United States."[24] *American Arabesque* complements Marr's research on the absorption of Orientalist references into the language of American identity, but it is fundamentally a study of a different kind.

Within the larger envelope of American Orientalism, discrete discourses exist for the figure of the Turk, the Moor, the Muslim, the Bedouin, and the Arab. In Barbary captivity narratives and Near East travel narratives, distinctions between Turks and Bedouins, as well as between Arabs and Moors, are central to understanding what is at stake in the comparisons American writers make between the United States and the Arabo-Islamic world. Furthermore, the pervasive romantic appeal of the Bedouin figure in nineteenth-century American literature is based precisely on the figure's pre-Islamic qualities and the connections many writers made between Bedouins' "primitive" life and the life of Abraham. But these distinctions between Muslim ethnicities, as well as between Islamic culture and Bedouin Arab culture, are significant not only because they speak to the creation of American racial maps but also because the first group of actual Arab immigrants to America were predominantly Christian. To fully appreciate the Orientalist narratives that these immigrants were both exploiting and revising, it is necessary to understand the nuances of that narrative and the ethnic, geographical, and cultural distinctions made in it. Tracking the conflations and separations of Arab, Muslim, Moor, Turk, and Bedouin in American discourse reveals the logic inherent in cross-cultural comparisons, such as between Bedouin and Native Indian, as well as the logic informing the creation of cross-cultural figures such as the American Moor.

Since the 1990s, a number of exemplary studies of American versions of Orientalism have been published, including Fuad Sha'ban's *Islam and Arabs in Early American Thought*, Malini Johar Schueller's *U.S. Orientalisms*, Scott Trafton's *Egypt Land*, Hilton Obenzinger's *American Palestine*, and Brian T. Edwards's *Morocco Bound*.[25] None of these books has dealt with the specificity of the image of the Arab, and most importantly none has dealt directly with the Arabic language and Arabic-language writers. If American Studies is truly to take its much-advertised global turn, its scholars must cultivate an appreciation for the languages from which foreign references are pilfered. It is only by developing this intercultural perspective that we can fully appreciate the dynamics of absorbing "foreign" and/or "exotic" references into American contexts. In order to reinvigorate a dialogue between American culture and Arab culture that was initiated in nineteenth-century Orientalist discourse, it is necessary to follow al-Jurjani's advice and pay close attention to how borrowed words maintain two simultaneous, and often opposed, meanings.

The methodological decision to include analyses of Arabic-language texts in my chapters allows me to explore the relationship between the figurative Arabs and/or Muslims of American Orientalist discourse and the Arabs and/or Muslims who used Orientalist discourses to figure themselves as Americans. It is a critical practice that acknowledges the limits of the tradition it is building on by both excoriating the terms that discourse employed to know the "other" and creating a new hermeneutic methodology of retrieving knowledge—knowledge that is not one culture's property or another's but rather is an overlapping and at times shared imaginary. As a generation of inquiry into Orientalism has taught us, there are multiple Orients as well as multiple Wests, often simultaneously conjured in the same figure. Our critical approach to these respective concepts must be as supple as al-Jurjani's approach to *majaaz*. It must be an approach that allows us to recognize, through the figure, a "shortening [of] the distance between East and West."

Figures of the Arab and Definitions of America

Two historical anecdotes serve as bookends for *American Arabesque*. The first takes place on the coast of North Africa at the turn of the nineteenth century. The second takes place in a U.S. court room at the beginning of the twentieth century. The story of the Mameluke sword focuses on the translation of an Arabo-Islamic referent into a key iteration of American national identity, the Marine hymn. The story of the *Dow* case examines how the first "Arab" immigrants to the United States narrated themselves into American citizens. These two moments delineate the historical sweep of *American Arabesque*. They also model two theoretical approaches to understanding arabesque representation: intercultural translation and intracultural translation. The former focuses on the use of the Arab and/ or Muslim figure from elsewhere to create national imaginaries; the latter focuses on Arabs and Muslims in America and their creation of counter national imaginaries. Both types of translation are intimately connected to the racial politics of American citizenship.

On April 27, 1805, the exiled ruler of Tripoli, Hamet Karamanelli, presented Lieutenant Neville Presley O'Bannon with a jeweled Mameluke sword in acknowledgment of the successful bayonet charge the young Marine from Virginia had led earlier that day against the fortified city of Derne. The ceremony took place on North Africa's Mediterranean coast, and the larger event it commemorated was eventually incorporated into the Marine hymn as a testament to the transatlantic reach of U.S. military power and political influence: "from the halls of Montezuma to the shores of Tripoli." Soon after the sword ceremony, O'Bannon raised the Stars and Stripes over Derne. The event marked a turning point in the United States' first extracontinental military venture and, as Marine lore holds, the first time the American flag had been carried and planted on the other side of the Atlantic. To this day, commissioned officers of the Marine Corp carry a replica of the same Mameluke sword that Hamet Karamanelli presented to O'Bannon on the shores of Tripoli.

The sword exchange still resonates in the American national memory as a heroic first chapter in the country's global crusade against despotism and its enduring commitment to spreading democracy to the far corners of the earth.[26] In other words, the Mameluke sword and the event it commemorates have been translated into an American national fantasy. Berlant, describing her definition of national fantasy, explains, "I mean to designate how national culture becomes local—through the images, narratives, monuments, and sites that circulate through personal/collective consciousness."[27] The Marine hymn is one of these transformative narratives, and in it Barbary becomes a productive site of American national identity. It is in this "fantasy" sense that the invocation "to the shores of Tripoli" uses affect to bind the individual citizen to the collective notion of national honor, integrity, and military power. But what if we were to read this national fantasy dialectically through the filter of Arab history and the Arabic language? What if we took a philological approach to the hymn's translation of the Mameluke sword into the Marine sword?

O'Bannon was a member of a small expeditionary force of eight Marines, a hundred or so European fortune fighters, and several hundred Bedouin Arabs. The group had been led across the Libyan Desert by an intrepid Revolutionary and Indian War veteran from Massachusetts, General William Eaton. Eaton's covert mission was to overthrow the acting ruler of Tripoli, Yusuf Karamanelli, and to replace him with his more pliable brother Hamet. The ultimate goal was to free the hundreds of American citizens held in Tripoli's slave prisons and rid the U.S. government of the need to pay tribute to a piratical state. In a matter of days after Hamet had handed the Mameluke sword to Lt. O'Bannon in Derne, his brother Yusuf precipitously began negotiations for peace with the United States. Far from being "chastised for his temerity" (as Eaton preferred) or removed from his position of tyrannical power, Yusuf ultimately signed a treaty that established him as legitimate ruler of Tripoli in the eyes of the U.S. government.[28] This treaty contained a secret proviso banishing Hamet from Tripoli and assuring his removal by securing his immediate family as Yusuf's hostages.[29]

In the years that followed the triumphant sword exchange in Derne, Eaton and Hamet remained connected through the written word. Hamet wrote many letters to the U.S. Senate complaining of his exile on an obscure Mediterranean island, his penury, and the unpaid debt that America owed him. When informed of the treaty negotiations that ultimately made Hamet an exile, Eaton, still occupying the Derne camp, wrote in distress to Samuel Barron, the commander in chief of U.S. forces in the Mediterranean. "Could I have apprehended this result of my exertions," Eaton complained, "certainly no consideration would have prevailed on me to have taken an agency in a tragedy so manifestly fraught with *intrigue*; so wounding to human feelings; and as I must view it, so *degrading to our national honor*."[30] In Eaton's view, the shores of Tripoli do not consolidate the righteous and masculine national subjectivity that so often affectively attaches itself to the Marine hymn. Instead Eaton narrates the United States' surreptitious retreat in the dead of night from Derne as "unmanly."[31] As concerns Hamet, Eaton remarks in his journal, "He falls from the most flattering prospects of a *kingdom*, to *beggary!*"[32]

How do we interpret the results of the U.S. military's actions in Barbary? Was it victory or defeat? Was it honorable or dishonorable? Tracking what Hamet's Mameluke sword signifies in both American and Arab cultural traditions provides a global perspective on the phrase "to the shores of Tripoli." Paying attention to the dynamics of translation, in other words, disturbs the exceptionalist national fantasy that the Marine hymn invokes. What emerges in its place is a narrative on American identity in which belonging and alienation (enfranchisement and disenfranchisement) are intrinsically bound together.

Mameluke refers to the organized bodies of slave soldiers employed by various Islamic armies from as early as the ninth century. The members of this corps, captured or bartered during their childhoods and raised as military orphans, eventually gave birth to two Egyptian dynasties. The first dynasty had consolidated its control over the state by the end of the thirteenth century. This generation of Mamelukes replaced the Arabo-Islamic caliphate with a form of military rule that placed power in the hands of central Asian, Turkish, Kurdish, and Caucasian soldiers. The Mamelukes' dynastic power originated in seizure, and their political aim was self-interestedly to perpetuate that power through clientage. To the Arab historian Ibn Khaldun, the advent of Mameluke control of Egypt is a signal event in the decay of the Arab *asabiyya* (group loyalty) that created the pinnacles of Arabo-Islamic civilization, the Ummayad and Abassid Caliphates.[33] Ibn Khaldun argues that the Mameluke dynasty marks a historical shift whereby Arabs will no longer be rulers of the Islamic *umma* (community) but rather will become the ruled. Seen through the perspective of Ibn Khaldun's theory of history, the Mamelukes revived an older form of natural kingship (*mulk*) but changed the terms of loyalty from tribal/ethnic bonds to military bonds.[34] By the beginning of the nineteenth century, the second Mameluke dynasty had taken control of Egypt, following the same policies as its original Mameluke predecessors.

The word *mameluke* is derived from the Arabic verb *malaka* (ملك), "to take in possession, seize, take over, acquire, lay hands (on); to dominate, control, be master (of)."[35] A *mameluke* is a slave or possession of someone, but a *malik* (derived from the same verbal root) is a king, and *mulk* is something that Ibn Khaldun theorized as natural kingship. In practice, the Mameluke dynasty combined these seemingly opposed states of being: they were both slaves and kings, both victims and administrators of imperialism. No man could become a Mameluke ruler who had not first been a Mameluke slave. The janissary body of the Mamelukes was not hereditary and theoretically could only be refreshed with new orphans. The Mameluke system meant that a boy seized on a military raid into the Caucus Mountains and raised as a slave could become the ruler of an Egyptian population to which he was not ethnically, racially, or culturally attached.

The transformation of the Mameluke sword into the U.S. Marine sword entails an act of transvaluation whereby an Arabo-Islamic symbol of slavery, imperialism, and dynastic hegemony becomes a symbolic expression of America's commitment to freedom and democracy. And yet O'Bannon himself hailed from a state in which slavery was legal, and the larger conflict in North Africa that came to be known as the Tripoli War gave birth to the U.S. Navy, impetus to the U.S. Marines, and still provides a quilting point for subsequent narratives of the United States' extracontinental military interventions in the name of overthrowing tyrants rather than appeasing them. The other narrative, the narrative that suggests the United States' own history of slavery, hegemony, and imperial aggression, remains as a ghostly complement to the New World symbol that American historiography was to fashion out of Hamet's Mameluke sword.

The proceedings from the court marshal of an American sailor aboard a ship sent to the Barbary Coast during the War with Tripoli provides a telling example of the gap many Federal-era Americans felt existed between the promise of revolutionary freedom and the reality of continued American bondage, between the affect of national fantasy and the lived experience of those still occluded from the values the national fantasy promoted. On June 23, 1804, Robert Quinn, the president of the sailors aboard the U.S. frigate *President*, was summoned to the bar at Hampton Roads for the crime of mutiny. The evidence against Quinn consisted of a letter he had written to Commodore Samuel Baron, commander of the U.S. naval squadron deployed to the Mediterranean to free American slaves held captive in Barbary prisons. The letter lists a series of complaints the common sailors had with their treatment and meal allowances. In the letter, Quinn uses the pointed terms of revolutionary rhetoric:

Tyranny is the beginning of all mischief and is generally attended with bad things at the latter end. Any Commodore or captain that had the least feeling or thought would not suffer this hard usage it is almost impossible for us to live. . . . Some of our friends in America and other parts shall know of this shortly and in time we hope to get redress—death is always superior to slavery—we remain your unhappy slaves.[36]

Quinn received cold satisfaction for his invocation of the language of the Revolutionary War and his appeal to its metaphors of freedom. He was sentenced to have his eyebrows shaved and to be branded on the forehead with the word "Mutiny." He also received 326 lashes equally apportioned among the crew of the different ships of the squadron. Eaton was one of the judges. Quinn and his fellow sailors had deployed to Barbary aboard an American ship rhetorically positioned as fighting tyranny and freeing slaves. Yet it is American commodores and captains he accuses of tyranny and slave driving.

The Marine hymn subsumes contradictions between the American rhetoric of liberty and the American history of bondage by appealing to the national fantasy of America's historical commitment to freedom. In other words, the hymn reinterprets the Mameluke sword, translating it into an affective iteration of American national identity. To put the Marine sword in dialectic with the Mameluke sword is to think through exchanges between America and the Arab world not only in terms of martial conquest but also in terms of intercultural translation. It is to reconstruct our understanding of national symbols with an eye toward their etiology. The cause of the sword exchange commemorated in the Marine hymn was the installation of Hamet Karamanelli, with the aid of the United States, as ruler of Tripoli. The result of the sword exchange was his disenfranchisement, exile, and alienation. The larger cause that had brought U.S. Marines to the shores of Tripoli was the enslavement of American citizens, who had been promised life, liberty, and the pursuit of happiness by the Declaration of Independence. As white slaves in North Africa, as well as the white seamen sent to rescue them, were well aware, these universal rights were far from universally applied in their home country.

The displacements involved in aestheticizing and refiguring Arab history, Arabo-Islamic expression, and the Arabic language as American cultural property create American arabesques. I categorize American representations of the Arab as arabesques because I recognize the fantasy quotient with which these images are imbued, but I am also arguing against dismissing them as merely "bad" or inaccurate representations. American arabesques define a spectrum of relations between American culture and Arab culture that have yet to be explored. Arabesque representation displaces the physical, material world in favor of an imagined world and imagined relations. The imaginaries created through arabesques speak to idealized visions of America, but they also speak to the real ideological, social, and racial fissures in the nation that must be ameliorated through imaginary projection. These imaginary projections, in turn, create new American identities. I approach the literary history of representing the Arab as a key that unlocks a larger story about how figures of the Arab and tropes of Arabness are used to construct definitions of American national identity, to mediate American racial differences, and to control the meaning of citizenship in the American context. But arabesques are not only figures of displacement; they are also figures of emplacement, particularly for groups within the United States that felt disenfranchised by nineteenth-century models of American citizenship.

A 1915 Fourth Circuit Court appeals trial, *Dow v. United States*, decided the question of Syrian race in the eyes of American law.[37] Guided by the Dillingham Report of the Immigration Commission, the Fourth Circuit appellate judge ruled that Syrian immigrants from the African side of the Mediterranean were "of mixed Syrian, Arabian, and even Jewish blood." Instead of being labeled Turkish and thus being subject to Asian immigration quotas, Syrian migrants to America were classified as "belong[ing] to the Semitic branch of the Caucasian race. Thus widely differing from their rulers, the Turks."[38] The decision ushered Syrian immigrants into the inner sanctum of American citizenship, even as it tacitly acknowledged the figurative nature of a racial category constructed from labile ethnic, national, and religious delineations. Legally recognized as white, Syrians became part of the American family, and the racial category of Arab disappeared from official tabulation.

The privileged place opened up for Syrians in the American legal conception of citizenship at the beginning of the twentieth century had its rhetorical genesis in nineteenth-century metaphors and figurations of Arabness. Literary tropes of Arabness not only influenced juridical definitions of American citizenship but also literally facilitated the transition of Arab immigrants from foreigner to American. The creation of very real American citizens out of Arab migrants, in other words, was abetted by fiction and figural representation. The *Dow* ruling legally sanctioned a distinction between Arab and Turk that American literature had been defining figuratively for over a century. Furthermore, by classifying Syrian ethnicity as a "Semitic branch of the Caucasian race," U.S. law codified the imaginative conduit between darkness and whiteness, as well as between foreignness and American citizenship, that tropes of Arabness had provided throughout the nineteenth century.

As the *Dow* case attests, the term *Arab* signified a mutable category in America, one that needed juridical policing. The definitions of *Arab* circulating in America contemporary with the *Dow* decision include, "A homeless child or street urchin"; "A Jew"; "A people of mixed breed, partially Indian"; "Any dark complexioned person, esp. if belonging to a group traditionally considered to be somewhat primitive in emotional matters; spec. a Jew or a Turk"; and "A huckster or street vendor, esp. those who posses a Central European or Middle Eastern cast of countenance."[39] The range of vernacular meaning for the word *Arab* meant that Syrian migrants encountered an array of potential identities—immigrant, Indian, Jew, Turk, primitive, Middle Eastern, Central European, mixed breed. These living Syrian individuals inherited imaginary subject positions that were engendered by arabesque representation. In negotiating their relationship to these subject positions, the Syrian migrants negotiated their relation to an American national symbolic that had already created a place for them in the national fantasy.

If one type of American arabesque involves the translation (often violent) of Arab and/or Arabo-Islamic words, images, spaces, and objects into American culture, another type involves the creation of alternative American identities based on "-esquing" these translations. This second type of arabesque is a conscious strategy of self-representation that reads a predominantly white American discourse on Arabo-Islamic culture against the grain. These arabesques blend not only the Arab and the American but also the real and the fictional. The figurative Arabs that appear on the pages of nineteenth-century American texts replace real Arabs in the American cultural imaginary and exert a representational pressure on the literal "Arabs" who eventually appear on American shores at the end of the nineteenth century. But it is precisely by playing into the existing American discourse on Arab identity that Syrian migrants to America made themselves "white." Exchanging their Syrian ethnicity for whiteness, these first-generation migrants demonstrate how Muslims and Arabs in turn-of-the-twentieth-century America readapted Orientalist discourses to their own purposes.

The physical arabesque pattern has acted as a medium of transference between cultures for centuries, connecting "Oriental" art and "Western" art through its tendril motifs (see figure 2).[40] The term *arabesque*, in turn, captures the way nineteenth-century American romanticism not only blended the real and the fantastic to reimagine the nation and the self but also borrowed its fantasies of national and personal difference directly from other cultural traditions. However, the term *arabesque* does not exist in Arabic. Sometime around the beginning of the seventeenth century, the word appears in the English language, by way of the French *arabesque*, which is borrowed from the Italian *arabesco*, which in turn is derived from the Latin *Arabus*. The "Arabian ornamental design" that the word *arabesque* references had been a source of European fascination since antiquity, exerting a particular influence on Renaissance artists as diversely situated as Albrecht Dürer and Raphael. Improvising on the "Arabian" design pattern, European artists over the ages created the related styles of the Romanesque, the Moresque, and the grotesque.

The history of intercultural translation, misinterpretation, and projection attached to the figure of the arabesque provides the impetus for the title of this book. *American Arabesque* tracks the exchange between American culture and Arabo-Islamic culture through five figures: the captive, the indigene, the arabesque, the Moor, and the migrant. Each of these figures is an arabesque in the sense that they (a) enact *romantic* engagements with the Arab world, (b) *blend* two languages of identity (American and Arab), and (c) create representative patterns of *mirroring/doubling*. An analysis of these arabesques illuminates the role that references to Arab and Arabo-Islamic culture play in shaping the contours of American belonging and ultimately the content of the U.S. national imaginary.

A Pattern of Representation

Chapter 1 focuses on the figure of the captive and argues for the discursive importance of North African slavery to the articulation of Federal-era American national identity. American captives in Barbary slavery extended Revolutionary War narratives on bondage and freedom to make arguments for their country's obligation to ransom them. In the process of claiming their own constitutional rights, these predominantly white, working-class sailors used Barbary types to establish comparisons

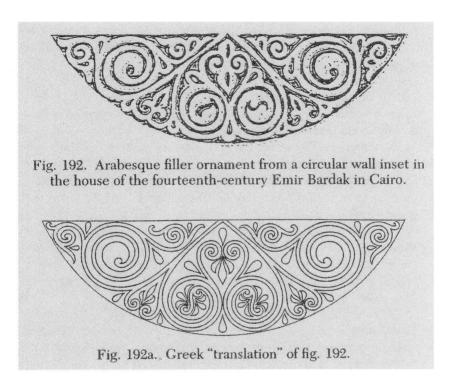

Fig. 192. Arabesque filler ornament from a circular wall inset in the house of the fourteenth-century Emir Bardak in Cairo.

Fig. 192a. Greek "translation" of fig. 192.

Figure 2. Arabesque filler ornament from a circular wall inset in the house of the fourteenth-century Emir Bardak in Cairo and Greek "translation." From Alois Riegl, *Problems of Style,* excerpted in Jules Bourgoin, *Précis de l'art arabe et matériaux pour servir à l'histoire, à la théorie, et à la technique des arts de l'Orient musulman,* 2 vols. (Paris, 1892), part 1, pl. 32.

between themselves and the disenfranchised in America's nascent democracy. Filtered largely through the experiences of James Leander Cathcart (Revolutionary War veteran, Barbary slave, U.S. diplomat, and student of Arabic, Turkish, and Lingua Franca), chapter 1 examines how Barbary was used rhetorically to interrogate the meaning and limitation of untested terms such as *democracy, equality, liberty,* and *patriotism* in the American context. The result is not only the importation of Barbary types into American racial maps but also the creation of cross-cultural comparisons that can be mined, retrospectively, for evidence of the nation's nascent multicultural consciousness.

John Foss, a sailor captured by the Regency of Algiers in 1793, demonstrates the relationships between America and North Africa that Barbary captivity narratives established for their readers.

> The Turks are a well-built robust people, their complexion not unlike Americans, tho' somewhat larger, but their dress, and long beards, make them more like monsters than human beings.
>
> The Cologlies are somewhat less in stature than the Turks, and are of a more tawny complexion.
>
> The Moors are generally a tall, thin, spare set of people, not much inclining to fat, and of a very dark complexion, much like the Indians of North America.
>
> The Arabs, or Arabians, are of a much darker complexion than the Moors, being darker than Mulattoes. They are much less in stature than the Moors, being the smallest people I ever saw. . . . As they are not allowed to trade in any mercantile line, nor even learn any mechanic art, they are obliged to be drudges to their superiors.[41]

In Foss's proto-ethnographic summary, four distinct inhabitants of the Algerian space are strung together as contiguous links in a cultural chain of being, each one's identity being determined in relation not only to the previous one but also to a racial identity recognizable from the American context.[42] Foss creates an arabesque pattern of representation by using Barbary to mirror American racial relations back to his readers. He employs similarity to establish the naturalness of America's racial hierarchies and reversal to establish America's cultural difference from Barbarous Africa. Thus, the Turks are "not unlike Americans" in racial complexion but also are "more like monsters than human beings" in their cultural habits (visible on the level of clothes and grooming). The Turk is a white American in reverse, monstrous instead of civilized, despotic instead of democratic, and barbarous instead of enlightened. Whiteness appears in Foss's Barbary racial grid as a universal marker of privilege and power, but Americanness remains a distinct and exceptional cultural identity for his reader, lest the comparison between Turk and American suggest other uncomfortable equivalencies.

However, the order and categorical differences Foss is attempting to establish through his grid of Barbary is in fact undermined by the latent equivalencies in his chart. The difference between Turk and American has to be quickly established because of the immediate similarity between the two. Perhaps even more disruptive to Foss's order than the Turk is the figure of the Cologlie, a hybrid entity that has no analogue in Foss's American racial mirror. The Cologlie, a child of a garrisoned Turkish soldier and a local Algerian woman, has no American double precisely because he or she represents the possibility of racial hybridity being integrated into an essentialist chain of being. Most tellingly, though, is Foss's categorization of Arab identity. Foss presents an Arab figure that is "much darker complexion than the Moors, being darker than Mulattoes." Yet the term *Arab* was applied in other contexts by other Barbary captives to a range of different American racial equivalents. Foss does not merely replicate the Barbary racial hierarchy; he translates it according to his particular conception of racial order.

The cross-cultural comparisons engendered by Barbary captivity reflect the national identity anxieties of the Federal era, anxieties centered on the meaning of democracy and the need to establish order, specifically racial order, out of revolution. In the decades that followed, tropes of the Arab were adapted by other American writers to new questions about American democracy and its limits. In the mid-nineteenth century, the genre of the Near Eastern travel narrative came into market prominence at the exact same time that the U.S. government was dramatically expanding its continental territory. In these narratives, the American frontier is mirrored in the Arabian Desert, and the politics of Indian removal are played out symbolically through travelers' ruminations about disappearing Bedouins. John Lloyd Stephens, the first American to write a Near Eastern travel narrative, demonstrates how representations of the Near East worked to rhetorically establish America's exceptional mandate. About midway through his account, Stephens describes the curse on Biblical Edom and Biblical Esau.

> Standing near the Elanitic branch of the Red Sea, the doomed and accursed land lay stretched out before me, the theatre of awful visitations and their more awful *fulfillment*; given to Esau as being the fatness of the earth, but now a barren waste, a picture of death, an eternal monument of the wrath of an offended God, and a fearful witness to the truth of the words spoken by his prophets.[43]

Stephens narrates his path across the Arabian Desert with intentional rhetorical echoes of an earlier Anglo-American settler colonialism that figured white Americans as New Israelites with a covenantal relationship to

American soil. By emphasizing the literal nature of the Old Testament's prophecies and their fulfillment in the ancient world, Stephens indexes the fulfillment narrative of New Testament–inspired Protestant interpretations of America as the New Israel. If the "curse" on Esau was fulfilled in Edom, it meant that by logical extension the chosen status of the Israelites would also be literally realized. Interpretations such as these were inspired by a Pauline approach to the Old Testament as a prefiguration of the New Testament and its history of salvation. Rejecting allegorical interpretation, Paul's epistles insisted on literal historical interpretations of both Old Testament figure and New Testament fulfillment. The fulfillment of the prophecy of Edom's destruction had implications for the New Israel of America. For the many Americans who believed in chiliastic rhetoric, the salvation and chosen status of the New Israel was confirmed in the plight of the figurative Esaus (i.e., Bedouins) located in the sands of Arabia Petraea.

Stephens's use of the Arab world to make arguments about American destiny creates an arabesque representation. His description of Edom establishes the naturalness of America's westward expansion through similarity and the uniqueness of America's exceptional mandate through reversal. The disappearance of primitive man in the face of civilized advance was a universal phenomenon, these travel narratives implied, visible in the Arabian Desert as well as on the American frontier. But America's colonial advance into its continental hinterland was differentiated from Ottoman colonialism, and American Manifest Destiny was distinguished from historical examples of imperial hubris through reversal. Whereas Edom is cursed, America is chosen, as evident in the Biblical story of Jacob and Esau being played out on America's own frontier.

Chapter 2 turns its attention to the figure of the indigene as it relates to the question of nativity and ownership in the American context. The writers detailed in chapter 2 are privileged rather than enslaved, moving relatively freely through Near Eastern deserts, cities, and ruins rather than being trapped in North African prisons and speaking to a domestic audience that is not as mindful of the question of American Revolution as they are of the question of American Empire. Yet the Near Eastern travel narrative, as the Barbary captivity narrative did more than a generation earlier, broached central questions of American national identity through representations of Ottoman colonial relations and Arabo-Islamic cultural stratifications. The Arab figure that reverberates most poignantly with the midcentury American national imaginary is the Bedouin. Americans in the Near East justified U.S. national expansion at its continental borders by employing pentimento representations of the Bedouin through which they discussed Native Indians. These representations created complex metaphors of white American nativity.

Yet the very figurative nature of these metaphors of nativity made them unruly and subject to co-option by "nonwhites" such as Jews and African Americans. Looking closely at Erich Auerbach's definition of *figura* in the context of Ibn Khaldun's fourteenth-century definition of the Bedouin, chapter 2 examines the stakes in translating a foreign archetype into a domestic stereotype. Read in an intercultural context, the translation of the Arab Bedouin into the American Bedouin does something more than stabilize white nativity in America and create a national symbolic that differentiates American Empire from its historical predecessors. This translation also, simultaneously, creates cross-cultural imaginaries that allow American readers to see Andrew Jackson mirrored in the Oriental "despot" Muhammad Ali and American expansionism mirrored in the hegemonic policies of the Ottomans toward indigenous populations.

The first two chapters connect parallel strains in American Studies scholarship: the effort to situate American culture within a global context and the developing critique of U.S. imperialism *prior* to the Civil War. My own analysis of Americans' antebellum contact with Arabo-Islamic cultures is coupled with attention to how these exotic encounters express white America's continental imperial imagination. What I discover, though, in this Eastern contact literature, is not the monocultural ethos underlying racial nationalism or the ruthless democracy of American imperial citizenship but rather textual moments when American citizens *confront* colonialism in America.[44] Placing narrative instantiations of national identity in the international contexts registered by both Barbary captivity narratives and Near Eastern travel narratives, in fact, disturbs the discourse of white privilege that several recent American Studies scholars have explored.[45]

The arabesques on which I concentrate in the first two chapters directly reference Arab culture. Edgar Allan Poe's arabesques refer not to the Arab world but rather to a romantic style the writer cultivates in an attempt to distinguish himself in a crowded literary marketplace. Washington Irving, for example, had dubbed his own stories "arabesque" before Poe published *Tales of the Grotesque and Arabesque*. However, though both Poe and Irving shared a fondness for the exotic and a propensity to invoke the supernatural in their short stories, the term *arabesque* held a different valence in their respective aesthetic sensibilities. Irving certainly had read more about Islam, Arabs, and Arabo-Islamic history than Poe had. He had published a biography of the Prophet Muhammad, as well as several histories of the Moors in Spain. He had even, unlike Poe, traveled to Andalusia and come in firsthand contact with Arabo-Islamic culture and ruins. But it is precisely Poe's lack of contact with primary sources and primary sites of Arabo-Islamic cultural production that makes his arabesque aesthetic so unmoored, so uniquely American. The physical arabesques in Poe's tales index his arabesque aesthetic. This aesthetic establishes conduits between accepted binaries, ultimately collapsing dichotomies to achieve Poe's signature modern affects of shock and terror.[46] Poe's arabesques link the theory and praxis of his romanticism, but they also translate an Arab cultural reference into an American idiom.

Poe's use of the arabesque to establish his romantic aesthetic provides a salient example of what happens when an Arabo-Islamic referent is translated out of its own cultural context and into American cultural property. At the beginning of his essay on interior décor, "The Philosophy of Furniture," Poe insists that the ideal American domestic space should be covered by arabesque patterns "of no meaning."[47] Though Poe's decorating advice is delivered tongue lodged in cheek, it has direct relevance to his own use of the arabesque pattern to model an art-for-art's-sake theory of literature. Poe evacuates material Arabs and Arabo-Islamic culture from the image of the Arab, replacing the real with the figural to create his idealized realm of "pure fiction." Poe's use of the term *arabesque* as code for his own theory of art effectively disconnects the image of the Arab from material Arab culture. It is precisely this aesthetic "sweep[ing] aside" of the material world that William Carlos Williams identifies as Poe's contribution to the creation of a national literature.[48] Seen through modernist criticism, Poe's arabesque consolidates the idea of America by presenting its unique literary voice to the world.

In chapter 3, I concentrate on the translation of the image of the Arab into a "unique" expression of American romanticism. In Poe, the figure of the Arab facilitates the experience of difference as sameness, the foreign as familiar, and the alien as domestic. In a sense, Poe cultivates the anxieties that are latent in the contact narrative's use of the image of the Arab to establish American national, cultural, and racial difference. Poe exploits those anxieties, refining them into an aesthetic instantiation of national terror based on the potential collapse of difference. Poe's domestication of the image of the Arab ultimately serves as an ironic acknowledgment of the impossibility of bounding a "unique" domestic national identity that is built through references to the foreign, the exotic, and the "other." Tracking the arabesque's movement from Arab cultural reference to uniquely American aesthetic demonstrates the role of translation in Poe's romanticism. Retranslating Poe's arabesque back into Arabo-Islamic cultural discourse, in turn, reveals resonances between Arab and American romanticism.

The design pattern that came to be called the arabesque in the Western world is known in Arabic as *tawreeq* (توريق), from the verb form of "to foliate" (ورق).[49] Whereas Poe's arabesque symbolizes a secular aesthetic, the *tawreeq* is intimately connected to sacred aesthetics. The *tawreeq* lends itself to poetic manifestations (*ghazel*) and musical manifestations (*muwashshah*) as well as ornamental design. Each of these *tawreeq* art forms strives to capture the Islamic concept of *tawHeed* (توحيد; unity) and to remind the viewer/listener of the oneness and utter transcendence of Allah. These theories of unicity receive especially poignant expressions in Islamic mysticism and the writings of Sufis such as Ibn Arabi. In translating an Arabo-Islamic referent into an instantiation of American literary nationalism, Poe not only strips the term of its original signification; he also fundamentally alters his audience's understanding of the term's cultural-historical significance to Muslims. Placing Poe's arabesque in an intercultural context, however, creates the possibility for appreciating how American and Arab cultural values interanimate each other.

At the same historical moment that Poe used the arabesque figure as code for his exploration of a primal aesthetic of sensation, Arab writers such as al-Tahtawi were beginning to modernize the Arabic language itself. In Poe's writing, the figure of the Arab indicates an emptying out of meaning from the form. In al-Tahtawi's writing, the meanings of the representational figures of the Arabic language are being expanded to include modern political concepts such as nationalism. To Poe, the arabesque figure is a sign of modernity because it has been stripped of content and only stands for itself. But to al-Tahtawi, Arab figures are keys to modernity because they demonstrate Arabo-Islamic culture's ability to incorporate foreign concepts into a familiar idiom. Ultimately, chapter 3 uses dialectics to move toward an intercultural interpretation of the arabesque and its relationship to national identity politics.

The first three chapters mark a trajectory of abstraction that culminates in Poe's arabesque, a figure that evacuates material Arabs and Arabo-Islamic culture from the image of the Arab. The birth of an indigenous form of American Islam (the Moorish Science Temple) and the nascent stirrings of an Arab American literary community (the *mahjar*), however, produce American arabesques that attempt to establish the material reality of Arab American and Islamic American identity. In the final two chapters, tropes of Arabness are reengineered to create subversive narratives of American belonging that nonetheless borrow their logic of representation from mainstream national fantasies. The arabesques that come under scrutiny in these final two chapters make manifest the racial and spatial reversals latent in the arabesques examined in the first three chapters. Nineteenth-century American arabesques contain anxious explorations of a potential America, an America that is multicultural, cosmopolitan, racially diverse, and internationally contextualized. In the figures of the American Moor and the Arab migrant, these potentialities are embraced, elaborated, and discursively instantiated.

Muslim identity provided disenfranchised American citizens, such as black Americans, with a counternode to European culture and cultural hegemony. As certain black uplift leaders pointed out, the Muslim is not only victimized by history but is also a historical victor, evidenced by the prominent histories of Egyptian Empire, Meccan revelation, and Islamic conquest. The founder of the Moorish Science Temple, Noble Drew Ali, tweaked nineteenth-century white Orientalist discourses on the Moor's in-between status to take rhetorical advantage of these counternodal possibilities. Drew Ali disclaims "Negro" and white identity alike in favor of a Moorish racial identity that draws on Arabo-Islamic history, references, and icons. The fiction of Moorish ancestry allowed Drew Ali to insist on a continuum between blackness and Americanness that was literal but rhetorically difficult to establish. Placing his community in the figurative position of Moor, Drew Ali reconceived the Middle Passage in terms of black triumph, conquest, and historical tradition rather than in terms of exploitation and memory loss.

The category of Muslim created by New World Islam prophets such as Drew Ali has very little to do with Islam. Instead, early black American Muslims were figural Muslims, modernist creations that borrowed references to the Arab and Islamic world to forge a new black American modality. Drew Ali's national fantasy of Moorish identity spoke to the real material and psychological needs of his community in particular and the rhetorical goals of black uplift discourse more generally. But his vision was not shared by all, and his categorization of black identity as Moorish came under perpetual duress from black uplift leaders who viewed him as a radical and/or a charlatan. Nevertheless, Drew Ali used the figure of the Moor to establish a counter American National Symbolic. Rewriting American historiography from the perspective of the Moor, Drew Ali rejected the elective model of national identity that the rhetoric of the Declaration of Independence had promised but never delivered on for people of color. Instead he turned toward an alternate form of nationalism, one that had resonance with the Anglo-Saxonist primordial-descent model of national identity that had justified American slavery, had driven America's westward expansion, and was to inform the restrictive American immigration laws passed in the 1920s. Mirroring the way that nineteenth-century white Orientalist discourse used the Orient as a screen to project national narratives and to configure New World racial hierarchies, Drew Ali used the figure of the Moor to establish a narrative of black American nativity and historical privilege.

The rhetorical reversal of a white American discourse on race is directly evident in Drew Ali's handling of the story of Ham. "Old man Cush and his family are the first inhabitants of Africa who came from the land of Canaan," relates Drew Ali's *Circle Seven Koran*. "His father Ham and his family were second."[50] Used throughout the antebellum period by racist apologists and proslavery advocates, the Biblical story of Ham had been marshaled as a defense of slavery for many years in American discourse. Drew Ali uses the Hamitic legacy in his *Koran* to ground the "lost-found" nation of American blacks in a locatable space and time, one that had been stripped from them by the experience of slavery. "What your ancient forefathers were," the *Circle Seven Koran* reads, "you are today without doubt or contradiction" (47:10). Drew Ali's *Koran* specifically challenges a history of American slavery, with its attendant erasure of historical memory, cultural identity, and a sense of homeland with a figure, Ham, associated with the justification of slavery. Through Ham, Drew Ali makes a direct claim on historical continuity for the African diaspora in America. Ham is just one of many North African figures that early twentieth-century black uplift leaders "-esqued" to create an aesthetics of black pride.

Chapter 4 examines the representation of Arabs, Islam, and Arabo-Islamic culture in early twentieth-century black uplift discourses. Borrowed from a Claude McKay poem about Morocco, the term *barbaresque* describes black intellectuals' aesthetic engagement with North Africa, as well as with the narratives of African American empowerment these engagements produced. The chapter centers on the birth of the Moorish Science Temple; its founder, Drew Ali; and his New Age religious text, *The Circle Seven Koran*. Drew Ali's co-option of Moorish identity, Islamic

history, and Moroccan nationality is contextualized by discourses surrounding the New Negro and the Harlem Renaissance. In particular,
chapter 4 examines W. E. B. DuBois's and McKay's treatments of Arabo-
Islamic culture, as well as the coverage of the Moors in the black press. The
chapter argues that the variations in these different writers' representation
of Arabs, Islam, and Morocco speak directly to central debates in black
uplift discourse about the politics of respectability, as well as to key class
divides between the talented-tenth and street-level black-empowerment
movements. Barbaresques ultimately could be mobilized for either spiritual or secular discourses on black identity, and charting their uses in the
first decades of the twentieth century reveals how intraethnic class and
religious reconciliation were often sacrificed on the alter of interethnic
racial reconciliation. However variously interpreted, though, barbaresques
opened a third space of identity. Through barbaresques, black intellectuals splintered the limiting binaries of black/white, African/American, and
savage/civilized and created new subject positions as well as new collective
histories.

The first Arab American novelist, Ameen Rihani, also retranslated
tropes of Arabo-Islamic identity familiar from nineteenth-century American literature to create a narrative of American continuity for a diaspora
group, Arab migrants to the New World. In his modernist novel *The Book
of Khalid*, Rihani invents a plot that mirrors the contact narratives discussed in the first two chapters. The novel begins with a description of
an image that the faux editors of the "discovered" novel have found on
the inside jacket of *The Book of Khalid*, an image "represent[ing] a New
York skyscraper in the shape of a Pyramid."[51] With a healthy dose of
humor, Rihani migrates his Syrian hero through a number of archetypal
American identities before finally allowing him to realize his Arab destiny. The relationship between America and the Arab world established
in nineteenth-century literature is reversed as the United States appears
as the contact zone and Arab identity is consolidated through projections
of images of America. Ultimately Rihani reads Western romantic literature's representation of Arabs contrapuntally to create a vision of pan-
Arab political representation, "The United States of Arabia," modeled on
the United States.

Chapter 5 concentrates on the emergence of Arab American literary
self-representation by moving through a historiography of Arab migration to America and toward an analysis of Rihani's literary and political
writings. As a first-generation Arab American, Rihani inherited the canon

of representation that *American Arabesque* details. His re-formation of that canon provides invaluable insight into the human ligatures connecting the experience of American immigration and the *geist* of Arab liberalism that ultimately found expression in the early twentieth-century pan-Arabia movement. Positioned at the headwaters of an indigenous Arab intellectual reawakening, the *nahdah*, and a migrant Arab political consciousness, the *mahjar*, Rihani articulates a vision of Arab identity that embraces arabesque self-representation as a form of empowerment. Rihani's figure of the Arab is built from both Arab and American literary traditions. The fictional editors in *The Book of Khalid* describe the novel as a "weaving" where "the material is of such a mixture that here and there the raw silk of Syria is often spun with the cotton and wool of America" (v). The book ends, however, not with Khalid's successful immigration to America but rather with his migration across the globe and eventually to the Arabian Desert. Rihani's goal is the formation of a pan-Arab identity that self-consciously blends Orient and Occident, modern and traditional, Islamic and Christian, America and Arabia to create *mahjar* or migrant identity. Rihani's use of literary logic to make arguments for the political recognition of Arabs provides a salient historical example of one man's belief in the power of figural representation to change the material world.

In closing this introduction, I want to acknowledge that this book is a first step, not a last word. Now more than ever before, Arabs, Muslims, and Arab Americans are part of the national conversation about what constitutes American identity. Now more than ever before, scholars of American Studies have an opportunity to enter that conversation. This book provides a history of American representation of Arabs, Muslims, and Arab Americans as well as a history of these groups' efforts at self-representation. In this sense, *American Arabesque* insists that current discussions about the relationship between being American and being Arab have significant nineteenth-century antecedents. But beyond its genealogical function, *American Arabesque* challenges us to recognize that Arabs, real and imagined, have always been part of American culture. Representations of the Arab have always influenced the way U.S. citizens have defined their "unique" national identity. The aesthetic sensibilities a culture produces and the market tastes these productions respond to provide invaluable information about how communities define themselves as discrete entities, as well as how they negotiate those definitions. This book is an examination of a particular kind of American aesthetic production, the image of the Arab in the long nineteenth century. The Arab immigrant, as well as the second-, third-, or fourth-generation Arab American, who reads these pages will recognize, I hope, his or her own story vibrating within the narrative of American race, nation, and literature that this book details. The larger point, though, is to demonstrate how profoundly provisional, contextual, and fluid all American identities are—how these identities, like figures of the Arab, are themselves aesthetic placeholders that translate imaginaries into realities and back again and back again in what we might call an arabesque pattern.

1

The Barbarous Voice of Democracy

For pre-Revolution settlers, tales of Indian captivity dramatized the stakes in the American experiment.[1] They also dovetailed generically with themes familiar from Barbary captivity narratives written by Europeans.[2] After the Revolutionary War, however, American citizens began writing their own accounts of Barbary captivity. White, working-class sailors who claimed no literary skill or pretension to fame produced the majority of postnational Barbary captivity narratives. These accounts were often circulated in support of subscription drives for ransom. Beyond the material support Barbary captivity narratives provided for actual slaves in Africa, the genre was clearly also a source of entertainment and intrigue for American readers. According to Paul Baepler, "Although the Barbary captivity narrative in English existed for more than three centuries, it caught the attention of United States readers primarily during the first half of the nineteenth century. Between John Foss's 1798 narrative and the numerous printings of James Riley's 1817 account, . . . American publishers issued over a hundred American Barbary captivity editions."[3]

Stories of American bondage in North Africa exploited the language of freedom that had inspired the American Revolution. But these stories also challenged the meaning of that freedom and, by extension, critiqued the presence of slavery in the United States. In other words, Barbary contact narratives exposed new citizens to literary images of bondage that resonated both with the unifying rhetoric of Revolution and with the divisive rhetoric of abolition. Of course, in Barbary, the roles of African slave and white American were reversed. Nevertheless, captives translated Barbary referents into American tropes of identity. Barbary types such as Turks, Arabs, and Moors allowed Federal-era readers to negotiate American racial classifications, the limits of American democratic inclusion, and ultimately the fantasy of America's exceptional difference through exotic proxies.

In the polyglot, polyethnic, and polytheist society that was the turn-of-the-nineteenth-century Barbary world, U.S. citizens encountered an Ottoman Empire whose racial stratifications, practices of slavery, and imperial aspirations served as both a model for the new nation and a threat to that nation's sense of identity. Through the figure of the captive, writers in the Federal era explored the continuum and the difference between Barbary and America. In particular, the claims for repatriation enunciated by American-citizen captives in a foreign land are based on an anxious recognition of their country's need to litigate the domestic relationship between master and slave. In turn, the language of national identification spoken by these captives often recognizes the citizenship rights of American "others." Contact with Barbary did not consolidate the relation between whiteness and U.S. citizenship but rather troubled that relation with specters of American multiculturalism. In the pages that follow, I examine why North Africa was then and continues to be now an integral semantic space for the expression of American values and ultimately the definition of U.S. national identity.

I begin with an examination of how and why the discourse surrounding North African captivity at the turn of the nineteenth century created literary configurations linking the United States and Barbary. American captives juxtaposed the spatially and culturally unique sites of America and North Africa, creating a range of imagined relations between whiteness and blackness, Christianity and Islam, democracy and despotism. Focusing largely on the firsthand account of captivity provided by James Leander Cathcart, I recover the intercultural dialectic that translates descriptions of Barbary bondage into discursive instantiations of American freedom, democracy, and social mobility. I use the phrase *barbarous voice of democracy* to describe the articulation of Barbary referents and references into enunciations of American patriotic values.

Next I place Cathcart's language of American patriotism within the context of a turn-of-the nineteenth-century transatlantic discourse on revolution, empire, and Napoleon. This transatlantic discourse sheds light on Cathcart's unique brand of cosmopolitanism, revealing the relationship between his ruminations on American patriotism while a captive in Barbary and his ruminations on American patriotism years later while serving as a U.S. government agent in the Louisiana Territory. Despite their obvious geographical separation, the physical spaces of Barbary and Louisiana, I argue, are treated with ideological continuity in Cathcart's writings. Both are spatially chaotic and historically abject, and both have the potential to be cultivated into the smooth spatio-temporality of empire. Cathcart's America is a mobile concept more than it is a geographically bounded space. But whether he is in Barbary or Louisiana, Cathcart's idealized vision of a coherent and culturally homogeneous America is constantly harassed by the multicultural and multilinguistic reality of the literal landscapes he surveys.

Cathcart's writings provide a particularly intimate account of the tension between the cosmopolitan and the local in Federal-era American national identity politics, but they also resonate with the writings of the Arab historian Abd al-Rahman al-Jabbarti. Al-Jabbarti wrote several accounts of Napoleon's invasion of Egypt. Each wrestles with tensions between the cosmopolitan and the local, and each confronts Enlightenment rhetoric with Arabo-Islamic values. Al-Jabbarti wrote his history in 1798, the same year a newly emancipated Cathcart was appointed special diplomatic agent to William Eaton in Tunis. The French occupation of Egypt that al-Jabbarti details ended in 1801, the same year Cathcart took an active role in recruiting Hamet Karamanelli out of Egypt and into the Libyan Desert to fight for the U.S. cause in the War with Tripoli. A month after the Mameluke sword exchange between Karamanelli and the U.S. Marines took place in 1805, the Albanian janissary Muhammad Ali seized power in Egypt, filling the vacuum left by the departed French. Ali came to be known as the founder of modern Egypt for his military, technological, and cultural reforms. In 1811, while Cathcart was still serving in the Mediterranean as U.S. consul in Madeira, Ali exterminated the Mamelukes forever in a famous massacre at the Citadel in Cairo. In 1819, while Ali was consolidating his hold on Egypt through cultural exchanges with France, Cathcart ventured into the Louisiana swamp on a mission to locate available timber resources from which to rebuild the U.S. Navy after the War of 1812.

Though certainly situated in distinct cultural milieus, Cathcart and al-Jabbarti are historical contemporaries. Both of them chronicle the historical forces that connect Europe, America, and North Africa in the Age of Revolution. Yet they come to quite disparate assessments of revolution's rhetorical meaning. In al-Jabbarti's account of the meeting between Western culture and Arabo-Islamic culture, the Enlightenment terminology undergirding Cathcart's patriotic values undergoes the rigors of the Arabo-Islamic interpretive method. Juxtaposing Cathcart's and al-Jabbarti's respective views on the encounter between West and East in the Age of Revolution productively challenges the assumptions inherent in

Enlightenment cosmopolitanism and gestures toward what Rajagopalan Radhakrishnan has theorized as a reciprocal defamiliarization.[4] As Susan Stanford Friedman puts it, discussing Radhakrishnan's work, "reciprocal defamiliarization unravels the self-other opposition that reproduces systems of epistemological dominance."[5] Both Cathcart and al-Jabbarti struggle to reconcile cultural incommensurability and ultimately fail, but in their struggles they point to the possibility for reconstituting a meaningful dialogue between American and Arabo-Islamic intellectual traditions based precisely on what is unknowable.

I end the chapter by examining the legacy of American contact with Barbary and the literature it produces. Barbary referents were vehicles for Federal-era American writers who wanted to express the tenor of national identity. Decontextualized and culturally orphaned, these Barbary vehicles acquired specifically American meanings that spoke to specifically American questions of national identity. In particular, I demonstrate the role that tropes and metaphors of Arabness play in ameliorating the impasses between the rhetoric of American freedom and equality and the U.S. government's exclusionary practices. The racially, socially, and sexually fluid figure of the captive is a rhetorical lynchpin in the transformation of particularistic American versions of democracy into universal expressions of freedom and equality. In turn, tropes and metaphors of Arabness provide conduits between captivity and freedom that symbolically code the passage as a movement from darkness into whiteness, from savagery into civilization, and from foreignness into American citizenship. As a symbol of national identification, the captive universalizes the reach of American values, but the movement from captivity to freedom is only accomplished by tropes that reparticularize those values. Nonetheless, a recovery of the intercultural dialectics that inform these tropes reveals alternate national imaginaries that American writers throughout the nineteenth century continued to explore through figures of the Arab.

A Dirty Cosmopolitan

During James Leander Cathcart's eleven years as a captive in Barbary (1785–1796), he maintained a lively correspondence with many of the most influential players in the new American republic's government. His collected papers attest to both his deep involvement in the protracted negotiations for the release of the American slaves held with him in Algiers and his abiding desire to have his efforts preserved for history in the most flattering possible light. On more than several occasions in his personal papers, he emphatically points to "proof" of his patriotic service, including a mention of a letter from the Swedish counsel in Algiers, Mr. Skoldebrand, in which, Cathcart says, "he acknowledges my success and hopes I may enjoy the gratitude of my country."[6] That gratitude was far from forthcoming, and Cathcart complained to his dying day of the debts (financial and otherwise) his country had left unpaid. One of these complaints appears in a sardonic note Cathcart scribbled at the bottom of a letter John Quincy Adams wrote to him in 1822. In the letter, Quincy Adams apologizes about a government position the former secretary of state was unable to wrangle for the former captive. Cathcart's handwritten comment reads, "I am left in my old age with a family of ten children unprovided for, not withstanding that I am master of the French, Spanish, Portuguese and Italian languages, God's will be done!!!"[7]

Cathcart saw himself by experience and training to be a perfect representative of the young, cosmopolitan republic. That experience and training were acquired during the time he spent in the Mediterranean as both captive and diplomat. "One article ought to be added to our Constitution," Cathcart wrote to then secretary of state Timothy Pickering in April 1800, "viz.: No person should be eligible to be a candidate for the Presidency of the United States before they reside six months in Barbary."[8] Cathcart's cosmopolitanism was not cultivated in school, honed in high-society fetes, or spoken in refined phrases. Rather, it was the product of years spent abroad as a captive, a sailor, and a tavern owner. Cathcart spoke a brand of what I am calling dirty cosmopolitanism,[9] a bottom-up universalism informed by the experience of slavery, dispossession, and exile.[10]

Born in Ireland in 1767, Cathcart joined the American Revolution at twelve years of age in 1779 and spent time in a British prisoner-of-war ship (which he escaped in 1782) before being captured off the coast of Algiers in 1785. The Spanish that Cathcart learned as an English captive served him well in Barbary, where he eventually climbed to the highest position a slave could hold in Algiers, secretary to the Dey. As secretary, Cathcart (having learned Arabic, Turkish, and Lingua Franca) acted as an intermediary between U.S. diplomats and Algerian government officials. Upon his release from Barbary captivity, Cathcart was appointed U.S. consul to Tripoli, and it was in that capacity that he suggested Hamet Karamanelli to General William Eaton as an "instrument" (Eaton's turn of phrase) that

America could utilize in its 1801–1805 War with Tripoli. By every means possible, honorable and dishonorable, Cathcart had managed to parlay Barbary captivity into a small if fleeting fortune (ample enough to buy the ship that sailed him home from North Africa) and ultimately into a career as a U.S. diplomat.

Immigrant, citizen, war veteran, slave, diplomat, avowed patriot, and inveterate critic of a nation he served in the Atlantic, in the Mediterranean, and on the Mississippi River, Cathcart left a body of writing filled with opinions that were largely ignored by his more influential contemporaries. This writing includes a closet Barbary captivity narrative published over a hundred years after its completion, diplomatic correspondences regarding the War with Tripoli that were more often than not dismissed as filled with prejudiced advice, and a government-sponsored survey of the Louisiana Territory that was promptly lost for close to half a century. Whatever his personal shortcomings, Cathcart participated in and provided copious comment on most of the major international events of the Federal era, including the Revolutionary War, the War with Tripoli, and the Louisiana Purchase.[11]

A consistent theme in Cathcart's writing is the struggle to manifest an idealized America defined by freedom, democracy, equality, transparency, and civilized order. This struggle is captured for Cathcart in both explicit and implicit comparisons between Barbary and the United States. When Cathcart first arrives in Barbary as a slave, he describes the country's landscape through a reference to American settlement. "The country except in their gardens and plantations which are all walled in, resembling the first settlements in America [i]s entirely uncultivated."[12] Cultivation, of course, was an operative metaphor of early American nation building, one found repeatedly in Thomas Jefferson's *Notes on the State of Virginia*, for instance. "I repeat it again," Jefferson wrote, "cultivators of the earth are the most virtuous and independent citizens."[13] In Jefferson's political economy, natural right and natural reason are literally "cultivated" by the free citizen's relationship to the soil. Jefferson believed that heterogeneity was a threat to this political ideal of cultivation. Speaking of potential American citizens who hail from foreign countries ruled by the monarchies that are the antithesis of natural right and natural reason, Jefferson argues, "These principles, with their language, they will transmit to their children. In proportion to their numbers, they will share with us the legislation." He continues, "They will infuse into it their spirit, warp and bias its direction, and render it a heterogeneous, incoherent, distracted mass."[14]

For Jefferson, American soil is a key component of national identification, but for Cathcart, American values can be cultivated almost anywhere. As a Barbary slave, Cathcart commented repeatedly on the potential of the landscape for commercial exploitation, if the population could only be given an enlightened government. "If this country was blessed with a good government which would promote the welfare of its subjects and encourage agriculture, arts and manufactures," Cathcart writes of Algiers, "it would become in a very few years a perfect paradise; it would also become a commercial nation of considerable import and from a 'Den of Thieves,' which it is now at present, it would rank among the civilized nations of the earth" (*Captives*, 88–89). Cathcart is certainly engaging in what we might call prospective colonialism, but he is also registering a more universal perspective on cultivation than Jefferson. Algiers, as well as America, can be cultivated and become a "perfect paradise." The formula is much the same: enlightened, progressive governance that creates order out of chaos. To cultivate Algiers would be to bring it not only social order but also historical order. Thus, if cultivated, Algiers would enter historical time and be counted among the "civilized nations of the earth."

The problem with Algerian society, in Cathcart's view, is that it lacks the progressive and homogeneous flow of time he associates with "civilized nations." This lack of order is nowhere more apparent in Algerian society than in the business sector. Cathcart, describing the slave prison, or Bagnio, where he owns a bar, complains:

> The jingling of chains adds horror to this dismal dungeon beyond conception, which with the stench and unnatural imprecations and blasphemy of some of its miserable inhabitants, makes it really a perfect pandemonium. I will now proceed to describe this receptacle of human misery. . . . They are perfectly dark and in the day are illuminated with lamps, and when full of drunken Turks, Moors, Arabs, Christians, and now and then a Jew or two . . . forms the most disgusting "Coup de Oeil" that can be imagined, . . . the place filled with smoke of tobacco which renders objects nearly impervious to the view, some wrangling with the tavern keepers for more liquor and refusing to pay for it, that upon the whole it must resemble the infernal regions more than any other place in the known world, especially when they frequently quarrel with themselves and proceed to blows and even murder often takes place in those receptacles of vice and immorality, which generally occasions the tavern keeper to lose all his property as the tavern is seized by the Regency and the tavern keeper sent to hard labor. (*Captives*, 126)

The antithesis of Enlightenment space, the Barbary Bagnio is a perfect "pandemonium" instead of a "perfect paradise." This pandemonium obscures clear vision but also impedes commercial order and due process. The mixtures precipitated by the Bagnio space are not only unwholesome; they are violently disruptive. The vision of chaos inherent in Cathcart's portrayal of the slave tavern within the prison suggests the captive's suspicions about the limits of multiculturalism. Cathcart's reaction to the cacophony of cultures mingled in the Bagnio reinforces, by contrast, the importance of homogeneity in creating "civilized nations." The passage also suggests that Jefferson's trepidations about the incoherency of a heterogeneous society were shared by other new American citizens. Appropriately enough, Cathcart names the tavern the "Mad House." If Americans fail to manage the relationship between the country's various constituent racial and religious elements, Cathcart implies, American society runs the risk of becoming similarly chaotic. Ethnic, racial, cultural, religious, and linguistic difference are all challenges to the spatio-temporal homogeneity of Cathcart's idealized community. Applying the language of Revolutionary American values to the social and racial reality of Barbary produces images that often reflect the barbarous potential of America as much as they project the potential of a cultivated North Africa.

The experience of enslavement in Barbary elicits, from Cathcart, a reinforcement of the Enlightenment values of order, progress, clarity, and transparency. Though these enlightened values are what distinguishes American society from Barbary society, Cathcart marks them not as peculiar or peculiarly beneficial to American democracy but rather as universal and universally beneficial. However, contact with Barbary also forces Cathcart to confront the particular claims of American identity. Barbary, in other words, provides Cathcart a screen through which to negotiate the meaning of America. This negotiation is evident in Cathcart's translation of his Barbary captivity back into an American discourse on freedom and bondage.

> Is it possible . . . an exile forever from my dear, but cruel Patria . . . ? . . . O! America, could you see the miserable situation of your citizens in captivity, who have shed their blood to secure you the liberty you now possess and enjoy: . . . you are the first that set the example to the world, to shake off the yoke of tyranny, to expel despotism and injustice from the face of the earth. The negroes have even had a share in your deliberations, and have reaped the benefits arising from your wise and wholesome laws and

regulations. . . . Have we sold our birthright? Are we excluded without cause from the privileges enjoyed indiscriminately by our lowest class of citizens? (*Captives*, 143–44)

In this passage, the appeal to the universal values of "civilized nations" is abandoned for the particular historical claim a U.S. citizen can make on his or her country. Eight years to the day after his initial captivity, Cathcart uses a journal entry to chide his country for neglecting its obligation to the citizens who fought in America's struggle for independence. Invoking the tone of a jeremiad, Cathcart reverses the Middle Passage, turning it into a white slave's journal of African captivity. The captive's voice, split between devotion and reprimand, calls forth from across the Atlantic, back to his unique *Patria*.

The figure of the captive appears in Cathcart's writing as a test case of the connection between the rhetoric of American Revolution and the actions of the new U.S. government. Patriotism depends on the abstraction of the individual into the collective idea of the nation. But if the nation fails to live up to its ideals, the bond between individual and collective that underpins national identity is broken. Read together with his description of the Mad House slave tavern, Cathcart's patriotic lamentation suggests two things: that a government's ability to deliver Enlightenment values such as justice, order, and due process to its citizens is what distinguishes "civilized nations" from Barbary pandemonium and that the U.S. government's ability to deliver freedom to its citizens is what distinguishes it from other "civilized nations." In this formula, the U.S. government's relationship to the exile, the captive, the prisoner, and the slave is central to expressions of the national fantasy of America.

"Have we sold our birthright?" Cathcart asks rhetorically, comparing the Barbary captive's situation not with the chosen Jacob but rather with the defrauded Esau. The story of Isaac's sons had deep significance for the many Federal-era Americans who identified with Israelites and thus with Jacob's lineage. Cathcart's point is that the American government's indifference to the Barbary captive's plight has transformed these American citizens into figurative Ishmaelites instead of figurative Israelites. Associated both literally and typologically with Ishmael, Esau represents an alternative condition of American exile, one that challenges a tradition that embraces the lineage of the exiled Israelites.[15] Instead of clever and blessed Jacob, Cathcart identifies the Barbary captive with brutish and shunned Esau. As a figure, Esau rhetorically opens a space in Cathcart's jeremiad for recognition of "other" Americans, specifically those who had been disenfranchised by the typological fathers of America's new covenant. Expressing his claims for repatriation from the position of captivity ultimately forces Cathcart and other captives to identify with various subaltern positions in the United States.

However, Cathcart's identification with American "otherness" is far from unambiguous in its democratic intentions. Though the journal entry mentions democratic values such as "shar[ing]" and liberal values such as "wholesome laws and regulations," it remains entirely unclear how Cathcart is configuring the relationship between race, freedom, and citizenship. As the lowest class, "negroes" are still hierarchically inscribed in a democratic system that putatively eschews hierarchies. Furthermore, it is uncertain whether Cathcart is referring to the "privileges enjoyed" by free men and women of color or whether he is referring to slaves whom he rhetorically positions as free. Neither group had full citizenship rights in America. Nevertheless, the Barbary milieu forces Cathcart to reimagine an America in which the social justice claims of African slaves are recognized, even if they are marked as the "lowest class of citizens."

The relationship between America and North Africa established through captivity is peculiar to Barbary contact literature. But the racial reversals inherent in Barbary enslavement also index the porous categories of identification that have always been part of the captivity genre in American letters. As Chris Castiglia argues in the context of female narratives of Indian captivity, "crossing cultures forced white women to question the constitutive binaries of civilized and savage, free and captured, Christian and pagan, race and nation, on which their identities were based."[16] Barbary slavery provides white, working-class sailors, such as Cathcart, with a set of experiences that reflect back onto the incompleteness of the Revolutionary War in the United States. These experiences produce meditations on the injustice still extant in the idealized nation, meditations in which the Barbary captive's sympathies often extend to forms of American victimization that cut across "constitutive binaries." In cutting across the "constitutive binaries" that defined their American identity, some of these captives redefined America not as a culturally homogeneous nation moving through historically homogeneous time but rather as a multicultural nation in which people experienced historical time quite differently because of their freedom or lack of it.

Barbary captivity narratives provide a literary forum in which suffering white, male, American citizens ventriloquize the sufferings of nonwhite, male, American "others." No captive spoke the syncretic language of equality more eloquently than the oft-maligned and perpetually ignored Cathcart. Far from the Enlightenment model of a statesman, Cathcart was often coarse and opinionated, as well as replete with a set of prejudices nurtured during half a lifetime spent negotiating the intricacies of power and influence in the Mediterranean. However, the captive-turned-diplomat's linguistic skills and range of contact with foreign cultures made him acutely sensitive to the multiphonic demands of freedom to be heard throughout the transatlantic world and its Mediterranean seam. As a result, Cathcart charts intercultural equivalencies that often challenge the dichotomies between America and Barbary, as well as between Christian and Muslim, that are found in many other captivity narratives.[17]

Tucked between Cathcart's letters to and from John Adams, Thomas Jefferson, James Madison, and Timothy Pickering is a yellowing and brittle scrap of foolscap (figures 3 and 4) with cursive writing on both sides. On the front upper half, above some rough numerical calculations, is the note, in Cathcart's hand, "Mohammadan prayer as learned by all Renegades" (converts to Islam), coupled with the suggestive comment, "this had like to have been a serious affair for me on July 25th, 1793."[18] In Barbary captivity narratives, the Renegado, a religious and cultural apostate, is a reviled figure. The temptation of "taking the turban" is one Cathcart explains and dismisses in his own captivity narrative. Yet his private notes display a fierce curiosity about the Renegado. On the back of the document is Cathcart's transliteration of the "Mohammadan" prayer from Lingua Franca into English.

The events of July 25 that Cathcart references cryptically in his note are documented more thoroughly near the end of *The Captives*, his posthumously published account of Barbary slavery. The "serious affair" Cathcart mentions evolves out of a confrontation he has with a Muslim *sheriff* (descendant of the Prophet Muhammad). On the day in question, the Muslim *sheriff* demands the "infidel" Cathcart vacate the seat he is occupying in the Mad House to let a "true believer" sit. Cathcart's response to this charge diplomatically employs both Arabic and English, as well as references to Arabo-Islamic and American cultural values.

As far as being without faith I believe in the faith of my forefathers (la illah, ila Allah), there is no God but the true God. But as I was not born in the same country that you was, I have not been taught the symbol of your faith, but I know it. You say "la illah, ila Allah wa Mahomed Arasule Allah, there

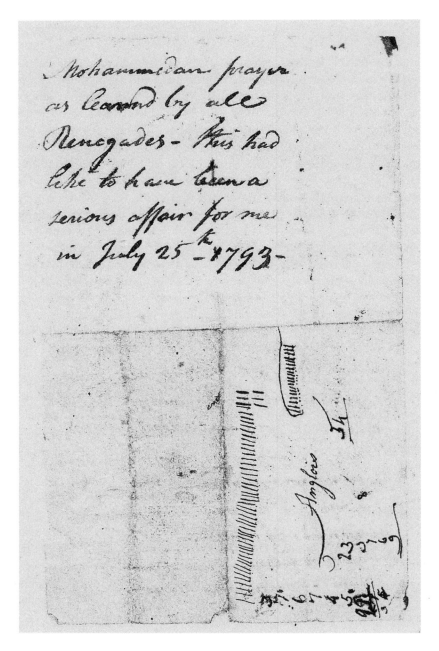

Figure 3. James Leander Cathcart, note, dated July 25, 1793. From James Leander Cathcart Papers, Manuscripts Division, Stephen A. Schwartzman Building, New York Public Library.

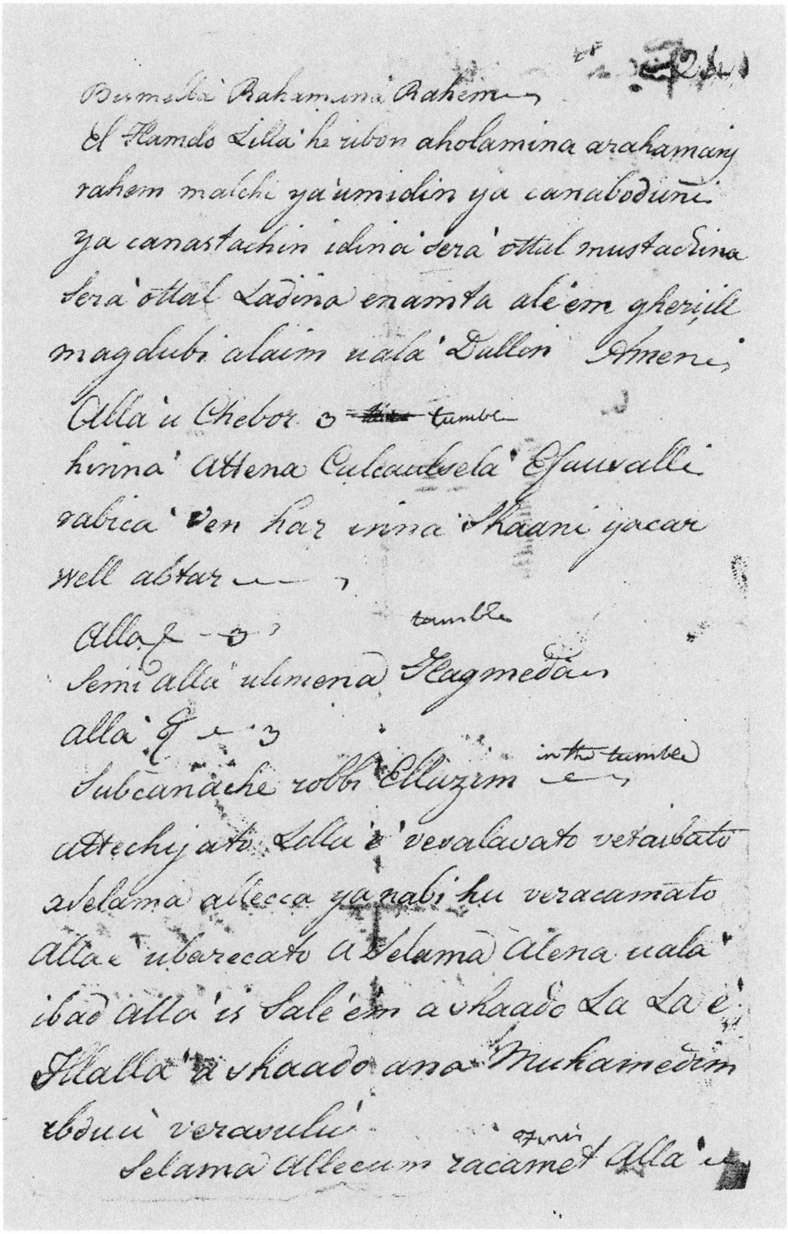
Bismilla Rahamana Rahem
El Hamdo Lilla he ribon aholamina arahamani
rahem malchi ya umidin ya canabodune
ya canastachin idina dera ottal mustadina
dera ottal Ladina enamta ale em gheriull
magdubi alaim uala Dallen Amen
Alla u Chebor 3 tamble
hinna Attena Culcautsela Esauvalli
uabica Ven har inna Skaani yacar
well abtar
tamble
Alla 3
Semi alla ulimena Hagmeda
alla 3
Subcanache robbi Ellazim in the tamble
Attechy ati Lilla e vesalavato vetaibato
aselama alecca ya nabi hu veracamato
Alla ubarecato A Selama Alena uala
ibad alla is Sale em a shaado La La e
Illalla a shaado ana Muhammedum
abduu verasulu
Selama Allecum racamet Alla e

Figure 4. James Leander Cathcart, note, "Renegado" conversion oath. From James Leander Cathcart Papers, Manuscripts Division, Stephen A. Schwartzman Building, New York Public Library.

is no God but the true God and Mohammed is his prophet." I do not know Mohammed as a prophet, but I believe him to have been a very great law giver, who converted millions of idolators and induced them to worship the only true God, as I do. (*Captives*, 146)

In an adroit rhetorical move, Cathcart recites the *shahada*, the profession of the Islamic creed, to establish his faith in Islam, if not his Islamic faith. It is an act of syncretism, not synthesis. Cathcart believes in the "only true God," as Muslims do, but he reserves the right to give that God a name that hinges on cultural context. By affirming his faith in both Allah and the God of Christianity in a single breath, Cathcart references the religious claims of two distinct languages of cultural identity without eclipsing either one's particularity. Cathcart translates the Arabic meaning into English but lets the transliterated Arabic words remain on the page for his reader, gesturing toward their ultimate incommensurability with English.[19]

Taken at face value, the intercultural equivalencies Cathcart establishes through his knowledge of the Arabic language, Islamic history, and the Mediterranean Lingua Franca (in which the conversation must have taken place) indicate his belief in a common morality, but not one that erases cultural particularity. Cathcart's response to the *sheriff*'s absolutist distinction between Muslim faith and Christian infidelity suggests a continuum between the two religions rather than a binary distinction. Cathcart provides a model of universal history that binds disparate global events (the advent of Christianity, the advent of Islam) in a common narrative of progress toward enlightenment (converting "idolators"). This intercultural language presents Arabo-Islamic and American-Christian identities as modulations of representation, not essential opposites.

Interestingly enough, though, the words Cathcart chooses to defend himself against the charge of "infidel" in his captivity narrative are not the same words he writes on the back of his reference to the event of July 25 in his scrap notes. What is written on the back of the scrap note is Cathcart's transliteration of the Lingua Franca oath of allegiance that the Barbary convert to Islam takes, an oath that begins with the *al-Fatihah*, or the opening words of the first chapter of the Qur'an: "In the name of God, the Compassionate and the Merciful—praise be upon Him." These words traditionally preface any task a faithful Muslim undertakes and are written at the beginning of almost any Islamically coded piece of literature. However, they are not the Islamic creed, nor does reciting them constitute an orthodox form of conversion. The verbatim Islamic creed that Cathcart recites in *The Captives* does not appear in the Renegado conversion mantra. Instead the Renegado mantra combines various snatches of Islamically coded phraseology.

Is Cathcart establishing a rough approximation between the Renegado's oath of conversion and the orthodox Muslim oath of conversion? Is he making a subtle distinction between his own, "accurate," knowledge of Islam and the inaccurate knowledge possessed by the Renegado, a distinction that would be apparent only to a person with knowledge of Arabo-Islamic history and the Arabic language? Or is he retranslating the Renegado oath to consciously craft a scene in which orthodox Arabo-Islamic identity and orthodox American-Christian identity mirror each other? Is he, in other words, choosing to juxtapose orthodox Islam and orthodox Christianity for an American reader? If so, why?

The Barbary experience produces a language of democratic identification with American "others" that depends on a moral universality that exceeds particularistic cultural and individual contexts.[20] The claim to justice that Cathcart fashions out of the Mad House confrontation with a Muslim *sheriff*, as well as through the "dear, but cruel Patria" lament, is spoken in a barbarous voice of democracy. It is a voice enunciated from the position of the slave who demands the same rights as the master. It is a voice that uses syncretism to transform heterodoxies and heterogeneities into shared cultural values. Cathcart's captivity narrative channels a dirty cosmopolitan ethics that informs his model of universal morality. Herein reside the multilingual possibilities of the vocabulary of freedom that emerges from American contact with Barbary.

The Barbarous Voice of Democracy

Forced into the position of the disenfranchised, many of the American sailors in Barbary captivity addressed the gap between the social fantasy of American freedom and democracy and the reality of continuing American slavery and dispossession.[21] In this sense, Barbary acted as a contact zone that pushed white American captives, and those who read about them, toward identification with the plight of African slaves in America. The captivity of white citizens changed the terms of the discourse on freedom and bondage in America. Revolutionary slogans about the metaphorical slavery of American colonists were replaced in newspaper print, magazine articles, and subscription drives with tales of the literal slavery of American citizens.[22] Accounts of captivity in Barbary created dialectics between the African slavery of white Americans and the American slavery of Africans. In the spirit of dialectics, the two slaveries were used to examine and compare the two cultures from which they emanated, often discursively collapsing the supposed differences between civilized America and barbarous North Africa. As the Barbary captive William Ray put it, "Petty despotism is not confined alone to Barbary's execrated and piratical shores; but the base and oppressive treatment can be experienced from officers of the American, as well as the British and other navies."[23] In some instances, dialectical considerations of slavery were used to rhetorically transform America into Barbary and Barbary into America. The title of Lewis Clarke's 1846 account of American slavery testifies to the rhetorical power of this inversion: *Narrative of the Sufferings of Lewis Clarke, during a Captivity of More than Twenty-Five Years, among the Algerines of Kentucky, One of the So Called Christian States of America.* The interpenetration of Barbary and America was the product of efforts to negotiate the inconsistencies between Revolutionary rhetoric and the reality of the American national experience.

Writing some forty years after Cathcart had gained his own freedom, William Lloyd Garrison found occasion to mention Barbary captivity in the preface he prepared for Frederick Douglass's *Narrative*: "An American sailor, who was cast away on the shore of Africa, where he was kept in slavery for three years, was at the expiration of that period found to be imbruted and stultified—he had lost all reasoning power; and having forgotten his native language, could only utter some savage gibberish between Arabic and English."[24] By referring back to the Barbary slavery of white Americans, Garrison places Douglass's narrative within a historical continuum of American captivity. He not only humanizes the African American subject, albeit in a troubling manner, by comparing him to the temporarily inarticulate white subject, but also makes an implicit claim for recognizing African Americans as American citizens. Garrison suggests that the narrative of black captivity in the American South is part of a more universal and unifying American experience. This experience extends the national memory across the Atlantic to the shores of North Africa.

Garrison's rhetorical model for the temporarily inarticulate American citizen was the most famous white man to be held in African slavery in the antebellum period (James Riley). However, his focus on Barbary "imbrutification" repeats the description of the postcaptivity state of the man who is credited with the only known African American account of Barbary from the antebellum period, Robert Adams. "Like most other Christians after a long captivity and severe treatment among the Arabs," wrote the 1816 English editor of Adams's Barbary captivity narrative, "he appeared upon his first arrival exceedingly stupid and insensible."[25] In his advertisement for Adams's narrative, the editor refers to him as an abstract "Christian," not as a black man, and thus plays to his readers' potential "universal" identification with the subject of the tale. The account was published in the *North American Review* (1817), but Adams may or may not have been the real name of the black sailor from New York, and the United States may or may not have been his birthplace. Though the account itself is of dubious authenticity, Adams parlayed the story of captivity among the "wild" Arabs of Barbary into food and shelter in London and eventually a passage back to the United States. Adams's white editors saw his narrative as a means of raising funds to explore the mysteries of North Africa's interior (one of the narrative's highlights is the "first" description of Timbuktu). Adams saw his narrative as a means of passage. But regardless of the individual motivations of Adams and his editor, they both knew that playing into the theme of Barbary captivity's decivilizing effect, its production of a "savage gibberish" even in a Christian, increased the account's emotional purchase.

In captivity narratives, cultural, somatic, and linguistic differences are often leveled to emphasize common humanity. This is the point of Garrison's interracial comparison between the inarticulate black slave in America and the inarticulate white slave in Africa. But the language produced by Barbary captivity is more pidgin vernacular than "savage gibberish." A hodgepodge of languages and cultural references, this vernacular informs the brand of dirty cosmopolitan ethics that Cathcart invokes to negotiate the divide between his American identity and his Arabo-Islamic context in his confrontation with a Muslim *sheriff* at the Mad House. The "savage gibberish between Arabic and English" that Garrison marks as the brutish language of the white captive in Africa I read as the language of a self reconciling itself to its other—as an articulation of the barbarous voice of democracy.

In discussing the linguistic origins of Lingua Franca and its relation to contemporary Creole and pidgin languages, Hugo Schuchardt points out that these dialects are "slave languages" as much as they are merchant languages, often learned in multilinguistic slave prisons and used to communicate between master and slave classes.[26] Cathcart bemoans the lack of clarity, honesty, and order that defines official Barbary society, and he critiques North Africa's barbarous mixture of languages, cultures, and customs while situated in its slave prisons. Yet his own ability to excel in this vernacular chaos and landscape of political intrigue is his strength. Vacillating "between Arabic and English" quite literally makes Cathcart's American diplomatic career.

Cathcart's experiences are singular, but his linking of Barbary and America through figurative antonyms of light and dark, cultivated and uncultivated, civilized and savage is representative. What is perhaps surprising, though, is the intimate relation of Barbary and America in Cathcart's political poetic. In Cathcart's writing, the reader sees antinomies before they are synthesized and witnesses the presence of American potential in North African space before this potential is translated into idioms of American patriotism. Instead of synthesis, Cathcart often offers juxtaposition. The difference is visible in the relationship between the rough transcription of the "Renegado Oath" and the crafted confrontation at the Mad House that appears in Cathcart's closet captivity narrative. Between the two documents something has happened: Cathcart has taken the material of Barbary contact and translated it into an expression of universal American values. What is important is not that the scene Cathcart creates syncretizes rather than synthesizes Arabo-Islamic values and American-Christian values (though that is important in a different respect) but rather that by juxtaposing the two documents we gain an appreciation for their difference. By juxtaposing translation (crafted scene) and original (scrap note) rather than superimposing one over the other we account for the stakes in translation and acquire a sense of the heterogeneities that are lost in the effort to craft an idealized expression of American national identity. Whether it is because he did not plan on publishing or because nobody paid much attention to him, Cathcart's writings work very much through this ethos of juxtaposition. The result is a representation of American subjectivity that acknowledges heterogeneity while fretting over its meaning for the good of the nation. Cathcart's expressions of patriotism are spoken in a barbarous vernacular that registers cultural, racial, and religious difference at the same time that it implicitly justifies American imperialism through reference to universal values.

Some fifteen years after the close of the War with Tripoli, Cathcart was commissioned by the U.S. Navy to survey the Louisiana Territory, which the government had acquired from Napoleon. The U.S. government, eager to replenish its naval fleet after the close of the War of 1812, charged Cathcart with taking account of the available timber resources in a region still largely unmapped and mostly hostile to the United States. In his report, *Southern Louisiana and Southern Alabama in 1819*, Cathcart presents himself not as a revolutionary whose country has deserted him but rather as an agent of an emerging empire. Tracking Cathcart's shifting definition of patriotism as he moves from captive to government surveyor and from Barbary to Louisiana reveals continuums between the rhetoric of American Revolution and the rhetoric of American Empire. This act of philological inquiry also demonstrates the tension between the local and the symbolic in Cathcart's distillation of national identity.

The Roots of Patriotism

Patriotism has its etymological roots in the difference that ancient Greeks made between themselves (a people attached to a *polis*) and barbarians (a people attached to a paternal line, or *patria*). The modern *patriot* first appears in late sixteenth-century French as *patriote*, denoting a person who loves his or her country. *Patriotism* begins to appear in the early eighteenth century, first in English and then by the middle of the century in French and German. The influence of eighteenth-century Enlightenment rhetoric is discernible in the new formation of patriot, as *patriotism* originally refers to a passion based not on love of the father land but rather on a commitment to universal values such as humanity, equality, and justice.[27] Common transatlantic "patriotic" causes were the antislavery movement and the penal-reform movement. The advent of the American Revolutionary War at the end of the eighteenth century gave patriotism a new, very specifically American valence, as the word *patriot* came to mean a person who actively defends his or her country against foreign occupiers (specifically the British). But this meaning of *patriot* was not confined to the American continent for long, as Spanish irregular forces resisting the occupation of their country by Napoleon in the Peninsular War came to be known as patriots. The definition of *patriotism* became slippery when eighteenth-century transatlantic discourses on enlightened revolution gave way to nineteenth-century transatlantic discourses on empire.

A shift in spatial and temporal context, as well as the change in Cathcart's official capacity, destabilized his own perspective on the meaning of *patriotism*. During Barbary slavery, Cathcart invokes his own "dear, but cruel Patria," speaking in a language of democracy that is intentionally broad and purposefully redolent of Enlightenment values. Cathcart uses the term *Patria* to bring the claims of black slaves in America as well as white sailors in Barbary to the rhetorical bar. Cathcart went into captivity a true believer in the democratic revolutionary ethos of the eighteenth-century Enlightenment, often sounding its claims in the pages of his captivity journal. While in Barbary captivity, Cathcart had even mused about the possibilities of fomenting a revolution in North Africa by uniting the various hinterland tribes against the Turkish rulers. Cathcart's visions of military ventures in Barbary were often specifically informed by European models of "enlightened" revolution. "What a pity such a character as Napoleon Bonaparte, with one hundred thousand men under his command, has not a footing in Barbary," Cathcart wrote early in his account of captivity. "With that force he would subdue the whole of Barbary" (*Captives*, 88–89).

Upon Cathcart's eventual return to the United States, he uses the word *patriotism* again in this eighteenth-century Enlightenment context. Castigating the ill-begotten wealth of a prominent Louisiana slave trader, Joseph Ervins, Cathcart comments, "he is now wealthy, & no person, or few, enquires how he became so, this is another proof, that wealth in a Republic answers the same purpose as Nobility in a Monarchy! but I hope there are some few among us, who think other wise, & who prefer virtue, & patriotism, in a tatter'd garment, to successful villainy in an embroidered coat."[28] Cathcart garbs himself in the simple authenticity of patriotism's humanist sentiment. He contrasts his rustic taste with the ostentatious "villainy" of the slave trade, recalling the revolutionary ethos of the war he has fought against an imperial monarchy in 1776. To be patriotic in this instance is to be enlightened in the sense that the American revolutionaries were representatives of freedom, democracy, and equality. But Cathcart has undergone a change since those revolutionary days.

In Barbary, Cathcart fantasizes about Napoleon-inspired revolutions that will transform the uncultivated jungle of Algiers into a garden, replacing despotism with democracy and barbarism with liberal government. In Louisiana, Cathcart operates as the agent of an "empire" he believes will accomplish just this task. As a result, Cathcart no longer consistently trumpets the revolutionary ethos of the eighteenth century, defined for many of his contemporaries by the figure of Napoleon. Rather, he embraces the nineteenth-century mandates of a prospective American empire. "On entering the Mississippi, (which in the language of the aborigines of the country is called 'Messachipi' which signifies the father of waters)," Cathcart writes at the outset of the government report, "the mind naturally expands in contemplation of the destiny which awaits it; the only grand outlet to the increasing commerce of an Empire, equal now to many, and in no distant period will be superior in wealth, population and resources to any in Europe" (*1819*, 16–17). Cathcart's movement from agent of democratic revolution to agent of imperial expansion engenders a shifting and shifty signification of patriotism in his Louisiana journal.

Cathcart's description of Louisiana in fact creates dialectics between his Barbary captivity and his Louisiana authority. Describing his reception in the backwaters and bayous, Cathcart writes,

> It is an incontrovertible fact, that we are view'd by every class of people (as spies) with a very jealous eye, upon a supposition that we have been sent here on purpose to collect information for the government, relative to the grants and claims of the land, & to inspect into the conduct of those who have given validity to them. . . . They therefore have determined it would seem, to place every obstacle in the way of our procuring land carriage, provisions & every other necessary, & their information is so contradictory, & in almost every instance palpably false, that it needs but little penetration to perceive, that it is studied on purpose to deceive. (*1819*, 102)

Cathcart complains that he is perceived as a government spy in what is ostensibly his own country. But to the squatters in Louisiana's backcountry, Cathcart *is* a spy for all intents and purposes, and Louisiana is not American. This squatter population is composed of freed African slaves, Native Americans, mixed African-Indians, and Spanish, French, Irish, and Scotch settlers, most of whose land claims are dubious in light of the Louisiana Purchase. In Cathcart's eyes, this "mongrel" population is uncultivated, disorganized, and hostile to enlightened government intervention. In other words, it looks a lot like Barbary. Impenetrability, chaos, disorder, and heterogeneity are as evident in America's backwaters as they are in a North African prison.

It is tempting to read Cathcart's embracement of the mandates of empire at the expense of revolutionary values as conditioned by his movement from the position of a slave to a position of relative authority—literally from the position of the surveyed to that of the surveyor. But captivity did not preclude Cathcart from surveying. He took assiduous notes on Algerian fortifications while a captive and often projected military battles onto the North African landscape. "So secure do the Algerines consider themselves from invasion," writes Cathcart, "that they have neglected to fortify a hill the Christians call Belvidere . . . [which] would undoubtedly be the first place an invading General would take possession of" (*Captives*, 88). While held as a slave, Cathcart mingles the perspective of the spy and the captive in moments of speculative military raiding.

A phrase Cathcart uses in his description of the Barbary Bagnio, "Coup de Oeil," the stroke of an eye, appears again in the Louisiana journal. Though it may seem an innocuous enough demonstration of Cathcart's linguistic range and cultural sophistication, the phrase carries in its military inference the sense of a tactical gaze that brings the terrain under view into strategic order. It is precisely the desire to order that motivates Cathcart's catalogues (of people, of plants, of geography) in both Barbary and Louisiana. Louisiana, like Barbary, lacks cultivation—both physical and social.

But the language Cathcart uses to organize the physical space and natural resources of Louisiana is a "barbarous" mixture of Latin, English, French, Spanish, Native American dialect, and even "the Turkish idiom." Cathcart refers to pumpkins by the French appellation given to them by the sixteenth-century trapper Jacques Cartier, "pompions." He refers to a canoe by the Carib phrase "Para agua." He contextualizes the reader's introduction to the Mississippi by providing both its "aboriginal" name, "Messachipi," and "aboriginal" signification, "father of waters." As much as Cathcart attempts to create order out of the swamp by applying Latin botanical names to trees and plants and posting placards on islands that claim the resources as government property, the vernacular reality of the region's lingua franca frustrates this new order and undercuts the U.S. government's claims with the claims of other histories, other presences.

Cathcart's political poetic of patriotism is ultimately ruptured in his Louisiana journal by vernacular slippages. These slippages shed light on the transnational contexts that shaped Federal-era America's terms of national identification. Describing the reports he has received of the far west region of Louisiana, Cathcart comments on the presence there of "bands of Pirates who wear any flag that suits them, but denominate themselves Patriots" (*1819*, 94–95). In the colloquial language of 1819 lower Louisiana, the term referenced a multitude of depredations that were committed under the cover of "patriotic" auspices. This final, ironic meaning of *patriot*, as "a person who claims to be disinterestedly devoted to his or her country, but whose actions or intentions are considered to be detrimental or hypocritical," had been around since the seventeenth century, but it gained renewed resonance in the transition from the eighteenth century to the nineteenth in light of the Peninsular Wars in Spain.[29] The word *patriot*'s ability to signify both itself and its ironic opposite acquires particular poignancy in the context of Cathcart's own "patriotic" efforts to bring Louisiana into the orbit of American imperial commerce and to bring America the full benefits of its territorial possessions.

At one point in the Louisiana journal, Cathcart encounters a native of the Adriatic city of Trieste who as a seaman traded with Turkey and the Barbary States. The two men exchange greetings in the depths of the swamp. "This reminds me of the following Turkish adage," Cathcart rejoins: "Dag a Dag consomes; Adan Adan conoscoer! (ie) Men may encounter, but mountains never meet!—" (*1819*, 27). The literal sense of Cathcart's adage is that man is mobile but mountains are fixed geographically. He also may be indirectly referencing the phrase "if the mountain would not come to Muhammad, Muhammad will go to the Mountain."[30] But the contrast between permanence and fluidity, as well as between man and nature, that Cathcart wishes to establish is in fact deconstructed by his own attempts to categorize the natural world he encounters in Louisiana. Cathcart's catalogue of bayous, plants, and land formations found in the swamp in fact points not to the permanence or fixity of the natural world but rather to the futility of the act of naming nature, of organizing it into a knowable grid. Fixing nature with the permanence of names is futile not only in the face of man's transitoriness and the tenuousness of his knowledge but also in terms of the natural environment's own physical movements.

The vernacular, in other words, always threatens to erode the sense of order established by the act of naming, just as erosion always threatens to undermine the maps that man charts and to change the landscapes he views. In this sense, the "Mountain and Muhammad" phrase is apt. If your first attempt does not succeed, try a different strategy. The classificatory language Cathcart imposes on Louisiana in 1819 is outdated within a few decades, as are many of the geographical features he enumerates. A reed cane that was once *Arundo Aquatica* is now known as a *Phragmites communis*. Cathcart's Cat Island no longer exists, having been reclaimed by the flooding of the Mississippi. The America that Cathcart presents in his Louisiana journal is a vernacular America—contingent, contaminated, fluid, and mongrel.

Cathcart creates in his Barbary captivity narrative a discourse on American national identity that universalizes American values, as well as connects white, male American citizens to their "others." From the distance of exile, Cathcart projected an idealized nation. In Louisiana, this ideal nation meets vernacular reality. If national identity depends on a coherent national culture with which to identify, Louisiana appears as foreign to America as Barbary. Yet it is America. Cathcart registers the threat to the national frame of reference that Louisiana poses by remarking on the gap between his definition of *patriotism* and the definition that circulates in the backwaters and bayous of the swamp. Registering the tension between the local and the national, Cathcart remarks on the populace's refusal to be abstracted away from their bodies and everyday experiences to the supposedly more stable symbolic order of America.

> Between Renthrops, & McCows, or Muggahs, there is a ridge of tolerable good live Oak, which we had not seen before, the proprietors of which would be glad to permit any individual to take it away gratis, merely to clear their land, but if the United States were to order the purchase they would not fail to demand an exorbitant price for it probably from 3 to 7 dol's per tree, for patriotism is a plant which does not grow in this climate, & Uncle Sam is consider'd fair game. (*1819*, 82)

Attempting to close the gap between local interest and national interest, Cathcart figures patriotism as a plant, naturalizing its sentiment as universal. But he also acknowledges patriotism's particularist valence. The Louisiana setting frustrates any translation of the particularity of Uncle Sam's values into the universal sentiment of patriotism. The name Uncle Sam came into existence as a direct result of the War of 1812, the same war that left the country in need of the timber resources Cathcart surveys.[31] But because patriotism does not grow "in this climate," it must be imported and cultivated. In this usage, patriotism is not equated with nationalism exactly and is not a universal humanism opposed to self-interest per se. Rather patriotism is described as allegiance to Uncle Sam, the figurehead of an emerging American empire. Patriotism, as Cathcart uses the term in this context, is an American political poetic that organizes a mutually beneficial relation between citizen and nation.

In Cathcart's captivity narrative, he takes the experience of slavery in Barbary and translates it into expressions of American national identification. But the imaginary America that Cathcart crafts in his Barbary captivity narrative is always in tension with American governmental practices that fall short of the nation's stated ideals. Cathcart not only demands that Revolutionary values must be applied equally to American citizens in Barbary as well as to American citizens in the United States. He also insists that these values must ultimately be universal and universally recognizable across cultural identities, lest the covenant between patriotic citizen and exceptional nation be broken. But in Louisiana, patriotism reappears as a particularist value, not a universal one, and citizenship is exclusive. The problem in Louisiana is that a large number of its inhabitants do not embody the ideal of a U.S. citizen. Discussing the potential of New Orleans as an "Emporium" to the world, Cathcart laments the French Creoles' lack of enterprise and comments that the needed improvements to Louisiana's infrastructure will not commence "before the majority [of the population] are native Americans, either from, or descended from natives of the Northern and eastern states" (*1819*, 17). If Louisiana is to be absorbed into the national symbolic, Cathcart suggests, it is going to have to be colonized.

Cathcart's often contradictory and ambivalent views on the relationship between local identity and national identity tracks with the transformation of a late eighteenth-century rhetoric of revolution into an early nineteenth-century rhetoric of imperialism. The Enlightenment tropes and metaphors that fueled the patriotism of American Revolutionaries were morphing into arguments for stability, coherency, continuity, and cultural homogeneity. Values that were previously marshaled rhetorically against tyranny, slavery, and colonial bondage were often discursively repurposed to support a system of government that abided slavery, that was viewed by many as tyrannical, and that was beginning to express its own colonial ambitions. Cathcart was cosmopolitan in experience and sentiment, but multiculturalism posed a direct threat to his sense of the national frame of reference. Fear of cultural incoherency and anxiety about the destabilizing effect cultural relativism would have on national identity linked Cathcart to prominent American Enlightenment thinkers such as Jefferson, but it also linked him to a more unlikely counterpart, half a world away.

An Arab View of Patriotism

While Cathcart fantasized about Napoleonic invasions of North Africa, the most renowned Arab historian of the era, Abd al-Rahman al-Jabbarti (1756–1825), experienced one firsthand. In 1798, the al-Azhar-trained

Egyptian sheikh al-Jabbarti wrote a historical account of the initial six months of the French occupation of Egypt.[32] A blend of defiance and admiration, al-Jabbarti's history of the French in Egypt captures the ambivalent relationship the nineteenth-century Arab world had with European modernity.[33] It also distills a decisive moment from which there was no return for the next generation of Arab intellectuals who came into contact with the West.[34]

Very early in al-Jabbarti's account of the French occupation of Egypt, he reprints a proclamation written in Arabic that the French circulate in Egypt. Beginning with the same words transliterated in Cathcart's "Mohammadan prayer," the document moves quickly to bind the Muslim profession of faith to an Enlightenment discourse on secular liberalism.

> In the name of God, the merciful, the Compassionate. There is no God but God. He has no son, nor has He an associate in His Dominion.
>
> On behalf of the French Republic which is based on the foundation of liberty and equality, General Bonaparte, Commander-in-Chief of the French armies makes known to all the Egyptian people that for a long time the Sanjaqs who lorded it over Egypt have treated the French community basely and contemptuously and have persecuted its merchants with all manner of extortion and violence. Therefore the hour of punishment has come.[35]

A few lines later, the proclamation goes on to promise the Egyptian people, "I have not come to you except for the purpose of restoring your rights from the hands of the oppressors and that I more than the Mamluks, serve God—may He be praised and exalted—and revere His prophet Muhammad and the glorious Qur'an" (*Chronicle*, 24, 26).

Napoleon sought to naturalize the French colonial presence in Egypt by printing his proclamation in Arabic and paying homage to the religious convictions of the Muslim populace. He also sought to justify French colonialism's advent in Africa by wedding free-market liberalism and political liberalism to a rhetoric of religious righteousness. Napoleon, in essence, claims to be a better Muslim than the Mamelukes he is ousting—"O ye Qadis, Shaykhs and Imams; O ye Shurbajiyya and men of circumstance tell your nation that the French are also faithful Muslims" (*Chronicle*, 26). Unlike Cathcart's pseudoconversion, with its syncretic approach to the competing Christian and Islamic claims to religious authority, the French proclamation synthesizes French identity and Muslim identity to produce

French Muslims. By enlisting the intellectual and religious elite (the *ulama*) in his cause, Napoleon planned to follow the path to hegemony paved by centuries of foreign invaders in the Orient before him—the Mughals, the Mongols, the Mamelukes, and so on.

Al-Jabbarti takes Napoleon's written attempt at self-patriation to task on the most elemental level of Arabo-Islamic cultural identity: language. Al-Jabbarti concludes his reprinting of the French proclamation in Arabic with a *tafseer* (literal exegesis) aimed at revealing the gap between French mimicry and Islamic authenticity—aimed at outing the French as *kuffar* (non-Muslims) and their figurative interpretation of Muslim identity as false. "Here is an explanation," al-Jabbarti writes, "of the incoherent words and vulgar constructions which he put in this miserable letter" (*Chronicle*, 27). Incoherency in language and vulgarity in linguistic construction are charges that carry deep cultural resonance for al-Jabbarti's literate, urbane Arab audience.

Al-Jabbarti's *tafseer* extends for several pages and makes the general point that the French are poor hands at writing the Arabic language— they lack style, they blend colloquial with classical vocabulary, they do not know the proper case endings for words, and they use unnecessary words where fewer words would produce a more refined sentiment. Al-Jabbarti's most general argument might be taken as, "These barbarians do not even know proper grammar. How can they rule a country?" But, more particularly, al-Jabbarti resists French colonial occupation by using Arabic to deconstruct French figurative claims to be culturally analogous with Egyptians. Reacting to the line in the proclamation which reads, "I more than the Mamluks serve God," al-Jabbarti points out, "There is inversion in the words which should read *innani a'budu Allah akthar min al-Mamalik*" (because I serve God more than the Mamluks do; *Chronicle*, 31). Al-Jabbarti's point is that according to the rules of good Arabic style, the sentence as written has a different meaning than intended, a meaning which because of the improper arrangement of its grammatical structure reveals the French as imposters. "However, it is possible that there is no inversion and that the meaning is 'I have more troops or money than the Mamluks' and that the accusative of specification has been omitted," al-Jabbarti proposes. "So his words 'I serve God' are a new sentence and a new lie" (ibid.). A literal interpretation of the sentence, al-Jabbarti argues, exposes the French colonists' true nature.

By referencing the "accusative of specification," a particular case ending a word takes that changes its desinential inflection, al-Jabbarti relies on an essential aspect of the Arabic language to make his point, something called *i'raab* (اعراب). *I'raab*, derived from the same root as the word *Arab*, means "expression," as well as "grammatical inflection." *I'raab*, many scholars argue, provides the fundamental link between language and cultural identity for the Arab people. Discussing the birth of *i'raab* diacriticals, the contemporary Arab poet Adonis relates the story of the seventh-century grammarian Abu'l Aswad al-Du'ali, who was the first person to systematize the case endings of the Qur'an. When al-Du'ali would recite passages of the Qur'an, he had his scribe mark different inflections with a system of differentiated dots. "These dots were the earliest indications of the case endings (*i'rab*) to guide the people to the correct pronunciation," Adonis explains, "and thence to the correct meaning of the Qur'an."[36]

For al-Jabbarti at the turn of the nineteenth century, using the wrong case ending indicates a misunderstanding of the Qur'an—it indicates Napoleon's status as cultural outsider, not insider. "The word *Muslimin* should be *Muslimun* in the nominative," complains al-Jabbarti, again referencing the sloppy use of *i'raab*. "The point of putting the word in the *nasb* (accusative) has already been mentioned," he continues. "There is another point namely: that their Islam is *nasb* (fraud)" (*Chronicle*, 32). Al-Jabbarti's charge of fraud works on several fundamental levels of cultural knowledge and presents an implicit contrast between his deep understanding of how the Arabic language works and the French writer's lack of understanding. As his deft play on words demonstrates, the Arabic root *n-s-b* in its grammatical meaning puts a noun in the accusative case and demands it take the *-in* instead of *-un* ending. But *n-s-b* (pronounced *nusb*) in its nongrammatical inflection refers to a graven image or an idol and thus is an indicator of heresy. The joke depends on its aural component for effect (the short *damma* vowel which changes *nasb* to *nusb*) and thus demonstrates precisely the inflective skill that the French lack. The French do not know *i'raab* because they are not literally Arab and thus cannot "express" themselves as Arabs. Al-Jabbarti promotes language as an essential aspect of Arab resistance to Western colonialism. Figurative representations, such as Napoleon's French Muslims, displace Arab culture. The Arabic language preserves Arab culture in the face of these displacements.

Whereas Cathcart presents himself as progressive, enlightened, and liberal, al-Jabbarti presents himself as a cultural conservative and as a defender of Islamic tradition. Yet both react with similar anxiety to heterogeneity and the threat of incoherency it poses to the national frame of reference. To al-Jabbarti writing at the turn of the nineteenth century, the vernacular "threat" to Arab culture represented by the French attempt to pass their secular humanist rhetoric of *liberté, égalité, and fraternité* off as compatible with Muslim orthodoxy is visible most clearly on the level of their bad grammar or, as he puts it, their "vulgar constructions." The French speak a corrupt version of the Arabic language that betrays their corrupt values. "They follow this rule: great and small, high and low, male and female are all equal," writes al-Jabbarti of the French creed of equality and liberty. "The women do not veil themselves and have no modesty; they do not care whether they uncover their private parts," he continues. "Whenever a Frenchman has to perform an act of nature he does so wherever he happens to be, even in full view of people, and goes away as he is, without washing his private parts" (*Chronicle*, 29). The French's mixing of classical and vernacular and the lack of refinement in their style all signal for al-Jabbarti, on the linguistic level, that the French creed of equality is tantamount to a call for an unwholesome blending of things that the Arabo-Islamic tradition keeps separate. The French creed of liberty is a license to behave as a barbarian. Al-Jabbarti rejects the French's "vulgar constructions" on every level. "They mix their foods," al-Jabbarti comments, in taking a brief break from critiquing the French's use of Arabic. "Some might even put together in one dish coffee, sugar, arrack, raw eggs, limes, and so on" (ibid.). What the French call equality and liberty (Enlightenment "patriotic" values) appear to al-Jabbarti as signs of a promiscuous cultural anarchy whereby the proper order of things is perverted, forgotten, ignored. This foreign anarchy threatens to undermine Arab culture through the vehicle of the foreigners' "vulgar" Arabic.

Napoleon's Arabic declaration in Egypt is calculated to import an eighteenth-century Enlightenment notion of patriotism to the Orient, one based not on nationalism but rather on a commitment to transatlantic humanist values such as equality and liberty. In an ironic twist, al-Jabbarti interprets this Enlightenment brand of patriotism as a kind of *patrios* and thus attaches the European notion of patriotism to a much older, ancient Greek connotation of a barbarian.[37] In al-Jabbarti's account, the French are the barbarians at the gate of the Islamic *umma* (world community), their claims of liberty and equality a kind of garbled mumble. Cultural identity in al-Jabbarti's history is a matter of linguistic purity and literal meaning. He undermines the French political rationale for ruling the Egyptian population by demonstrating the slippage of their Arabic terms into other meanings, meanings that contradict their stated intentions.

Napoleon attempted to represent the French as Muslims in an act of cultural translation that depended on the Enlightenment's universalist secular values being transmuted into Islamic values. Al-Jabbarti uses the full range of Arabic's figurative power to expose the cultural inconsistencies in this act of translation.

Cathcart promotes the civilizing influence of Enlightenment values; al-Jabbarti marks these values as barbaric. But both, in their way, are arguing for cultural consistency and continuity. Both are threatened by the specter of multiculturalism, and both seek to reestablish the smooth, empty time of empire when confronted with an "outside" cultural threat to their notion of communal self. Cathcart is writing from the spring of American empire and al-Jabbarti is writing from the autumn of Arabo-Islamic empire, but that is only one among many ways we might view their relation. They are each more than vanguard and rearguard, respectively. However cosmopolitan Cathcart's sensibilities may be, his frame of reference for American national identity is still quite provincial: "natives of the Northern and eastern states." However provincial al-Jabbarti seems in relation to Western influence, he is writing in defense of an incredibly cosmopolitan Arabo-Islamic cultural tradition. Cathcart writes in a teleological tradition often associated with Western historians. Al-Jabbarti, as an Arab historian, would have been quite familiar with Ibn Khaldun's cyclical theory of empire. Yet this dichotomy is specious as well. Cathcart, the cantankerous former slave, and al-Jabbarti, the discomfited cultural elite, are both grappling with the spatio-temporal disjunctions of the turn-of-the-nineteenth-century transatlantic world. Both are trying to dismiss the heteroclite cultural elements that threaten the terms by which they define their cultural selves, even as they are registering these heteroclite elements on the most basic level of interaction—language. Cathcart cannot rid America of its vernacular declivities any more than al-Jabbarti can preserve the purity of the Arabic language from contamination by contact with Western values. For Cathcart and for many others who wrote Barbary contact narratives in the Federal era, the figure of the Arab was a key rhetorical shuttle in their efforts to bridge the gap between their rebel and citizen identities. These writers' representations of the Arab spoke directly to their desire to amend rifts between the revolutionary promise of America and the governing realities of the United States. In the process, they incorporated images of the Arab into the idioms of American national identity politics, effectively severing representations of the Arabo-Islamic world from the tradition that al-Jabbarti warned was under threat from the West.

Troping the Arab

Barbary captivity created figurative relations between North African culture and American culture. But the figure of the Arab itself was an American arabesque, a willful misinterpretation of Arab identity in the service of creating an American narrative on national identity. Tropes and metaphors of Arabness supply rhetorical ameliorations to the questions about the rifts between the rhetoric of American democracy and the exclusionary practices of the U.S. government raised by Barbary captivity narratives. Arabness, in other words, provides a symbolic figuration of the American promise that is foreclosed in the actual experiences of many Americans. These tropes and metaphors, read against their intentions, though, also create the possibility of thinking through a less exclusive imaginary of American belonging. For the remainder of the chapter, I focus on how American contact with Barbary shaped the representation of Arabness in American literature.

In 1797, Royall Tyler wrote a fictional captivity narrative entitled *The Algerine Captive*. In it, Tyler crafts a bathing scene that invokes the anxiety of cultural conversion referenced in many Barbary captivity narratives. Tyler's hero, Updike Underhill, has been invited to leave the fields of slave labor in Algiers and join the Muslim Mollah at the Muslim college for a series of discussions comparing Islam and Christianity.

> Immediately upon my entering these sacred walls, I was carried to a warm bath, into which I was immediately plunged; while my attendants, as if emulous to cleanse me from all the filth of errour rubbed me so hard with their hands and flesh brushes, that I verily thought they would have flayed me. . . . I was then anointed on all my parts, which had been exposed to the sun with a preparation of a gum, called the balm of Mecca. This application excited a very uneasy sensation, similar to the stroke of the water pepper to which "the liberal shepherds give a grosser name." In twenty-four hours, the sun-browned cuticle peeled off, and left my face, hands, legs and neck as fair as a child's of six months old.[38]

The application of the "balm of Mecca" to Updike ultimately allows him to regain his essential whiteness by peeling off the darker cuticle of slave-labor skin. The balm from Mecca figuratively Arabizes Updike's body in preparation for his potential rebirth as a Muslim but also as a free white man. Arabness ultimately outstrips a narrow association with Islamic identity and becomes a bridge between seemingly binary identities. Updike's figurative Arab skin provides a passage not only from slavery to freedom but also from darkness to whiteness. By becoming Arab, Updike can emancipate his body from slavery and return to white subjectivity. It is the same path the Mollah, himself a European convert to Islam, has taken.

The temporary nature of Updike's Arabization allows him to navigate between the position of slavery and freedom, darkness and whiteness, Christianity and Islam, without ultimately sacrificing his own cultural identity. By presenting Arabness as an applied outer shell of identification (a balm) that can be discarded, Tyler captures a host of anxieties about cultural conversion that circulate under the terms "taking the turban" or "turning Turk" in authentic Barbary captivity narratives. In the end, Updike chooses the fields of slave labor over the comfort of the Muslim college not because his faith wins out but rather because the Mollah's logic tests his faith too strenuously.[39] Unable to refute the Mollah's unfavorable account of the Christian enslavement of black Africans in America, Updike sacrifices his body so that he may remain master of his mind. Though this sacrifice nominally upholds the distinction between savagery (body) and civilization (mind), it also cuts across that distinction by presenting the Mollah's logic as superior to Updike's logic. Updike trades the civilized space of the Muslim college, where he is cleaned to whiteness, for the barbaric fields of slave labor, where he becomes increasingly dark and brutish.

Updike remains patriotic by refusing the temptation of physical freedom. In doing so, though, he brings the positions of master and slave into shifting relations, as well as introduces a potential critique of American Christianity. Arabness provides Tyler with a trope through which to examine the meaning of being American. It is a literary figuration that speaks to the larger dynamic of cultural exchange and erasure that *American Arabesque* charts. Once Updike establishes his allegiance to America, his Arab skin disappears. Tyler uses the "balm of Mecca" to present Arabness as a figurative condition that one can explore and refuse. But the Arabs in invented tales of Barbary captivity operate as proxies for American ethnic types. The fictive encounter between American and Arab allows American readers to negotiate their democratic ideals by reimagining themselves in perverse situations.

Eliza Bradley, whose 1820 fictional captivity narrative sold through several editions as "authentic," describes her imagined capture by North

African "natives" in terms that borrowed heavily from American readers' familiarity with Indian captivity narratives.

> About two hours after the party had departed in search of water, they returned nearly out of breath, and apparently much affrighted, and informed us that they had been pursued by a party of *natives* (some of whom were mounted on camels) and that they were but a short distance from us! . . . Their appearance, indeed, was frightful, being nearly naked, and armed with muskets, spears and scimeters.
>
> Our company having no weapons with which to defend themselves, they approached and prostrated themselves at the feet of the *Arabs* (for such they proved to be) as a token of submission. This they did not, however, seem to understand, but seizing us with all the ferocity of *cannibals*, they in an instant stripped us almost naked.[40]

Bradley invokes the white settler identity of the American colonial through her encounter with the "natives" on shore. But she also registers the ambivalent nature of the boundary between settler and native in the post-national-independence period. Bradley's imaginative inversion of the roles of settler and native in Barbary dramatizes not only anxieties over revolution (racial or otherwise) and the morbid desire to fantasize about the outcome but also a collective cultural need for negotiating the inequities in American democracy.

Whereas white Americans often saw themselves uncomfortably mirrored in the figure of the master "Turk," in the figure of the "Arab" they saw that *other* part of the American population staring back at them. Representing the "Turk" as both illegitimate usurper and legitimized hegemon, American writers offered their readers a split image of themselves—an image that highlighted the conflict between white Americans' imaginative cultural opposition to the English during the Revolutionary War and their very real cultural affiliation with English ancestry. American readers could see themselves in the "Turk," and they could see the English in the "Turk." Though writers used the figure of the "Turk" to facilitate discourses on the evils of patriarchy, tyranny, and usurpation, these indictments threatened to reverse and become unconscious critiques of America's own despotic practices.

The "Arabs" in Bradley's fictitious description, on the other hand, are originally called "natives" and then referred to as "Arabs" before finally being labeled "cannibals." Bradley allows her figure of the Arab both to fit neatly within and to vacillate between the ethnic trope of Native American and African American. Though the Federal-era U.S. government recognized neither of these groups as "Americans," they nevertheless occupied the literal and imaginative American geography. They were a presence that white Americans had to acknowledge subconsciously, and their claims for inclusion in the national identity were often litigated through imaginative projection. When the white American readership of Bradley's story came across this passage, they could imagine themselves staring at the native presence in their own country, as well as at members of the African diaspora who had gained a natal claim to American identity.

A few lines after the encounter, Bradley describes the "hot contest" that erupts between the Arabs who are claiming the whites as "property." Bradley consciously inverts African slavery in the United States. By the end of the passage, Bradley elides the difference between whites and Arabs, as the "nearly naked" natives strip the whites until they are "almost naked." All that is left of white difference is the fig leaf of civilization—a metonym that in fact links whites and natives. Master becomes slave in Bradley's encounter, as the whites "prostrated themselves at the feet of the Arabs."

Bradley's fictive captivity narrative makes clear what is implicit in Cathcart's real account. In the Barbary milieu, the white American occupies the place of the subaltern. The reversal allows for identification with American "otherness" and gestures toward both inclusion and the anxiety elicited by the possibility of inclusive national identity. Cathcart uses syncretism to link the experiences of white, working-class sailors in Africa with black African slaves in the United States. Figurative Arabness creates imaginative conduits between these subject positions. These conduits allow for literal transformations rather than the exploration of mutually shared experiences. The translation of Barbary tropes into the American cultural milieu demonstrates their function in American racial politics. Situated in the American context, Barbary tropes become devices for policing the expansion and contraction of whiteness. Relinking Barbary tropes back to the context from which they were wrested, however, reveals American whiteness to be a contaminated category, haunted by the ghosts of the "otherness" it has incorporated into itself.

American Arabs

Imaginative constructions of Arab identity are found in both real and fictitious accounts of Barbary captivity. These representations of the Arab elsewhere have a profound influence on the representation of Arabness in the American context and ultimately on American categorizations of racial identity. Allan Austin, in his book *African Muslims in Antebellum America*, chronicles the lives of seventy-five African slaves on American plantations who identified themselves as Muslims. Many of these men were literate because of Qur'anic training, and as Austin relates, this literacy "gave them some standing in the New World, particularly among those who decided that the literate slaves must be Moors or Arabs because they would not credit such a possibility as literacy in an African."[31] In this plantation context, the construction of the term *Arab* ostensibly supports racism by allowing white Southerners to maintain categorical prejudice against black Africans through practices such as marking "outstanding" Africans as Arabs, instead of recognizing their visible African heritage. Although some of these West African slaves were indeed Muslim, they were not Arab or Moor.

The marking of an African as a Moor, in fact, did as much to unsettle racial categories as it did to maintain them. Sylviane Diouf, in her analysis of the history of African Muslims enslaved in the Americas, explains how the unique American system of slavery created Moors and Arabs out of sub-Saharan Muslims.

> Because the American system of racial classification did not recognize intermediate strata—mulattos, for example—there could only be inferior blacks and superior whites. Within these limits, a particularly "intelligent black" had to stop being black and become ersatz white. He could be one solely by becoming an African white, that is, an Arab. The only Africans that could qualify for this co-optation were the Muslims, as their religion and their literacy in Arabic could be touted as tangible proof of their Arab origin. With the whitening of the "elite" slaves, the basis on which slavery rested was not threatened. Blacks were still subhumans and thus fit to be enslaved, whereas the Moorish princes, warriors, and fellow slave traders could elevate themselves to the highest positions within the rigid boundaries of the rigid slave society.[42]

Diouf details how the imaginary marker of Arab and/or Moor created differential power relations both between slave and master and between slaves. Through innovative approaches to the historical archive, Diouf, as well as Austin and Michael Gomez, have convincingly demonstrated that Muslim slaves held positions of power on the plantation (such as overseer) disproportionate to their relatively small numbers. Many of these Muslim slaves who were marked as Arab and/or Moor became characters in stories by white, Southern American writers, characters such as Joel Chandler Harris's "Arab" Bilali Mahomet and Cyrus Griffin's "Prince, the Moor," based on the Fulbe slave Ibrahima abd al Rahman. Other slaves such as Omar ibn Said and S'Quash were also transformed into Arabs/Moors by antebellum journalists writing for newspapers such as the *Providence Journal* and the *Wilmington Chronicle*.[43]

The willful misinterpretation of Arab identity was a prominent feature of antebellum American images of the Arab. When the term *Arab* is applied to actual Africans residing in antebellum America, it operates as a discursive bulwark separating African and white culture, but it also opens up a catachrestic space—a space where, as Gayatri Spivak has put it in a different context, "words or concepts are wrested from their proper meaning." The interpretive slip that marks black Muslims on the plantation as Arabs creates "a concept metaphor without an adequate referent."[44] In the American context, the term *Arab* accrues value that cannot be fully absorbed by its referent.

American representations of Arabs are what John Michael has called "figments of the imagination."[45] These figments create the imaginary scene necessary for white Americans to confront their anxieties about the exclusivity of particularistic formations of American citizenship. The Arab of Federal-era American literature is largely figurative, a symbolic position where identity is negotiable and the signifier is free-floating. The Arab is a tropic meeting point; as Žižek says, "We identify ourselves with the other precisely at a point at which he is inimitable, at the point which eludes resemblance."[46] A conceptual metaphor without a stable referent, the image of the Arab operates as a conduit for the white American captive to identify with the disenfranchised Native and the enslaved African precisely at the point of nonresemblance. In the fictional narratives of Barbary captivity that emerged on the American market, such as Tyler's *The Algerine Captive*, the white subject self does not resemble or imitate the "dark-skinned" other but rather occupies the subjective position of the other. The figure of the Arab is the vehicle through which this subjective identification occurs. In this formulation, a new position of subjective enunciation opens up, and the "other" of American national discourse is granted a voice of response and authority, albeit one that is still filtered through white consciousness.

In Barbary captivity narratives, Arabs are figured as both masters and subalterns. They supply a return to whiteness (the balm of Mecca) and stand in for blackness ("the darkest people I ever saw"). They represent civilization (the Muslim college) and primitiveness (the tribe). Through the figure of the Arab, American writers highlighted the potential democratic bond between white and black, settler and indigene, male and female, savage and civilized. Assuming a figurative Arabness, in turn, allows white writers to move symbolically between these mutually exclusive positions and, like Cathcart in the Mad House, not ultimately sacrifice the privilege of their racial and cultural status. These American arabesques mediate between what is "Arab" and what is represented as Arab in the American context, but they also mediate between what is American and what is "other."

The figuration of Arabness in the context of Barbary slavery demonstrates the ambivalent desire to synthesize the positions of master and slave, as well as the recognition that a mediating term was necessary to achieve this synthesis. But whereas the figure of the Arab in American literature gestures toward the synthesis of lordship and bondage in the American literary imaginary, Cathcart's dirty cosmopolitan vernacular vacillates between the positions of the subjective actor in history and the mute object on which history is enacted, with a full appreciation of their mutual exclusivity. When Cathcart arrives in Algiers, his captors bring him and his fellow Americans to the homes of several prominent Algerians, who are "curious to see Americans, having supposed [them] to be the aborigines of the country" (*Captives*, 11). The mistake that the Algerian viewers make in assuming that Americans are aboriginal inhabitants of the United States highlights the role of white citizen as usurper. Even as Cathcart positions himself as the mute object of surveillance on whom history is enacted, he also acknowledges the white American citizen's role as historical agent of colonialism. As an object of contemplation, the white citizen takes the place of the aboriginal inhabitant of America and literally stands in for his country's native population when Cathcart appears in Algeria. What I have been elaborating throughout this chapter by means of these Barbary captivity narratives is not only the split in subjectivity where Cathcart embodies both himself and the nation but also a splintering of subjectivity where the exile sees himself as embodying the plight of many, different exiles.

In Cathcart's image of himself being surveyed by curious Algerians, the captive conjures his nation's fraught national identity by imagining himself simultaneously as subject and object of history, as disenfranchiser and disenfranchised, as white colonizer (usurper) and aboriginal colonized (usurped). Exile in Barbary forces Cathcart, and other captives, to see themselves in the other. This is true of most contact literature; however, the peculiarity of Barbary captivity speaks directly to America's nascent national identity, particularly the question of lordship and bondage as the discussion moves from the metaphorical to the literal plane. In America's Federal-era literature, Barbary serves as a kind of ghostly proxy, allowing readers to examine the stakes in the nation's turn from revolution to empire building. Accounts of slavery in Barbary rebound into ruminations on America and leave the nation's claim to be representative of universal humanist values haunted by its functional failures to grant citizenship to "others." The specter of multiculturalism hangs over these accounts of Barbary, providing a counterimage of an America that is discontinuous with the nation's physical borders, as well as its rhetorical claims.

Though Cathcart's fugitive journal was not published in the Federal era, the experiences he relates in it are emblematic of that period. The images of racial, religious, and social role inversion engendered by American captivity in Barbary pry open a discursive space for fictional writers on captivity, and later for American romantics who used Oriental imagery, to explore American subjectivity from the margins. The pluralistic potential of American identity that emerges anxiously at salient moments in these Barbary captivity narratives expresses claims for inclusion of the disenfranchised groups who were physically present in, but psychically excluded from, the new American nation. And yet as these claims are translated from the Barbary context into the American context, the nodes of intercultural exchange that they mark are erased. The arabesques that Cathcart and other captives from North Africa create out of their experiences in Barbary become American cultural property and establish American categories of race, nation, and citizenship. In recent years, these distillations of American values have both been pitted against rude constructions of Arab identity (9/11) and conjured as a rationale for the support of Arab citizens' universal rights (the Arab Spring). The language, tropes, and fantasies of American difference produced by contact with

Barbary continue to underwrite the enduring national symbolic evoked in the phrase "to the shores of Tripoli." In the late spring of 2011, the literal shores of Tripoli once again became a proving ground for the universal applicability of the American values first put to the test of their "global" reach in the Federal era.[47]

2

Pentimento Geographies

The New York lawyer John Lloyd Stephens wrote the first American version of a Near Eastern travel narrative. Europeans had been describing their travels in the Orient since the Middle Ages, but Stephens's particularly American perspective on the region made his account an instant success with his domestic audience. *Incidents of Travel in Egypt, Arabia Petraea, and the Holy Land*, published by Harper and Brothers in 1837, sold through its first printing within a year despite a nationwide financial panic brought on by Jackson-era speculation. Within two years, the book had sold twenty-one thousand copies, ultimately staying in continuous print until 1882.[1] Edgar Allan Poe enthusiastically reviewed Stephens's book, commenting that it was "equally free of the exaggerated sentimentality of Chateaubriand, or the sublimated, the *too* French enthusiasm of Lamartine on the one hand, and on the other from the degrading spirit of utilitarianism."[2] Herman Melville went so far as to reproduce Stephens as a character in his novel *Redburn*.[3] Though Stephens subsequently wrote several other travel narratives about Europe and South America, his account of Near Eastern deserts, ruins, and lost cities was far more influential on his nineteenth-century contemporaries. Written in a matter-of-fact style, Stephens's book capitalized on his American audience's growing archaeological interest in the Holy Land and its environs. But his book also appealed to American readers because its foreign references often registered their domestic anxieties.

Something of a captain of industry in hiking boots, Stephens went on to found the American Ocean Steam Navigation Company and become president of the Panama Railway Company. Stephens's direct involvement in the advancement of steam and rail on the American continent may seem odd given his concerns about the introduction of rail and steam power in the Sinai Desert.

A railroad is about to be constructed across the desert, over the track followed by the children of Israel to the Red Sea. The pasha had already ordered iron from England for the purpose when I was in Egypt, and there is no doubt of its practicability, being only a distance of eighty miles over a dead level; but whether it will ever be finished, or whether, if finished, it will pay the expense, is much more questionable. Indeed, the better opinion is, that the pasha does it merely to bolster his reputation in Europe as a reformer; that he has begun without calculating the cost; and that he will get tired and abandon it before it is half-completed. It may be that the reader will one day be hurried by a steam-engine over the route which I was now crossing at the slow pace of a camel; and when that day comes all the excitement and wonder of a journey in the desert will be over. There will be no more pitching of tents, or sleeping under the starry firmament, surrounded by Arabs and camels; no more carrying provisions, and no danger of dying of thirst; all will be reduced to the systematic tameness of a cotton factory, and the wild Arab will retire farther into the heart of the desert, shunning, like our native Indians, the faces of strangers, and following forever the footsteps of his wandering ancestors. Blessed be my fortune, improvement had not yet actually begun its march.[4]

Nominally Stephens offers a vision of what the Sinai Desert might look like in the years to come. But the passage touches on topics so central to the question of U.S. continental expansion that American readers would be hard-pressed not to imagine their own country being discussed alongside Egypt. Slavery, Indian removal, and mechanized continental expansion were all sources of intense debate in 1830s America, and they all find their way into the narrative picture Stephens draws of the desert. The cotton factory, the disappearing Indian, and the railway—none of these is actually present in the scene Stephens witnesses firsthand, but they are all present in his description. Curiously, though, the spectral American destiny Stephens sees lurking within the Sinai Desert is not yet manifest in American space either. In 1835, when Stephens set out on his trip east at the advice of his doctors, Peter Cooper's *Tom Thumb*, America's first steam locomotive, had appeared in Maryland only five years earlier. Asa Whitley's resolution to Congress supporting the building of a railway to the Pacific was still ten years away. Nonetheless, Stephens was prescient about the coming of the railroad in America. Though there were only very limited amounts of train tracks already laid in the United States when Stephens left, talk of a transcontinental railroad was in the air before he returned, and the topic picked up momentum through the advocacy of several prominent newspapers throughout the 1840s and '50s.[5]

On the other hand, Stephens's narration of the disappearing Indian is less prescient than prematurely wistful. The Indian Removal Act passed in 1830, but there was still resistance to its implementation throughout the 1830s and '40s, as evidenced in the Black Hawk War (1832), the Second Creek War (1836), and the Seminole War (1835–1842). When Stephens published his book, the term "Manifest Destiny" had not been coined, and Native Americans still inhabited both the western frontier and areas east of the Mississippi in large numbers. Yet in his account of potential Sinai modernization, Stephens represents the Indian to the reader as already receding from view. Furthermore, though Stephens was personally opposed to slavery, the transformation of America's cotton industry from a chattel economy to a systematic "factory" economy was more than thirty years away.

Stephens's description of the Arabian Desert is consistent with midcentury American travelers' penchant to see their own country's social and cultural politics latent in the sights/sites of the Near East. Beginning by locating his readers in a colonial American moment identified with the Israelites' exodus from Egypt and journey across the Red Sea into exile, Stephens ends the passage with a national vision of a modern, industrial economy denuded of its atavistic reliance on slavery and its atavistic population of indigenes. I call this effect *pentimento* both because it describes a visual field in which one image is visible beneath another and because of the word's association with penitence. Travel accounts of the Near East, I argue, are redolent with repentance over the colonization of the American West. This repentance is often discernible in cross-cultural analogies that express regrets about the fading indigene and the loss of a pastoral economy. In Stephens's account of Sinai, the physical facts of the Near East eventually recede from the foreground. The reader is left, by the end of the passage, to contemplate the disappearance of the Indian in American space and to wax nostalgic about the costs of American westward expansion.

Within the narrative picture of the Near East that Stephens paints, a second picture of a potential America is faintly perceptible. The appearance of the Bedouin Arab catalyzes the motion by which this secondary picture, this American scene, moves from background to foreground in the mind's eye of the reader. But the Bedouin figure does not only provide a visual analogy for Native Indians in the American West; it also acts as a living visual analogue for Biblical patriarchs such as Abraham. In short, American writers traveling in the Near East used the figure of the Bedouin to negotiate several, often competing, metaphors of American settlement. The translation of the Bedouin into American frontier geographies is the focus of this chapter.

Starting with the groundbreaking work of Richard Slotkin, critics have continued to demonstrate the central importance that representations of Native Indians have had in creating American national myths.[6] This chapter investigates how placing American national narratives in a global context disturbs a familiar interpretation of the cultural politics of representing the indigene. The presence of the Indian in Near Eastern travel narratives is not merely evidence of the writers' preoccupation with domesticating the exotic or with their desire to project U.S. colonial imperatives onto a global field. The conceptual relationships between Bedouins and Indians explored in these travel accounts index alternative American imaginaries. In these travel narratives, the Near East operates not only as a site where imperial fantasies are played out and racial hierarchies are justified. The Near East also provides an opportunity for American writers to enunciate counterimperial narratives, to explore the contradictions in American national identity, and to reimagine the limits of racial identification. The transformation of Bedouins into Indians and Indians into Bedouins creates cross-cultural equivalencies that can be mined for evidence of the subversive national imaginaries that are embedded within mainstream iterations of white settler colonialism.

I begin by providing a historical overview of Bedouin representation that places in perspective mid-nineteenth-century American writers' interaction with the figure. I then describe how travel writers co-opted the Bedouin figure into American narratives about the western frontier and American tropes of identity. These tropes include the frontiersman and the colonial settler, as well as their ghostly counterparts the savage and the Biblical patriarch. I end the chapter with an extended look at the representation of one of the most famous icons of Arab culture in mid-nineteenth-century America, Petra. Petra's appearance in both Herman Melville's short story "Bartleby" and Frederic Edwin Church's landscape painting *El Khasne'* attests to the influence that midcentury Near Eastern travel narratives had on the Orientalism of later American artists. Pairing descriptions of Petra offered by Americans with a much earlier description of the Arabian Desert offered by the famous Arab traveler Ibn Battuta, however, challenges some of the central rhetorical premises of white settler colonialism.

The Bedouin

> The Bedouins are a savage nation, fully accustomed to savagery
> and the things that cause it. Savagery has become their character
> and nature. They enjoy it, because it means freedom from authority
> and no subservience to leadership. Such a natural disposition
> is the negation and antithesis of civilization. All the customary
> activities of the Bedouins lead to wandering and movement. This
> is the antithesis and negation of stationariness, which produces
> civilization.   —Ibn Khaldun, *Muqaddimah*[7]

Ibn Khaldun's *Muqaddimah*, a fourteenth-century introduction to his
multivolume world history, posits a simple thesis: empires rise and fall
because history is cyclical and all created things decay. "The past resem-
bles the future," Ibn Khaldun advises, "more than one drop of water
another" (*Muqaddimah*, 12). The rise and fall of a specific tribe's imperial power takes place over the course of four generations at the most. The
Bedouin is an integral agent in this imperial drama and, fresh from the
desert, plays the role of new conqueror. However, the conquering Bedouin
tribe's group loyalty and desert mentality weaken with each generation in
power because of the deleterious influences of urban life and luxury. In
Ibn Khaldun's formula, the Bedouin is not merely the savage relic of a pre-
civilized past but also a natural man whose vitality, independence, and
strength of communal spirit contrast sharply with the complacency, deca-
dence, and erosion of communal ties indicative of urban life. "Sedentary
life," Ibn Khaldun notes, "constitutes the last stage of civilization and the
point where it begins to decay" (94). Ibn Khaldun's Bedouins "are closer to
the first natural state and more remote from the evil habits that have been
impressed upon the souls of sedentary people through numerous ugly
and blameworthy customs" (94). The Bedouin stands for the negation of
certain intrinsic features of civilization, but he also keys the development
of civilization. The Bedouin exemplifies Ibn Khaldun's emphasis on the
interplay between the modern and the primitive.[8]

When reform-minded nineteenth-century Arab political theorists such
as Rifa'a al-Tahtawi and Khayr al-Din sought to reinterpret the Islamic
state's relationship to its citizens (Muslim and otherwise), they did so
through Ibn Khaldun's concept of *'asabiyya* (عصبيّة).[9] *'Asabiyya* comes
from the root *'asb*, meaning "to wind, fold, tie, bind." Ibn Khaldun uses
'asabiyya to mean mutual affection and willingness to fight and die for

one another. More simply put, *'asabiyya* is tribalism. But it can also mean the type of power that emanates from that group feeling, what Ibn Khaldun calls natural kingship. Ibn Khaldun argues that *'asabiyya* is necessary to form any kind of stable state but that the strongest manifestation of *'asabiyya* is the tribal blood ties of the savage Bedouin. The process of civilization transforms the natural *'asabiyya* of the savage Bedouin tribe into a form of political *'asabiyya*, based not on blood bonds but rather on imitation and clientage. For Arab intellectuals writing five centuries later, Ibn Khaldun seemed to offer an Islamically grounded approach to modern nationalism. Ibn Khaldun's particular interest is the salutary influence of Islam on Arab civilization, but his exploration of *'asabiyya* broaches the classic question of political thought: the legitimacy of power. He approaches the topic of legitimacy through the figure of the savage, folding the conceits of primitivism into narratives of the modern state.

Of course, American citizens in the mid-nineteenth century confronted a set of historical circumstances vastly different from those confronting Arabs in the fourteenth century. Nevertheless, the question of modern statecraft and its relationship to putatively "savage" populations is at the heart of mid-nineteenth-century discussions about the definition of American democracy and American empire. Juxtaposing the two different historical moments and their respective treatment of the savage Bedouin figure demonstrates something essential about the life of literary images, about the way they manage to fracture linear spatio-temporal narratives and to create continuities between seemingly disparate times and spaces. Ibn Khaldun's relevance to nineteenth-century Arab philosophers of the modern state provides just one example of the nonlinearity of a certain historical imaginary's influences. Bringing Ibn Khaldun's historical imaginary to bear on mid-nineteenth-century American literature locates Americans' national conversation about identity in a longer historical fetch and within a larger global discourse on primitivism. I do not wish to decontextualize mid-nineteenth-century American primitivism but rather to recontextualize it through juxtaposition and comparison. The benefits of recontextualization, I firmly believe, outweigh the risks of decontextualization.

The savage, as a rhetorical figure, plays a key role in the discourses both supporting and challenging the legitimacy of mid-nineteenth-century American continental expansion. The ambivalence and ambiguity attached to representations of Indians in American culture are well documented.[10] The relationship of this history of representation to a history of representing Bedouins has received little to no critical attention. Yet Near

Eastern travel narratives written by Americans in the mid-nineteenth century are rife with comparisons between Native Indians and Bedouins. These comparisons are not merely primitivist conflations. They are significant negotiations with the question of the legitimacy of the American state, a question particularly relevant in light of midcentury debates about westward expansion. These debates, largely between those inclined toward Republican constraint and those inclined toward Democratic expansion, directly influenced the translation of Arab Bedouins into American geographies. To understand the stakes in this translation, it is important to detail the movement between archetype, stereotype, and *figura*.

The Bedouin archetype that Ibn Khaldun describes provides a model (Gk. *archetypon*: "model, pattern"). The fixity of the Bedouin's character resides in the consistent historical pattern he establishes. Specific individuals and whole groups stop being Bedouins for Ibn Khaldun when they stop living nomadic desert lives. The individual can change even if the type remains consistent as a historical force. In Ibn Khaldun's version of colonization, savage Bedouins wrest control of dynasties from effeminized urbanites. But the difference between the urban and the primitive is part of interplay; it is not absolute. Individuals are mutable even if the historical forces they play a role in are not. "Man is a child of the customs and things he has become used to," Ibn Khaldun asserts. "He is not the product of his natural disposition and temperament" (*Muqaddimah*, 95). It follows that the Bedouin archetype may be filled by a wide range of actors, irrespective of race, ethnicity, religion, and the like. Individuals themselves are not inherently, or permanently, Bedouin.[11] One way of saying this is that the term *Bedouin* is a typology but not an ethnicity.

Ibn Khaldun wrote his *Muqaddimah* in a period of "hemispheric interregional history," to borrow Marshall Hodgson's phrase.[12] A distinguishing feature of this period is the advance, often violent, of Turkish-speaking Muslim herding peoples from Central Asia into the central lands of Islam. Within this historical template, Ibn Khaldun's nomadic savage remains a destructive yet romantic figure. It is an archetype associated with his literate, urban, Arab audience's tribal ancestry yet still a relevant force in their contemporary lives (if only as a group against whose attack you needed to protect your caravan). The tribal, nomadic, oral, and martial cultures that poured into the Near East, pillaged cities, and ended dynasties in the thirteenth and fourteenth centuries were largely Mongol and Turkish-speaking horsemen from the Central Asian Steppe. Regardless of this fact, Ibn Khaldun explores the historical processes that these foreign elements enact in his contemporary world through the figure of the Bedouin (بدوى/ *badawee*), who is most readily associated with Arab ancestry. But when Ibn Khaldun speaks of Bedouin culture (عُمْران بدوى/*'umran badawee*), he uses the term primarily as it was used in the Qur'an, to indicate "primitive." Derived from the root ب-د-و, which means "beginning, appearing, initiating," Bedouin contrasts with civilized (حضارة/*HaDaara*) to form a pure typology.[13] Though the Bedouin was certainly associated with the original desert-dwelling way of life of the Arabs from Arabia, Bedouin attributes were not racial but rather behavioral for Ibn Khaldun. The Bedouin pattern of conquest that he narrates could be fulfilled by a range of ethnic groups that were not Arab. Indeed one of the major influences on Ibn Khaldun's thesis of civilization was the series of conversations he had with the Mongol conqueror Tamerlane at the gates of Damascus.[14]

In the nineteenth-century American context, the Bedouin archetype elaborated by Ibn Khaldun some five hundred years earlier provides a convenient stereotype for American "savages," most notably Indians. Homi Bhabha has argued persuasively that colonial discourse is defined by ambivalence and that the stereotype is this discourse's major discursive strategy. Bhabha asserts that the colonial stereotype "is a form of knowledge and identification that vacillates between what is always 'in place,' already known, and something that must be anxiously repeated."[15] While U.S. citizens in the mid-nineteenth century were not colonizing the Near East, they certainly were colonizing the American West. The repeated substitutions found in the Near Eastern travel genre—Bedouins for Native Americans, the Nile for the Mississippi, the desert for the frontier—reflect the ambivalence of midcentury American readers' interest in the American West. Writers such as Stephens use the Bedouin to lament the "disappearance" of Native Americans on the western frontier, while simultaneously representing that "disappearance" as the inevitable march of progress. Discussing the stereotype, Bhabha refers to "that 'otherness' which is at once the object of desire and derision, [as well as] an articulation of difference contained within the fantasy of origin and identity."[16] American travel writers were not merely finding justifications for domestic continental expansion abroad. They were not only using geographic metaphors to universalize the contest between forces of metropolitan modernization and those of tribal nomadism. These writers used representations of Bedouins to structure their fantasies of national origins.

But Bhabha's definition of stereotype does not fully account for the multiple and often mutually exclusive positions the Bedouin occupies in the drama of U.S. colonialism. Rather than being a node of fixity that is always already known and must be repeated, the Bedouin operates as a mutable figure. The figurative range of interpretive possibilities that travel writers attach to Bedouins destabilize the rhetorical arguments they enlist the figure to support. Travel writers may have used the Arab Bedouin to create stereotypes of American Indians, but the Bedouin figure itself remains fluid. In order to analyze the motion between foreign archetype and domestic stereotype, I am arguing that the Bedouin represents a *figura* of the primitive in the drama of nation building.[17]

The word *figura* has been associated with new manifestations of the familiar since its original employment in pre-Christian Roman documents. Erich Auerbach points out that "the changing aspect of the permanent runs throughout the whole history of the word."[18] Consistent over time and transportable across location, the *figura* works as a plastic form, amenable to any number of localized national identity politics even as it translates those politics across a global imaginary. The Bedouin can and does inhabit multiple positions in a range of different narratives of nation formation—Native American, Abrahamic patriarch, Argentine gaucho, Mongol invader.[19] The Bedouin is amenable to this range of identities precisely because of the *figura*'s transformational properties. Ibn Khaldun, for instance, uses the Bedouin to articulate a theory of tribal affiliation that could be applied to historical actors who were not themselves Bedouins but rather were nomadic Turkic peoples. In the nineteenth-century, American writers used the figure of the Bedouin to describe the fate of American Indians. The *figura* constantly introduces a new formation into the familiar form. The *figura* is model *and* copy, archetype *and* replica.

The young Swiss explorer Johann Ludwig Burckhardt was a major source of information about Bedouins for nineteenth-century travel writers. Trained as an Arab linguist at Cambridge and employed by the British exploration group the African Association, Burckhardt represents the academic-oriented ethos of Eastern discovery that seized Westerners in the nineteenth century. He had a profound influence on those who followed him east, especially Stephens. Burckhardt's own biography is brief but eventful. He "discovered" Petra in 1812, penetrated Mecca dressed as a poor Syrian merchant the year following, and died of dysentery in Cairo while awaiting a caravan for the Fezzan in 1817. Stephens read Burckhardt's posthumously published books with the keen eye of a man who knew he would be traveling through the same foreign spaces. Stephens's own impressions of Bedouin culture were colored by Burckhardt's earlier account of traveling through the Arabian Desert.

Burckhardt's *Notes on the Bedouins and Wahabys*, published in 1831, offers a telling description of the Aeneze tribe. Burckhardt begins by disassociating the Aenezes from other Bedouin tribes and ends by establishing the figure of the Bedouin as the ideal of freedom and independence.

> The following sketches relate exclusively to the Aenezes; these are the only true Bedouin nation of Syria while the other Arab tribes in the neighbourhood of this country have, more or less, degenerated in manners; several being reduced to subjection, while the free-born Aeneze is still governed by the same laws that spread over the Desert at the beginning of the time of the Mohammedan era.[20]

As Burckhardt's "true Bedouin," the Aeneze model the traditional culture and natural freedom by which other Bedouin tribes must be judged. The archetype of tradition and freedom, the Bedouin figure was a natural rhetorical pairing with the Native Indian of North America, and Burckhardt indicates as much when he compares their respective methods of tracking footsteps, "a talent the Bedouins posses, in common with the free Indians of America" (*Notes*, 1:374). Natural freedom and traditional cultural practices were, of course, the rhetorical engines driving noble savage theories about Native Indians in the American context, and Stephens could not have missed the connection. Burckhardt defines the Bedouin type by his spatial context, the desert. For Stephens, penetrating the Arabian Desert allowed him to enact several different American settler archetypes: the frontiersman, the primitive the frontiersman was displacing, and the covenantal colonist.

Travel writers who co-opted the Bedouin of the Arabian Desert for narratives about American settlement transformed the figure into both Indians and Jews. This double identity speaks to dueling narratives of American settler colonialism. The first is a discourse of settlement that emphasizes democratic American expansion. The second is a colonial discourse of settlement that emphasizes covenantal American identity. Functioning as a *figura*, the Bedouin of Near Eastern travel narratives, however, does not ameliorate democracy and exceptionalism as much as it emphasizes the discontinuities between these two visions of American colonialism. Even as writers such as Stephens rhetorically employ the Bedouin to support visions of American progress and civilization, the archetypal *figura* from which the figure is derived can simultaneously reveal haunting nightmares of American ruin and savagery by pointing to other potential shapely correspondences over time. Thus, the Bedouin-as-Indian analogy begs the

American-settler-as-despotic-Turk analogy, and the Bedouin-as-living-patriarch analogue transforms covenantal American settlers into potential savages. When writers translated the Arab Bedouin into American geographies, they created narratives that did more than marginalize Native Americans and authorize white Americans to take their land. They created a range of reverberating relations between archetypes of American colonialism, such as the savage, the Jew, the frontiersman, and the covenantal settler. The echoes between these different figures threatened to undercut the logic of racial nationalism and to reveal other potential visions of America, as well as other interpretations of continental colonialism.

The Savage

The use of Indians to locate American readers' sense of national identity in descriptions of the Near East remained commonplace in the genre Stephens initiated in 1837 and Mark Twain exhausted in his 1871 sardonic send-up *Innocents Abroad.*[21] At first glance, locators of insular national identity politics, such as Indians, in exotic contact narratives seem to naturalize American continental expansion by projecting the rhetorical premises of continental imperialism across a global field.[22] Stephens, describing his progress through the desert separating Egypt from the Holy Land proper, announces,

> In the present state of the world, it is an unusual thing to travel a road over which hundreds have not passed before. Europe, Asia and even the sands of Africa, have been overrun and trodden down by the feet of travelers; but in the land of Idumea, the oldest country in the world, the aspect of everything is new and strange, and the very sands you tread on have never been trodden by the feet of civilized human beings. The Bedouin roams over them like the Indian on our native prairies. (*Incidents*, 284)

Differentiating between civilized and uncivilized feet allows Stephens to employ landscape descriptions of the Near East to make claims about the natural expansion of "American" space. Stephens uses the figure of the Bedouin to establish/expand the literal ground of the United States. He announces that the Bedouin roams over the sands of Idumea (Edom) "like the Indian on *our* native prairies" (emphasis mine). Stephens employs the hypermasculine voice that has been associated with the Western explorer since Mary Louise Pratt's foundational work theorizing travel narratives as contact narratives.[23] But the claims to ownership of the U.S. frontier that he establishes through his "seeing eye" have more to do with the context of his national affiliation than with gender politics.

Sarah Rogers Haight was a contemporary of Stephens, as well as a fellow New Yorker and a prominent socialite. She was also the wife of Richard Haight, who was president of the American Oriental Society and a contributor to its journal. Sarah Rogers Haight joined her husband on one of his Oriental journeys, producing two highly readable volumes of epistles entitled *Letters from the Old World*. Sarah Rogers Haight's account was meant to be a counterweight to her husband's impressions, and the book was aimed largely at women who shared her social class. At the outset of her narrative, Haight tells her readers that she has accompanied her husband on his Eastern jaunt as civilizing and feminizing influence. Her class pretentions aside, Haight clearly enjoys roughing it, delighting in the "novel and amusing" mode of travel in the Arabian Desert, where, she explains, "a hundred little incidents occur daily . . . which I never would have experienced when rolling over the Macadamized roads of Europe in a well-appointed chariot and four."[24] Despite the difference in gender, audience, and purpose of trip, Haight and Stephens use the Bedouin to make similar claims about the American frontier. Commenting on the Arab tribes she encounters near the Valley of Jordan, Haight writes, "They live in rude tents, and are as wild in their appearance as the savages of *our* Far West" (*Letters*, 2:130, emphasis mine).

Stephens and Haight both convert the Native Indian into an interloper on "native" American prairies through a kind of rhetorical shell game that dismisses Indian claims to the land even as it acknowledges Indian presence on the land. The figures these writers use to compare Bedouin and Indian bear close scrutiny. The associative logic of simile ("like" and "as") transfers the Bedouin into a figurative American space and the Indian into a figurative Near Eastern space, but it also transforms the literal North American frontier into white American space. Stephens and Haight offer geographical visions of the Near East that extenuate an emerging domestic discourse on the vanishing American Indian. "A vague and self-justifying form of social Darwinism," explains Arnold Krupat, "this dominant ideology (from perhaps 1830 or so until as recently as 1934) claimed as a necessity of nature the ascension of Indian savagery to white civilization."[25] American writers of different political persuasions bifurcated the discourse of savagism into on one hand a rhetoric that claimed Indians were unredeemable savages and on the other a rhetoric that posited Indians as noble savages. The upshot of both strains of savagism is a teleological view of history whereby Indians are doomed to disappear. But, as Michael Rogin details in *Fathers and Children*, when contact with Indians became more infrequent in the experiences of white Americans, the symbolic importance of Indians to white Americans' sense of national identity increased. The discourse of savagism insisted on the disappearance of Indians while simultaneously licensing their incorporation into the national symbolic.

American discourses on the fading native naturalized the removal of physical Indians from the frontier at the same time that it supported the nostalgic preservation of Indians through representational modes that abstracted them from material American culture. One of the most significant and telling examples is the "Indian Gallery" paintings that the self-taught artist George Catlin undertook in the 1830s. Expressing the desire to "lend a hand to a dying nation" by rescuing "from a hasty oblivion what could be saved for the benefit of posterity," the Pennsylvania lawyer-turned-painter claimed that his paintings were "preserving" the North American Indians' "primitive looks and customs."[26] The first American artist to record the Plains Indians in their own territories, Catlin initially traveled up the Mississippi into Indian Territory with General William Clark in 1830 and then continued his travels through various Indian countries in the years 1831–1837. After completing his project, Catlin exhibited his portraits in major cities along the Ohio River and on the East Coast, from 1837 to 1839, precisely the time when Stephens's book was selling through its first few editions. The more than five hundred oil paintings in Catlin's "Indian Gallery" forcefully express his belief, stated explicitly in his journals, that the encounter on the American frontier between whites and Indians was resulting in the permanent destruction of Indian culture.[27] The rhetorical overlap between the "disappearing" Indians evoked by Catlin's contact with the U.S. frontier and the "disappearing" Indians invoked by Stephens's contact with the Arabian Desert demonstrates the relationship between representing the Indian and representing the Bedouin in American discourse. U.S. readers in the mid-nineteenth century were told repeatedly and through multiple mediums that they could look at primitive Bedouins and see Indians, but also that they could look at primitive Indians and see Bedouins. Catlin's "Indian Gallery" paintings also, however, indicate the difference between Indian stereotype and Bedouin *figura*.

The Indian mimicry of white ways is the theme of one of Catlin's paintings, a portrait of a man named Wi-Jun-Jon (figure 5). The canvas is split into two panels. The left panel depicts the Indian before his trip to Washington, D.C. In it, Wi-Jun-Jon dresses traditionally and faces the viewer with a look of solemnity. The right half of the canvas displays Wi-Jun-Jon after his visit to Washington, D.C. He is attired in white American fashion, a top hat has replaced his headdress, an umbrella has replaced his pipe, and coat and pants have replaced his traditional garb. In this latter representation, Wi-Jun-Jon's back faces the viewer, and as a final statement on his corruption, two bottles of liquor can be seen protruding from his rear pockets.

The painting is a dramatic example of how nostalgia discursively privileges Catlin's Indians at the same time that it normalizes their physical removal from the modern world. The painting mocks Wi-Jun-Jon's entrance into American society under the guise of lamenting the loss of authentic Indian cultural identity. Catlin's depiction of Wi-Jun-Jon posits the Indian as a colonial stereotype whose identity is permanently fixed. Despite the Indian's attempts at assimilation, he remains trapped in his "otherness." He adheres to Bhabha's definition of *stereotype*, which insists that the difference between the "other" of colonial discourse and the colonizer must remain intact no matter what the behavior or attributes of the colonized subject. Bhabha argues that the consistency of the other and his continued production of an "inappropriate" mimicry of the colonizer provides the continuing justification for the "civilizing" project of colonialism. The "ambivalence" of the colonial stereotype means that the Native Indian is not only premodern savage doomed to eradication by the advance of America's civilizing enterprise but also noble progenitor of an authentic American identity.

However, when Catlin's representation of the Indian is contextualized by Near Eastern travel narratives, the figure ceases to operate as a colonial stereotype. The American Indian was just one of multiple archetypes of the primitive that Jackson-era writers explored and often connected to one another. The connections between "primitive" peoples charted by Near Eastern travel writers produced justifications for western expansion through global analogy, but they also displayed the desire to map American destiny through Biblical geography. Thus, the American Indian was often associated with the Jew and in some cases argued to be a descendant of the lost tribes of Israel. Near Eastern travel narratives simply mirrored domestic settler narratives and their tendency to look at American space and see Biblical space. In domestic settler narratives, the covalence of American space and Biblical space provided typologies that naturalized colonialism through Biblical analogy. However, the projection of these settler typologies back into Near Eastern geographies created looping

Figure 5. George Catlin, *Pigeon's Egg Head (The Light), Going to and Returning from Washington* (1837–39), oil on canvas, 29 × 24 in. Reproduced with permission from Smithsonian American Art Museum, Washington, D.C.

relations between Indians and Bedouins and Jews, and Indians and white settlers, and Jews and Bedouins.

The Biblical Patriarch

Catlin was close friends with the most prominent American Jew of the nineteenth century, the journalist, entrepreneur, diplomat, playwright, and proto-Zionist Mordecai Manuel Noah. The two former Pennsylvania lawyers exchanged letters often, and during an 1837 lecture that Noah held at New York's Clinton Hall titled *The Evidences of the American Indians Being the Descendants of the Lost Tribes of Israel*, Noah read from one of Catlin's missives. "The first thing that strikes a traveler in an Indian country as evidence of their being of Jewish origin, (and it is certainly a very forcible one)," Catlin wrote, "is the striking resemblance which they generally bear in contour, expression of head, to those people." "In their modes and customs," the letter continues, "there are many striking resemblances, and perhaps as proof, they go much further than mere personal resemblance."[28] Noah used Catlin's comments as supporting evidence for his thesis. "If these are the remnants of the nine and a half tribes which were carried into Assyria," asks Noah of the Indians, "and if we are to believe in all the promises of restoration, and the fulfillment of the prophecies, respecting the final advent of the Jewish nation, what is to become of these our red brethren, whom we are driving before us so rapidly, that a century more will find them lingering on the borders of the Pacific ocean?" (*Evidences*, 37).

Noah's appeal to his New York audience dovetails the language of Protestant millennialist eschatology and Democratic expansionist ideology. Noah skillfully manages to capture the figurative assumptions of both salvationism and savagism through his own act of exegetical interpretation about "the final advent of the Jewish nation." In effect, Noah borrows the premises of a domestic narrative about American settlers' covenantal identity and uses it to argue for the Jewish colonization of the Holy Land. Noah's plea for sympathy for the "red brethren" is a rhetorical prop. The real aim of the talk is to raise "12 or 13 million with the co-operation of England and France" in order to "purchase Syria from the Egyptian Pasha" (*Evidences*, 39–40) and to install a Jewish state in the Near East. As to the fate of the material Indians whom Noah deploys in the service of his extracontinental colonial ambitions, their physical presence in the new Jewish state is extraneous to their symbolic role in its establishment.

"Possibly, the restoration may be near enough," Noah concludes with per-siflage, "to include even a portion of these interesting people" (*Evidences*, 37). Though he nominally laments the dislocation of Indians to the mar-gins of the physical nation, the result of Noah's assumptions about the frontier is the inscription of Indian removal into his prospective vision of the American West. This prospective vision of American space, in turn, licenses the purchase of Near Eastern land from Mohammad Ali for a Jewish state. Mirroring the translation of Bedouins into American geog-raphies, Noah translates the Indian into a Near Eastern geography in an effort to claim a colonial mandate.

The difference between the figures of speech Noah uses to compare Indi-ans and Jews and those Stephens and Haight use to compare Indians and Bedouins is significant. In Noah's account, Indians are not *like* Israelites; they *are* Israelites. Because the substitution is literal, Noah can directly conflate a narrative of Zionism with a narrative of American colonialism. Whereas Stephens and Haight use similes to translate Bedouin Arabs into visions of American continental colonialism, Noah reads Indians as Jews to make an argument for Jewish colonialism in the Ottoman-controlled Near East.

Figurative discourses on American space had a profound influence on the material history of American colonization. Both Noah and Stephens were members of Tammany Hall, and both were active in mid-nineteenth-century New York City Democratic politics. They may or may not have come into contact at the Hall's "wigwam" in the 1830s and '40s. Neverthe-less, they share a larger Jackson-era propensity to map American identi-ties through reference to Biblical figures. For the American traveler in the Near East, though, contact with Biblical space often disturbed the settler metaphors culled from Biblical analogy, providing other possible configu-rations of the colonizer-colonized relationship. Stephens, in his own travel account, often refers to Bedouin Arabs as appearing unchanged from the pages of the Bible. Describing contemporary Bedouins, Stephens draws on the familiar Biblical patriarch.

> In fact the life of the Bedouin, his appearance and his habits, are precisely the same as those of the patriarchs of old. Abraham himself, the first of the patriarchs, was a Bedouin, and four thousand years have not made the slightest alteration in the character of these extraordinary people. Read of the patriarchs in the Bible, and it is the best description you can have of pastoral life in the East at the present day. (*Incidents*, 214)

If the substitution of Bedouins for Native Americans underwrote narrative visions of America's national future, the substitution of Bedouins for Biblical patriarchs evoked narrative visions of a prenational past.

Since the outset of seventeenth-century Puritan colonial settlement, narrative conflations of Biblical geography and New World geography have been instrumental to establishing a uniquely American subjectivity. Before the *Arabella* had ever touched New World shores, John Winthrop delivered a sermon on its deck, prefiguring the wilderness of America as a chiliastic New Jerusalem: "Wee shall finde that the God of Israell is among us, when ten of us shall be able to resist a thousand of our enemies; when hee shall make us a prayse and glory that men shall say of succeeding plantations, 'the Lord make it likely that of *New England*.'"[29] Utilizing exegetical methods of interpretation, Puritan leaders mapped Biblical geographical names onto the landscape of the New World and transformed a physically foreign milieu into a familiar one. This invocation of Biblical geography created a recognizable figure of colonial American nationalism, the covenantal settler. Narratives that manifested the Biblical Near East in America confirmed and amplified the link between the exceptional status of the Jews and their covenantal relationship with God and the exceptional status of the Puritan community and its relationship to God.

These early American writers, in the process of identifying their community's uncertain destiny with the destiny of well-known Biblical figures, established the presence of the Near East in America as simultaneously tropic and literal. The exegetical imposition of a Near Eastern map onto the physical American landscape established imaginary historical contiguities between Puritan settlers and Biblical Israelites. Transoceanic metonyms translated the Old Testament into geographies of New World fulfillment. As John Winthrop insists, Puritans were settling "a citty upon a hill," not exiling themselves in a "howling wilderness."[30] Geographical metaphors, in other words, created the figurative ground of the New World. This strand of religious rhetoric was far from obsolete once America became the secular United States. The rhetoric of covenant was just as integral to continental expansion as was the secular rhetoric about democracy and progress. Hilton Obenzinger points out that Protestant doctrines on the Jews "provided originary models for America's narratives of continuing settlement and expansion: if the elect though cursed *ur*-nation of Israel could be restored, so too could fallen Anglo-America, the typological new Jews, be 'restored' as a racialized chosen people."[31] White continental settlers who assumed the tropic status of a "racialized chosen" created an alibi for Indian removal.

But if the Bedouin was associated with both Indian and Biblical patriarch in American travel narratives, then a conundrum arises. How could the Bedouin be substituted for the racial other, the typological Indian, to be removed by westward expansion and be a living stand-in for the racially privileged remover, the typological new Jew of America? As a simultaneous mythical father and literal indigene, the Bedouin figure brings America's colonial and national narratives to a logical impasse. In the displaced tableaus of American destiny located in these travel narratives, the *figura*'s evocation of shapely correspondences rather than direct transformations allows several narratives to compete for attention without eclipsing one another. Biblical figures created American ground, but contemporary Near Eastern figures had to be distinguished from American figures because the comparison ultimately underwrote America's exceptional difference. This difference between Near Eastern and American figure supported America's geographical narrative of fulfillment, which stood in contrast to a consistent narrative of Near Eastern ruin to be found in the genre.

The *figura* of the Bedouin, with its spectral replicas of primitives and uncanny doubling of origins, however, presented American readers with a series of potentially disruptive intercultural relations. As *figura*, the Bedouin connects not only savages to Biblical patriarchs, and Indians to Jews, but also American settlers to savages, as well as American colonialism to the Ottoman Empire. Whether or not contemporary readers recognized these potential contaminations of distinct settler binaries, they are there for us to recognize. The transpositions of Near East and America that allow travel writers to establish associations between Bedouin and Indian ("like our Native Indians") simultaneously conjure the possibility of a host of associative connections between American continental expansion and Ottoman colonialism, as well as between Andrew Jackson and the Egyptian pasha Mohammad Ali. These potential alternative perspectives on the United States and its policy of westward expansion open up an imaginative space in the travel genre for subversive visions of U.S. geography and historical destiny to become visible through a form of Orientalist gazing. I want to explore that space and elaborate on the possibilities for reinterpreting the terms of American identity through the latent imaginaries it harbors.

Doubles and Reversals

> Thence we traveled to Ma'an, which is the last town in Syria, and
> descended through the Pass of al-Sawan into the desert of which the
> saying goes "He who enters it is lost, and he who leaves it is born."
> —Ibn Battutah, *RiHla*[32]

In the quotation that opens this section, Ibn Battutah offers a perspective on origins that differs in kind from Euro-American narratives of romantic nationalism. It is culled from a Bedouin proverb about the desert space that Stephens was to traverse some five hundred years after the Moroccan adventurer. Whereas narratives of romantic nationalism focus on the collective search for origins in a primordial past, Battutah's quotation emphasizes the personal struggle with the primordial space of the desert—"he who enters it is lost, and he who leaves it is born." Ibn Battutah's own literary career in the West had been born only about a decade before Stephens departed for the East. Though Ibn Battutah's *riHla* of his journey (lasting close to thirty years and covering over seventy-three thousand miles across an Islamic world that extended from North Africa to China and included India and parts of Europe) had been transcribed by Ibn Juzayy in the middle of the fourteenth century, the book had been unknown outside the Islamic countries until the nineteenth century. In 1829, Samuel Lee, a British Orientalist, published the first English translation of Ibn Battutah's *riHla*, based on an abridgement of the narrative that Burckhardt had acquired in Egypt close to twenty years earlier.

Stephens's weak health, foreign status, and dependence on Alouin tribal guides whom he did not trust made his own trip across the Sinai desert an arduous one. But, as if fulfilling the Bedouin proverb, when he emerged from the shifting sands of desolation dressed not as an American traveler but as the Cairo merchant Abdel Hassis, Stephens had lost one identity and been born into another one. "Indeed, I played the Turk well," announces Stephens, "and, if I could have talked their language, dressed as a Turk, they could not have judged from my appearance that I had ever been outside the walls of old Istanbul" (*Incidents*, 224–25). There was no question of passing for Stephens, of course, and the language which he did not speak was translated for him by his constant man servant, a Maltese dragoman named Paul. The purpose of Stephens's change of clothes and performance of "Turk" identity is closer to minstrelsy than passing. But in "playing the Turk" in the Sinai desert, Stephens brings the connection between American imperialism and Ottoman imperialism into sharp focus. Stephens does not dress as the subaltern Bedouin; he dresses as the hegemonic Turk—leaving the "Bedouin shirt" for his "man" Paul to wear.

The comparison between Turkish and American hegemon latent in Stephens's text is in keeping with the manifest connections Stephens makes between Bedouins and Indians. "Mohammad Ali had endeavored to reduce these children of the desert under his iron rule," Stephens explains in reference to the Bedouins of Sinai, "but the free spirit of the untameable could not brook this invasion of their independence" (*Incidents*, 170). Though Stephens offers Ali as an example of hegemony and the Bedouin as an example of romantic resistance to tyranny, a mid-nineteenth-century American reader might as easily substitute Indian for Bedouin here and be left contemplating the politics of Indian removal.[33] In his treatment of Near Eastern space and Ottoman colonial structures, Stephens employs recognizable Orientalist tropes that have a tendency, retrospectively, to boomerang into critiques of American imperialism. The Near Eastern travel genre's sympathetic identifications with the Bedouin's plight, even when they appear in suspect idealizations of the fading indigene, have unruly consequences when these Bedouins are translated into American space and transformed into Indians. The Bedouin reference has the potential to transform the American geography of modernization into a geography of despotic dispossession. The analogy linking Bedouins and Native Indians, in other words, threatened to mark Americans as Turkish despots seizing land from brave indigenes.

There is a long history in American Orientalism, stretching back to the Federal era, of labeling American "extremist" and/or autocratic political figures "Turks."[34] While this particular form of critique does not rupture any of the cultural prejudices or racial binaries inherent in Orientalist discourse, it does demonstrate that Orientalist imagery was often mustered in the service of anti-imperial politics. Rather than unambiguously promoting U.S. continental expansion, Near Eastern travel narratives also dramatize the cultural cost of modernization in America by projecting expansionary anxieties onto their presentations of Arab peoples, Bedouin culture, and Ottoman colonial relations. It is not only that romanticizing the Bedouin had implications that were discontinuous with Indian removal, for domestic discourse also romanticized the Indian. It is also true that the Near East provided a literary space where colonial dramas could be played out with neutral actors, and readers could identify the stakes in imperial expansion without overtly engaging in domestic politics.

There is, of course, no question that Muhammad Ali and Andrew Jackson were confronting quite disparate historical circumstances and controlling quite distinct political machineries. But nevertheless, the landscape of Mohammad Ali's Egypt and the landscape of Andrew Jackson's United States were undergoing similar material changes in the 1820s and '30s.[35] Thus, Ali's modern nation-building measures offer an enticing parallel to U.S. nation building during the period. Stephens's criticism of Ali's despotic acquisitiveness and his authoritarian pugnacity, in turn, offers a potential critique of the democratic failures of Andrew Jackson's policies. For example, Stephens gives a lengthy description of Ali's "extermination" of and "treachery" toward the Mamelukes, a description that could easily describe Jackson's slaughter of the Seminole Indians of Florida in the ongoing Seminole War or his backsliding promises to the Choctaw in the recently concluded Creek War. Stephens then goes on to say,

> Since that time [Ali] has had Egypt quietly to himself; he has attacked and destroyed the Wahabees on the Red Sea, and subdued the countries above the Cataracts of the Nile, to Sennar and Dongola. He has been constantly aiming at introducing European improvements; he has raised and disciplined an army according to European tactics; increased the revenues, particularly by introducing the culture of cotton; and has made Egypt, from the Mediterranean to the Cataracts, as safe for the traveler as the streets of New York. It remains to be seen whether, after all, he has not done more harm than good, and whether the miserable and oppressed condition of his subjects does not counterbalance all the good that he has done for Egypt. (*Incidents*, 25)

Ali's territorial acquisitiveness was consistent in many ways with the U.S. policy of territorial expansion at its borders, a policy that was justified by the rhetoric—mouthed by Jackson himself—of "subduing" Indian tribal threats to American border integrity and acquiring access to the natural resources necessary for white settler economies. The fact that Ali was engaging in some of the same nation-building tactics as Jackson by "subduing" a Wahabee tribal threat and acquiring access to the natural resources of the Nile may or may not have been lost on a mid-nineteenth-century American reading audience that included many inclined toward models of Republican restraint in relation to the frontier. The reference to "the streets of New York," where prominent Republican-minded individuals such as Philip Hone, Noah Webster, and Thomas Cole lived, only makes the connection between American destiny and Near Eastern space more vivid, however, for present-day readers.

American travelers often described the despotism of Muhammad Ali in order to highlight the enlightened democratic model of expansionism practiced by the U.S. government.[36] "The canal of Alexandria is a noble work for this semi-barbarous country," writes Haight, "but the manner of its construction was one of *wholesale iniquity*, and none but the most hardened tyrant would have conceived of the idea" (*Letters*, 94). Haight's dismissal of Ali's material modernization of the Egyptian landscape is in keeping with Stephens's suspicions about the railroad coming to Sinai. Ali's claim to be a modernizer, Haight suggests, is speciously built on models of tyranny and despotism. Significantly, whereas Stephens had mentioned the "tameness of a cotton factory" in passing, Haight puts a fine point on the market anxiety submerged in Stephens's account of Egyptian modernization. She indicates that the completion of the Alexandria canal means that "the forty miles of the canal . . . were navigated by cotton bags in an incredibly short space of time" (*Letters*, 96). As a competitor to U.S. cotton, Egyptian cotton posed a threat that both Stephens and Haight eagerly dismiss.

The chiastic relation between America and the Ottoman Empire established in these travel narratives, however, draws attention to the connection, not the difference, between the American and the Ottoman version of imperialism. Narratives about the European settlers' colonial mission in the New World, as well as white America's midcentury colonial expansionism, evidence in both Stephens's and Haight's descriptions of Ottoman colonialism in the Near East. "The modern Pharaoh," Haight announces in reference to Ali, "has but to will it, and any scheme, however visionary, is immediately put *en train*; and if he has not the *Children of the Captivity* to make bricks for him, the *Land of Goshen* still teems with slaves quite as degraded and oppressed as the ancient Israelites" (*Letters*, 95). Though Haight's ironic tone is meant to emphasize the gap between Ali's title as modernizer and his "antiquated" practice of employing slave labor, the irony extends to a critique of the American system of farming cotton through slave labor. Haight's quip does not ironize Ali as much as it ironizes America's claim to be the New Israel in the face of its own pharaonic practices of slavery.

Reading Orientalism against the Grain

The translation of Near Eastern racial tropes into American space under-wrote the rhetoric of settler colonialism both in the prenational and postnational periods. When American figures are used to re-create Near Eastern ground, however, the categories of racial difference these fig-ures create begin to be infiltrated by their figurative doubles and ghosts. Reversing the relationship between Biblical figure and American ground, Haight describes how she will reimagine the Nile through the vehicle of "our noble Hudson" once she returns to America. "Should perchance, an Indian be seen gliding past on his canoe, or stealing his way among the trees, then indeed would the illusion be complete; and the swarthy son of Shem, like the Nubian on his raft of reeds, or sauntering among the columns of Philae's ruins, would, by adding reality to fancy, give the last finishing touches to the picture" (*Letters*, 171). In her pictorial prevision of the Hudson as Nile, Haight associates the Indian, whom she marks as the "swarthy son of Shem," not with the Bedouin but with the Nubian. A sight of the Indian on the Hudson, in other words, is analogous to the sight of a Nubian on the Nile, and the effect adds "reality to fancy." Using the description "sauntering," Haight implicitly associates the Nubian with the Christian pilgrims from whom the word *saunter* (*Sainte-Terre*: Holy-Lander) is derived.[37] A number of different people can inhabit the position of Holy-Lander, just as a number of different spaces can fill the figura-tive role of the Holy Land. Thus, the association of Indian/Nubian adds reality to the transposition of Hudson/Nile. But in the process, American racial typologies are revealed to be labile. By associating Shem, the puta-tive ancestor of the Semites, who included both Arabs and Jews, with the Native American and the Native American in turn with the black Nubian (in this model a descendant of Ham), Haight creates a nonhierarchical chain of relations that depend on geographical context, not racial identity, for their value. In other words, she presents racial identity not as essential, immutable, and permanent but rather as figurative.

The translations of the Near East into American racial categories splin-ter the material "Orient" from the representation of the "Orient" in the U.S. context. But they also reveal American racial categories to be figura-tive abstractions built out of a globalized imaginary of difference. If the Indian is a swarthy son of Shem and American settlers identified with Biblical Israel and Biblical Israelites, then a connective tissue—tenuous enough but there—is established not only between Indians and white

Americans but also between white Americans and Africans. Given the fact that West African Muslims who were literate because of Qur'anic training were also marked as Arabs and/or Moors on many antebellum plantations, the construction of Arabness in nineteenth-century American racial discourse provides a trope where whites, Indians, and Africans all circulate.[38] The figurative use of the term *Arab* to describe a range of American outsiders, however provisional that use may be, offers an opportunity to imagine the transvaluing of nineteenth-century American racial hierarchies from within the discourse of Orientalism.

The conflation of Near Eastern space with American space and the refraction of American destiny through Orientalist tropes had consequences that are discontinuous with "democratic" justifications of white advance into the American continent. These consequences were visible to mid-nineteenth-century writers. For instance, when the slave David F. Dorr traveled with his master to Egypt and the Holy Land in the 1850s, he employed a recognizably Orientalist mode of imperial gazing, but not in the service of white hegemony. In the preface to *A Colored Man round the World*, Dorr explains that he "has the satisfaction of looking with his own eyes and reason at the ruins of the ancestors of which he is the posterity."[39] Dorr repeats the white American traveler's desire to link his own national destiny with Biblical geography. That is, both Dorr and a writer such as Stephens look past a Near Eastern present with living humans and functioning societies in order to see their own past. Such visualizations project Western narratives of identity onto Oriental space. But Dorr's imperial gaze operates not in the service of white settler colonialism but instead in the service of a nascent Afro-Arab transnationalism that linked African Americans to ancient Egyptians. Thus, Dorr explains, "If the ruins of the author's ancestors were not a living language of their scientific majesty, this book could receive no such appellation with pride. Luxor, Carnack, the Memnonian and the Pyramids make us exclaim 'What monuments of pride can surpass these?'" (*CM*, 11). Claiming the scientific legacy of the Egyptians as African American cultural property, Dorr demonstrates both his own intelligence (he has been reading the latest literature on archaeology) and the black race's historical claim to a tradition of inquiry predating the white man's scientific discoveries. Dorr's reinterpretation of the narrative meaning of the Near East from an American slave's perspective reveals that the transnational imaginaries feeding American nationalisms could be simultaneously Orientalist and antihegemonic.[40]

The view of U.S. geographical destiny that appears in midcentury Near Eastern travel narratives does not necessarily promote a Manifest Destiny underpinned by racial nationalism. For example, the Mississippi River was a common reference point for Americans traveling on the Nile, and, as Scott Trafton argues, "the semiotic and ideological links between the Nile and the Mississippi were formative links for the iconography of Western expansion."[41] While travelers from the North usually used the opportunity to comment on slavery in general, one traveler from the South saw, in the Nile river economy, an opportunity to implicitly support the peculiar institution. Randal W. MacGavock, Democratic mayor of Nashville, personal friend of Jackson, and future Confederate army commander, comments that on the Nile "the banks are low and caving, and the general appearance of the country [is] very much like the lower Mississippi."[42] MacGavock does not stop with the physical similarities between the two rivers; he moves on to remark that though this area, "the cotton region," of the Nile is poorly cultivated, "one of our southern planters might come here, and . . . with our mode of cultivation produce the finest crop in the world."[43] The Southern mode of cultivation, of course, depended on slavery, and MacGavock uses the Near East geography to justify its utility in the American South, as well as to project American cultural practices (and superiority) across a global geography.

Though Dorr too traveled on the Nile, he does not compare it to the Mississippi. Rather, Dorr compares the Mississippi to a "taste" of the Jordan River: "We took a bath in the Jordan, and tried some of its water with *eau de vie*, and found it in quality like Mississippi water" (*CM*, 186). Because the Israelites had made a difficult and hazardous journey from slavery in Egypt to freedom in the promised land by crossing the Jordan, the river had acquired folkloric value in antebellum African American culture. Comparing the "quality" of Jordan with the "quality" of the Mississippi, Dorr may be making a subtle reference to the quality of freedom both represent. The Jordan, rather than the Nile, serves as Dorr's reference point for a Mississippi River he himself had to cross to move from bondage, in Louisiana, into freedom, in Ohio.[44] In the Jordan passage, Dorr, who throughout the text connects with the very same Egyptians who enslaved the Israelites, identifies himself with the figurative position of a people unjustly oppressed by a "princely" class. Dorr's reference to Egyptian princes who refused to release Israelites from slavery corresponds with Phillis Wheatley's invocation, over half a century earlier, in a letter to

Samson Occam, of "our modern Egyptians" in reference to white owners who denied their slaves freedom.[45]

Both references are part of a long tradition in African American discourse that explains the plight of Africans in America through the trope of Israelites in Egypt. As the historian Michael Gomez explains, "the nature of the identification was not always precise: at times it was associative and turned on the notion of parallel experiences; at other times it was appropriative, driven by the conviction that what was recorded was prophetic and predictive of both a time to come and a time that had already come."[46] Metonymic and metaphoric connections between African Americans and Israelites both circulated in African American discourse: the former naturalized the African presence in America through association, and the latter naturalized black extracontinental colonialism through transformation. But whether the African-descended population in America was figured in these discourses as like the Hebrews or directly as Hebrews, the effect was the same: using figurative interpretation to ground the diaspora in a recognizable history.

Dorr refers to his own master's "princely promises" (*CM*, 12) to manumit him after the completion of their three-year journey abroad—promises that were not kept. But whereas Dorr's reference is associative, black-nationalist writers such as Martin Delany used appropriation. Conjuring Egypt in his 1859 novel of slave insurrection, *Blake; or, The Huts of America*, Delany positions black slaves as Israelites on the threshold of deliverance.[47] Describing the novel's hero, Henry, and his spreading of the spirit of slave insurrection, Delany writes, "from plantation to plantation did he go, sowing the seeds of future devastation and ruin to the master and redemption to the slave, an antecedent more terrible in its anticipation than the warning voice of the destroying Angel in commanding the slaughter of the firstborn of Egypt."[48] Positioning the white master as the Egyptian oppressor, Delany taps the same rhetoric of victimization and divine covenant that early American settlers and contemporary proponents of continental expansion deployed through exegesis. But he translates this rhetoric of white privilege into the language of a nascent black nationalism. At another moment in *Blake*, following the marriage of a slave couple by a black clergyman, the parson addresses a song to the slave women in the audience. "Daughters of Zion! Awake from thy sadness!" the parson exclaims. "Awake for thy foes shall oppress thee no more" (*Blake*, 156). These women are not *like* daughters of Zion; they *are* daughters of Zion. The means to end white oppression of the black population in Delany's text is not only revolution but also a colonization specifically modeled on Zionism.

Delany's vision of ethnic nationalism is both antiracist and proimperial. This is the case not only in Delany's novel but also in his political treatise *The Condition, Elevation, Emigration and Destiny of the Colored People of the United States* (1852). The novel focuses on the seizure of Cuba by violent means and the transformation of the Caribbean island into a black nation, and the treatise focuses on an expedition to East Africa that promises to elevate and enlighten Africans. *The Condition* even raises the possibility of building a trans-African continental railroad. In *The Condition*, Delany explicitly connects his vision of black nationalism and the importance of rhetorically co-opting the figure of the Jew. "There have in all ages, in almost every nation, existed a nation within a nation," Delany explains. "Such also are the Jews, scattered throughout not only the length and breadth of Europe, but almost the habitable globe, maintaining their national characteristics, and looking forward in high hopes of seeing the day when they may return to their former national position of self-government and independence."[49] As Paul Gilroy has pointed out, "Delany looks immediately to Jewish experience of dispersal as a model for comprehending the history of black Americans, and more significantly still, cites this history as a means to focus his own Zionist proposals for black American colonization of Nicaragua and elsewhere."[50]

Delany's black-nationalist readings of scripture are consistent with a Jackson-era propensity to enunciate American destiny through Near Eastern figures. Delany's co-option of the language of Zionism came at the end of a period of American continental expansion. This expansion was driven, in large part, by a rhetoric that harnessed the figure of the Israelite to drive the nation's colonial aspirations and to justify its imperial actions against a people of color. The rhetorical reversal of the roles of Israelite and Egyptian in Delany's writing was part of his revolutionary strategy. In *Blake*, the political arithmetic that Henry offers his wife, Maggie, as a lesson evidences this strategy. "Whatever liberty is worth to the whites, it is worth to the blacks," Henry explains. "Therefore whatever it cost the whites to obtain it, the blacks will be willing and ready to pay" (192). Far from reproducing a narrative of American exceptionalism garbed as African American exceptionalism, Delany's focus on the Jew is part and parcel of his global contextualization of the traffic in another diaspora, African slaves.

Dorr can hardly be described as espousing the same black-nationalist politics as Delaney in his conflation of blacks and Israelites. By playing both sides of the Israelite/Egyptian fence, however, Dorr does co-opt Near East figures for his own vision of American destiny. He uses these Near Eastern figures to represent himself as both hegemon and subaltern, as enslaved and enslaver, as oppressor and oppressed. Through the vehicle of the Near East, Dorr reveals the overlapping and contradictory colonial positions with which American travelers in general identified.[51] In a complex moment in Dorr's narrative, he tells the reader of his desire to see beneath a Turkish woman's veil. When he is told by his guide that this is impossible, a discussion ensues in which Dorr dabbles with the idea of purchasing the woman. Informed that that too is impossible because he is not a Muslim, Dorr offers to extend the requisite sum to his guide so he can purchase the woman. "He said he did not know how it could be done," Dorr continues. "I asked him if he thought the girl would admire me; he had no doubt about that, and added, I need not have any uneasiness about that, as I could make her love me after she was mine, she was obliged to obey me after Turkish laws, and no man can change the laws but Abdul Medjid, the Sultan" (*CM*, 123–24). Promiscuously playing with the power to buy and sell humans, Dorr provides a subtle critique of American slavery by establishing an Orientalist form of gazing. In effect, Dorr conflates the dissipated, corrupt, and despotic rule of the Turkish sultan with the rule of law in the American South. Both are provincial and absolutist, and both subject human beings to the will of others, stripping them of their humanity. But Dorr also uses this encounter with Turkish culture to demonstrate that a black man has the same freedom of movement, ability to gaze, and power to purchase as a white man does.

In *A Colored Man round the World*, Dorr focuses not on the collective deprivations of slavery but on his individual talents as equal or superior to any white man. In the face of narratives that insist on the black man's savagery and primitiveness, Dorr uses Egypt to establish a historical continuity for his own sophistication, education, and power. At the end of his preface to *A Colored Man round the World*, Dorr tells the reader about his escape from bondage in New Orleans and flight "westward, where 'the star of empire takes its way'" (*CM*, 12). Echoing George Berkeley's famous phrase, Dorr uses the rhetoric of Manifest Destiny to undercut racial nationalism. Dorr, who on the one hand identifies with Israelites in a moment of African American nationalism and local resistance, on the other hand identifies with Egyptians in a moment of pan-African internationalism that celebrates Egyptian imperial power. Dorr demonstrates that alternatives to hegemonic American geographical imaginations could become legible through Orientalist representations of the Near East. Indeed, he shows that various interpretations of American empire lurked behind the images of the Near East that American traveler writers projected out to their readers.

The American Frontiersman and Pentimento Petra

Writers of color such as Dorr used the Near Eastern travel genre to establish a gentile masculinity that emphasized their mastery of leisure. White writers such as Stephens were equally adamant about using the Near Eastern milieu to establish their claim to a primitive masculinity that emphasized hardship. The pinnacle of this hardship for Stephens was his arduous and challenging journey through the Arabian Desert. Stephens begins his travel narrative by acknowledging the effects of technical modernization on the genre, concluding by marking his specific intervention:

> In the present state of the world it is almost presumptuous to put forth a book of travels. Universal peace and extended commercial relations, the introduction of steamboats, and increased facilities of traveling generally, have brought comparatively close together the most distant parts of the world; and except within the walls of China, there are few countries which have not been visited and written upon by European travelers. The author's route, however, is comparatively new to the most of his countrymen; part of it—through the land of Edom—is, even at this day, entirely new. (*Incidents*, v)

The "epoch of annihilated space," as Hawthorne was to put it in *The Blithedale Romance*, threatened to make the discovery ethos of the travel narrative hackneyed.[52] Stephens's contribution to the crowded genre, however, is his "new" route through the desert separating Egypt from the Holy Land proper, what he marks as "Edom." The most striking details of Stephens's account collect around his visit to the "lost" Arabian city of Petra, and he makes much of his role as the first American to penetrate its enclave. So do reviewers such as Poe.[53] Unlike Egypt and the Holy Land, the Arabian Desert was a space that did not possess a recoverable Western history. The timeless desert under Stephens's gaze enters into the historical flow of time that was absent prior to the "civilized" Western man's arrival. That is why, for Stephens, Idumea (Edom) is both ancient and new, both "the oldest country in the world" and a place where "the aspect of everything is new and strange" (*Incidents*, 284). The Eastern desert is unlike the Eastern city, with its layers of ancient empires and civilizations crowding the "seeing man's" vision, literally jostling his descriptions with the voices of those who have come before him, described before him, conquered before him. In the urban East, the Western man is always belated. Not so in the Eastern desert.

Petra, in particular, is a charged Orientalist icon in the mid-nineteenth century. The city, historically inhabited by a Nabatean civilization whose ancestors were from Arabia and whose modern descendants were Bedouin Arabs, was formerly an important trading hub for Near Eastern caravans. However, Petra had disappeared from Western consciousness for a millennium and a half until Burckhardt brought it back into "history" by "discovering" it in 1812. Since that date, the city held an eerie fascination for Europeans and Americans alike, inspiring everything from adventurous travelers to popular poetry.[54] The history of Petra that was introduced in 1812 was a decidedly Orientalist history. For Americans in particular, Petra was not only a well-exploited popular symbol of empire and ruin; it also served as a physical marker of the Nabatean people's historical transition into sedentary, urban existence. The Nabateans had evolved from roving tribal bands subsiding on raids of caravans to wards of a caravan center that profited off the taxes that traders paid for the services they received. In essence, Nabateans had successfully managed the movement from nomad to urban capitalist some two millennia before debates raged in the United States about the fitness of putatively nomadic Indians for inclusion in the civilized, capitalist state. The fact that "rediscovered" Petra now lay ensconced in the wastes of the Arabian Desert and was once again habituated by nomadic Bedouins only lent complexity to the historical lesson that the location and its inhabitants held for American citizens confronting national debates about continental expansion, Indian removal, and industrialization.

I turn to Petra at the end this chapter on the figure of the Bedouin because it speaks directly to the legacy of midcentury American travel writers' representation of Arabs in American romanticism. Though Bedouin figures themselves are often absent in American romantic treatments of the Orient, the phenomenology of double vision activated by the *figura*'s law of correspondence remains an integral part of American Orientalism. Petra held a different message from other Near Eastern landscapes, and its adoption into an American aesthetics of ruin hints at its lingering presence in the imagination of American romantic writers who had read descriptions of it in travel narratives. Herman Melville, who had referred to the "wonderful Arabian traveler" Stephens as "haunting" in the beginning of *Redburn*, for instance, revisited the New York lawyer's "Stony

Arabia" in a late short story, "Bartleby the Scrivener." In "Bartleby," Melville places Petra in the bustling center of American capitalism.

> Think of it. Of a Sunday, *Wall Street is deserted as Petra*; and every night of every day is an emptiness. This building, too, which of weekdays hums with industry and life, at nightfall echoes with sheer vacancy, and all through Sunday is forlorn. And here Bartleby makes his home; sole spectator of a solitude which he has seen all populous—a sort of innocent and transformed Marius brooding among the ruins of Carthage![55]

In an attempt to conjure sympathy for the inscrutable and recalcitrant scrivener, the narrator of Melville's story of Wall Street imagines Bartleby's view from his law office on a Sunday. Superimposing emergent American capitalism and forlorn Arab ruin, the well-intentioned lawyer creates a visual image wedding the American landscape of modernity to a Near Eastern landscape of antiquity. What becomes visible within the picture of Wall Street is Petra. The viewer can see beneath the surface image another image, in fact, another intention, bleeding through. In Bartleby's eyes, the *narrator* suggests, the iconic landscape of American finance and progress transforms into the Orientalist icon of hidden treasure and ruin. Adopting the voice of liberal paternalism, the lawyer philosophizes that what is available to a certain class of citizens seems unattainable to another.

The dynamic scene crafted by the narrator's double vision provides a simultaneous narrative of imperial rise and of imperial ruin. The reader is asked to acknowledge that inherent in Wall Street *is* the ruin of Petra. The ruin is both retrospective and prospective, as the loss of a pastoral Native American economy, which has been replaced by the capitalist economy represented by Wall Street, and the future collapse of Wall Street itself are latent in the anamorphic view of Wall Street "deserted as Petra." The narrator associates desertion, ruin, and wistful regret with his subaltern, Bartleby, who stands as an antiquated remnant, "the last remaining column of some ruined temple," in the midst of a modern industrial economy where increasingly mechanized clerical work has lost its former status.[56] Melville, however, indicates that the ruin visible once the surface veneer of Wall Street has become transparent is far more democratic. It is precisely, in fact, the narrator's interpretive shortcomings that make him unable to decipher the hieroglyphic that is Bartleby. Despite all his good liberal intentions, the narrator approaches Bartleby through a complex of sentimentalized emotions such as Christian humanism, nostalgia, pity, and melodrama—but never as his equal. Both pentimento suggestions of Petra's meaning reveal Bartleby catalyzing the collapse of foreground American space into background Near Eastern space.

Given the latent literary ambitions of Melville's narrator, it is not surprising that Melville makes his description of Wall Street redolent of the pictorial-mode conceits fostered by 1830s and '40s writers such as Irving, Cooper, and Bryant and capitalized on by travel writers such as Stephens. As Donald Ringe has argued, the pictorial mode provides verbal landscape sketches crafted to elicit an emotional response.[57] In the New York lawyer's case, that emotional response is melancholy. The narrator transforms Bartleby into an "innocent" Marius brooding at the ruins of Carthage. This transformation suggests that the scrivener's fate as an exile from the modern industrial world is melancholy. Melville, however, suggests a more sweeping imperial repentance by indicating that the shared fate of all empire is ruin. In this second interpretation, Marius is not innocent but rather indicative, and the narrator has missed the point of his own image.

Though the image of Marius brooding at Carthage could have been drawn from a number of sources, among them John Vanderlyn's 1807 painting of the same name, Melville's visualized reference to Petra had been culled directly from Stephens. The early *Redburn* passage describing Stephens emphasizes visualization.

> For I very well remembered *staring* at a man myself, who was pointed out to me by my aunt one Sunday in Church, as the person who had been in Stony Arabia, and passed through strange adventures there, all of which with *my own eyes* I had read in the book which he wrote, an arid-looking book in a pale yellow cover.
>
> "See what *big eyes* he has," whispered my aunt, "they got so big, because when he was almost dead with famishing in the desert, he all at once caught *sight* of a date tree, with the ripe fruit hanging on it."
>
> Upon this, *I stared* at him till I thought *his eyes* were really of an uncommon size, and stuck out from his head like those of a lobster. I am sure *my own eyes* must have magnified as I stared. When church was out, I wanted my aunt to take me along and follow the traveler home. But she said the constables would take us up, if we did; and so I *never saw* this wonderful Arabian traveler again. But he long haunted me; and several times I dreamt of him, and thought *his great eyes* were grown still larger and rounder; and once I had *a vision* of the date tree.[58]

The repeated references to sight, seeing, and eyes dance between subject and object position, blending the sight of the Arabian traveler with the vicarious act of traveling achieved through reading and finally culminating in a vision that conflates Stephens's adventures with the narrator's romantic self-making. "With what reverence and wonder people would regard me, if I had just returned from the coast of Africa or New Zealand," the narrator comments in relation to his meeting with Stephens. "How dark and romantic my sunburnt cheeks would look; how I would bring home with me foreign clothes of a rich fabric and princely make, and wear them up and down the streets."[59] Melville admired Stephens greatly, but he also understood that Stephens's geographical vision was shaped by an era that laid waste to America's indigenous populations and transformed so much of the continental frontier from pastoral space into urban space. Whether or not Melville mourned those losses, he took Stephens's descriptions of Petra and in "Bartleby" shaped them into a consciously literary image that spoke to the central conflicts in midcentury American national identity. Melville's use of Petra to manifest a landscape of pessimism out of the landscape of American optimism, however, did not mean that the ancient Arab ruin was stable in its romantic message.

Installed above the fireplace in the Sitting Room at Fredric Edwin Church's private estate in the Catskill Mountains, Olana, and adorned with a frame designed by Church himself is the painter's most famous "Oriental study," entitled *El Khasne' Petra* (figure 6). A gift to his wife and the only painting mentioned prominently in his will, *El Khasne'* held immense personal significance for Church, in large part because he had made the arduous journey to the lost city of stone himself in February 1868. The El Khasne structure transmitted through Church's oil stands at the end of a narrow cleft in the mountains, called the Siq. The Siq served as the only entrance to Petra for travelers of Church's era. A view of this "treasury" was the highlight of any Westerner's trip to Petra in the nineteenth century, and its aspect is the visual subject of the two major European artists who preceded Church at the location, David Roberts and Edward Lear.[60] Church rendered his own detailed image of the salmon-colored, striated rock facade from the position of a viewer still ensconced in the shadowy enclave of the Siq. This perspective repeated the thematic approach taken by both Roberts and Lear. However, Church's painting and his own musings on its aesthetic influences offer a uniquely American tale of interpretation and misinterpretation. This tale elucidates the connection between Stephens's *Arabia Petraea*, Melville's story of Wall Street, and the resiliency of a narrative of American optimism built in large part on nineteenth-century American landscape painting.

In the late 1860s, Church and fellow late Hudson River School painter Sanford Robinson Gifford were among a number of cultural luminaries who made the Holy Land circuit after the end of the Civil War. But visiting Petra was an experience couched in a different discourse than that of visiting other Holy Land sites, in large part because Petra's associative power did not evoke Christianity but rather secular meditations on archaeology and aesthetic meditations on the romance of decay. Gerald Carr's exhaustive review of Church's Petra correspondences offers this synopsis of the artist's own purpose in visiting the site:

> Church's and Reverend Dodge's letters contain further clues to the artist's purposes, among them Church's references to Scripture and to "terrible prophecies." . . . Yet Petra itself was not a site sacred to Judeo-Christian tradition, and neither Church nor Dodge seem to have regarded it as such. They did not, for example, associate the Sik with Moses or discuss the Sik in terms of Wady Mousa, the "Valley of Moses," in which Petra is situated. Instead they applied the later designation (as did other travelers of the day) to the ravine through which they first approached El Khasne'. Their descriptions of El Khasne' per se focus on its "wild" surroundings and on the high finish of its architecture, its excellent state of preservation despite partial disfigurement, and its undiminished power as a source of self-generating light. In other words, Church and Dodge regarded the building as intrinsically significant, a spellbinding creation characteristic of that locale and of nowhere else.[61]

Church's emphasis on Petra as both a "source of self-generating light" and a site of exquisite desertion distills the peculiar attraction of the lost Arabian city for nineteenth-century Americans who wanted to find in it a comment on empire. Particularly in the Jackson era and the years immediately following, Petra's dual capacity for meaning captures the dueling narratives of American empire: the one justifying American imperial expansion at its borders through the rhetoric of enlightened self-generation, and the other pointing to the fatuousness of imperial rhetoric evinced by a world landscape dotted with the resplendent ruins of imperial ambition. However, while many of these midcentury, antebellum American writers and artists felt compelled to weigh in on one side or other in regard to American national expansion, Church completed his painting

Figure 6. Frederic Edwin Church (1826–1900), *El Khasne', Petra, 1874*, oil on canvas, 60.5" × 50.25", framed. Accession: OL.1981.10.a.b. Reproduced with permission from Olana State Historic Site, Hudson, NY, New York State Office of Parks, Recreation and Historic Preservation.

of Petra in the postbellum year of 1874, when the question of the West and national borders had largely been settled. Indeed, between the years of 1860 and 1870, a new word had entered the American lexicon, as codified by Webster's dictionary—*imperialism*.[62] The "spirit of empire" definition attached to this word replaced empire's older autocratic associations with more benign and democratic associations. Church's *El Khasne'* painting combines the seemingly opposed antebellum narratives on empire into a single aesthetic.

Thomas Cole, Church's mentor, had hung a series of metaphoric landscape paintings entitled *The Course of Empire* in a New York gallery only months before Stephens's travel narrative appeared in print. Cole, socially conservative and Whiggish in political sentiment, viewed his landscape series as a warning to an American populace increasingly enamored with the idea of western expansion. However, as Carr opines, "One could say that with *El Khasne'*, through the medium of scientific archaeology, Church combined and distilled *Consummation* and *Desolation* from Thomas Cole's *Course of Empire*."[63] Church reconciles the rhetoric of imperial advance and the rhetoric of imperial ruin through the medium of his "enlightened" painting. Imbued with both a luminous romantic sensibility and the enlightened scientific accuracy of detail for which Church was famous, *El Khasne'* translates the pessimistic political mood of his mentor Cole's series *The Course of Empire* into a message of aesthetic triumph. Church had personally survived the dangerous trip to Petra and had artistically responded to the challenge of capturing a site that had been called by previous travelers "impossible . . . by any sketches to convey to the mind of a person who has not visited [it]."[64]

Ultimately, the superimposition of sentiment over history in Church's Orientalist painting reveals much about the role of the narrative of American optimism in transforming the message of American Orientalist aesthetics. Though Church had commented about Petra in a March 10, 1868, letter that it was "the strangest scene of desolation I ever saw," and though he had commented in 1885 that Cole's painting *Desolation* "had as much poetic feeling as I ever saw in Landscape Art," Church's own sense of artistic achievement in *El Khasne'* perhaps motivated him to reinterpolate his master's conservative political message into a romantic aesthetic that unabashedly celebrates a narrative of acquisitiveness.[65] Cole's antinationalist narrative about desolation becomes the postcard romance of penetration and panoptic possession in Church's desolation painting.[66] Carr argues that *El Khasne'* "became a synonym for Olana," Church's Near Eastern–inspired home located in the Catskill Mountains. Through this synonym, Church appropriated the ancient Arabian site and transplanted it to the American space of upstate New York. This process of transplantation reinterprets Petra's historical narrative in an act of American home building in much the same way that the Near Eastern travel narratives of a generation earlier translated Bedouins into American dramas of frontier colonial expansion.

In Melville's story, the image of Petra acts as the catalyst for the transformation of a discourse of American optimism, the bustle and hum of Wall Street, into a discourse of American pessimism, a forlorn scene of

Marius brooding at the ruins of Carthage. Yet in Church's hands, the image of Petra becomes a vehicle to transform the pessimism of Cole's *Desolation* into a nostalgic meditation on desolation. Church's reinterpretation/misinterpretation of the American narrative on Petra creates the possibility for adorning his American home with an exotic purchase, while still situating that home within the national landscape that he helped make famous and that in turn solidified nineteenth-century conceptions of national identity. The Oriental artifacts, objects, architecture, and paintings in Church's Olana are cultural capital divorced from their cultural context and put to the service of American national identity.

Ultimately, Church's act of appropriation produces the kind of "optimistic interpretation" that continues to imbue Americans' vision of their own national landscape and supports the rhetorical justification that the national landscape provides for the American nation's international interventions in Arabo-Islamic homelands today. In the nineteenth-century, Arabs, much as Indians in post-Indian-removal America, are cultivatable as cultural capital but invisible as a culture. While images of Arabs, Arab space, and Arab architecture are repeatedly marshaled to the service of the iconography of American national space and the rhetoric of the expanding national geography, physical Arabs are ignored, treated as inconveniences that need to be removed, or narrated as disappearing in the face of Western progress. If one looks closely at Church's *El Khasne'* painting, though, the two shadowy Bedouin figures lurking in the lower left corner, melded as they are with the natural surroundings, serve as a reminder of the continuity of local resistance to foreign countries' appropriations of Near Eastern space for their own national identity politics. The irony is that the two men who modeled for these Arab figures were Church's upstate New York neighbors.

In returning to Petra and to the desert sands of Arabia Petraea, I want to return to Stephens, the first American to penetrate its enclave, and to his claim that "the very sands you tread on have never been trodden by the feet of civilized human beings." Sometime close to the year 1325, Ibn Battutah found himself on the border between Egypt and the Arabian Desert on his way to Mecca to perform his first *Hajj* (حج), an event that is essential to the *riHla* genre. Battutah took the opportunity to remark on the method the local Bedouins used to secure the border between Egypt and Syria (the same border Stephens crosses with Bedouin guides some five centuries later). "At nightfall they smooth down the sand so that no mark is left on it," Ibn Battutah relates, "then the governor comes in the morning

and examines the sand." "If he finds any track on it," Ibn Battutah continues, "he requires the Arabs to fetch the person who made it, and they set
out in pursuit and never fail to catch him."[67] Ibn Battutah describes the
Bedouin practice of *athr* (أثر). *Athr* translates as "track/trace/vestige," and
it refers to the method by which skilled Bedouin trackers read impressions
in the sand. Through those impressions, Bedouin trackers divine a whole
world of information about the person or beast that left them.[68] Reading
athr is a form of literacy that inverts the terms of Stephens's dichotomy
between civilized and uncivilized. "Many secret transactions are brought
to light by this knowledge of Athr," marveled Burckhardt in his own early
nineteenth-century account of the practice. "The Bedouin can scarcely
hope to escape detection in any clandestine proceeding," Burckhardt
explains, "as his passage is recorded upon the road in characters that every
one of his Arabian neighbors can read" (*Notes*, 377).

Stephens, faced with the desert script legible to his Bedouin counterparts, is the illiterate barbarian, unable to read the historical record
impressed on the land itself. Instead Stephens's narrative focuses not on
the living history of the desert but rather on a secondary derived meaning
of *athr*: the relic, remnant, or ancient monument. It is in these inhuman
"footsteps" of ruins that Stephens sees the marks of civilization and the
evidence of history. He remains blind to the meaning of the human footsteps that contextualize these secondary traces. Ibn Battutah's fourteenth-
century *riHla* illuminates a highly civilized and advanced Islamic society
that stretched across multiple linguistic and cultural borders. It puts the
lie to Stephens's civilized-feet claim and offers us a metaphor for thinking
through local strategies of resistance to the footprint Western man wishes
to leave, be it on Arab lands now or Native Indian lands in the nineteenth
century. The Crusoe-esque smooth desert sands of Stephens's imaginary find a historical response in Ibn Battutah's anecdote. This response
reminds us of Ibn Khaldun's admonishment that "the knowledge that
has not come down to us is larger than the knowledge that has" (*Muqaddimah*, 39). The trace of this forgotten knowledge, like the *athr* left in the
desert sand, is as inscrutable to Stephens as the "ruin" Bartleby is to Melville's own New York lawyer. And yet the impression of this trace remains
embedded within America's cultural landscape for those who care to decipher it—a trace that can be cultivated to reveal an alternative account of
American history, space, and identity formation.

3

Poe's Taste for the Arabesque

While the first two chapters detail American literature's direct engagement with Arabo-Islamic culture, chapter 3 examines the incorporation of that world into a self-referential American aesthetic. In Edgar Allan Poe's oeuvre, the American arabesque undergoes a fundamental change in its meaning. This change has a legacy in the poetics of both Eastern and Western modernism. Poe's arabesque is an abstraction of the Arab world, but in modernist aesthetics, the foliate pattern comes to represent the impulse to figural abstraction in general. William Carlos Williams, devising his own genealogy of modernism in the poem *Paterson*, alludes to the importance of figural representation and its connection to Arab art:

The neat figures of
        Paul Klee
                fill the canvas
but that
        is not the work
                of a child.
the cure began, perhaps
        with the abstraction
                of Arabic art
Dürer
        with his *Melancholy*
                was aware of it—
the shattered masonry. Leonardo
        saw it,
                the obsession,
and ridiculed it
        in *La Gioconda*.
                Bosch's

congeries of tortured souls and devils
   who prey on them
      fish
swallowing
   their own entrails
Freud
   Picasso
      Juan Gris.[1]

Visually displaying his own taste for fragmentation, Williams traces the modernist penchant for figural play back to the "abstraction / of Arabic art" visible in Dürer's treatment of the line as an ideal form. Dürer provides an excellent example of Arabic art's abstraction from one culture and narrative instantiation of another. As M. Norton Wise points out, "Dürer had become the personification of Germanness at a time when the Germans had discovered the gothic as their own, a wellspring of their unifying national character even though political unity eluded them."[2] In this formulation, the "abstraction / of Arabic art" into the gothic line play associated with Dürer provides a narrative foothold for German romantic nationalism.

In Dürer, the line itself is a form of Platonic writing, and the line's capacity for movement between the written and the graphic symbolizes the artistic ideal of metamorphosis. The associated artistic style of the gothic grew out of Dürer's line play and was retrospectively attributed to Dürer in the nineteenth century as a distinctly German style. Marked by the advent of the 1828 Dürerfest celebrating the three-hundred-year anniversary of his death, the Dürer Renaissance in Germany resurrected the artist as an icon of national identity and co-opted his linear abstractions into an iconography of Germanness at roughly the same time Poe was cutting his own literary teeth. By the time Poe complains about the charges of "Germanism" being leveled against him in the preface to *Tales of the Arabesque and Grotesque*, the gothic had become a symbol of autochthonous German culture.

Roughly a hundred years after the Dürer Renaissance took place in Germany, Williams resurrects Poe as an icon of American literature and place in his book *In the American Grain*. Describing Poe's unique aesthetic, Williams emphasizes figural reinterpretation as a formative component of expressing a new identity. "With Poe words were figures," Williams insists, "an old language truly, but one from which he carried over only the most elemental qualities to his new purpose which was to find a way to tell his soul."[3] The motion between abstract representation and the creation of a new language to which Williams alludes through reference to Dürer's lines in *Paterson* returns in *In the American Grain* as an explanation of Poe's transformation of an "old language" into a "new purpose." Poe's invention of tradition, for Williams, is captured in the translation of familiar figures into a highly personal idiom. Williams acknowledges that figural representation is an old form of expression, one translated across cultural traditions. But he also insists that the abstraction of a figure inspires a new, culturally specific language.

Poe's conscious construction of a figural alternative to the real world is precisely what makes him an icon of American literary nationalism to early twentieth-century critics such as Williams.[4] Thus, it is not Poe's representation of a real America that is important to Williams but rather Poe's "voluntary lopping off of [America's] lush landscape" (*AG*, 227). This "lopping off" signals the emergence of "a juvescent local literature" (*AG*, 216). Williams declares, "it is a new locality that is in Poe assertive, it is America, the first great burst through to expression of a re-awakened genius of place" (*AG*, 216). Genius of place is not identifiable in Poe's choice of subject matter or native material but rather in his originality, in his will to a "fresh beginning and need to sweep aside all colonial imitation" (*AG*, 219).

The word "genius" is not accidental in Williams's assessment of Poe, and its employment purposefully suggests secular models of romantic inspiration. Marking a change in the word's meaning that began in the eighteenth century, "a genius," Talal Asad writes, "was [now] the product of nature, and what he produced was 'natural,' albeit singular." "For this reason," Asad asserts, a genius "could be appreciated by a cultivated audience exercising judgments of taste."[5] The theme of cultivation is central to Williams's assessment of Poe's "genius of place." He argues that Poe's creation of a "local" literature is possible because Poe's criticism has "clear[ed] the ground" and prepared the way for America to be "cultivated" (*AG*, 224).[6] Poe, as a former critical arbiter of American taste, provides Williams, a current critical arbiter of American taste, with continuity for his theory of national literature. Using Poe as a seed, Williams nurtures a literary theory of American self into fruition. Williams cultivates a cult of Poe in order to identify a uniquely American aesthetic tradition, establishing for his audience standards of taste that, in turn, link national identity to literary affect.

Asad demonstrates in his genealogical study of modernism that the discourse surrounding "the cult of genius" translates the language of religious rapture into the language of secular humanism, thus establishing dichotomies between nation-states regulated by external religious forces and nation-states, such as America, governed by a rationality that is putatively internalized in each citizen.[7] In both the narrative of the exceptional romantic writer, around which the cult of the genius collects, and the narrative of the historically exceptional nation, myth operates as the fictional grounding for secular values that Asad argues "are sensed to be ultimately without foundation."[8] Romantic myths of American literary autochthony are generated by the desire to have the spiritual show forth in the actual, to have physical words "tell his soul," as Williams put it in regard to Poe. These romantic myths represent, for Asad, the profound intermingling of rationality and imagination in the history of secularism.

To read Poe's arabesque as a secular translation of a sacred Arabo-Islamic symbol, then, is to misread the way the secular and the sacred, the rational and the romantic, are profoundly mingled. The false dichotomy between rational/secular modes and mystical/religious modes of value making on which Asad focuses is one that Poe's own use of the arabesque both indicates and exploits. In "The Philosophy of Furniture," the arabesque is a material sign of a cultivated secular taste. In tales such as "Ligeia," the arabesque is an amorphous affect used to cultivate an experience of the occult. Though the critical and the literary may have been distinct genres in Poe's mind and perhaps even in his readers' minds, the rational conceits of the former structured the aesthetic affect of the latter. When the occupant of the "Philosophy of Furniture" is relocated to Poe's tales, the ordered display of eclecticism that defines his rational interior-design choices turns disorderly, creating the possibility for taste to transform into terror. The disorder is caused by the same graphism that defines Poe's "genius of place" for Williams. The stable and static arabesque design turns three-dimensional in these tales, indexing the movement of the word off the page and into the reader's body as stirring affect.

Williams's critical account of Poe presents him as the lamp of a sovereign inspiration. This inspiration is literally internalized in the image of the artist telling his soul through figures. But these figures are borrowed or, more properly, abstracted from another context. In the case of the arabesque, Poe's most prominent and poignant figure, this abstraction is a form of cultural translation. Reading Williams's "abstraction" as code for a form of cultural translation instills an appreciation for the profound alienation that Abdelfattah Kilito argues is inherent in the transfer of Arabic cultural products into Western cultural paradigms. "Naturally literary memory is different for Arabs and Europeans," Kilito asserts. "In both cases, it rests on a certain foundation, a primal model, a particular conception of time and space."⁹ To demonstrate his point, Kilito relates a story about Ahmad Faris al-Shidyaq, a mid-nineteenth-century Arab scholar and major figure in the modernization of the Arabic language. Born in Lebanon to a Maronite Christian family, al-Shidyaq converted to Protestantism and then Islam over the course of a life that also saw him obtain citizenship in London and live for years in France. Al-Shidyaq ultimately sought his fortune in Paris, the place where he was to publish his major works as well as to become active in the social life of the city. The poet had garnered patronage in the Arab world through the traditional practice of writing praise poems to influential men. At one point during his residence in France, al-Shidyaq tried his hand at the same game in Paris. However, in attempting to praise the French monarch Louis Napoleon through poetry, al-Shidyaq abandoned the traditional erotic introductory section of an Arab poem, the *ghazel*. "In order to assure the acceptance of his poetry," Kilito explains, "he disrupted the familiar order of the poem, . . . he amputated his poetry, castrated it so as to approximate European taste" (*ML*, 78). The *ghazel*, meant to conjure a poetic mood for the reader/listener by focusing on the often unrelated charms of a departed woman or a young boy, disappears in al-Shidyaq's French praise poem.

Al-Shidyaq's "castrated" attempt to praise Louis Napoleon through poetry was actually his second try. His first poem uses the traditional *ghazel*. Both were returned to al-Shidyaq without the recognition he had hoped. Arguing that al-Shidyaq's two poems stand in metonymic relationship to all Arabic poetry, Kilito asserts that their rejection is a rejection of Arab poetics on the whole. The lesson Kilito takes away from this anecdote about translation, both cultural and literal, is that "outside its familiar sphere, Arabic literature has no currency—indeed, has no existence" (*ML*, 81).

Kilito's anecdote about al-Shidyaq demonstrates the epistemic violence that results from the cultural translation of Arabic art into the forms of Western modernism referenced in *Paterson*. Arabic art appears in its Western representations as something alien to Arab history and aesthetics. As Kilito suggests in a particularly piquant image of the erotic *ghazel*'s removal from al-Shidyaq's second poem, Arabic art appears in its Western manifestations as something "castrated." Kilito's choice of words speaks more directly to the violence of translation than does Williams's "abstracted." While the "abstraction" of Arabic art recognizable in Poe's figural method establishes what Williams calls a uniquely American "genius of place," the "castration" of Arabic art forms discernible in the writings of nineteenth-century Arab poets such as al-Shidyaq dislocates Arab identity.

The infiltration of Arab references into American literary sources helps create what critics such as Williams call a uniquely American literary aesthetic. But the opposite is true in the critical response to the presence of Western references in the work of nineteenth-century Arab writers. Just as Williams had in the early years of the twentieth century, modern critics turn to Poe again and again as a source of contemplation about what makes American literature unique. In contrast, many modern Arab critics such as Kilito turn toward Arab Renaissance writers such as al-Shidyaq to discuss how the uniqueness of Arab literature was betrayed in the nineteenth century. In the writings of respected Poe scholars such as G. R. Thompson, Poe's arabesque appears as a sign of his unique aesthetic sensibility and his romantic genius.[10] To critics such as Kilito, Arab Renaissance writers' use of Western forms signals an unfortunate mimicry of the West and an abandonment of a uniquely Arab literary tradition. Placing an American Renaissance writer, such as Poe, in the context of the Arab Renaissance reveals the extent to which American romanticism is a cultural translation. But it also illuminates how American romantic aesthetics can be used to read Arab cultural forms dialectically.

Though the golden years of the Arab Renaissance, known as the *nahda* (النهضة), are usually marked as the turn of the twentieth century, its intellectual roots are located in Poe's contemporary historical moment, in what Albert Hourani has called the "Liberal Age" of Arabic thought.[11] Specifically, in the wake of the French occupation of Egypt (1798–1801), discussed in chapter 1, Muhammad Ali realized that European military superiority flowed, in large part, from its modern scientific knowledge. In an effort to rectify the "gap" in modernity between Egypt and Europe, Ali sent educational missions to France in the 1820s, with an eye mainly toward military advancement. In 1831, the Azharite imam Rifa'a al-Tahtawi returned from his mission in France to establish a school for translation in Cairo that was primarily aimed at disseminating modern European science and thought to Egyptian readers.[12] The texts translated were initially heavily weighted toward the military sciences, but slowly and surely al-Tahtawi and his growing body of students translated European literature, philosophy, and history books. Al-Tahtawi's efforts represent the most important translation of European knowledge into Arabic since the translation of Greek philosophy undertaken during the Classical era over seven centuries earlier.[13]

Al-Tahtawi's account of his five-year stay in Paris, *Takhlis al-Ibriz fi Talkhis Bariz* (The Extraction of Pure Gold in the Abridgement of Paris), published in 1835 and revised in 1849, was the first comprehensive treatment of European society and culture to be written in Arabic. The *Takhlis* was the forerunner to the account al-Shidyaq wrote a generation later. Taken together, the two represent a turning point in Arab literature's relation to the West. Though many prior travel accounts of Europe existed in Arabic, the *Takhlis* is, in the words of Daniel Newman, unique in its efforts "to provide a detailed discussion of European civilization and, particularly, its political concepts (e.g., the republic, democracy) and institutions (e.g., Parliament)."[14] The book introduces many new terms into the sacred Arabic language (such as *steamship*), as new sciences required new words and new readerships (Ottoman technocrats rather than Islamic literati) demanded a more streamlined and simplified style. In addition, al-Tahtawi applies old terms such as *freedom* (*Hurriyya*/حُرِّية) and *homeland* (*waTin*/وَطَن) to new concepts. These concepts were influenced by European political thought as well as notions of nationalism bounded by nation-state borders instead of a wider affiliation with the Islamic community (*umma*/أمّة).[15] The Arabic language itself was thus undergoing a radical post-Classical-period innovation in the mid-nineteenth century, and al-Tahtawi was at the spearhead of the changes.[16] The intellectual forerunner to the reformism of *nahda* thinkers who emerged in the next generation, al-Tahtawi encompassed the major themes of the Arab Renaissance: selective appropriation of European ideas, Arab nationalism, and anti-Ottoman ideology.[17]

While the *nahda* represents a strain of liberal reformism and intercultural dialogue in Arab thought, it is also a reaction to both Western colonialism and, later, Western literary forms. This reaction occasions a cultural reentrenchment in romanticized visions of the Arab past usually associated with the heroic Bedouin character traits celebrated in pre-Islamic poetry. Al-Tahtawi provides insight into this mid-nineteenth-century turn toward Bedouin idealization:

> The issue of personal honour which makes the French and the Arabs similar to each other consists of the perception of the ideal of manhood, the

fact of telling the truth and other qualities of [moral integrity and] perfec-
tion. . . . These days [the noble character of Arabs] has waned and melted
away as they suffered the hardships of oppression and the calamities of
time. . . . [But] there are some who remain faithful to their *original* Arab
nature, . . . [and the freedom which Westerners value] was also part of the
character of the Arabs in *past times*. (*Takhlis*, 365; emphasis mine).

Arabs, in al-Tahtawi's description, have more in common historically with
the French than with their Turkish colonizers. But these shared noble
qualities are largely absent in the present-day Arab and must be relocated
in the "original" Arab of "past times."

Arab thinkers' pre-Islamic nostalgia has many of the characteristics of
Western romanticism. The confluence of late eighteenth-century European
romantic models of a national identity based on *volk* practices and the mid-
nineteenth-century Arab *nahda's* construction of an Arab self that stands
outside of time results in what the modern Arab critic and poet Adonis
describes as the double dependency at the heart of the crisis of Arab
modernity: "a dependency on the past, to compensate for the lack of creative activity and a dependency on the European-American West, to compensate for the failure to invent and innovate by intellectual and technical
adaptation and borrowing" (*Arab Poetics*, 80). In both these formulations
of Arab identity, modernity is foreclosed to the figure of the Arab, with the
result that authentic Arabness is either only locatable in an ancient past or
necessarily corrupted by its borrowings from contemporary Western culture. For Adonis, the modernity that appears in Arab society through the
nahda is something "imported from abroad" and ultimately an imitation.

Adonis identifies the problem of Arab modernity as one of imitation.
The solution is not just a question of eliminating Western forms but also
of eliminating the mimicry of pre-Islamic poetry. Adonis's criticism of
imitative poetry leads him to seek his own "cure" for Arab identity in a
genealogical reconfiguration of Arab modernity that can be read against
Williams's "abstraction / of Arabic art." Viewing poetry as "a beginning,
not an imitation" (*Arab Poetics*, 51), Adonis insists that the modernization
of Arab poetry can be retrospectively located in the eighth- and ninth-
century switch from a pre-Islamic oral form to a written form influenced
by Qur'anic studies. "The poet not only had to avoid imitating pre-Islamic
poetry," explains Adonis, "but also had to break new ground in terms of
expression, in exploring his own soul, and in his approach to inanimate
things and the world around him" (*Arab Poetics*, 50–51). The importance

Adonis places on a poet who explores "his own soul" in order to "break new ground in terms of expression" resonates richly with Williams's decision to emphasize the figural qualities in Poe's writing.

Both Adonis and Williams scan their respective cultural heritages for examples of writers who shake off old models in favor of an aesthetic of innovation. Both critic-poets designate the figural aspect of language as the key to resisting imitation and creating the new. "Language here does not only create the object," insists Adonis; "it creates itself in creating the object" (*Arab Poetics*, 73). For Adonis, as for Williams, the employment of language as a self-referential and self-sustaining reality keys the creation of a nationally distinct literature. This literature, in turn, provides a grounding discourse of national identity. Rather than find origins, though, these respective poet-critics construct beginnings that place their own work within a recognizable aesthetic tradition.[18]

It is true that Poe abstracts Arabs in the service of producing Western modernity. But the American writer is also the progenitor of an aesthetic legacy that Adonis identifies as producing his own, authentic, Arab poetic modernity. Adonis explains:

> I should acknowledge here that I was one of those who were captivated by Western culture. Some of us, however, went beyond that stage, armed with a changed awareness and new concepts which enabled us to reread our heritage with new eyes and to realize our cultural independence. I must also admit that I did not discover this modernity in Arabic poetry from within the prevailing Arab cultural order and its systems of knowledge. It was reading Baudelaire which changed my understanding of Abu Nuwas and revealed his particular poetical quality and modernity, and Mallarmé's work which explained to me the mysteries of Abu Tammam's poetic language and the modern dimension to it. (*Arab Poetics*, 80–81)

Adonis credits the Symbolists Baudelaire and Mallarmé with opening his eyes to a nonderivative Arab modernity. He locates this authentic Arab modernity in the eighth- and ninth-century politics of *ihdath* (احداث; innovation), represented by the Arab poets Abu Nuwas (d. 810 CE) and Abu Tammam (d. 845 CE). These poets eschewed imitation of pre-Islamic Bedouin forms and subjects and created a modern, metropolitan language of experience.

In assessing the importance of Poe's writing, Williams emphasizes his figural approach to signifiers, his ability to make them material entities as well as vehicles for communication. Abu Nuwas's ninth-century poetry evidences the same modernist concern with the materiality of the signifier. Though Adonis does not mention it specifically, a poem Abu Nuwas addressed to his on-again, off-again lover Jinan speaks directly to the point about Arab modernity that Adonis makes through the vehicle of the Symbolists Baudelaire and Mallarmé.

> Make many deletions, Jinan, when you write,
> and delete the word, when you do, with your tongue,
> and passing deletingly over a word
> draw close to your beautiful lips,
> for I hold, when running over the lines,
> the cancelled something up for a lick:
> That—is a kiss from you from afar
> which I steal while keeping here to my room.[19]

Abu Nuwas's poem, with its tweaking of the traditional *ghazel* form, represents a shift from an oral to a text-based experience of the world. Placing presence and absence in dynamic tension (as was the norm for the *ghazel*), Abu Nuwas fractures temporal and spatial constraints in his search for communion. Via the written word, the body becomes an unbounded vehicle of desire rather than the limit of experience. And yet that written word is itself absent of meaning and entirely symbolic because it has literally been deleted. Through the medium of a written language that can be erased but still remains as a trace, Abu Nuwas both captures and destroys the physical world.

Instead of celebrating the heroic ideals of the desert life, such as stoic resolve and tribal honor, Abu Nuwas's poetry is concerned with word play and the metaphysics of being. In pre-Islamic poetry, the distant woman was the medium of a Bedouin poet's erotic ingress (*nasib*/نسيب), but she was usually discarded by the time the poet delivered his final message/boast.[20] In Abu Nuwas's poem, the distant woman, Jinan, remains at the end of the poem.[21] In poems such as the one quoted, Abu Nuwas revised the traditional tropes of pre-Islamic Bedouin poetry into the language of the cosmopolitan litterateur. Language in Abu Nuwas's poem is not only oral sensation; it is a physical entity that can be transferred, erased, and manipulated on the page. To Adonis, Abu Nuwas's figural approach signals a modernity that has always been latent in written Arab poetry but, like Poe's "genius of place," requires critical rediscovery.

Adonis's search for a strain of modernity in Classical Arabic poetry, via the handmaiden of modern European Symbolism, has a striking relationship to the Orientalism of Western romantics. Romantics often located models of modern folk consciousness, noble savagery, and natural men in primitive Bedouin culture and pre-modern Oriental practices. Adonis locates models of Classical-era Arab modernity through modernist European Symbolists. The Western Orientalist taps Arab folk culture to reinterpret the modern. Adonis employs the modern to reinterpret the supposedly premodern Arab. In the spirit of intercultural hermeneutics that Adonis uses to reinvigorate ancient Arab poetry, this chapter turns to the arabesque, a topic in Poe criticism that has received much attention in the context of American modernism but almost no truly intercultural analysis of the kind that approaches modernity as a global flow of ideas that moves between East and West. I want to turn now to reading Poe's short story "Ligeia" alongside the classic Arab story of love, loss, and spectral renascence, *Layla and Majnun*. Viewed through the arabesque, the two stories work in dialectic, connecting the romantic traditions of two cultures and dissolving the binaries of secular and sacred, rational and romantic.

Ligeia and Layla

Poe's tale "Ligeia" begins with the drug-addled narrator describing his continued attachment to the dead and departed Ligeia, a woman who had tutored him in "wisdom too divinely precious not to be forbidden"[22] Having replaced the dark Ligeia with the light-skinned Lady Rowena, the narrator now resides in an isolated room of a decaying castle in the English countryside.[23] Describing the lavishly decorated bridal suite he has created for himself and his new wife, the narrator proclaims that "in the draping of the apartment lay, alas! the chief phantasy of all" (*CT*, 661). This draping repeats the "taste" for the arabesque elaborated in "The Philosophy of Furniture." Covering the carpet, the ottomans, the bed drape, the bed itself, and the curtains, the upholstery is "spotted all over, at irregular intervals, with arabesque figures, about a foot in diameter" (*CT*, 661). In keeping with Poe's insistence that every element of a prose tale be written with a mind toward "the single *effect* to be wrought out," the arabesque operates as a clue to the reader that the physical furnishings the decorator has chosen reflect the state of his mental furniture.[24] The rigidity of the arabesque as cultivated "taste" gives way here to the plasticity of an unfettered imagination. When the narrator of "Ligeia" explains the significance of the arabesques, a gothic window into his unquiet mind opens:

> But these figures partook of the true character of the *arabesque* only when regarded from a single point of view. By a contrivance now common, and indeed traceable to a remote period of antiquity, they were made changeable in aspect. To one entering the room, they bore the appearance of simple monstrosities; but upon a farther advance, this appearance gradually departed; and, step by step, as the visitor moved his station in the chamber, he saw himself surrounded by an endless succession of the ghastly forms which belong to the superstition of the Norman, or arise in the guilty slumbers of the monk. The phantasmagoric effect was vastly heightened by the artificial introduction of a strong continual current of wind behind the draperies—giving a hideous and uneasy animation to the whole. (*CT*, 661)

The animation of the arabesque allows superstition and guilt to replace rational order and repose. In this transformation of a material signifier of rational order into a dematerialized sentiment, Poe exploits the arabesque's dual and dueling meanings in his oeuvre.[25] As object, it is a sign of rationality; as sentiment, it is a sign of the occult.[26]

The aesthetic structural duplicity of the arabesque has implications for Poe's romantic nationalism. In "The Philosophy of Furniture," Poe uses the arabesque to model the reformation of American taste. The essay begins by claiming that "the Yankees alone are preposterous" among the nations of the world in design choices. It ends with a "room with which no fault can be found," in which "repose speaks in all."[27] Taste must be internalized, the essay implies, before it can be externalized. Taken as either comic bagatelle or serious attempt at the aesthetic education of Americans, "The Philosophy of Furniture" approaches the question of national identity through taste. If handled with sophistication, Poe suggests, the encounter with one's own internalized taste provides the contemplative space necessary for both personal and national self-fashioning. The arabesque covers all surfaces in Poe's remodeled American interior, but Poe's insistence that the pattern has "no meaning" allows him to abstract it from the cultural context to which it nominally refers and to render it amenable to American national identity construction.

If the arabesque of the bourgeois domestic American interior is a mute figure symbolizing a cultivated national space, then the baroque arabesque of the decadent foreign interiors found in Poe's tales enact the discourse of extranational violence that remains hidden beneath the mute figure of nation. Moving from static "monstrous" design pattern into mobile "ghastly forms," the change in the arabesque in "Ligeia" has textual and metatextual significance. It both foreshadows the Lady Ligeia's ghostly reincarnation and schematizes the goal of the tale of sensation. For the dark and displaced Ligeia of the story's title, the first wife whom the narrator struggles both to memorialize and to eradicate, eventually returns through the vehicle of the arabesque and usurps the place of the fair-skinned Rowena.

"Ligeia," a tale that narrates the return of a dark and displaced woman who makes counterclaims on a domestic sphere newly occupied by a fair-skinned woman, has obvious racial implications.[28] These racial undertones serve to emphasize a larger theme of transference—physical and psychological. The arabesque patterns cast by a saracenic censer play a central role in linking the world of the living with the world of the dead in "Ligeia," but these patterns also link the world of objects to the world of sensation. The animation of the arabesque in "Ligeia" leads to an unbinding of libidinal energy, to the appearance of a phantasmagoria latent in the fetishized objects populating the room. A synergistic interaction between the censer, the arabesque patterns covering the drapery, and the static world of objects ultimately remanifests the narrator's ideal object, the human Ligeia. "I gazed with unquiet eye upon the sarcophagi in the angles of the room, upon the varying figures of the drapery and upon the writhing of the parti-colored fires in the censer overhead. My eyes then fell, as I called to mind the circumstances of a former night, to the spot beneath the glare of the censer where I had seen the faint traces of the shadow" (*CT*, 660). Ligeia's shadow, brought into relief by the writhing "saracenic" patterns emitted from the censer, moves from the world of suppressed memory into the world of physical objects. In forcing herself from the narrator's subconscious into the material world, Ligeia ultimately occupies the light-skinned Lady Rowena's corpse, masking it with her own features. The corpse in "Ligeia," invested with significance by the narrator and transformed by the arabesque pattern, stares back at its interlocutor with an inscrutability that begs to be interpreted. The narrator's loss of faith, his special brand of melancholic *acedia*, finds a response in the reappearance of the person to whom his faith was originally bound—Ligeia. The interpretive act elicited by the cathected corpse allows the world once again to acquire feeling for the mourning subject. In this process, the formerly hollow object, the corpse now draped with the arabesque pattern cast throughout the room, undergoes a fundamental shift in meaning—it becomes transformed into sensation itself. It is a sensation released from the subject and now bound to the object. The effect of this reification is the creation of a self-reflexive mirror for the viewer in the corpse. The melancholic narrator stares at Rowena's body only to see the object of his solipsistic obsession, Ligeia.[29]

Poe's "Ligeia" dramatizes rebirth, or at least the potential for rebirth. The tale explores the very theme of autochthonous renaissance that draws Williams to Poe's "American" legacy. Furthermore, the allegorical function of the corpse in Poe's story (the way its symbolic message subsumes its materiality) also speaks to the larger mid-nineteenth-century American literary ethos of rebirth. But the corpse's allegorical function has resonance with a tradition in Arab literature as well. I want now to turn to a discussion of a different kind of transference and a different kind of cultural translation. So far I have suggested that an appreciation for the aesthetic imperatives of the American Renaissance, as well as modernism, enriches our understanding of Poe's use of Oriental tropes in the tale "Ligeia." But the tale acquires something of a different meaning when read in the context of an Arab literary tradition.

The seminal story of artistic creation in Arab culture is the story of the poet Qays or Majnun Layla ("mad for Layla"). It has many versions, but its basic form is a tale about a poet who falls madly in love with his cousin, Layla. When Layla's father refuses Majnun's advances on his daughter, the poet exiles himself to the desert and sings of his love for Layla. Over the course of time, he goes mad, and when Layla finally goes out to meet him in the desert, he cannot recognize her because he has been consumed with the image of his own love and become obsessed with his own suffering. Layla dies in despair, but Majnun's songs of love are overheard by shepherds and eventually make their way into general circulation.[30]

Majnun Layla is a story of exile, alienation, obsession, and solipsism. In these respects, it has much in common with Poe's short story "Ligeia." In addition, Majnun, whose name comes from the Arabic word for a demonic force (*Jinn*/جِنّ), has much in common with the love-crazed, self-isolated, and perpetually mourning narrator of Poe's tale, a man who claims that he has been possessed by a "demon." Of course, the particulars are transformed in radical ways, and the endings of the two narratives have quite different takes on the moment of the beloved's return. But the dark and mysterious Ligeia, who acts as the pivot point of a cautionary tale about excessive passion and the power of the imaginary to overcome the real, strikes me as a potential reworking of Majnun's Layla. In viewing Poe's exploration of renascence in "Ligeia" through the optic of Arab literary hermeneutics, I am putting American and Arab romantic traditions into dialectic tension in order to explore the tropic connections between the two.

Ligeia/Layla is a source of obsession that is ultimately externalized in forms of creative imaginary. In the "Ligeia" narrator's final vision of Rowena as a remanifested Ligeia, we have an example of a central trope in the Arabic love lyric, the *khayal* (خيال). *Khayal* can be translated as "disembodied spirit, ghost, specter, imagination, phantom, vision, shadow, trace, dim reflection." The "faint traces of a shadow" that ultimately manifest Ligeia's image for the narrator call the *khayal* directly to mind. The word *khayal*'s archaic meaning grows out of the Arabic love lyric, and the role the apparition of the poet's beloved plays within it. As Michael Sells explains in reference to the *khayal*, "In whatever form we try to seize her, she eludes us. She cannot be possessed. To attempt to possess her, or seize her in a particular image is more than idolatry. The desire for possession violates the *adab* (taste, literature, manners)."[31] Poe's narrator, by trying to possess the shadow of his beloved, violates *adab*, both a chivalric code of "good manners" and the Arabic code of "literature."

Khayal is directly related to the Arabic word for imagination. Ligeia is a *khayal* in every sense of the word, and the appearance of her specter/trace/dim reflection in Poe's tale signifies the fundamental connection the American writer made between the artist's imaginative faculties, the narrator's haunted reflection, and the reader's terror. Through the spectral figure of Ligeia, Poe binds writer, fictional character, and reader together on the plane of the imaginary. It is an imaginary that knows no bounds, whether of time or space, and thus not only is Ligeia a *khayal*, but the tale itself acts as a *khayal* that can reenact the syzegetic connection between artist, character, and reader at any time, anywhere. Though Poe himself most probably had no knowledge of the Arab literary trope, it is through the *khayal* that we can link his aesthetics of sensation back to an aesthetic tradition in Arab romantic poetry.

Connecting Sacred and Secular Aesthetics

The *khayal* has its genesis in pre-Islamic poetry. But in the verses of Sufi mystics such as Ibn Arabi, *khayal* operates as a spiritual metaphor, indexing divine rapture and love through descriptions of earthly passion and desire. Poe's Byronic antihero seeks to obtain forbidden knowledge through his own *khayal*, Ligeia. The Sufi mystic also seeks knowledge, something known in Sufi hermeneutics as *ma'rifa* (معرفة; gnosis), through spectral visions and metaphors of rebirth. According to R. W. J. Austin, *ma'rifa* is "an immediate recognition and grasp not of something new or strange but rather of the state and status of things as they really are, have always been, and eternally will be."[32] The difference between Poe's Byronic antihero and the Sufi mystic resides in the lack of religious value that the American writer affords his hero's quest for knowledge. Whereas Poe uses the *khayal* Ligeia to establish an occult world where man is profoundly alienated and faith in the divine is replaced with object fetishism, the *khayal* in Sufi mysticism establishes correspondences between the material and the divine. As Austin explains, *ma'rifa* "involves the knowledge of oneself that is, at the same time, knowledge of the divine Reality of which one is, latently and essentially, inescapably an aspect, which is the meaning of the saying 'Whosoever knows himself, knows his Lord.'"[33]

The magnificent in Sufi theology is God. *Ma'rifa* insists not on transference from one state to the other but on the identity between the visible reality and the divine Reality, as well as between man and God. Much like figurative language in al-Jurjani's theory of metaphor, *ma'rifa* reveals the essential unity of seeming binaries. When binaries collapse into one another in Poe's tales of terror, the revelation of an absence of difference between seemingly opposed states of being evokes anxiety and terror, not a sense of divine connection. The sublime, in other words, has no sacred revelatory value in Poe's tales. Poe's sublime entails a confrontation not with divinity but with an otherness that is contradictorily perceived as sameness. The anxiety that emerges from this confrontation is symptomatic of a secular ethos of individualism that is absent in Sufi hermeneutic explorations of fear.

One of the most important contributions that the twelfth-century Muslim theologian Muhammad al-Ghazali (d. 1111/505) made to the teaching of Islam was the reintroduction of the element of fear to religious contemplation.[34] Al-Ghazali's spiritual autobiography, *al-Munqidh min al-Dalal* (*Deliverance from Error*), is marked by a dramatic episode in which "a door of fear" opens up to him and forces him to reevaluate his earthly activities as a religious teacher and cleric in Baghdad. Explaining the moment when he realizes that his religious practices are aimed at garnering him worldly fame and prestige, al-Ghazali tells his reader, "so I became certain that I was on the brink of a crumbling bank and already on the verge of falling into the Fire, unless I set about mending my ways."[35] Fear does not intensify into terror for al-Ghazali, but it does indicate the importance all Muslims should place on preparing themselves for an afterlife that is already present. Al-Ghazali internalizes the struggle that the faithful have with their faith, modeling an interior life that should be more important for a Muslim than the exterior world.

Largely responsible for the legitimization of Sufism in mainstream Islam, al-Ghazali's theorization of fear as an impetus to piety usefully contrasts Sufi hermeneutic tradition with Poe's romantic use of the arabesque to establish terror. Writing about the benefits of Sufi asceticism in *Ihya 'Ulum al-Din* (*The Quickening of the Science of Religion*), al-Ghazali argues,

> It is indeed evident that the attainment of the beatitude of meeting God in the hereafter can be only by the acquisition of love of Him and intimacy with Him in this life. But love is acquired only by knowledge, and knowledge [*ma'rifa*] only by continual reflection (*bi dawaam al-fikr*). And intimacy is acquired only by love and continual remembrance (*dawaam al-dhikr*). And persistence in remembrance and reflection is facilitated only by lopping off the love of this world from the heart, and that is not lopped off save by renouncing the pleasures and appetites of this world.[36]

Al-Ghazali marks the discontinuities between the "pleasures and appetites of this world" and attainment of beatitude in the hereafter. He insists that it is only by "lopping off the love of this world from the heart" that faithful Muslims obtain a clear vision of their purpose in life. Williams lauded Poe for his "voluntary lopping off of [America's] lush landscape" and creation of a figural substitute for the real. Al-Ghazali encourages the faithful to see the physical world itself as that which is figural and the spiritual world as that which is real.

This contrast signals something other than a religious versus a secular approach to the sublime. It marks an important difference in the aesthetic use of fear. For al-Ghazali, fear (خَوْف/*khawf*) creates an interface between the temporal and the transcendent. "The renouncement of such [worldly] desires," explains al-Ghazali, "is impossible except by bridling the passions, and by nothing is passion bridled as it is by the fire of fear, for fear is the fire which burns the appetites" (*Munqidh*, 36). Fear brings one closer to transcendent knowledge in al-Ghazali's thought. "How can fear not possess excellence," al-Ghazali insists, "when by it one acquires purity . . . and piety and self-conquest, i.e., the virtuous acts which bring one very near to God!" (*Munqidh*, 36). Fear elides the difference between the visible and invisible world, allowing the faithful to approach the divine through the everyday.[37]

Poe's tales can hardly be read as religious heuristics, but fear, or more precisely its intensification into terror, has an essential function in tales that refer to the arabesque, such as "Ligeia," "The Fall of the House of Usher," and "The Masque of the Red Death." Each of these domestic terrors challenges a metaphysics of corporeal transcendence. In fact, the terror in these stories often emanates from bodies that refuse the teleology of death, be they Lady Ligeia, the Lady Madeline, or the Red Death party crasher. Describing Ligeia's preparation for burial, Joan Dayan explains, "She, like the narrator, is being prepared for a more terrible visitation: her body remains where it is, to be alternately activated and exhausted in tune with the narrator's oscillating thoughts about the lady he sees and the one he remembers."[38] Rather than transcendence, Poe's domestic terrors focus on immanence by collapsing the line not only between life and death but between individual subjectivities. In these tales, bodies do not transcend the physical world; they refuse to leave it once they die. Poe and al-Ghazali both employ fear as a response to epistemological anguish. For al-Ghazali, fear motivates him eventually to follow the Sufi path, to practice mystical contemplation as a form of *dhouq* (ذوق; taste). In al-Ghazali's account, fear is a religiously grounded response to his epistemological skepticism.

Poe, in contrast, systematically pushes fear beyond its rational limit, into terror. Terror is not only Poe's signature romantic affect; it also defines his alteration of romance's signification. A scene from "The Fall of the House of Usher" demonstrates how Poe revised the romantic medievalism of a writer such as Irving into his own unique aesthetic.[39] As the narrator reads to Usher from a medieval romance about the gallant knight Ethelrod, the sounds written on the page correlate with the sounds of the actual movements of the prematurely buried Lady Madeline unscrewing her coffin lid and climbing the stairs: "for there could be no doubt whatever that, in this instance, I did actually hear . . . a low and apparently distant . . . screaming or grating sound—the exact counterpart of what my fancy had already conjured up for the dragon's unnatural shriek as described by the romancer" (*CT*, 244). The passage thematically collapses the boundary separating text and reality. The words in Usher's book enter the "real" world of the reader, performing as the onomatopoetics of terror. It is a process that ripples outward, for the reader *within* Poe's tale acts as an analogue for the reader *of* Poe's tale, modeling the affective experience of terror that the writer has designed his fiction to produce. Sensation replaces sentiment when the fate of Usher usurps the fate of the knight Ethelrod as the focus of the romance's action.

Al-Ghazali and Poe both use fear to structure interiority, creating a space where questions about immanence and transcendence are confronted, borders dividing the invisible and the visible world are collapsed, and values are potentially reversed. Fear pushes al-Ghazali toward divine wisdom, the knowledge that here is a preparation for "there," but it pushes Poe's characters toward earthly horror, toward skepticism that there is any "there" other than here. The epistemological impasse in Poe's tales is eventually answered by a terror that embodies the reader and makes the text a living thing. Yet al-Ghazali's "door of fear" and Poe's sensational terror both act as a dissolvent, an agent that reveals the inherent connection between the tangible and the intangible, between illusion and reality, and between the present and the eternal. Al-Ghazali uses this dissolution to remind the Muslim reader that earthly life is a dress rehearsal for a hereafter that is already present but invisible. Poe maintains that the here and now of this world may be ultimately inescapable.

Poe's Arabesque Reconsidered

With a rudimentary understanding of Islamic mysticism, it is now possible to reapproach Poe's arabesque with an appreciation for the formal violence it enacts. The arabesque conducts Poe's principle of sensation in "Ligeia," progressively building a tension that ultimately releases itself in the reader's experience of "shock." However, this progressive use of the arabesque, in both theory and praxis, to achieve "shock" is at odds with the Islamic interpretation of the Arab foliate pattern's (*tawriq*) nonprogressive nature. As an infinite pattern without development, the Arabo-Islamic ornament diffuses aesthetic tension rather than build it. Through agglutination of foliated forms in its field of representation, the *tawriq* encourages persistent movement of the eye across the visible patterns, a movement that ultimately encourages the mind to take flight from the artwork itself. Accordingly, *tawriqs* in Islamic art often appear in truncated forms at the edge of a field of representation, encouraging the viewer to move off the finite and toward the infinite. Grasping and understanding each foliated pattern may provide an emotional release, what the ethnomusicologist Lois Ibn al Faruqi has called the principle of *dafqah* (outpouring), but this release does not produce shock or terror.[40] Quite the opposite. The *tawriq* is a meditative form in Islamic aesthetics, one meant to inspire thoughts of the divine. In Poe's aesthetics, it provides the formula of romantic tension. The difference in the arabesque's and the *tawriq*'s function is in many ways the difference in the respective meanings of taste and *dhouq* (taste).

The affect of terror created by the convolutions of Poe's arabesque stands in stark contrast to the original affective purpose of the *tawriq*. The art historian Ernst Kuhnel writes about the Islamic ornament that "it is obviously the decorative intention that the eye of the viewer is not arrested by the pleasant detail, but that it is delighted by the kaleidoscope passing of an ever-changing and disappearing harmony of unreal forms."[41] The pleasing detail and kaleidoscope harmony of the original "Arab spirit" is perverted into "an endless succession of ghastly forms" in the "Ligeia" interior. In Poe's formal world, the arabesque pattern does not accrete meaning; it undergoes a catachresis.

The self-replication encountered through Poe's arabesque represents a formal change in the grammatical structure of the Arabo-Islamic pattern. In Islamic mysticism, the *tawriq* expresses a mirror motif, but one that has quite different aesthetic aims than Poe's mirrors. Muslim artists often refer to the *tawriq* pattern as a reference to creation being a reflection of the divine names on the dark ground of nothingness or a symbol for the heart acting as a mirror that has to be polished repeatedly in order to assimilate the splendor of divine beauty. Both these conceptualizations of the *tawriq* ultimately bring viewers into contemplation of Allah, not themselves. This Islamic concept is captured in a section of the Qur'an's Surat al-Baqarah, oft repeated by Sufi mystics: "to Allah belong the East and the West: whithersoever ye turn, there is Allah's face, for Allah is all-Embracing, All Knowing" (2:115). In Sufi hermeneutics, the mirrored structure of the *tawriq* represents the essential unity of the world's constituent pieces. In Poe, the arabesque is both a medium through which to express his individualism (his unique aesthetic, his unique market appeal) and a message about the modern anxieties unleashed when individualism is threatened by a collapse between self and other.

The Sufi mystical writer Ibn Arabi, in his thirteenth-century masterpiece *Fusus al-hikam* (*The Bezels of Wisdom*), addresses the collapse of subjective and objective poles of identification, the same collapse Poe explores through the arabesque pattern.

> In one sense the Reality is creature, so consider
> In another He is not, so reflect.
> Who grasps my saying, his perception will not dim,
> Nor may one grasp it save he be endowed with perception.
> Whether you assert unity or distinction, the Self is Unique.
> As also the Many that are and yet are not.[42]

Ibn Arabi describes how the conflation of subjective and objective positions provides the Muslim a vision of unity that is enlightening, not terrifying. As William Chittick explains, Ibn Arabi's major methodological contribution to Islamic theology was his harmonization of reason and imagination (a goal with which Poe would happily associate himself). Reason, based on differentiation and discernment, held that God was incompatible with worldly things, a doctrine known as *tanzih* (incompatibility; تنزيه). This is the assertion of "distinction" that Ibn Arabi references in the preceding quotation, the anti-anthropomorphism behind the claim that "He" (God) is not creaturely. Imagination, on the other hand, perceives identity and sameness, and hence through it we see God's presence rather than his absence in worldly things. This is a doctrine known as *tashbih* (similarity; تشبيه). Those who believe in *tashbih*, Sufi mystics who adhered to a theory of unveiling (*kashf*/كشف), assert the "unity" mentioned in Arabi's poem. They believe that "Reality is creature."[43]

Despite Ibn Arabi's and Poe's quite different aesthetic goals, both explore the connections between opposites through the figural method. Ibn Arabi rejected the stance of theological authorities for whom declaring God similar to creation was a heresy, arguing that *tashbih* was the necessary corollary of *tanzih*. He sought to reconcile traditionalist and rationalist interpretive approaches through figurative interpretation. For Ibn Arabi, the Perfect Man could become the perfect image of God.[44] The Perfect Man is he who combines in himself both heaven and earth in a realization of *wahdat al-wujud* (وحدة الوجود; Oneness of Being).[45] This is a person who is "at once the eye by which the divine subject sees Himself and the perfectly polished mirror that perfectly reflects the divine light" (*Bezels*, 35). Regarded by Islamic historians as the most influential commentator on Islamic mysticism, Ibn Arabi approached the Qur'anic text as, in Austin's words, "a mirror to the reader, in that the [reader] will perceive in it only what his own spiritual state permits him to see" (introduction to *Bezels*, 19). Ibn Arabi was fond of perverse formulations that challenged readers to open their inner eye. The contradictions and oppositions in Ibn

Arabi's writings are meant to guide the initiate toward a "perception" of unity. Metaphoric language that weds seeming opposites is central to the achievement of this "perception." To Ibn Arabi, metaphor enhanced the Qur'an's mystical qualities and allowed readers to see it as text with open-ended meanings. This approach to the Qur'an is perverse in the sense that it goes against traditional Islamic approaches that hold that the Holy Qur'an is a book of answers and fixed certainties rather than a book that opens horizons of new thought.

In Poe's romantic arabesque, the Islamic religious function of the *tawriq* is not perverse but perverted. Poe strips the arabesque of its religious significance and reinvests it with the secular anxieties about individuality, distinction, uniqueness, and/or sovereignty. This process is in fact dramatized within "Ligeia." But so is an arabesque aesthetic that uses figurative language to create conduits between opposites. The characteristic tension in Poe's tales between life and death, immanence and transcendence, pleasure and terror, and the real and the imaginary is resolved not in a dialectical synthesis but rather in a process of cathexis exemplified by Ligeia's occupation of Lady Rowena's corpse. Poe evacuates the presence of Allah in his arabesque. As a result, the viewer of the arabesque in Poe's fiction is not brought into contemplation of the divine through self-reflection but rather stays mired in self-contemplation. Terror is not grounded in a fear of God, as it is in al-Ghazali, but rather in fear of oneself. The promise of spiritual unity offered in Sufi mystical approaches to the image of the mirror, such as those suggested by Ibn Arabi, doubles back onto the viewer in "Ligeia" as a threat of profound spiritual isolation.

The "alien presence" that infiltrates the home space in Poe's tales of terror is born out of the decorator's own decorative impulse. The "alien presence" emerges out of the subject's effort to create a screen of subjectivity in an aesthetic world without religious underpinning. And yet the secular terror Poe conjures is dependent on religious conceits. For Ibn Arabi, the collapse of the subjective and objective poles of identification captured in his images of the mirror precipitates a realization that all distinction, difference, and contrast are illusory. This conflation brings the realization that humanity is but a facet of a single Being, whose reality commissions all derivative being and experience. For Poe, the collapse of the subjective and objective pole is indicative of a modern world voided of religious authorities and littered with religious pieties that have lost their value. The arabesque in this sense acts as a ruin.

In discussing the significance of the ruin to understanding the transformation of material objects into art, Alois Riegl differentiates between what he calls "historical value" and "art value."[46] In Riegl's grammar of the visual arts, the monument in the past age has "historical value," and the ruin in the present age has "art value" precisely because it has survived its historical context and exists only for aesthetic truth. But if the arabesque in Poe's domestic terrors represents on one hand an act of forgetting, an act of replacing historical narrative with aesthetic representation, it is on the other hand an incomplete act of forgetting that always threatens, through its mutable forms, to recall the history it has been summoned to erase. The displaced almost always returns in Poe's tales, and the dead often refuse to die. This movement from erasure to remembrance creates the affect of terror in Poe's domestic tales. It is a movement captured in the arabesque's transformation from static to mobile image. It is also a movement that points to the fundamental connections between Western romantic uses of the arabesque, Arab romantic uses of the *tawriq*, and Islamic religious uses of the *tawriq*.

The Arabo-Islamic *tawriq* is inspired by the Islamic concept of *tawhid* (unity). In Poe, it appears as an allegorical fragment, borrowed from Arab culture and reinterpreted within a different cultural context. In turn, the arabesque in critical approaches to Poe provides a vehicle for discussing the fragmentation of the artistic sphere from the didactic, religious, and political sphere—for modernity. What had been in Islamic interpretations a principle of unity becomes in Poe's aesthetics and the critical canon surrounding Poe a principle of fragmentation. This literary principle, in turn, has a political application. Definitions of the secular nation-state insist that, unlike a society built on religious principles, in America, religion and politics, private belief and public ethic, personal morality and state law are distinct spheres.

Using the aesthetic as a space where the threatening aspects of Islam as a competitive source of revelation can be neutralized has long been a tactic of Western approaches to Arabo-Islamic cultural material. This aesthetic neutering of Islamic religious signification has a special relationship to nineteenth-century romanticism. The project of modernity, Asad argues, employs proliferating technologies that generate "new experiences of space and time, of cruelty and health, of consumption and knowledge." The notion that these new experiences imply direct access to reality, Asad goes on to say, is "arguably, a product of nineteenth-century romanticism, partly linked to the growing habit of reading imaginative literature—being enclosed within and by it."[47] Produced by transnational nineteenth-century romanticism, the emergence of a distinct genre of imaginative literature in mid-nineteenth-century America had the immediate effect of reinforcing readers' belief in the disenchanted nature of their contemporary Western society. The mid-nineteenth-century emergence of imaginative literature also had the retrospective effect of enchanting the "premodern" past. This premodern past was attractive and readily retrievable in the proliferating Oriental tales that appeared in nineteenth-century American magazines.[48]

For the American reading public in a golden age of magazines, the Orient acted not only as an escapist realm of premodern fantasy and nostalgia but also as a location that structured conceits about the nation's modern, secular identity. The replacement of religious icons with literary icons or, to put it otherwise, the substitution of the role of aesthetic taste for the role of the religious in promoting a unifying experience of belonging is one of the major innovations of the modern secular state and its print culture. It is an innovation intimately connected to Poe and to his historical moment. Poe's translation of the arabesque into American literature creates what critics refer to again and again as his modern aesthetic. But what violence does this translation enact on the Arab culture from which the arabesque is abstracted? What relation does this translation have to the development of Arab literary modernity? On the other hand, how can the arabesque be used to distinguish Arab aesthetics from Islamic aesthetics, as well as to reveal the continuities between American romanticism and both these aesthetic traditions?

Adonis sees the problem of modernity in the Arab world as a problem of language. Language in the Arab perspective, explains Adonis, "is not a tool for communicating a detached meaning; . . . it is meaning itself because it is thought" (*Arab Poetics*, 82). What was once the sign of the Arabs' presence and creativity, Arabic, has now become, in Adonis's view, a corrupt and degraded form. The result is that the modern Arab "appears ignorant of what has given him his identity, or who he is" (ibid.). Adonis explains that for the pre-Islamic *Jahiliyya* poet, who served as the early Arab grammarians' resource for "pure" Arabic language, poetry was a communal activity that linked poet to tribe. Poetry was first and foremost oral, and the poet's "basic preoccupation was . . . that his poem must correspond to what was in his listener's soul," for "what was in his listener's soul was part of the common code" (27). Adonis asserts that this *Jahiliyya* poetry "was judged according to how far it could arouse *tarab*, a state of musical delight or ecstasy, and the poetics was founded on what could be called an aesthetics of listening and delight" (27). This experience of aural delight carried over into the early Islamic community of Arabs and still informs much of that community's relationship to the Qur'an. Thus, the problem of modernity in the Arab world in general, and Arab poetics in specific, comes back to questions of the sacred and the profane. "If we remember [language's] relationship to the sacred, and more precisely to the Qur'an," Adonis admonishes, "can we not see in the current ignorance surrounding its usage or in the call for it to be modified by dialectal structures which separate it from the sacred, a sort of declaration of a changed awareness and identity?" (82–83).

Adonis's conservative meditation on the Arabic language provides a linking point between Poe's arabesque and modern Arab poetics. The problem Poe explores through the arabesque is the same problem Adonis explores through Arabic, the gap that has emerged between language and experience, between the word and identity. If we view the arabesque in this intercultural context, it appears to have a function very similar to the sacred capacities of the Arabic language itself (whether or not the user is Muslim). Poe's arabesque, estranged from its original context, functions in American culture as translation divorced from meaning. It has figural value instead of informational content. In a similar vein, the aural qualities of the Qur'an operate as ecstatic sounds independent of meaning, for one need not speak Arabic to appreciate the beauty and religious rapture of Qur'anic recitation. I am claiming that Poe's arabesque is the translation of Arab culture into American culture, a translation that in its catachrestic quality creates entirely new cultural forms that are often independent of meaning and reliant on direct experience. A return to a world in which the word and sensation have become covalent again is certainly indicative of Poe's art-for-art's-sake aesthetic. But this return also speaks directly to Islamic notions of the primary importance of the aural and to Adonis's emphasis on the importance of "pure" Arabic language.

A Tell-Tale Coda

In M. H. Abrams's highly influential critical analysis of romanticism, *The Mirror and the Lamp*, the author posits a thesis as direct as it is powerful.[49] Prior to the romantics, Abrams argues, literature was largely conceived as a mirror that reflected the world. In contrast, romantic writing was conceived as a lamp pouring light outward. The image of the writer as a solitary and radiant force illuminating the world with his creative power is one that Poe would have embraced and that his later critics did embrace for him. Walt Whitman figures Poe as a glowing light whelmed by the welter of a storm when he refers to him as a "lurid dream" in a November 1875 *Washington Star* article.[50] James Russell Lowell, Charles Baudelaire, Henry James, and William Carlos Williams all employed a favorite romantic trope of creative illumination in referring to Poe as a "genius." And yet within Poe's oeuvre, it is not lamps but mirrors and mirroring motifs that consistently develop his own, arabesque, theory of romanticism. Rather than mimetically reproducing the world as it is, Poe's mirrors produce uncanny doublings that blur the distinction between the real and the imaginary. The relationship between inspiration and transference in Poe's romanticism is thus a vexed one. It is a relationship triangulated by a third conceptual object, the veil.

Though *The Mirror and the Lamp* is Abrams's most acclaimed book, it was a later work of romantic literary criticism, *Natural Supernaturalism*, that he called his most important.[51] In *Natural Supernaturalism*, Abrams examines the influence of Biblical and theological thinking on secular literature, ultimately defining romanticism as the transference of religious expression into secular expression. Abrams's analysis focuses on Judeo-Christian sources, but the scope and resonance of his insight is usefully broadened by considering the presence of Islamic references in Western romantic traditions. Infusing Poe's Oriental references with their Arab and Islamic significations makes his romantic arabesque appear not as the creation of autochthonous genius or the result of mimetic transference. Rather it provides a key to interpreting what happens when the light of Western inspiration shines on the veiled mirror of Eastern culture. The image that returns is a figural interpretation of what lies beneath that veil; it is an American arabesque.

Located in the very middle of Poe's "The Tell-Tale Heart" is an encounter between the anomic narrator and the patriarch of the house. In this encounter, the narrator illuminates the old man's rheumy eye with a "single dim ray" shot from a lantern. The eye, a natural and metaphysical mirror, stares at the narrator in a veiled form that refuses to reflect humanity back to him. We can think of this moment of encounter between lamp and mirror as analogous to the image of the mirror that Ibn Arabi often uses, an image that relies not on the specially coated glass mirror of today but rather on the metal mirror of his own day. This metal mirror had to be expertly polished in order to preserve its reflective qualities. The more skillfully the metal surface was polished, the more the otherness of the mirror was reduced to a minimum or effaced for the reflecting consciousness. But, as Austin explains, "To the extent, however, that the mirror reflects a dulled and distorted image, it manifests its own otherness and detracts from the identity of the image and subject."[52] The identity of image and subject is the key to Ibn Arabi's epistemology. Linking reason and imagination harmonizes the traditionalist doctrine of *tanzih* with the Sufi doctrine of unveiling, or *tashbih*. To think of God as either present or absent, Ibn Arabi argues, is to see with only one eye. Perfect knowledge requires that you see with both the eye of reason and the eye of imagination.

The violence in "The Tell-Tale Heart," of the narrator against a man who was "like a father" to him and with whom he sympathetically shares the experience of terror, can be located in the absence of identity between image and subject—in the imperfect polish of the mirror that the old man presents to the viewer. It is an absence of identity that emerges with the revelation of a dull and rheumy eye/mirror that distinctly "manifests its otherness." Here the eye of reason and the eye of imagination are radically split and pitted against each other. Here the mirror is veiled. "I saw it with perfect distinctness—all a dull blue, with a hideous veil over it that chilled the very marrow of my bones; but I could see nothing else of the old man's face or person; for I had directed the ray as if by instinct, precisely upon that damned spot" (*CT*, 304–5). This intertwining of gazes—the one prosthetic and mechanical, the other occult and obscured—reads like an encounter between the lantern of Western Enlightenment rationality and the veil of Eastern mysticism.

If the encounter between lantern and veil speaks to the transnational phenomenon of Orientalism, it also has a very particular valence for American Orientalism. Confronted with the interpretive ray of lantern light, the human eye in "The Tell-Tale Heart," a symbol of nineteenth-century America's stress on seeing (its *eidos* of vision, illumination, rationality, and penetration), stares back at the viewer with a blind impenetrability that excites rage and madness. The old man's eye is an object that both refuses to be disenchanted by the lamp light of reason and refuses to provide vision itself. Doubly impenetrable, the blind and veiled eye clings stubbornly to an obscurity that is reversible for the viewer and the viewed. The symbolic interconnectedness of organic life envisioned in Emerson's image of a "transparent eye-ball" evaporates in Poe's tale.[53] What remains is the image of an eye milky with blindness and parasitically attached to its host, as though it were a "vulture eye."

There is a lesson about transnational exchange to be drawn from this encounter with a rheumatic eye that refuses to act as a mirror. This lesson suggests that the "deep time" of cultural influence does not always produce smooth transitions from the Persian poetry of Hafiz to the transcendentalist writings of Emerson.[54] Tracing the lines of intercultural influence does not always reveal aesthetic "twins" in whose work we can recognize a universal aspect of American culture participating in the development of localized identity across the map. This intercultural influence just as often produces the interpretive violence that characterizes the life of the image of the Arab in American discourse—an interpretive violence that does not create global communities out of spatially separated individuals but rather abstracts certain individuals away from their history, culture, and identity in order to rhetorically clear a space for other imagined communities to flourish.

Although "The Tell-Tale Heart" makes no mention of Arabs, its use of certain transatlantic Orientalist tropes to structure its sentiments of violence, fear, anxiety, and guilt over usurpation demonstrate the central argument I am making about American literature's catachrestical use of the image of the Arab. Disconnected from any Eastern context and displaying no primary knowledge of the Orient as such, Poe's Oriental imagery is quite consciously put to the service of creating a variously located American milieu of fantasy. This fantasy milieu had nothing to do with Eastern contact or colonies and everything to do with North American contact and the foundational myths of American identity. The figure of the Arab in Poe is shaped by transnational flows of imagery, but it tells an American story of nativity. What disappears in this story and what is too often ignored in the critical canon surrounding Poe's Orientalism is any engagement with Arab culture on its own terms. And yet this American adoption of the image of the Arab into the iconography of its domestic colonial dramas has a formative impact on definitions of Arabness that eventually influence modern Arab self-definition.

The point of this chapter, then, is not that the arabesque is transformed from an aniconic religious image to an icon of secularized romantic irony in Poe's aesthetics but that this transformation is a distillation of the cultural politics of American Arabism. American Arabism is a symptomatic discourse that allows citizens to employ images of the Arab both to confront questions of origins, nativity, indigenousness, belonging, and ownership and to structure their own sense of national and personal sovereignty. In Poe's arabesque, in the critical literature surrounding Poe's arabesque, and in the Western intellectual history attendant to the arabesque pattern, the image of the Arab becomes a source of speculation on origins of one kind or another and ultimately a literary instrument in creating the imagined community of America. In the course of this speculation, the image of the Arab is disassociated from actual Arab peoples and culture and transformed into a trope of aesthetic contemplation. This transformation from culturally situated material human to decultured figural device in Poe's poetics is indicative of what happened to the image of the Arab circulating in the realm of American literature proper in the mid-nineteenth century. But it is also a transformation that is reversible. It is by being attendant both to the materiality of the arabesque pattern and to the formal qualities of the Arabo-Islamic design called the *tawriq* that I have attempted to hark to the heartbeat of a dialectic between American and Arab culture that has been buried, as it were, beneath the floorboards of literary history.

4

American Moors
and the Barbaresque

Standing on the shores of Morocco just prior to returning to Harlem in the 1930s, the Caribbean writer Claude McKay pays
romantic homage to the Barbary Coast almost a century and a half
after the word *Barbary* circulated in American print culture as an
indicator of savagery and slavery. "The Moroccans are a magical barbaric people," McKay announces, "if one isn't too civilized to appreciate the subtlety and beauty of their barbaresques."[1] Federal-era American captives in North Africa used the term *Barbary* as a discursive
tool to establish the civilized mandates of the new, slave-owning, U.S.
nation. In the process of projecting nascent nineteenth-century American racial hierarchies across a global field and presenting American
secular democratic values as universal, these working-class sailors also
anxiously acknowledged their country's multicultural composition.
McKay, in the post–World War I Jim Crow years, tropes Barbary in
order to blend the categories of civilized and savage and undercut the
logic of segregation.

By "-esqueing" Barbary, McKay twists the trope of barbarism, associated with Africa, into a question of taste—a transhistorical and transspatial marker of civilization. Barbary captives used aesthetic categories such
as appreciation for architectural beauty and literacy to differentiate their
civilized status from the barbarous status of their North African captors.
McKay disassociates taste and civilization, opening up a semantic space
of appreciation for the barbaric. Improvising on the discourse of primitivism, McKay vernacularizes Barbary, changing it into a "barbaresque"
that speaks to African subtlety and beauty, as well as the limits of civilized
America's cosmopolitan artistic sensibility. To further complicate the
twist on the Barbary trope McKay enacts, his ode to Moroccan "barbaresques" is followed by a formalist poem that indulges in blatant images of

Orientalist fantasy, including a line that praises dancing "fatmahs shaking their flamenco feet."[2] McKay seizes the right to gaze on African culture with the eyes of civilized distance, as well as with the sympathies of primitive taste. In doing so, McKay situates himself as a black Orientalist who both inherits and revises a white discourse on civilized superiority. Rather than use North Africa as a screen through which to negotiate the anxieties of white privilege in America, as Barbary captives did, McKay uses North Africa to explore the privileges of blackness.

This chapter borrows McKay's term "barbaresque" and applies it to the representations of Arabs and Islam found in early twentieth-century black discourses on American national identity. These representations are hardly consistent and often speak directly to differences in theories on self-representation, as well as to the aesthetic divides that these differences engender. For instance, W. E. B. DuBois, champion of the "talented tenth," mines African Islam as a source of racial pride, especially in the late *The World and Africa*, and occasionally co-opts Arab history as African history. On the other hand, McKay, voice of the "debauched tenth," offers more fraught accounts of the relationship between Arabness and Africanness. His engagements with Arab race and Islamic culture ultimately allow him to narrate a form of black Orientalism and a form of primitivism. Despite their differences, both DuBois and McKay contributed to an uplift discourse that used representations of Arabs and Islam to rewrite the history of black identity in the New World. In the early twentieth century, a range of black writers created their own American arabesques, often reformulating romantic origin narratives familiar from white Orientalist discourse.

The most salient figure of black engagement with Arab and/or Islamic culture is the Moor. *Moor* was a term used in American vernacular discourse since the eighteenth century, but it gained a new purchase in the context of early twentieth-century black uplift discourse. In an effort to invest black American identity with historical continuity, New Negro and Harlem Renaissance writers often turned to North Africa and Islam. So did a wealth of street-corner prophets who traveled north and west with the Great Migration. This chapter pays close attention to one of the most mysterious and biographically elusive street-corner prophets, Noble Drew Ali, founder of the still-extant Moorish Science Temple. Though black intellectual elites such as DuBois held street-corner prophets such as Drew Ali in low regard, the two men shared a common interest in co-opting narratives about North African civilization for the service of black

American uplift. A powerful counterweight to images of African primitivism, North African history from the pharaohs through the advent of Islamic kingdoms provided early twentieth-century black writers with proof of African civilization, cultural sophistication, and imperial power. The connection between this "sophisticated" African identity and Arab or Arabo-Islamic identity is often murky, mutable, or invented but is nonetheless key to various rhetorical efforts both to extend the color line and to prove black humanity to a larger white audience.

The goal of extending the color line and appealing to white audiences, of course, was not shared by everyone who employed the figure of the Moor. DuBois, Drew Ali, and McKay all use references to the Moor as part of their explorations of racial identity and race relations, but they come to quite distinct conclusions. McKay's complex representation of Morocco in the context of his commitment to the ethnic renewal of the Harlem Renaissance exists in tension with the representation of Morocco located in the writings of Drew Ali, for instance. Drew Ali's Morocco is a very different discursive touchstone than McKay's Morocco. Whereas McKay represents Morocco as barbarous, Drew Ali represents it as the pinnacle of human civilization. Whereas McKay revels in the aesthetic appeal of Moroccan primitivism, Drew Ali uses Moroccan culture to model black middle-class respectability. However, both writers trope Morocco to create new black modalities. These new modalities disaggregate African culture from white models of historical knowledge.

The conflicts between embracing primitivism and cultivating cultural sophistication that McKay exploits in his own engagements with "barbaresques" are central to debates about the goals and methods of early twentieth-century black uplift discourses. How the figure of the Moor was "-esqued" by writers involved in movements such as the New Negro, the Harlem Renaissance, and black internationalism is the focus of this chapter. Reading the differences between DuBois's and Drew Ali's engagement with the figure of the Moor alongside the differences between McKay's and Drew Ali's engagement with the figure of Morocco/Barbary clarifies the way class divides affected the longevity, success, and reception of African American sociopolitical movements. The figure of the Moor was mobilized for both spiritual and secular discourses on black identity. Tracking its uses in the first decades of the twentieth century reveals how intraethnic class and religious reconciliation were often sacrificed in black uplift discourses on the altar of interethnic racial reconciliation.

The Prophet Noble Drew Ali

Black newspapers across the Northeast and Midwest had been sporadically covering the Moorish Science Temple since 1927, mostly exhibiting curiosity about their leader, a man who claimed that Americans of African descent were in reality Moors from Morocco. But in March 1929, the alternative religious movement caught the full attention of the black press. The event that sparked the increased coverage of the Moors was their involvement in a bloody confrontation with Chicago police. As a number of black newspapers reported, the confrontation resulted in the fatal shooting of two police officers and the arrest of the group's leader, Noble Drew Ali. Adding to the intrigue was the report that the shoot-out was precipitated by the murder of one of the Moorish Science Temple's members by a rival faction. What was Noble Drew Ali's role in the murder, if any? Who were these Moors, and what did they preach? Why did they call themselves Moors? Why did they wear Islamic headgear such as the fez and the turban? Upon Noble Drew Ali's release and subsequent death from mysterious causes only a few months later, the Moorish Science Temple factionalized, and the plot thickened. The story of Drew Ali's death and the temple's schism was carried on the front page of the *Chicago Defender* and in feature articles in the *Pittsburgh Courier*, as well as in the *Philadelphia Tribune*. This news was largely ignored in white owned and operated press outlets, as was Drew Ali himself.

The elaborate filigree of hagiographic detail that has accumulated around the historical picture of Noble Drew Ali traces out the marginalia of a tale as romantic as any found in Oriental fantasies. Generally recognized as being born in North Carolina on January 8, 1886, Timothy Drew may or may not have been the son of former slaves or of a Moroccan Muslim father and a Native American mother. He may or may not have been the descendant of Bilali Mahomet, a Muslim slave who lived off the coast of Georgia on a Sapelo Island plantation and wrote one of the few nineteenth-century American documents in Arabic.[3] True or apocryphal, the details of Drew Ali's early biography create a pattern recognizable from oral histories of folk heroes who symbolize resistance to institutional power. These details include being adopted by a tribe of Cherokee Indians when his mother died, falling in with a band of Roma gypsies to escape an abusive aunt, traveling with a circus as a magician, sailing around the world as a merchant seaman, and working as a railway man.[4]

If this early biographical information plays on and plays up Drew Ali's propensity to find community with the dispossessed, the story of his coming into the realization of his prophethood focuses on his empowerment through the acquisition of coded titles, tools, and names. These codes speak to an affiliation not with the dispossessed but with a rising class of black bourgeoisie and spiritual entrepreneurs, as well as with men such as Marcus Garvey, to whom Drew Ali refers as his own John the Baptist. The prominence of Egypt, Mecca, and the pyramids as well as the names Sharif and Noble in the oral history surrounding Drew Ali suggests a connection between his Moorish Science Temple and fraternal organizations such as the black Masons and the black Shriners.[5] By the turn of the twentieth century, over five million Americans had joined some six hundred different fraternal orders. The nomenclature and symbols used by alternative black versions of the white fraternal organizations that were growing exponentially in the last decades of the nineteenth century provide a clue as to why the Islamic names and Arab cultural references that Drew Ali employed had a purchase in the African American community. These symbols and codes spoke of ambition and success, be it class or race based, to a group of migrants who had come north to find a better life for themselves and their families. Founded in the United States in the eighteenth century by the Caribbean-born Prince Hall, black Freemasonry provided a common point of reference for many upwardly mobile and politically conscious members of the African diaspora.[6]

Globally contextualized by movements such as black nationalism, Freemasonry operates as a conduit for and conductor of pan-African consciousness. Just as black Freemasonry offered both an alternative to racially exclusive white Freemasonry and a continuation of the secret societies and social clubs that had always played a prevalent role in the cultural life of West Africans, its outgrowth the black Shriners (founded in 1893) also filled social, economic, and political needs for the African American population.[7] A more exclusive group than the black Freemasons (a member must be a thirty-second- or thirty-third-degree Mason), the Ancient Egyptian Arabic Order, Nobles of the Mystic Shrine, adopted many of the same Islamically coded regalia, rituals, and iconography as their white counterparts, the Ancient Arabic Order, Nobles of the Mystic Shrine. Most notable is the wearing of the familiar fez, the use of a Qur'an, and the invocation of both Allah and Muhammad in rituals of Shriner initiation. The founder of the Shriners, Billy Florence, claimed to have journeyed to Mecca, where he received a secret document that forms the basis of the group's charter. It is a story that shares an inordinate amount of specific details with the origin story of Drew Ali's Moorish Science Temple.

Sometime after Ali's sixteenth birthday, he is said to have traveled to Egypt, where he met the last priest of an ancient cult of High Magic who took him to the pyramid of Cheops, blindfolded him, and abandoned him there. When Drew Ali found his way out of the pyramid unguided, he was immediately recognized as a potential adept and initiated under the name Sharif Abdul Ali. Drew Ali is also said to have traveled to Mecca, where he met Abdul Aziz al-Saud, the future ruler of Saudi Arabia. It was either in Egypt or in Mecca, depending on the oral history one chooses to privilege, that Drew Ali came into possession of the *Holy Koran of the Moorish Science Temple of America* (*The Circle Seven Koran*), a document that covers, among other things, the lost years of Jesus's wanderings in Asia. Upon Drew Ali's "return" to the United States, he founded the Canaanite Temple in Newark, New Jersey, in 1912 or 1913, preaching his doctrine in basements, empty lots, and street corners with the help of a mysterious fabric salesman named Dr. Suliman (who may or may not be the founder of the Nation of Islam, W. D. Fard).[8]

The first in a series of worship centers that came to be collectively known as the Moorish Science Temple, Newark Temple was joined over the next decade by temples in Richmond and Petersburg, Virginia; Charlestown, West Virginia; Pine Bluff, Arkansas; Baltimore, Maryland; Youngstown and Cleveland, Ohio; Lansing and Detroit, Michigan; and Philadelphia, Pittsburgh, Milwaukee, and Chicago. Membership is said to have reached thirty thousand at some point before Ali's mysterious death in 1929.[9] Though the movement's first temple was located in Newark, Drew Ali put down his most permanent roots in Chicago. He established a Moorish Science Temple there in 1925 (the same year as the peak of the Harlem Renaissance), moving its base of operations from Newark. From the Chicago headquarters, Drew Ali ran the day-to-day operation of the temple. He supervised the production of a Moorish Science publication named *The Voice of the Prophet* (figure 7), which did everything from reprint sections of *The Circle Seven Koran* to endorse politicians to supply a Moorish society page written almost entirely by women in the movement. Drew Ali also distributed the many Moorish Science products that this publication advertised for mail order from Chicago, products such as antiseptic bath compound and mineral healing oil. There is still a Moorish Science Temple in use in Chicago's Ukrainian Village, and its members

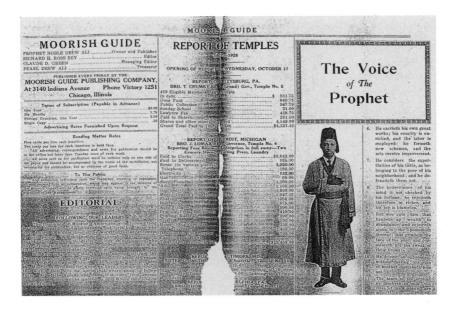

Figure 7. The Voice of the Prophet. From Moorish Science Temple Papers, New York Public Library, Schomburg Center for Research in Black Culture.

still open the door in observance of the prophet's directive "keep my temple doors open, and I will drive them in."[10]

The Circle Seven Koran

The first known publication of *The Circle Seven Koran* appeared in 1927, two years after the temple's move to Chicago and two years before Drew Ali's death, though the work is purportedly much older. *The Circle Seven Koran* is largely a plagiarized document, lifted practically verbatim from two sources that had their own prominence in New Age and Rosicrucian movements. The first source, *The Aquarian Gospel of Jesus the Christ*, covers chapters 2–19 in *The Circle Seven Koran*. The second source, *Unto Thee I Grant*, covers chapters 20–44. The final chapters of *The Circle Seven Koran*, chapters 45–48, appear to have been written by Drew Ali himself and deal directly with the Asiatic origins of the Moors. I focus on these final chapters, but by way of background, I want to provide a bit of information on the two appropriated sources.

The Aquarian Gospel is liberal and mystical theosophical in perspective. The book's topic is Christ's sojourn in India during the years that the Gospel loses track of him, from adolescence to thirty years of age. Attributed to an obscure figure from Ohio, Levi H. Dowling, the book is supposedly transcribed from akashic records in 1908 but has an earlier 1894 French source, *La Vie Inconnue de Jesus* by Nikolai Notovitch. Notovitch, a Russian Jew who converted to Christianity, claims to have discovered the manuscript for his book in a Tibetan monastery in Ladakh, convincing a monk to translate its contents to him while he was nursing a broken leg there. From these two very similar sources, Drew Ali's text differs only in changing the name "God" to "Allah" and stripping Jesus of his blue eyes and blond hair. *The Circle Seven Koran*, in fact, spends much more space discussing Jesus than it does Allah or Muhammad and has a very clear Christian New Age underpinning.

Unto Thee I Grant is a Rosicrucian text with more obscure origins. Sri Romathario, the editor or reviser, claims that the English version of the manuscript dates back to 1760 but also that the original may be a Tibetan translation of a work by the Egyptian pharaoh Akhenaton. Regardless of its sources, the sections of Drew Ali's *Koran* that he lifted from *Unto Thee I Grant* focus on proper behavior and etiquette as it applies to young people, young married couples, and children. Patriarchal in tone and content, these sections are mostly devoid of the central theological arguments made in the first half of Drew Ali's *Koran*.[11] In the final section of *The Circle Seven Koran*, Drew Ali's own voice comes to the fore, speaking directly to the questions of racial identity and cultural heritage that are at the center not only of early twentieth-century New Negro identity politics but also of American debates about immigration and national identity more generally.

Drew Ali was not alone in his direct employment of Islam as a means to attract individuals who felt disenfranchised within their own national boundaries. A few streets down from Ali's Moorish Science Temple headquarters in Chicago, another putatively Islamic organization was seeking congregants from the African American community, the Ahmadiyya movement. Formally founded in 1900 by Ghulam Ahmad from the Punjab, India, and introduced to America in 1920, the Ahmadiyya movement was, unlike the American Moors, transnational in scope as well as philosophy. The Ahmadiyya movement found that it appealed to the same Great Migration African American population from which the Moors drew their congregants. Not surprisingly, then, Ahmadiyya missionaries in the United States, such as Muhammad Sadiq, received attention in the black press of the period as well. In the articles where Sadiq is quoted, he links his pan-Islamism with pan-Africanist rhetoric. Similar to Drew Ali's Moorish Science Temple, the Ahmadiyya incorporated elements of *The Aquarian Gospel of Jesus the Christ* that were rejected by mainstream Muslims as heretical.

Drew Ali's emphasis on the term *Moor* as the key to unlocking the secret of black American identity, however, distinguishes his doctrine both from indigenous black spiritualist movements tinged with New Age religious syncretism and from foreign Islamic missionary movements such as the Ahmadiyya. In *The Circle Seven Koran* and elsewhere, Drew Ali insists that all Africans are originally descended from the "ancient Canaanites from the land of Canaan" (*Circle*, 47:1). "The 'Negro,' as they were called in this nation, have no nation to which they might look with pride," wrote Drew Ali in a note at the end of a copy of the *Circle Seven Koran*; "their history starts with the close of the Civil War or more properly with his being forced to serve someone else."[12] Drew Ali situates black Americans not in white history or American history but in their own, as he puts it, "Moorish" history.

Respected and insightful historians such as Michael Gomez, Edward Curtis IV, Brent Turner, and Sherman Jackson have all looked to Noble Drew Ali as a potential bridge between the orthodox forms of Islam that came to America with the importation of West African slaves to the New World and the indigenous black American Islam that sprang up in American cities in the 1920s and 1930s, but my interest is in Drew Ali's innovative reinterpretation of the term *Moor*. Drew Ali uses the term *Moor* to translate Arabo-Islamic history into African American history and ultimately to link Africanness and Americanness. The orthodoxy or lack thereof of the Moorish Science Temple is not the focus of this chapter. Rather, my analysis considers the instrumentalization of the term *Moor* in Drew Ali's reconstruction of American history. I am concerned with the way in which the term *Moor* links literary language with political language, romanticism with citizenship, and a transnational imaginary with national identity politics. Drew Ali places Africa, Egypt, and Moorish identity, in particular, at the core of his alternative vision of American citizenship. By choosing to identify American Moors with Moabites and Canaanites, Ali claims descent not from Jewish Biblical patriarchs but from their Biblical enemies, consciously creating a counterdiscourse on American origins from within the seedbed of American Orientalism. This counterdiscourse posits America not as a New Israel but rather as ancient Morocco, an interpretive shift that had major consequences for how Drew Ali reinterpreted the Atlantic passage and thus reinterpreted black American identity.[13]

The American Moor

Drew Ali's ontological and epistemological reinterpretation of black American identity through the vehicle of the figure of the Moor begins with a relocation of Africa and an insistence on African nativity in the New World. In chapter 47 of *The Circle Seven Koran*, entitled "Egypt, the Capital Empire of the Dominion of Africa," Drew Ali binds the African and American continents together through the vehicle of Egypt, a move conversant with the rhetorical conflations of the two spaces that I discussed in chapter 2. But rather than lingering in Egypt, a trope present in a number of other forms of black nationalist rhetoric and internationalist thought, Drew Ali quickly moves to the Maghreb. In an imaginative geographical move with radical historical consequences for the remapping of black identity in the New World, Drew Ali makes the Americas and Morocco covalent by closing the Atlantic Ocean.

> The Moabites from the land of Moab who received permission from the Pharaohs of Egypt to settle and inhabit North-West Africa; they were the founders and are the true possessors of the present Moroccan Empire. With their Canaanite, Hittite, and Amorite brethren who sojourned from the land of Canaan seeking new homes. Their dominion and inhabitation extended from North-East and South-West Africa, across great Atlantis even unto the present North, South, and Central America and also Mexico and the Atlantis Islands; before the great earthquake, which caused the great Atlantic Ocean. (*Circle*, 47:6–7)

Here, the Atlantic, the space of the middle passage, is not only a historical wound; it is also historical suture. Caused by "the great earthquake," the opening of the Atlantic highlights the centrality of the Mediterranean in Drew Ali's reconfiguration of African American identity. What is significant in this recounting of history and reallocation of geographic belonging is the figuration of Moroccans (cum Moabites) as original inhabitants of the New World. These inhabitants predate European settlers by thousands of years. The Atlantic, a space of repressed memory and forced removal for Africans according to European history, becomes something else in Drew Ali's account of Pangaeaic continental connection. It becomes the space that both divides Moorish Americans from their original African heritage and instantiates their American origins. Drew Ali's reinterpretation of the meaning of the Atlantic in the narrative of Africans' journey to America denies the primacy of slavery to African American identity and reaches back farther into history for a new origin story, a new beginning. Once the watery Atlantic is transformed into a land bridge, Africans come to America as conquerors, not slaves. In using the figure of the Moor to relocate not only black Americans' origins but also the Atlantic Ocean and the American continent itself, Drew Ali coopts the power of Orientalist discourse to rewrite, reimagine, and rediscover American history.

In place of a history of slavery, Drew Ali substitutes a *volk* identity that keys on the notion of descent and immutable cultural heritage that is transferred in one's blood. "There is no one who is able to change man from the descendant nature of his forefathers," the *Circle Seven Koran* states, "unless his power extends beyond the great universal Creator Allah Himself" (47:11). Rewriting American historiography from the perspective of the Moor, Drew Ali rejects the elective model of national identity that the rhetoric of the Declaration of Independence had promised but never delivered on for people of color. Instead he turns toward an alternate form of nationalism that had resonance with the Anglo-Saxonist primordial-descent model of national identity. This descent model of belonging justified American slavery, drove America's westward expansion, and was to inform the restrictive American immigration laws passed in the 1920s. Embracing a Hamitic legacy that rejects the term *Negro* as a form of false consciousness, Drew Ali's *Circle Seven Koran* enunciates a new black American consciousness, but he also leaves many of the American stereotypes of sub-Saharan African identity intact.

Remapping Race

In turning toward Africa as a source of race pride and historical ballast, Drew Ali's Moorish Science Temple had much in common with the pan-Africanist movements that were gaining traction in the early years of the twentieth century. But there is a major difference between Drew Ali and his contemporaries here. Drew Ali sought to situate black Americans not as Africans but as indigenous Americans, and his nationalism was not Africanist but rather an alternative version of American nationalism. To this end, Drew Ali not only flew both the American and the Moorish flag in his Moorish headquarters (figure 8), but he also issued his congregants "nationality and identification" cards or "passports" that both presented them as American citizens and laid claim to an alternative vision of how that citizenship was constituted.

The front of the card is adorned with Muslim symbols and the bearer's "free" name written in English and Arabic. At the bottom of the card, a line states, "The bearer is a registered Moslem." On the back of the card, a line on the bottom reads, "I hereby do declare that you are a Moslem under the Divine Laws of the Holy Koran of Mecca, Love, Truth, Peace, Freedom and Justice." As if to situate this alternative form of "Moslem" national belonging within the mainstream American notion of nationality, the card also reads in bold, "I AM A CITIZEN OF THE U.S.A."

Though the dueling identities of an American citizen who operates under secular laws and a "Moslem" citizen who operates under divine laws may seem to be at odds, they are naturalized in Drew Ali's vision of Moorish citizenship. The relationship of "Moslem" and American national identity to each other is clarified in *The Circle Seven Koran*. Chapter 46, entitled "The Divine Origin of the Asiatic Nations," lays out the foundation for the psychological and physical geography of black American identity that Drew Ali sought to remap.

1. The fallen sons and daughters of the Asiatic Nation of North America need to learn to love instead of hate; and to know their higher self and lower self. This is the uniting of the Holy Koran of Mecca, for teaching and instructing all Moorish Americans, etc. 2. The key of civilization was and is in the hands of the Asiatic nations. The Moorish, who were ancient Moabites, and the founders of the Holy City of Mecca. 3. The Egyptians who were the Hamathites, and of a direct descendant of Mizraim, the Arabians, the seed of Hagar, Japanese and Chinese. 4. The Hindoos of India,

Figure 8. Prophet Noble Drew Ali, founder of the Moorish Science Temple of America, and secretary, in his office, January 8, 1928. Photographer: L.L. Foster. Reproduced with permission from the New York Public Library, Schomburg Center for Research in Black Culture.

the descendants of the ancient Canaanites, Hittites, and Moabites of the land of Canaan. 5. The Asiatic nations of North, South, and Central America: the Moorish Americans and Mexicans of North America, Brazilians, Argentinians and Chilians in South America. 6. Columbians, Nicaraguans, and the natives of San Salvador in Central America, etc. All of these are Moslems. 7. The Turks are the true descendants of Hagar, who are the chief protectors of the Islamic Creed of Mecca; beginning from Mohammed the First, the founding of the uniting of Islam, by the command of the great universal God—Allah. (*Circle*, 46:1–7)

As a "lost-found" nation, black Americans are "fallen" and must be redeemed. The fall is very specifically the loss of Moorish national identity and the attendant self-abnegation and self-loathing that Drew Ali identifies with his admonition that the Moors "need to learn to love instead of hate" through acts of historical and spiritual self-recovery. Locating and claiming that Moorish nationality again brings redemption. Because the Moors had "strayed after the gods of Europe," Drew Ali claims that they "honored not the creed and principles of their forefathers." This religious backsliding results in a loss of identity that Drew Ali directly conflates with a loss of nationality. As punishment for their "straying," "the nationality of the Moors was taken away in 1774 and the word negro, black and colored were given to the Asiatics of America who were of Moorish descent" (*Circle*, 47:14–17).

Drew Ali provides a narrative that accounts for the loss of Moorish identity without disturbing the basic historical outlines of American nation formation. The narrative contends that the Moorish flag was hidden in the basement of the White House along with a "mandate for the land" that acknowledged Moorish claims to ownership of parts of North America. These pieces of apocryphal Moorish history are, in turn, rendered both invisible and visible (to the adept) in a national narrative of white American identity. The tale of George Washington and the cherry tree becomes in Drew Ali's allegorical reading of American history a tale of the dispossession of the Moors, with the chopping of the tree as a coded message about the first American president's seizure of the Moorish nation's flag—a red flag with green accents.[14] In Drew Ali's alternative origin story of the nation, the flag's seizure points to the temporary loss of Moorish national identity as a kind of Biblical punishment. Blending rhetorical elements of American jeremiad and Sufi unveiling, Drew Ali's history of American blackness uses Arabo-Islamic figures to reread central narratives of white American identity, revealing hidden meanings. The result is a vision of Moorish identity that is not assimilated or erased by American identity but rather integrated into existing narratives of American history.

Whatever the factual merits of this alternative American chronology of events, it is a powerful act of imaginative historiography. The term "Moslem," as Drew Ali uses it, signifies non-European and encompasses the "Asiatic" nations of all the Americas, as well as Arabians, Egyptians, Indians, Japanese, and Chinese. These are precisely the peoples who would be excluded by an Anglo-Saxonist rendering of a descent (rather than consent) model of American national identity. In Drew Ali's racial map, Moorish Americans, as descendants of Moabites by way of Canaanites, are a particularly important group (having founded Mecca) within the larger fold of Asiatics and the even larger envelope of "Moslems." Drew Ali's inclusive category of Moslem implies that the struggle for recognition extends past the bounds of black identity and toward a more expansive color line. The prophet's choice of the term "Moslem" to extend the color line beyond the United States and beyond blackness per se distinguishes his employment of African roots rhetoric from black nationalist movements that focused on Egypt or Ethiopia, making his category of outsider more expansive.[15] Drew Ali reinterprets the meaning of blackness by turning toward Arabo-Islamic history and civilization. He does so not in the service of an internationalist back-to-Africa movement but rather in the context of a black American nationalist movement.

The Arab and the African in New Negro Self-Representation

The amount of newspaper coverage devoted to Islam and Arab-African links in the period of the Harlem Renaissance indicates that there was a growing curiosity about these subjects in the black American community. The news coverage of the Moorish Science Temple in the *Chicago Defender*, the *Pittsburgh Courier*, the *Philadelphia Tribune*, and the *Baltimore Afro-American* resonated with the increased attention to Oriental material in these press outlets. One man who drove this coverage was Joel Augustus Rogers, the Jamaican-born journalist, historian, and author, as well as the early twentieth century's great popularizer of African history. He was also the period's most persistent interrogator of accepted theories of race. His first book, *From Superman to Man*, self-published in 1917, stages a conversation between a black Pullman porter and a racist white Southern politician. The porter uses references to historical, biological, and anthropological sources to systematically debunk the politician's theories of black inferiority. In the late 1920s, Rogers wrote a series of journalistic articles on his travels around the globe for the *Pittsburgh Courier*. These articles were part of his lifelong commitment to challenging Eurocentric views of history and uncovering evidence of "Great Black Men." Rogers's globe-trotting dispatches often focus on race relations within Islam and Islam's appeal to American blacks. "Words 'American Negro' Unknown to Arabs, Says J. A. Rogers," reads an April 16, 1927, *Courier* headline (2). "Says Islam Faith Knows No Color Line," reads the headline of a June 25, 1927, *Courier* article from Rogers (A1). Other black press outlets picked up on the domestic side of the issues Rogers raised. "Sees Islam Making Bid for Converts," announced a March 14, 1927, *Chicago Defender* article that focused on "the converts among Negroes of our larger American cities" (A1).

Though Rogers's articles all appeared in the same year that Drew Ali published the *Circle Seven Koran*, black press explorations of Islam, Arab race, and the increase in black American converts had begun a few years earlier with coverage of the Indian Muslim proselytizer Sadiq and continued with examinations of Africa's role in world civilization. Rogers may have been a forerunner in the field of researching African cultural history in the context of American race relations, but he was certainly not alone by the time the Harlem Renaissance started gaining momentum. Sounding a theme that was a familiar refrain in both Drew Ali's Muslim uplift teachings and secular black uplift sermons, an October 11, 1924, *Chicago Defender* banner reads, "Civilization in Africa at One Time Superior to Ours." Discussing ancient Arabia's contributions to civilization, the author, F. E. Bowles, asserts that "Negro blood spread into the Arabian race" because of slavery and intermarriage. He continues, "Many Arabs have made names for themselves along many lines—Is it because of their Negro blood or in spite of it?" Bowles concludes his musings on Afro-Arab connections by furnishing the example of the "greatest of the Arabians, . . . Antar, the Arabian Negro warrior, poet and hero" (A9). Antar, a sixth-century pre-Islamic poet as well as the subject of multiple European tales of Arabian romance, had been born a slave to an Arab father and an Ethiopian mother. Improvising off this story of mixed Arab-African origins, Bowles transforms Antar into a representative "Negro."[16]

Popular black press writers such as Bowles were echoing discourses circulating among the intellectual elite in the black uplift movement, especially those associated with the New Negro movement. The New Negro movement placed its faith in the ability of DuBois's "talented tenth" to provide representations of black identity that would change white opinions of blackness. Alain Locke, editor of the collection of works published under the title *New Negro*, framed the movement as an attempt to prove black humanity to a largely white readership. Respectability and achievement were keys to Locke's conception of black self-representation. Locke's second essay in the volume, "Enter the New Negro," makes it clear that, in the words of David Levering Lewis, "migrating peasants were expected to leave the immediate future (of the black race in America) to the upper crust."[17] Locke's vision of black uplift had the New Negro as its avant-garde but ultimately "sought to graft abstractions from German, Irish, Italian, Jewish and Slovakian nationalisms to Afro-America."[18] Yet despite the obvious Eurocentrism of Locke and other talented-tenth leaders, Arab and Islamic references were important tools in translating black civilization and sophistication to white audiences. The March 1925 special edition of *Survey Graphic*, dedicated to representing the "young generation of Negro writers," in many ways signaled the launch of the Harlem Renaissance. It was tellingly titled "Harlem: Mecca of the New Negro."

In *The Souls of Black Folks* (1903), DuBois posed the "problem" of the color line as the "problem" of the twentieth century. This problem centers on "the relation of the darker to the lighter races of men in Asia and Africa, in America and the islands of the sea."[19] As David Louis-Brown points out, this "lesser-known second clause of DuBois's most famous pronouncement pushes the color line beyond the United States, sketching out a global approach."[20] One of the most important results of DuBois's insistence on globally contextualizing the color line is that "it calls on African Americans to forge a political identity that goes beyond their particular ethnic identity."[21] Similar to Drew Ali, DuBois also turned to Arabo-Islamic civilization to reinterpret the meaning of blackness in the American context.

DuBois revisited both the subject of Islam and the histories of Near Eastern and North African space repeatedly in his life, touching on them in writings as diverse as *The Negro* (1915), *Black Folk Then and Now* (1939), and *The World and Africa* (1946). Jason Young asserts in his examination of DuBois's continued fascination with Islam as a foil to Christianity, "DuBois saw in Muslim societies throughout the Middle East and North Africa complex societies comprised of varied races, religions, and cultures that might serve to guide the United States in the twentieth century into more equitable social and racial interactions."[22] Whereas the street-corner prophet Drew Ali directly co-opted the nomenclature, iconography, and history of Islam as American cultural property, DuBois used Islam as a comparative apparatus that could potentially advance the situation of the African diaspora in the Americas. DuBois employed Islam rhetorically, as white Orientalists before him did, to reform American practices and reconstitute American racial categories.

For DuBois, it was not enough to promote contemporary representative men and women. It was also important to mine the historical past for representatives of black civilization and cultural sophistication. This often meant channeling the historical achievements of Egypt, Islam, and the early Arab empires into a narrative stream about black American history. Commenting on the relationship between Arab racial identity and African racial identity in *The Negro*, DuBois states that African and Arabian contact "has been so close and long continued that it seems impossible today to disentangle the blood relationships." He concludes that Arabs "are too nearly akin to Negroes to draw an absolute color line."[23] The blurred distinction between Arab and black cultural/racial identity indicates DuBois's desire to co-opt Arabian history to the service of black American historical empowerment. As such, the racial interpenetration of Arabs and "Negroes" in DuBois's writings on Africa is correlated with a geographical interpenetration of Africa and Arabia. Commenting on Islam in *The World and Africa*, DuBois claims that the religion "arose in the Arabian deserts, starting from Mecca which was then part of the world which the Greeks called Ethiopia and regarded as part of the African Ethiopia."[24] The use of Islamic history to revise Western historical accounts of African barbarity recalls Dorr's mid-nineteenth-century travel narrative, *A Colored Man round the World*, and repeats the earlier writer's tendency to establish Afro-Arab historical ties that ultimately serve New World black identity politics at the expense of any meaningful alliance between contemporary New World black populations and contemporary Arab populations. DuBois goes so far as to claim, in *Black Folks Then and Now*, that North Africans historically were "not, in fact Arabs; they were Negroes with some infiltration of Arab blood."[25]

In many cases, the blurred racial locus between Arab and black identity promoted by black intellectuals such as DuBois repeated and played to the white American population's inability to differentiate between racial others. This is a point the *Chicago Defender* made by picking up an article from the *Baltimore Sun* on October 12, 1929. Under the title "Some Confusion," the article relates the story of a "Negro named Williams" addressing a "radical meeting in Brooklyn on the Palestine situation." The article goes on to relate the following story about Williams's fate after someone in the audience shouted, "He's an Arab": "whereupon the assembled multitude went after Williams with such earnestness that police resources were necessary to rescue him from the mob." The original *Sun* article pivots from the theme of racial indeterminacy to the racial masquerade of minstrelsy by suggesting, tongue in cheek, that "Al Jolson would be a good fit for a play involving the prophet Muhammad." Linking whiteness, blackness, and Arabness through the Jewish minstrel Jolson, the *Sun* creates its own mixed interpretation of racial identity, one that the *Defender*'s black readers most likely read with less laughter than suspicion.[26] But it is the article's final lines that speak most saliently to the divide between the minstrel humor that papers with predominantly white readerships tried to elicit through the theme of racial masquerade and the project of extending the color line that both DuBois and Drew Ali took seriously. "And if the Arabs feel that their cause suffers in New York from a majority against them," the article's author asks rhetorically, "why not take over in a body the speakers for the Society for the Advancement of Colored People?" (A2).

DuBois's willingness to rewrite African history, as well as to reconfigure African American historical knowledge, through the handmaiden of Arabo-Islamic history had much in common rhetorically with the New World Islam of Noble Drew Ali. However, unlike DuBois, Drew Ali does not turn to indigenous African material in an attempt to resuscitate the importance of Africa to a sense of black identity. Rather he makes Africa covalent with America and reinterprets narratives already in popular American circulation to reveal their esoteric meanings. This difference in use of the figure of the Moor ultimately points to the difference between a class of intellectual elites who sought to rehabilitate the term *Negro* by investing it with historical significance and a class of spiritual entrepreneurs who eschewed the term *Negro* altogether. This second group, which included Drew Ali but also Father Divine and Sufi Abdul Hamid, turned to Arab and/or Islamic references to instantiate black identity as unique and different, not to explain its significance to white America. For Drew Ali, translating Arabo-Islamic history into African American historical knowledge meant eschewing the term *Negro* as one foisted on the African diaspora in America.

Whatever DuBois's differences with Locke, he saw Islamic history and Arabo-Islamic culture as a way to challenge what the term *Negro* meant and to reinscribe a new "Negro" identity. Drew Ali used Islamic history and Arabo-Islamic culture to figuratively reinterpret blackness itself and discard the identity of "Negro" entirely.[27] Employing the word *Moor* as an organizing principle of racial identity, Drew Ali translated Islam into a New World black idiom as a way to translate blackness into American culture. Locke emphasized the importance of framing representations of black identity for white audiences. Drew Ali preached his gospel of Moroccan identity to an all–African American congregation. Drew Ali's conceptualization of Moorish race gestured toward a "colored" collective that was also part and parcel of DuBois's intellectual program, if not necessarily Locke's program. But DuBois's insistence on reinterpreting blackness through the paradigms of moral and material uplift often led him to muddy the distinction between Arabness and blackness in the service of creating a continuum between contemporary African American identity and African identity in the past.

DuBois's and Drew Ali's respective Orientalist reinterpretations of New World black identity both seize the term *Moor,* but they interpret the term differently. DuBois claimed that medieval Spain was "conquered not by Arabs, but by Berbers and Negroes" who were under the military leadership of Arabs.[28] Moors, in his figuration of the term, are a heterogeneous mix of Arabs, Berbers, and West Africans. Moorish history, to DuBois, is "Negro" history. Drew Ali claimed that no such thing as "Negroes" existed at all and that all Americans of African descent were in fact Moors misnamed. Representations of Arabo-Islamic figures appear in both DuBois's and Drew Ali's writings as a conduit between identities—"Negro" and Arab, Islamic and African, American black and African black. These American renderings of the Moor allow the figure to operate as a link between American racial classifications and transatlantic affiliations. But Drew Ali's interest was essentially nationalistic, not transnational. Drew Ali remade Islam into a black American religion largely aimed at precisely the dislocated black under- and middle class whose voices Locke wanted to keep sidelined. Whereas Locke sought reconciliation with white American culture and DuBois was thinking through forms of black internationalism, Drew Ali marked his congregation of American Moors as a culturally distinct national group living within the larger fold of the United States.

The Question of Class

Though Islam offered intellectual elites such as DuBois a powerful tool through which to critique the gap between Christian ideals and Christian practice, these same intellectual elites had little patience for the religious movements that swept through lower-class black American neighborhoods. The black press coverage of the Moorish Science Temple shoot-out and schism and Drew Ali's arrest and death reflects many of the prejudices that black intellectual elites held toward popular religious movements in the black community. This coverage tended to salacious insinuation and conspiratorial suggestion. The March 23, 1929, *Pittsburgh Courier* headline blares, "Murder Exposes Moorish Leader's Amours" (10). The article refers to the Moorish Science Temple as a "cult" and leads with information about Noble Drew's alleged three "secret" wives, the youngest of whom the writer claims was forced to marry at twelve years of age. In the *Courier's* October coverage of Drew Ali's death, articles refer to the Moorish

Science Temple as a "racket" which "duped members."[29] Black press outlets such as the *Courier* were as ready as mainstream American newspapers to label the Moorish Science movement a cult. It took the *Atlanta Journal-Constitution* six months after the fact to register the events revolving around the March Chicago shoot-out, but when it finally did, the September 12, 1929, heading read, "Negro Cultists Battle Police."

Black newspapers paid much closer attention to the Moorish Science Temple than did their white counterparts, in part, because the questions about black identity raised by the Moors were particularly pressing for uplift-minded African Americans in the 1920s. The New Negro movement had begun in the 1890s.[30] By the time Drew Ali had formed his Moorish Science Temple in 1925, however, many of the New Negro's goals were highly contested within the African American community. While more moderate and mainstream black intellectual voices, such as DuBois, often emphasized middle-class respectability, formal education, and refined artistic sensibility as keys to overturning stereotypes and achieving black empowerment, other, more radical voices contested both these claims and their aims.

The coverage of the Moorish Science Temple in the black press is symptomatic of the struggles to define the goals and methods of black American uplift in the late 1920s and early '30s. The *Chicago Defender*, which had published articles that were initially sympathetic to Drew Ali, stopped taking the movement seriously after the 1929 events. Just two years earlier, the paper had referred to Drew Ali in a November 17, 1927, article as "Prophet, founder and head of the Moorish Divine Movement," mentioning the "splendid uplift work being done" by his followers, as well as his intimate connection with Marcus Garvey (5). Perhaps in keeping with the demise of Garvey's own reputation in the eyes of many African Americans over the second half of the 1920s, *Defender* articles that followed in the wake of Ali's death routinely referred to the Moorish Science Temple as a "cult" but never again as an uplift movement. The *Defender*'s language registered more than Garvey's fall from grace, though; it registered class schisms within the black community that often turned on interpretations of what "back to Africa" meant culturally.

The delegitimizing of Moorish Science visible in The *Defender*'s changed nomenclature hinges on an altered interpretation of the origin of the Moors' practices. Intervening in a debate about primitivism within the black uplift movement of the period, the *Defender* writer Dewey R. Jones reinterprets the Moors' claims to be of African heritage as a form of savage cultism. Under a December 10, 1932, heading, "Voodoo Rites of the Jungles in Odd Contrasts with Background of the City," Jones revisits the Moorish Science Temple's 1929 scandal in the context of "religious cults which had beginnings in Africa" and "still make use of human sacrifice" (9). The juxtaposition of African jungle and American city in the article's title gestures to the contradiction between modern progress and primitive return. By "revealing" the cult origins of the Moors, Jones marginalizes their discourse of uplift and "reveals" its regressive elements. Jones locates the Moors' practices not in "civilized" North African civilization but rather in the African "jungle."

It is precisely the religious claims of the Moorish Science Temple that made them a "cult" in the eyes of black newspapers with predominantly educated middle-class and upper-middle-class readerships. The Moorish Science Temple's sacred interpretation of Moorish identity made it a target of a critique largely motivated by class dynamics. No less than was the case with Father Divine and Sufi Abdul Hamid, the Moors' religious fervor was associated by many in the upper echelon of black society with low economic class and ignorance. These were decidedly not "representative Negros" in the eyes of the black intelligentsia. Whether out of genuine suspicion of popular religious movements led by charismatic leaders or out of a desire to control the terms of the discourse of Afro-Arab continuity, mainstream black intellectuals largely dismissed movements such as the Moorish Science Temple, even though there was significant overlap between Drew Ali's turn to Arabo-Islamic history and the use that respected leaders such as DuBois made of Arabo-Islamic history. For DuBois, who had some but ultimately limited sympathy for popular cult movements, religious significations such as Muslim and Jew were appropriate as figural devices but not as spiritual identities. For Eurocentric thinkers such as Locke, the Jew was a far more palatable model of identity formation for the American black than was the Arab or the Moor.

Drew Ali's turn toward the figure of the Moor as a link between the African identity and the American experience of blacks in the New World is an implicit rejection of the dominant narrative in black American discourse that had achieved this rhetorical aim earlier. This dominant narrative wedded Africans to Jews. In the context of early twentieth-century racial uplift politics, the narrative about the covalence of Jews and black Americans acquired a distinguishable class dynamic that was only latent in the eighteenth and nineteenth centuries. In chapter 2, I examined an antebellum African American discourse on Jews and explored the alternative mappings of America and American space that emerged from the symbolic associations and conflations between Jews and dispossessed Africans circulating in that discourse. African Americans' rhetorical seizure of the symbolic power of the figure of the Israelite and/or Jew was part of a larger black Atlantic discourse on Jews to which I turn our attention now.

Olaudah Equiano, in his 1789 spiritual autobiography, *The Interesting Narrative of the Life of Olaudah Equiano*, compares the manners and customs of his African tribe, the Eboe, to those of ancient Israelites. Equiano claims that both peoples share a common approach to circumcision, ritual purification, feasting, and child naming.

> And here I cannot forbear suggesting what has long struck me very forcibly, namely, the strong analogy which even by this sketch, imperfect as it is, appears to prevail in the manners and customs of my countrymen, and those of the Jews, before they reached the Land of Promise, and particularly the patriarchs, while they were still in that pastoral state which is described in Genesis—an analogy, which alone would induce me to think that the one people had sprung from the other.[31]

As Vincent Carretta notes, Equiano's linking of Africans with Jews "reflects the widespread belief among both supporters and opponents of the slave trade that, in the words of John Gill (1697–1771) . . . '. . . all Africa and a considerable part of Asia were possessed by the four sons of Ham and their posterity.'"[32] John Gill, whom Equiano cites in the *Narrative*, was only one of many Europeans who speculated on the meaning of Ham and Hamitic peoples in terms of contemporary questions such as slavery. Discussions of Ham and the subject of Africans' connection to Jews were to be found in the abolitionist writings of Granville Sharpe (1735–1813), Thomas Clarkson (1760–1846), and the African-born writer Ottobah Cugoano (1757?–1791+).[33]

The bone of contention between those who would use the story of Ham to liberate Africans from slavery and those who would use it to justify the enslavement of Africans was whether or not Ham's descendants were cursed, like him, for having mocked Noah. Genesis states that Noah, once he awakes from his drunkenness and realizes what Ham has done to him, curses Ham's son Canaan. "25 And he said, Cursed be Canaan; a servant of servants shall he be unto his brethren. 26 And he said, Blessed be the LORD God of Shem; and Canaan shall be his servant. 27 God shall enlarge

Japheth, and he shall dwell in the tents of Shem; and Canaan shall be his servant" (9:25–27). Discussions of Noah's three children and the fate of their descendants were essential to the racist typologies informing pseudoscientific disciplines such as physiology and anthropology—disciplines that now have legitimacy but were born out of the late eighteenth-century application of scientific language and methods to Biblical exegesis.[34] Professionally trained African American social scientists such as Zora Neale Hurston attempted to co-opt the language of science in order to reverse the terms of racist identification promoted by "scientific" discourses. Hurston's position allowed her, in Louis-Brown's words, to "use the social scientific practice of ethnography to mend a rift between professional and everyday scientific discourses."[35] While Hurston's refusal to dismiss Southern folk practices such as voodoo as superstitions challenged New Negro class (and geography) prejudices, Drew Ali's audience was not the urban elites but rather precisely the Southern "folk" who had migrated north and often brought their "superstitions" with them. Drew Ali's Moorish science, esoteric and passed on from generation to generation through secret documents and oral traditions, was much closer to folk conceptions of privileged knowledge than were the scientific discourses valued by the New Negro emphasis on material and moral improvement.

Equiano's own rhetorical effort to place his original African culture in the context of Judeo-Christian history and morality by invoking the power of analogy and the authority of Biblical scholarship is part of the *Narrative*'s ethos of development. This ethos is consistent with New Negro talented-tenth discourses on advancement. In the course of the *Narrative*, Equiano moves from pre-Christian pagan to Christian and from slave to successful entrepreneur, arguing, through synecdoche, that what can be achieved spiritually and economically by the individual African can also be achieved by African society as a whole. In Equiano's interpretation of Genesis, the Hamitic legacy is not the creation of fixed and essential racial characteristics which are passed down over the centuries and mark certain people as eternal slaves. Rather, the story of Ham points to race as a mutable entity whereby a person's pigmentation can change over the course of centuries from white to black, just as one's national affiliation can change from Jewish to Eboe. Equiano uses the popularly circulated Atlantic discourse on Ham to trace African racial heritage back to an ancestor whom Africans have in common with Europeans, Noah.

More than a century after the publication of Equiano's *Narrative*, Drew Ali returned to the story of Ham as a means not to link whiteness and blackness but rather to separate them through the categories of Asiatic identity and European identity. Equiano argues for mutability, Drew Ali for continuity. In Drew Ali's reinterpretation of the Hamitic legacy, the African diaspora is associated not with Jews but with their historical enemies Canaanites. The name *Canaan* predates the book of Genesis, and its appearance in the Jewish origin story owes itself to a history of Hebrew imperialism that is literally codified in the writing of the Old Testament. It is a story with which the essayist Eliot Weinberger begins his own quixotic exploration of racial classification.

> In the second millennium B.C.E., the coast of Palestine is known as Kinahna, for the people there make a purple dye called *kinahhu* from the shells on the beach. In the 12th century B.C.E., the land is conquered by the Philistines coming east from across the sea and the Hebrews ("the people from over there") coming west from the desert. The people of Kinahna, and all other subjugated groups—Amorites, Hivites, Perizzites, Girgashites, and Jebusites, among them—become known indiscriminately as Kinahnites, the Canaanites.[36]

Weinberger's genealogy of Canaan suggests that Equiano's effort to associate Eboe Africans with Jewish patriarchs in their "pastoral state" does not challenge the racialized logic of imperialism inherent in the Genesis codification of Israel's origins. Instead Equiano shifts the African subject's associations, binding him or her to the Israelite narrative of conquest and divine mandate rather than binding him or her to the narrative of subjugation associated with the Canaanite figure.

In *The Circle Seven Koran*, by contrast, Drew Ali repeatedly draws on the figures of Biblical curse and exile who are not Jews—Canaanites, Amorites, Hittites, Moabites, Hagar, Ham—and links them with current racial "others" to be found in an increasingly multicultural United States: Mexicans, Hindus of India, Turks, South Americans, and so on. Drew Ali recognized that race was a myth, and he seized control of the discourse to fashion his own mythology of identity. Drew Ali's New World racial typologies did not play directly to white audiences' sense of race hierarchy or to New Negro attempts to redefine themselves in Eurocentric terms. He seems to have cared little for white America's vision of the racial ladder, except to reverse it. His creation of a privileged Moorish identity did, however, pick up on African racial hierarchies and exploit their extensions into antebellum American discourse.

The Fulbes and American Blackness

The Moorish identity that was at times foisted on slaves by antebellum white observers keen to differentiate between educated Africans and "barbaric" Africans was an epistemic reconfiguration of identity in which slaves often participated because it spoke to their African-based notions of racial difference. This is particularly true for an ethnic group from West Africa known variously as Fula, Fulbe, Futa, and Pulaar. Georgia diplomat and linguist William Brown Hodgson wrote about the Fulbes in his 1844 *Notes on Northern Africa*:

> The Foulahs are not negroes. They differ essentially from the negro race, in all characteristics which are marked by physical anthropology. They may be said to occupy the intermediate space betwixt the Arab and the Negro. All travelers concur in representing them as a distinct race, in moral as in physical traits. To their color, the various terms of *bronze, copper, reddish*, and sometimes *white* has been applied. They concur also in the report, that the Foulahs of every region represent themselves to be *white* men, and proudly assert their superiority to the black tribes, among whom they live.[37]

Hodgson's observations in Africa were amply supported by anecdotal evidence in the American South, where white observers often commented on the Fula/Fulbe sense of superiority to other slaves. Ibrahima Abd ar-Rahman, a Fulbe slave from Futa who lived on a plantation in Natchez, Mississippi, from 1790 to 1829, told Cyrus Griffin "explicitly, and with an air of pride, that not a drop of Negro blood runs in his veins."[38] In an attempt to secure ar-Rahman's release from slavery, a number of white luminaries in the Natchez community, including Griffin, advocated on behalf of the "Unfortunate Moor" to both the president of the United States, John Adams, and the secretary of state, Henry Clay. Though evidence was produced to contradict the assumption that ar-Rahman was from Morocco, the association was advantageous to the cause of the slave's release, in large part because Morocco itself was considered to be an advantageous Mediterranean political ally. Clay indicated as much in a February 1828 letter to Griffin regarding ar-Rahman's potential manumission. "The President is obliged by your attention to the subject of the Moorish slave," wrote Clay, "the object of the President being to restore Prince, the slave mentioned, to his family and country for the purpose of making favorable impressions in behalf of the United States."[39]

Ar-Rahman's family and country were thousands of miles from Morocco, located in the interior of West Africa, not on its Mediterranean coast in the north. But the employment of the moniker *Moor* was instrumental in securing ar-Rahman's release, and both he and his advocates used it to their advantage. When ar-Rahman eventually met Adams and Clay in person, both men marked down the event in their diaries by referring to ar-Rahman as a "Moor." Prince's request for a return to Africa, however, had now been altered: he no longer desired to return to his "native" Morocco; instead he insisted on being shipped by the American Colonization Society to Liberia, much closer to his home. He got his wish, only to die days after arriving on African shores and before he ever saw his homeland again.

Ar-Rahman's story of "passing" as a Moor demonstrates how the ethnogenic imaginary of white Americans was often manipulated by slaves. But this act of passing also speaks to the interdependent discursive nature of the Moor in the antebellum American construction of the term. It is useful here to juxtapose the Fulbe origin story with the construction of the term *Moor* in order to understand how African tales of ethnogenesis found resonance with the racial imaginary of many white Americans. "Originating long ago in present-day southern Mauritania, many of the Fulbe claim descent from the Arab general 'Uqba b. Nafi, who in 667 led Muslim armies as far south as Kawar in the Fezzan," explains Michael Gomez. "This clear fiction reflects the larger truth of their mixed ancestry, resulting, in some instances, in the view of non-Fulbes as inferior."[40] In the Fulbe origin story, Arab blood distinguishes the group from other sub-Saharan Africans.

The Fulbes' Arab origin narrative is rhetorically conversant with the use of the term *Moor* by white Americans to mark certain Africans as having civilizing Arab blood and thus explaining (away) their superior intelligence and character. "The aristocratic or pastoral background of some West Africans, combined with the aforementioned agricultural expertise of others," writes Gomez, "meant that Muslims were, in the eyes of the host society, better suited to domestic or supervisory roles, a determination that widened the schism between Muslim and non-Muslim."[41] The Moors of American vernacular, be they Fulbe or other Muslims, were often treated as superior to other slaves and given roles of leadership and power over them in part because their own ethnic and religious convictions reinforced and were reinforced by plantation hierarchies and American racial logic and in part because they were said to look more phenotypically European.[42] Many Muslims had been slave holders them-selves in Africa, and Fulbe ethnocentricity is well documented.[43] The plan-tation schism between Muslims and non-Muslims repeated an indigenous African schism between the two groups.

Drew Ali's construction of a Moorish identity, in effect, repeats many of the same civilizational hierarchies and racial prejudices that were intrin-sic to both a Fulbe and a white American discourse on the cultural supe-riority of Arabs to sub-Saharan Africans. The category of the American Moor emerges from the intertwined history of white European/American misinterpretation of African ethnic identity and the carryover of African racial and religious hierarchies into the New World. In Noble Drew Ali's own approach to the figure of the Moor, he alights on a rhetorical tool that redefines blackness in the American context while still gesturing back to an African ancestry. In a sense, Drew Ali's alternative American histori-ography created the Mediterranean Moor's transatlantic cousin. But it is also true that Drew Ali's Moorish cosmology of black American identity marginalizes sub-Saharan African culture and repeats some of the very same cultural prejudices that were present on the antebellum plantation and bled into postbellum class stratifications.

In 1929, after Noble Drew Ali died and the Moorish Science Temple leadership splintered, the form of romantic black nationalism that Drew Ali expressed through his construction of an American Moor figure was taken up by new and more militant movements with their own ori-gin stories. These origin tales also reconfigured African American roots through Islamic codes, most notably in the case of the Nation of Islam. The term *Moor* and the idea of Moroccan nativity to America, however, remained peculiar to Drew Ali's heterodox version of African American Islam. Nevertheless, Morocco still circulated in the romantic thought of early twentieth-century black cosmopolitanism, both as a literal Mediter-ranean site and as a mobile and imaginative space of hybridized identity. Morocco's betwixt and between location, literally and imaginatively, begs the question of the sustainability of the Afro-Arab transnational alliance toward which Drew Ali's Moorish Science version of New World Islam gestures. If DuBois's political thought demanded that the color line be extended and Drew Ali's religio-nationalist reinterpretation of Ameri-can blackness imagined that extension through the term *Asiatic*, how did the fiction of the Harlem Renaissance approach the connection between blackness and other colors? What role, if any, did the figure of the Moor play in mediating these imaginative extensions of the color line?

Ray Is "Beaucoup Oriental"

Toward the end of Claude McKay's 1929 novel without a plot, *Banjo*, the question of DuBois's expanding color line and very particularly the question of the possibility of building links between the African diaspora and the Arab diaspora come directly into focus through the literary vehicle of romance. The scene takes place in the apartment of the novel's only significant female character, the mysterious Latnah, who speaks fluent Arabic and holds her own counsel. Latnah's racial identity has remained a question up to this point in the novel, and she has been imaginatively coded as an Arab, an Indian Coolie, and as more generally Oriental. Disappointed in her romantic pursuit of the inconstant Banjo, Latnah invites his friend and fellow black cosmopolitan drifter Ray back to her apartment to partake in an opium-smoking session. As the scene unfolds, both characters explore the question of their own racial origins, as well as cautious fantasies of a potential link between blackness and Arabness. It is precisely the Orientalism of the scene that allows these fantasies of Afro-Arab community the space to breathe.

"Take fruit. It good with fruit," she said.

"I know that," Ray replied.

"You know all about it," she smiled subtly. "I think is leetle Oriental in you."

"Maybe. There's a saying in my family about some of our people coming from East Africa. They were reddish, with glossy curly hair. But you have the same types in West Africa, too. You remember the two fellows that used to be at the African Bar during the summer? They looked like twins and they were heavy-featured like some Armenians."

"I think they were *mulattres*," said Latnah.

"No, they weren't mixed—not as we know it between black and white today. Perhaps way back. I heard they were Fulahs."

"We all mixed up. I'm so mixed I don't know what I am myself."

"You don't? I always wonder, Latnah, what you really are. Except for the Chinese, I don't feel any physical sympathy for Orientals, you know. I always feel cold and strange and far away from them. But you are different. I feel so close to you."

"My mother was Negresse," said Latnah. "Sudanese or Abyssinian—I no certain. I was born at Aden. My father I no know what he was nor who he was."[44]

In their respective explorations of ancestry, both Ray and Latnah touch on nodes of contact between blackness and Arabness—the ethnic identity of Fulah for Ray and the historical spice-trade crossroads of Aden for Latnah. Latnah's jest that Ray has a little Oriental in him becomes, by the end of the conversation, her assertion to him that "You beaucoup Oriental" (283). Ray, in turn, takes the jest seriously and explores a speculative link between himself and Latnah that hinges on the suggestion of an Oriental identity in his past. Both characters mark the impossibility of retrieving a certain account of their ancestry and thus implicitly acknowledge that their attempts at historical retrieval are really acts of imaginative historiography. For Latnah, the act of genealogy leads to a dead end: she is Arab because she speaks Arabic, yet she knows not if she actually has Arab blood in her—only that she has black blood. Yet she is not accepted among Ray and Banjo's Marseilles drifter crowd as either black or white. Latnah's Arabness is pure speculation, and thus her racial identity remains suspended. Banjo has her "tangled up and lost in the general color scheme" (170). Latnah herself tells Banjo, "I no black woman," to which he replies, "You ain't white" (175). Instead of being black or white, Latnah is always coded as Oriental. She is first introduced to the reader through another character, Malty, a West Indian who associates her with the Indian coolies he used to see as a child back in the Caribbean.

While Malty's fantasy about Latnah as coolie replicates an Orientalist conflation of Asiatic identities recognizable from both black and white versions of the discourse, Ray's approach to the mystery of her in-between identity employs Orientalism in a different vein. Ray uses Orientalism to try to find the join between himself and Latnah. In the hodgepodge of an ethnic identity that is "all mixed up," Ray's act of imaginative genealogical reconstruction links his New World identity back to Africa. He substitutes a family legend about the Fulahs for a version of mixing that depends on blending black and white into *mulattres*. This family legend grounds Ray in an Afro-Arab history of contact as much as it does in a history of contact between Africans and the Americas. But it also ties him to a history of African ethnocentricity that often translated into plantation hierarchies in the Americas. It is a moment of expanding the color line that paradoxically depends on a narrative of Arab superiority to Africans. In response to this personal gesture of expanding the color line, Latnah acknowledges Ray, in turn, as having a share of Oriental identity. It signals a moment of mutual respect, the kind that would be necessary for the speculative extension of the color line on which DuBois insisted as the most important question facing the black community at the beginning of the twentieth century. It also indicates the complexity of that extension by highlighting the term *Fulah* and its fraught historical associations with African ethnocentricity, legends of Afro-Arab connection, and plantation myths about the Moorish and/or Arab ethnicity of Muslim slaves.

As a number of recent critics have pointed out, DuBois himself explored the potential of this larger colored collective in *The Dark Princess* (1928). *The Dark Princess* is a narrative of international romance that brings together an Indian woman and a black African man in a love plot with implications for the redrawing of a global black political identity. A year after DuBois's *Dark Princess* appeared in print, McKay published *Banjo*. Both novels display the influence of Marxism and the anticolonial movements of the early twentieth century on their respective explorations of a larger, global coalition of the "colored." But McKay's *Banjo* ends not with the romantic coupling of two "dark" people of different ethnicities but rather with the foreclosure of that possibility. On the novel's last page, when Ray approaches Banjo with the possibility that the Afro-Arab Latnah, whom both men know romantically, might accompany the two of them on their travels, Banjo refuses. He comments, "a woman is a conjunction. Gawd fixed her different from us in moh ways than one" (326). Given DuBois and McKay's disagreements on central questions of New Negro discourses such as the importance of the cult of middle-class respectability and the importance of race consciousness, the difference between the result of their respective explorations of cross-color romance is significant.

While the statement Banjo gives about Latnah at the end of the novel has usually been read by critics in terms of its masculinist implications, the "conjunction" Latnah represents has something to do with her ethnic identity as well. With Banjo's refusal to include Latnah, he preserves the masculinist community of vagabondage, but he also denies the possibility of creating a meaningful connection between two disparate dark ethnicities, the Arab and the black. Banjo's denial of a place for Latnah is especially important given the book's earnest explorations of the potential for globally contextualized "colored" community building. This refusal, in other words, has political, social, and cultural implications that go beyond sexism. Latnah's erased/obscured paternity leaves her out of the color scheme as Banjo understands it. In turn, Latnah's avoidance of the fate of the tragic mulatta that befalls so many black heroines in the Harlem Renaissance oeuvre must be read in terms of something other than sexual dynamics. Latnah is no victim, and she demonstrates as much with her willing use of a knife that scares the male characters.

Independent, a survivor, and culturally more sophisticated than any of the women and most of the men in the novel, Latnah's conjunction of East African and Arab ethnicities marks her as a source of ethnic-pride narratives peddled by racial uplift prophets such as Drew Ali. Yet Banjo rejects her. Abyssinia, Ethiopia, and Arabia were used by many people in the New Negro movement and black New Age spiritualist movement to replace sub-Saharan Africa and West Africa as locations of black identification. Is Banjo's rejection of Latnah also a rejection of the class politics inherent in these rhetorical conjunctions, as well as a rejection of the white Orientalist tropes these narratives readapted to black nationalism? Is Latnah too civilized for Banjo's politics of blackness? Is she code for the white models of identity McKay saw hidden beneath the black rhetoric of uplift peddled by Locke? The figure of Latnah, with her acceptance by Ray and her rejection by Banjo, returns us to questions about the relationship between Arabness and blackness in early twentieth-century black cosmopolitan discourse, albeit as viewed from a different angle. These questions are best approached not through DuBois's voice of idealistic romance but rather through McKay's primitivism. McKay's writing focused on libidinous excess, vernacular wisdom, and frank displays of sexuality. He offered these bottom-up portrayals of "Negro" identity as a "new" form of race pride, one that contrasted with both the elitism of black intellectuals and the inhibitions of the dominant white society.

Civilizing the Barbarian

The witticism contained in Claude McKay's quip about Moroccan "barbaresques" that began this chapter plays both on a white Western history of marking North Africa as barbarous and on the possibility of establishing a counterdiscourse to that history through a cultivation of the primitive. The comment comes near the end of McKay's 1937 memoir and just prior to the writer's announcement to the reader that he is leaving Africa to return to America. Despite his obvious attachment to Morocco, a place he compares favorably on more than one occasion to his home in the West Indies, McKay explains that he feels compelled to become a firsthand participant in the "Negro Renaissance" taking place in Harlem. Before textually enacting this migration from primitive Africa back to modern and "renewing" America, however, McKay ironically juxtaposes savagery and civilization in this statement about Moroccans being a "magical barbaric people." McKay's "-esqueing" of the barbaric locates cultural capital not in the civilized, metropolitan, European-inflected language of cosmopolitanism but rather in the primitive, tribal, and vernacular language of dirty cosmopolitanism circulating among the drifter class of itinerate workers, sailors, hustlers, and vagabonds that he celebrates in *Banjo*.

The dig contained within McKay's Morocco quip is partially aimed at his critics among the black intellectual elite. Many of these elites panned McKay's own penchant for primitivism in books such as *Home to Harlem* and *Banjo*, arguing that these booze-drenched, sex-infused portrayals of black identity and community played to racist stereotypes and did nothing for the uplift movement. Reviewing *Home to Harlem* in the *Crises*, DuBois had complained that McKay's focus on "drunkenness, fighting and sexual promiscuity" was so disturbing that it made him "feel . . . like taking a bath."[45] McKay had little patience for these kinds of critiques, motivated as they were by the middle-class cult of respectability. His novels are replete with race men who fail to understand race as a lived experience rather than an ideology one learns from race-conscious rhetoric.

McKay's overly "civilized" characters often come under withering criticism from their more rough-edged counterparts for imitating the manners, rhetoric, and behavior of the very white world that denies them civilized equality. Goosey, a young race man with "book larnin," hears just such a line of criticism from his more worldly companion Banjo as the two are preparing to depart Marseilles together for what Goosey has called "The United Snakes." In this farewell, Banjo informs Goosey that he will not be returning with him to America after all but rather will be staying behind in defiance of government orders to leave France. Banjo explains, "Ise a true-blue travelingbohn nigger and I know life, and I knows how to take it nacheral. I fight when I got to and I works when I must and I lays off when I feel lazy, and I loves all the time becausen the honey-pot a life is mah middle name" (*Banjo*, 305).

Presenting a vernacular approach to questions of race identity and national affiliation, Banjo contrasts his natural flow with the goose step of ideological rigidity that defines the language of the educated but naive Goosey. Trying to regulate his companions' use of vernacular, Goosey pleads at one point, "I wish yo-all would say corn bread instead of corn pone. Corn pone is so niggerish" (*Banjo*, 159). Banjo's colloquial expressions directly challenge the contained identities and set ideological positions that Goosey holds dear. "In speaking of Negro people Goosey always avoided the word 'Negro' and 'black' and used, instead, 'race men,' 'race woman,' or 'race'" (*Banjo*, 115). As "a true-blue travelingbohn nigger," Banjo identifies with both internationalism and blackness while rejecting the logic of essentialism that animates both racism and race-based nationalism. Using the forbidden word that has marked him in Goosey's opinion as ignorant, Banjo establishes his own approach to questions of identity as more "nacheral" than those of the race man. Banjo voices a form of what Brent Hayes Edwards has called vagabond internationalism. "This is the internationalism of the defective: the unregistered, the undocumented, the untracked," explains Edwards, "an ab-nationalism, as it were, of all the 'Doubtful.'"[46] This vagabond internationalism, I would suggest, is expressed in the dirty cosmopolitan vernacular out of which the arabesque aesthetic emerges.

Working, like Poe, from a fascination with the grotesque as an aesthetic form, McKay crafts a new Mediterranean lingua franca for his drifter class in *Banjo*, a dialect that mixes snatches of wisdom, insight, and rhythm from the larger Atlantic world that flows into and out of Marseilles. The piquant colloquialisms that inflect Banjo's speech perform precisely the rhythmic acts of invention and reinvention that inform his own ethics of living as well as the general ethos of the vernacular. His refusal to conform to civilized norms of behavior that separate work from pleasure and adhere man to fixed patterns is reflected in his refusal to conform to the norms of civilized English pronunciation and grammatical construction. The coupling of a motion that denies particularistic belonging ("traveling") with an instantiation of that belonging ("born") into a single word ("travelingbohn") allows Banjo to create a moment of vernacular self-identification that pushes the grotesque toward the will to autochthonous invention. "Travelingbohn" is an arabesque word in its fantastic mixture as well as adhering to an arabesque aesthetic of creating conduits between apparent opposites.

But if McKay's "barbaresques" share an affinity with Poe's arabesques in terms of their formal structure and aesthetic goal, they also signal a shift in the perspective on the image of the Arab that this chapter marks. Poe's arabesques are disembodiments of the Arab and abstractions of material culture into a dematerialized sensation. McKay's barbaresques are pleas for the gross materiality of experience. The strain of romanticism evident in McKay's fascination with "barbaresques" connects him aesthetically to almost every writer I have discussed thus far in this book through at least two interrelated discursive sources, primitivism and Orientalism. McKay, however, turns the cultural hierarchies and racial prejudices inherent in these discourses to his own account, providing insight into the meaning of the Arab from the perspective of a black cosmopolitan discourse. Where, one might ask, does the Oriental fit into McKay's vagabond internationalism, and on which side of the color lines drawn by black internationalism does the Arab fall?

Located, as Edwards remarks, "against the grain of nationalism,"[47] McKay's version of internationalism is supported by his own words in the memoir *A Long Way from Home* but also by the words and actions of certain characters in *Banjo*—the lumpen figure of Banjo, the newly working-class figure of Jake, and the writer/intellectual Ray. In the farewell-to-Goosey moment discussed earlier, ethnic nationalism is juxtaposed against vagabondage. As Banjo contradictorily announces his commitment to vagabondage by telling the group, "this nigger ain't gwine no place," the four black men divide by sympathy. "Jake grinned. Banjo grinned. Ray grinned. Goosey alone was glum" (*Banjo*, 306). Vagabondage as the vernacular iteration of internationalism finds voice in Banjo. He explains to Goosey that "the wul' goes round and round and I keeps right on gwine round with it. I ain't swore off nothing like you. United Snakes nor You-whited Snakes that a nigger jest gotta stand up to everywhere in this wul', even in the thickest thicket in the Congo" (*Banjo*, 304). Banjo turns Goosey's neologism of the "United Snakes" against the race man, calling him "You-whited Snakes" and insinuating that prejudice is not the province of whites alone or of the United States. Putting faith in the individual, not the nation, Banjo insists on the universal nature of black people's struggle but avoids the kind of ethnic nationalism that would romanticize Africa or demonize America.

Banjo's insistence that whether he is in the United States or in the Congo, his battle is the same sounds curiously discordant when pitched against the tenor of McKay's own opinions on Africa in the memoir. Morocco, where McKay completed *Banjo*, was appealing to the writer in large part because there he claimed to feel relatively free from the demands of race and its attendant forms of nationalism. "For the first time in my life I felt myself singularly free of color-consciousness," McKay comments on Morocco. "I experienced a feeling that must be akin to the physical well-being of a dumb animal among kindred animals, who lives instinctively by sensations only, without thinking" (*Long Way*, 300). In this complicated expression of freedom, McKay posits Africa as a kind of primitive utopia. It is a statement that ultimately dovetails with the quotation on Moroccan "barbaresques" which comes some twenty-five pages later. In both instances, McKay presents several recognizable tropes of the African as primitive, only to turn those tropes into a celebration of primitivism and an implied condemnation of civilized society. "But suddenly I felt myself right up against European intervention and proscription," McKay explains by way of finishing the thought on color consciousness (ibid.). This European intervention and proscription is the demand that the British consulate makes on McKay to declare his nationality as either British or American.

The freedom of Africa for McKay is suddenly impinged on by the civilized menace of a European nationalist discourse that would divide him from his "nacheral" affiliations and associations and impose a Euro-American history of colonialism and slavery on his identity. In speaking about the residents of Tangier, McKay comments, "they are all remarkably free of any color obsessions or ideas of discrimination. They are Africans" (*Long Way*, 334). Yet what does McKay mean by "Africans"? Surely he recognizes that North Africa was populated by Berbers, Arabs, and sub-Saharan Africans, by peoples whose ancestors came both from Africa and from Arabia. In McKay's memoir, there are two types of people to be found in Morocco: Europeans and Africans. Is he conflating Arab, Berber, and sub-Saharan African peoples into a single group, into a colored collective? Or is he only identifying with the black African population in Morocco? At one point, he intimates, tacitly, that Moroccans might not consider themselves black. "I did have 'white friends'" in Morocco, McKay announces and then parenthetically adds, "(if the Moors do not object to the use of the phrase)" (*Long Way*, 334). Slyly McKay acknowledges the context dependence of the terms *black* and *white* and implicitly differentiates Moors from blacks at the same time that he lumps them together in opposition to the "white colony." The figure of the Moor here is a mutable entity, one that has the potential to slip between whiteness and blackness even as it can contain Arabs and Africans in one trope.

The peaceful coexistence of Arab, African, and Berber identity in McKay's figure of the Moor of Morocco is contrasted by the conflict between Arabs and blacks in McKay's novelistic description of life on the other side of the Mediterranean. In the dive districts of the Marseilles port where *Banjo* is set, the tension between Arab and black identity is acknowledged simultaneously with the fact that both identities are marked as colored. "Although the Cairo was a colored bar, the Negroes hardly ever went there," the novel explains. "Negroes and Arabs are not fond of one another—even when they speak the same language and have the same religion" (*Banjo*, 166). Linguistic and religious affiliation are overridden by ethnic difference in *Banjo*, and the communities that form in Marseilles are, like the bars in the port, coded by ethnic markers: the Cairo Bar, the British-American Bar, the African Bar. Latnah's own mixed and confused ethnic heritage is precisely what makes her an outsider. She belongs at none of the bars because she belongs to no one race. Latnah's freedom from racial classification makes her independent but also deprives her of community.

Despite McKay's protests about European civilization's propensity to categorize people, he recognized the importance of the kind of group identification that leads to nationalism. "It is a plain fact that the entire world of humanity is more or less segregated in groups," McKay announces in a memoir chapter entitled "Belonging to a Minority Group."

> The family group gave rise to the tribal group, the tribal group to the regional group, and the regional group to the national group. There are groups within groups: language groups, labor groups, racial groups and class groups. Certainly no sane group desires public segregation and discrimination. But it is a clear historical fact that different groups have won their social rights only when they developed a group spirit and strong group organization. (*Long Way*, 350)

Acknowledging the necessity of group identification for a cause (be it ethnic nationalism, communism, or other labor collectives), McKay justifies the personal abandonment of the principles of vagabondage, individuality, and race-ideology suspicion that he placed in the mouth of his vernacular hero Banjo. His memoir ruminations on the importance of group belonging rhetorically pave the way for precisely the return to America that Banjo rejected. "For my part I was deeply stirred by the idea of a real Negro renaissance," McKay explains.

> The Arabian cultural renaissance and the great European renaissance had provided some of my most fascinating reading. The Russian literary renaissance and also the Irish had absorbed my interest. My idea of a renaissance was one of talented persons of an ethnic or national group working individually or collectively in a common purpose and creating things that would be typical of their group. (*Long Way*, 321)

Couching his return to Harlem in an internationalist context, McKay nevertheless endorses forms of nationalism and ethnic nationalism. But my main concern here is not to litigate the claims of nationalism versus internationalism in McKay's oeuvre but rather to locate the role of the Arab figure in negotiating these conflicts and, in turn, to locate those negotiations in the much wider discourse of black cosmopolitanism to which McKay was contributing. To do this, it is useful to mark the moment in the memoir when McKay announces his intentions to leave Morocco, a moment that immediately follows his quip about barbaresques, which itself immediately follows a story McKay has related about hiring dancing Moroccan girls to perform at his Tangier home for a two-day party. "When at last I decided to return to America," McKay informs the reader, "in homage to them I indited: 'A Farewell to Morocco.'"

> Oh friends, my friends! When Ramadan returns
> And daily fast and feasting through the night,
> With chants and music honey-dripping sweets,
> And fatmas shaking their flamenco feets
>   My thoughts will wing
>   The waves of air
>   To be with you.[48]

One might wonder who the "them" is of McKay's homage—is it Moroccans, is it barbaresques, is it the dancing girls?—but the poem that follows, replete with references to notes "haunting me like a splendid dream," make it clear that McKay is conjuring an Orientalist "honey-pot a life" in his farewell to North Africa. The religious ceremony of Ramadan, whose purpose is to reinforce faith through modes of denial, is transformed in McKay's poem into a reason to celebrate sensuality. McKay's Moroccan poem associates him with a discourse traditionally aligned with the white colonist gaze. But if the content of McKay's "Farewell to Morocco" poem reinvents Banjo's vernacular philosophy on pleasure into an oriental reverie, its classical form holds a message of civilized restraint.

Located in Morocco, on the other side of the Mediterranean littoral from Banjo's Marseilles, McKay answers Banjo's vernacular farewell to Goosey with a high-culture farewell to Africa. Bidding good-bye to Morocco in the voice of Renaissance literacy, McKay's return to America forms a chiasmus with the dirty cosmopolitan language Banjo uses to reject a return to America. The figure of the Moor is located precisely in the oceanic cross enacted by a juxtaposition of these two farewells, farewells that reverberate across the Mediterranean and stretch out over the Atlantic, wedding the shores of Barbary to those of Europe and the Americas in entanglements of migration. Situated geographically between Europe and Africa and rhetorically between civilization and savagery, the Moor has always operated in Western literature as a liminal figure, one that has mediated the relationship between races as well as the relationship between race, ethnicity, and national identity from as far back as medieval stories about the Crusades. For black intellectuals in the early twentieth century, the Moor's interstitial position posed particular questions about the relationship of Arab Africa to black Africa, as well as about the relationship of Arabness to blackness and blackness to Islam.

McKay's own multiple and contradictory representations of the connection of Arabness to Africanness, contained in both the novel *Banjo* and the memoir *A Long Way from Home*, indicate that these questions were not resolved as much as they were posed by the figure of the Moor. What is clear is that Harlem Renaissance literature, such as that produced by McKay and DuBois, resonated with New Age spiritualist writings, such as that produced by Noble Drew Ali, in their mutual fascination with Moroccan civilization. In McKay's "Farewell to Morocco" poem, he refers to himself as both a "captive" and a "prisoner," repeating the dominant tropes of Barbary savagery circulating in nineteenth-century American literature. However, McKay is a "willing" captive and prisoner not of a barbarous culture but rather of the music and dancing conjured by highly cultured activities attending the Ramadan feast. McKay's poem is dedicated to the civilization of Barbary.

A Pan-American Postscript

On January 16, 1928, Calvin Coolidge, the president of the United States, addressed the Pan-American Conference assembled in Havana, Cuba, in the same year that the Harlem Renaissance reached its peak. Reminding his audience of the hemisphere's common migratory ancestry, Coolidge marked the West Indies, McKay's home, as Columbian outposts of the new civilization of the Western Hemisphere:

> The Great Discoverer brought with him the seed of more republics, the promise of greater human freedom, than ever crossed the seas on any

other voyage. With him sailed immortal Declarations of Independence and Great Charters of self-government. He laid out a course that led from despotism to democracy. . . . In the spirit of Christopher Columbus all of the Americas have an eternal bond of unity, a common heritage bequeathed to us alone. . . . This is the destiny which Pan America has been chosen to fulfill.[49]

Coolidge's Columbian "promise" of inter-American unity follows a recognizable New World schema: as civilization moves west, humankind moves progressively toward enlightened government and individual freedom—from despotism to democracy. Ignoring the differentiated way in which the Columbian legacies of "human freedom," "self-government," and "independence" had been historically experienced by people of color, women, and religious minorities in the Americas, Coolidge's formulation dissolves racial, religious, and cultural particularities under the universal sign of pan-American destiny. Through this universal sign, Coolidge weds the language of civility to the philosophy of mercantilism. It is a vision of American expansion remarkably consistent, in its way, with DuBois's own vision of an expanding color line.

Noble Drew Ali is reported also to have been in attendance at the Pan-American Conference. As the story goes, he traveled to Havana in order to register the Moorish Americans as an indigenous nation, located within the territorial boundaries of America but owning a cultural ancestry that had origins on both sides of the Atlantic. This cultural ancestry, in Drew Ali's formula, included a pan-Asiatic ethnic identification, a North African national origin, and an Islamic religious tradition. In each of these Arabo-Islamic nodes of cultural identity, Drew Ali enunciates a model of American belonging that looks east, not west, for its authority. Contemporaneous with Coolidge's projection of the idioms of the Western world as American universals, Noble Drew Ali announces an alternative Columbian legacy that harks back to the arrival of Europeans on the shores of the New World. As Michael Gomez puts it in the prologue to his book *Black Crescent*, "In 1492 Christopher Columbus crossed the Atlantic and with him came Islam. Among his crews were Muslims who had been forced to profess the Christian faith; it is highly probable that Islam remained embedded in their souls."[50] Gomez refers directly to figures such as Ladinos and Moriscos. He points out that for those who had practiced the art of dissimulation as a form of cultural survival in Old World milieus such as Iberia, "the New World provided the opportunity to unmask."[51] The closeted Muslim Ladinos and Moriscos were joined over the next three hundred plus years by thousands of West African Wolofs, Mandingas, Fulbes, and others who were also Muslim.

The theme of unmasking, the shedding of external Christian practices to reveal the esoteric Islam within the hearts of these New World transplants—these first Muslims in the Americas—provides a counterpoint to the discussion of Noble Drew Ali, a man who used Islam as a form of masking. The Islam that Drew Ali espoused was exoteric in the sense that it employed Islamic symbols, codes, and nomenclature in the service of a decidedly American-influenced (one could even say Christian-influenced) version of identity politics and racial uplift. However tenuous the association of Noble Drew Ali with these first Muslims in the Americas may be, though, the presence of the term *Moor* in American vernacular usage draws the two phenomena together rhetorically. These original West African Muslims' homelands became spaces of amnesia in American history. Many of them came to be known as Moors in America. These men and women, initiating a discourse on the American Moor that Drew Ali inherited and reinvented, point to a discursive America born as much in Mediterranean passages as in Atlantic passages. But they also gesture east, back across the Atlantic, to an American history that happened elsewhere and to the desire in the early twentieth century to bring that elsewhere home to the American continent.

Drew Ali, DuBois, and McKay all explored the possibility of fusing America and Africa through figures of the Moor and/or Morocco. They came to quite different conclusions. Their respective conclusions were generated by their different visions of reconciliation. Concerned with intraethnic reconciliation, Drew Ali used Moorish identity to create an imaginative geography that wedded African American identity with both African ancestry and Arabo-Islamic culture, but he kept it distinct from white Euro-American culture. Both DuBois and McKay, whatever their differences on representing the "Negro," use the figure of the Moor to explore interethnic relations. The class divisions and religious discomforts that separated the uplift programs of the intellectual elite and the street-corner prophets of 1920s black America are brought into relief by each group's differential use of Moroccan figures and Arabo-Islamic history. Though this is largely a question of audience, it also points to the fact that the construction of the figure of the Moor works to create and perpetuate spaces of historical amnesia for the African diaspora in the Americas, even as it is rhetorically positioned as a tool of historical recovery.

5

Arab Masquerade

Mahjar *Identity Politics and Transnationalism*

The first four chapters of this book address an American discourse on Arabness that the first generation of Arab immigrants to America inherited. The ways in which this discourse prefigured Arab American identity and the ways in which a group of Syrian migrant intellectuals challenged that discourse are the focus of this final chapter. Until quite recently, historians have tended to read the story of the pioneer Arab migration to America through a narrative of the Arab that existed in American literature prior to the actual presence of Arabs: the story of the street Arab. This story uses the figure of the peddler to tell a tale of transition—from savage to civilized, from darkness to whiteness, from foreigner to citizen. As with Barbary captivity narratives and Near Eastern travel narratives, Arabness is a temporary state in the street Arab tale, and once one becomes American, one is no longer Arab. A coterie of first-generation Syrian migrants to America, by inserting themselves into the American discourse controlling the definition of Arabness, however, enunciated their own forms of literary representation and myth, inventing a system for inventorying and controlling the meaning of the term *Arab*. Focusing on these *mahjar* intellectuals situates the Arab experience in America in a global context and shifts the narrative emphasis from the teleology of "becoming American" to a more complex accounting of the multiplicity of identities migrants inhabit.

The chapter begins with a historiography of Arab migration to America that emphasizes the role literature plays in erasing the Arab identity of Syrian immigrants. I then provide a counternarrative on the Arab presence in America that stresses migration rather than immigration and transnational affiliation rather than national affiliation. This counternarrative emerges out of the *mahjar* sensibility cultivated by writers such as Ameen Rihani, the first Arab American novelist and a lifelong advocate of pan-Arabism. Concentrating on the forms of Arab masquerade that Rihani explores in his novel *The Book of Khalid*, the chapter moves into an analysis of the relationship between American Orientalism and Arab American self-representation. The literary strategies of self-representation that Rihani employs ultimately translate into the political strategies informing pan-Arabism. The chapter ends with a reconsideration of the legacy of Arab American literature that revivifies the importance of *mahjar* writers and their transnational paradigms of identity.

Syrian Immigration

> *Arab*, to go huckstering. 1948, Baltimore, MD.
> — H. L. Mencken, *The American Language*[1]

The first "Syrians" who came to and through America in the late nineteenth century were mostly Christian men from rural villages hived into the Lebanon mountain range.[2] Many of them earned their money in a trade they inherited from German Jews in America: pack-peddling. Pack-peddlers carried a large suitcase filled with "notions," often on their backs and often from places such as New York City to places such as Vicksburg, Mississippi, or Sioux Falls, South Dakota. These suitcases were called *kashshies* (a corruption of *caixa*, the Portuguese word for box). The narrative of the Syrian pack-peddler is so central to the way in which the pioneer generation has been historicized that no scholarly account of the years between 1880 and 1924 exists in which the figure does not appear prominently. A pioneer-generation anecdote relates that the first words a Syrian in the New World learned were "Buy sumthin', Ma'am?"[3]

With rare exceptions, earlier historians of Arab immigration in America have argued that the pioneer-generation migrants were remarkably successful in their effort to integrate into an unhyphenated American culture.[4] Elaine Hagopian and Ann Paden begin the preface to their 1969 study on Arab American assimilation by remarking on early Arab immigrants' "tendency to acculturate rapidly and assimilate to the American environment."[5] Sameer Abraham and Nabeel Abraham, in their introduction to a 1985 study of Arab American communities, note that Arab Americans' lack of visibility in American society can be attributed partly to "the fact that they were generally well integrated, acculturated, and even assimilated into mainstream society."[6] Alixa Naff comments on the "rapid assimilation of Arabic-speaking immigrants before World War I" into American society, in the introduction to her 1985 book on the role pack-peddling played in the early Arab immigrant experience.[7] "If political and economic events had not reactivated Arab immigration" in the post-1967 years, Naff asserts in *Becoming American*, "Syrian-Americans might have assimilated themselves out of existence."[8]

This assimilation view dominated the historical account of the Arab presence in America for over a generation and created something of a self-fulfilling prophecy. By repeating the tropic representation of Arab identity circulating in nineteenth-century American literature, these historical studies of Arab migration fit seamlessly into a larger American story of immigration. The literary and the historical representations of Arab erasure, in other words, reinforce each other. Both tell an American story, and both represent Arabness, in that American context, as a disposable identity. The most powerful literary trope for this historical account of Arab ethnic erasure is the street Arab.

American writers had used the popular trope of the street Arab to demonstrate the amenability of Arabness to transformation into Americanness since the middle of the nineteenth century. This trope gained increased relevance in American cultural discourse during the peak years of foreign immigration, 1880–1924. Not coincidentally these years also mark the advent of Syrian migration to America. Though these pioneer Syrian immigrants would not necessarily have identified themselves as Arabs at first, the street Arab narrative prefigured their potential assimilation into American culture through its representation of an Arab identity that was mutable and transitional. But prior to the advent of Syrian migration to America, the term *street Arab* had not referred to Arabs at all.

The term *street Arab* received perhaps its most recognizable usage in the up-by-the-boot-straps children's stories penned by Horatio Alger, Jr. In Alger's 1871 *Tattered Tom; or, The Story of a Street Arab*, the street Arab appears as a primitive type in a Protestant-inspired narrative of missionary redemption. Describing Tom (his only female protagonist), Alger writes,

> Arab as she was, she had been impressed by the kindness of Captain Barnes, and she felt that she should like to please him. Still, there was a fascination in the wild independence of her street life which was likely for some time to interfere with her enjoyment of the usages of a more civilized

state. There was little prospect of her taming down into an average girl all at once. The change must come slowly.[9]

The polarities of "wild independence" and civilization that Alger erects make it clear that, as Tom moves from the figurative position of Arab and into the position of "average" American girl, she plays out a capitalist allegory of social progress. Entrance into a "civilized state" necessitates a move from itinerate begging into professions that depend on capital accumulation and investment. Tom's ascendancy of the social ladder begins when she invests her begging profits in newspapers and changes her role from mendicant street sweep to budding entrepreneur. Tom begins the story by demanding of a dandy she meets on the street, "Gi' me a penny," but she quickly adjusts to entrepreneurial ownership and eventually even speculates in gold. By the story's conclusion, Tom has been rescued from the street by Captain Barnes, who has taken an "interest" in her; inserted into a bourgeois family environment; and finally rediscovered by her lost mother, who turns out to be a wealthy heiress. The novel ends when the "slow" change from primitive nomad to modern citizen is complete: the marginal, wild, and wandering Arab joins the nineteenth-century American "civilized state" as a normalized civilian.[10]

Appearing before the period of mass immigration to America that began in the 1880s, Alger's street Arab is not a literal foreigner but rather a metaphorical one. Describing the first glimpse of Tom, Alger racializes her appearance without marking her as a racial other: "The child's face was very dark, and, as might be expected, dirty; but it was redeemed by a pair of brilliant black eyes."[11] As Tom moves from the position of figurative Arab and into the position of Protestant American member of the civilized state, she is symbolically whitened, in a bath given to her by Captain Barnes's sister, and gender stabilized, by being dressed in female clothes and dubbed "Jenny." Figurative Arab identity played the same transitional role almost a hundred years earlier in fictional Barbary captivity narratives such as *The Algerine Captive*. With Tom, as with Updike before her, Arabness is a temporary state and a potential conduit from darkness to whiteness, from cultural outsider to cultural insider, and from savagery to civilization. But whereas Tyler employed these binary positions ironically to send up the civilizational prejudices of his American audience, Alger employs them quite seriously as part of the pedagogical message of his children's stories.

The *street Arab* narrative presents Arabness as a transitional node that ultimately must be transcended. Alger's stories predate the Syrian-immigrant presence, but his narrative provided a powerful template for subsequent historians of Arab immigration to America to narrate the process of assimilation. Discussing the second-generation Arab Americans' attitude toward their pioneer Syrian-immigrant parents, Naff writes, "most of them conceive of that period in Horatio Alger terms in which poor illiterate immigrants, with little or no English, succeeded by ingenuity and hard work. References to Alger are, of course, apt."[12] These "apt" references enforce the idea that Syrians integrated successfully into American culture through hard work, but they also support the narrative of ethnic erasure. In Naff's historical account, as in Alger's literary account, Arabness is a transitional node of identity.

The theme of redemption attached to Alger's Tattered Tom carries over in subsequent uses of the term *street Arab* to refer to actual immigrants. As in Alger, the turn-of-the century use of the term *street Arab* does not refer to Arabs at all. Rather, it refers to an indigent child whose nascent capitalist spirit makes him or her a potential member of the civilized U.S. state—if his or her primitive Arabness can be eradicated. The street Arab's tropic characteristics—motion, transition, and passage from one state to another—exist in continuum with a history of representing Arabs in American literature that goes all the way back to the beginning of the nineteenth century. Turn-of-the-century immigrants were just another in a long line of nineteenth-century American "others" that writers marked as figurative Arabs.

Jacob Riis, in his 1890 *How the Other Half Lives*, trained a light on the crowded living conditions of New York's tenements and slum streets, revealing in flash photographs and often describing in highly moralistic terms the experience of America's immigrant population.[13] Taken as a whole, Riis's *How the Other Half Lives* offers a jeremiad vision of modernizing urban America characterized by moral backsliding and the potential for redemption.[14] A key figure in the drama is the street Arab (see figure 9). When Riis, himself a Danish immigrant, describes the street Arab, he blends Protestant ethics with a tale of American assimilation.

> His sturdy independence, love of freedom and absolute self-reliance, together with his rude sense of justice that enables him to govern his little community, not always in accordance with municipal or city ordinances, but often a good deal closer to the saving line of "doing to others as one

would be done by"—these are strong handles by which to catch the boy and make him useful. Successful bankers, clergymen, and lawyers all over the country, statesman in some instances of national repute, bear evidence in their lives to the potency of such missionary efforts.[15]

Riis's street Arab must be caught before he can be taught. Using the language of missionary uplift, Riis marks the American immigrant child as a primitive with latent values that can be cultivated for a successful transition into American identity. Though the name *Arab* refers to the urchin's nomadic ways, Riis's description plays up the metaphorical association between the street Arab and the Bedouin archetype. Furthermore, by marking the Arab's "sturdy independence," "love of freedom," and "self-reliance" as a Biblical code of ethics, Riis uses Mosaic law to link the street urchin's figurative Arabness to potential Americanness. Because these Biblical character traits are shared by both figurative Arabs and successful Americans, the street Arab is a particularly good candidate for missionary conversion. Indeed, with the benefit of these "missionary efforts," Riis promises that the street Arab will become a productive member of the American nation's body politic as a potential banker, lawyer, clergyman, or statesman.

Although Riis did not invent the term *street Arab*, he did attach it directly to immigrant children and the rhetoric of American assimilation in ways only suggested in earlier uses of the figure. Within the confines of Riis's social justice narrative, however, the street Arab does not enact a Franklinesque revolution in social status. The tenement children who stare back at the viewer through the sepia glow of Riis's flash photographs could not have their racial and social alterity cleansed away by a bath from Captain Barnes's sister, and it would take at least a generation for their ethnic identities to be integrated into the phantasm of American citizenship.[16] While the physical bodies of these European immigrants were eventually marked as "white" and/or "civilized," the moniker *Arab* remained a trope of primitiveness. Both Alger's and Riis's street Arabs, divorced from any material connection to actual Arabs, become object lessons, not on Arab identity but rather on American identity—both individual and national. Both Alger and Riis use the metaphor of Arabness to promote a Protestant ideology of national character. In the metaphor of the street Arab, Arabness is the vehicle, Americanness is the tenor, and literature is the aesthetic promotional tool. Though earlier historians of Arab immigration to America invoke the peddler, it is in fact largely a Protestant-inspired story of the street Arab that they tell.

Figure 9. Jacob Riis, *Street Arabs in Sleeping Quarters*, ca. 1890. Photograph reproduced with permission from Jacob A. Riis Collection, Museum of the City of New York.

In the book *Inventing Home*, Akram Khater challenges the emphasis in pioneer-generation histories on the making of "new man" Americans out of Syrian immigrants. Arguing that "large numbers of immigrants rejected 'America' as an idea and reality," Khater contends that instead of assimilation, these immigrants preferred a complex process of "mixing and matching what they brought with them and what they saw in the streets and homes of America."[17] These pioneer migrants were often forced to internalize the dichotomy of the "traditional" and the "modern" that they encountered in American culture and through American cultural institutions that tried to "reform" their practices of child rearing or marriage. But most Syrian migrants interpreted themselves as "modern." Khater's emphasis on a transnational understanding of Syrian immigration leads him to deprivilege the American context and finally to conclude that "what we see among the immigrant communities in the Americas is the rise of a class whose members tried to distinguish themselves as different (culturally and socially) from middle-class America as well as from peasant Lebanon."[18]

Naff and other late twentieth-century historians of pioneer Arab immigration to America tell a story about American immigration largely bounded by the physical parameters of the nation. Khater and a few other contemporary scholars of Syrian migration tell a story about how Arab immigrants conceptualized America and brought that concept with them outside the borders of the physical nation. The American immigrant narrative tends to present Arabness not as a negotiation between cultural discourses but as a story of coming to terms with American assimilation. However, Khater demonstrates that many Syrian migrants, far from losing the trappings of their ethnic identity and assimilating out of existence, chose to return to Lebanon rather than stay in America. Others made the trip back and forth between the two locales, establishing what Khater describes as the modern Lebanese middle class. These middle-class Syrian migrants with feet in two worlds form the core of the intellectual group on which I focus my attention in the pages that follow. This group of intellectuals referred to themselves as the *mahjar* (المهجر; the Arab diaspora, Arabs living abroad) from the Arabic root هجر (to emigrate). Many of these *mahjar* intellectuals were concerned with fair treatment in their host country, but they ultimately identified themselves with an entity that offered them a sense of affiliation that did not require ethnic erasure. Through them, I tell an alternative story of Arab migration to America in which literature and figurative representation open up a third space of identity that is affiliated neither with Syria/Lebanon nor with America but rather with the transhistorical and transspatial idea of a pan-Arabia.

This *mahjar* group of Arab migrants to the Americas, as a response to both formal and informal modes of exclusion in their host country, developed forms of Arab nationalism that were routed through their own experiences with transnational movement. "The boundaries of the Arab nation in the prewar period were configured along a space-time axis that was powerfully rooted in the experience of migration," explains Sarah Gualtieri. "In spatial terms the *mahjar* was positioned within the imagined community of Syria," but in "temporal terms, the *mahjar* became a symbol of the future and the Arab modern."[19] Gualtieri's identification of the migrant's altered time-space axis helps explain why immigration narratives that privilege the telos of assimilation ultimately fail to account for the full range of *mahjar* potentiality. These immigration narratives tend to elide the multiplicity of identities, spaces, and temporalities the *mahjar* intellectual juggled. The ideas of civic participation and the citizenship regimes that Syrians encountered in their migrations gave impetus to their conceptions not only of Arab or American identity but also of pan-Arabia. Though most of these intellectuals were Christians from Syria, many of them conceived of an Arab identity that included Islam and indeed all those who spoke Arabic. The expansive idea of Arab identity that emerged out of the experience of migration to the Americas was indebted in many ways to American discourses on the Arab. Attention to migrant rather than immigrant identity politics emphasizes the relationship between an international Arab Renaissance and American national debates about immigration, assimilation, and racial identity. Though the Arab identity crafted by a group of transnationally minded Arab intellectuals in America represents a path not taken by most Arab immigrants to America, it also represents an opportunity to imagine different futures from the archive of the past. In particular, explorations of pan-Arabism draw attention to the cross-pollination between the language of American and Arab national identity politics.

The Mahjar

Histories of pioneer Syrian immigration to America that emphasize assimilation and ethnic erasure split literal Arabs from literary Arabs, leaving the trope of the Arab unchanged. An icon of Yankee mercantilism, the peddler lends itself to the story of becoming American. However, *mahjar* intellectuals, who were children of the liberal reform spirit that characterized the *nahda*, used the peddler figure to subvert the story of becoming American and to establish an identity that was compatible and integrated with Americanness but not transitional. In 1927, at the end of the era of pioneer immigration, Salloum Mokarzel, a prominent publisher and personality in New York's Washington Street Syrian community, wrote an article on the history of Syrians in America. In it, he proposes that a statue be erected "to the enterprising spirit as symbolized by the pioneer peddler." A. Hakim, known as "the Sage of Washington Street," took this suggestive ode to Syrian entrepreneurship and miniaturized its nostalgic sentiment: "Little book-ends of a peddler's figure should grace every cultured Syrian's home; or a little statuette in bronze could be a graceful and appropriate ornament for every Syrian executive's desk; or still a handsomely engraved picture of the pioneering peddler could be framed and hung in a conspicuous position in offices and homes."[20] The ornamental peddlers that Hakim would have strategically placed in the sites of Syrian success in America stand as curios of a cultural identity that existed without the support of a political body.

At the turn of the twentieth century, the Syrian peddler in fact stood between two political bodies: Ottoman and American. If asked, a majority of these migrants from Greater Syria identified themselves first by clan or by village and, only after these associations, then perhaps by the more general appellation "Syrian."[21] Intellectuals such as Mokarzel eventually fought to have their Lebanese identity recognized, as well as to have Lebanon itself recognized as an individual nation. But "Syria" was a name initially foisted on these migrants from Lebanon by an Ottoman Empire from which, by and large, they distinguished themselves not only through religion but also through language and culture. The general resistance to Ottoman affiliation within this first wave of what came to be known as "Arab" immigrants to America was expressed clearly in the Syrian American press's responses to a series of court cases that ultimately decided Syrian ethnicity in the eyes of American law. Reacting to a 1914 lower-court decision that had denied George Dow's application for citizenship on the basis of his "darker" racial features, the Syrian community, with the help of the active Syrian press in America, rallied around "defending the rights and the honor of all those who speak Arabic and are born under Asian skies."[22] The implicit idea behind this notion of speaking one language while living in a "foreign" country is that a culturally unique identity can exist in a diaspora and that Arabs from Greater Syria constituted just such a diaspora.

Mahjar writers, in particular, had a complex relationship to discourses on Americanization, assimilation, and hyphenated ethnic identification. As the name *mahjar* suggests, these intellectuals were far from unambiguous advocates of American assimilation. The number of articles published in the Syrian press about the importance of maintaining the use of the Arabic language in the New World attests to the importance *mahjar* intellectuals placed on retaining their cultural identity in the face of forces of American assimilation.[23] In fact, as many as twenty-one of the dailies, weeklies, and monthlies published for the Syrian community in the United States were initially printed only in Arabic.[24] As the nineteenth century gave way to the twentieth and as Arabic-language newspapers were replaced with English-language newspapers, many of the Syrian intellectual elites looked back with nostalgia to an earlier moment in the short history of the community.

The peddler was prominent in these recollections, standing not as a figure of transition from one identity to another but as a monument to an identity that seemed in danger of being lost. An icon of the Syrian pioneer to *mahjar* intellectuals, the peddler is transformed into an example of American assimilation in too many of the historical accounts of Syrian immigration. But the peddler who loses his or her ethnicity stands in stark contrast to the message provided by the peddler statue Mokarzel would have erected as a foundational monument of Syrian/Lebanese *mahjar* identity.

In Mokarzel's and Hakim's formulations of *mahjar* community, the peddler is a sign not only of motion away from Lebanon but also of emplacement in America. The figure is an indicator of diaspora as a material fact but also of the necessity to create a functional American fiction of origins. Not only was the figure a ready-made symbol of Yankee American mercantilism, but it also gestured back to the theme of migration that *mahjar* intellectuals linked, through the act of naming, to an Arabo-Islamic history. The peddler marks the transition from one national identity to another. Standing between the old world and the new, the peddler is an identity to be discarded once "offices" and "executive desks" have replaced the road, once Syrians have become Americans. But Syrian/Lebanese identity itself is not sacrificed in this formula.

The Syrian/Lebanese community's adoption of the peddler figure as symbol of its American identity speaks to a negotiation between a nineteenth-century American discourse on Arabs and the early twentieth-century literary enunciation of Arab American identity. Lisa Suhair Majaj asserts in her work on Arab racial identity and classification,

> In addition to using Christian identity to assert their intrinsic affinity to white American society, Arab-American authors also made strategic use of the "exoticism" of their Holy Land origin. In doing so, they drew on the overlapping paradigms of racial essentialism, assimilation and cultural pluralism that structured cultural interaction in the American context. While the essentialism that viewed races and ethnic groups as totally distinct set Arabs apart from European Americans, it also allowed them to assert their "uniqueness" (transposed onto a cultural and spiritual plane) as exotic emissaries from the Holy Land.[25]

Majaj identifies the dovetailing of turn-of-the-century American racial politics and *mahjar* identity politics. The double strategy that these *mahjar* authors employ means emphasizing both their similarity with white

America and their difference as exotic Arabs. The result is discernible in the nostalgic embracement of a peddler figure that repeats the redemptive and transitional nineteenth-century narrative of the street Arab as well as inaugurates a Syrian history in America. *Mahjar* intellectuals such as Hakim and Mokarzel posit a version of identification that does not dissolve their Syrianness into Americanness but rather juxtaposes the two imaginaries.

Of course *mahjar* intellectuals did not always agree on what to name themselves and where to locate their transhistorical identities. In the first Arab American novel, for instance, the literary representation of Arab identity ultimately serves as an argument for political recognition of both Arabia and Arab migrants. *The Book of Khalid* was written by Ameen Rihani. Mokarzel knew his fellow *mahjar* migrant well and had published Rihani's writings in his English-language newspaper, the *Syrian World*.[26] However, the two men eventually had a falling out, specifically over the question of affiliating the *mahjar* diaspora with Lebanon or with Arabia. Mokarzel ultimately argued for the importance of Lebanese identity, whereas Rihani set his sights on promoting the idea of pan-Arabia and establishing a narrative on transnational Arab identity.

Ameen Rihani

Rihani enjoyed an eclectic career. In addition to being the unofficial ambassador between the Arab world and the West in the interwar years, Rihani published in both English and Arabic consistently throughout the first four decades of the twentieth century. He translated Arab poetry into English, wrote his own poetry in Arabic and English, completed two separate Arabian travel narratives published simultaneously in Arabic and English, and penned numerous critical reviews of art, literature, and U.S. diplomacy, appearing in both Arab American periodicals and the hip art and culture magazines spawned by the Jazz Age. A child immigrant to America in 1888, Rihani spent his adult life splitting time between living in his native Lebanon, touring the lecture circuit of the United States, and visiting remote redoubts of the Arab world, such as Yemen, Saudi Arabia, and Iraq. Rihani used each of these manifestations to literary effect, reclaiming the term *Arab* from Orientalist discourse and retranslating the figure of the Arab found in both American and Arab traditions.

Rihani's most stunning act of cultural translation is his first and only novel, *The Book of Khalid*. Rather than translate Arabic and Arabo-Islamic culture *into* English, Rihani presents his audience with a book that juxtaposes American and Arab references. This form of translation as juxtaposition treats the two cultural traditions he engages as coequals. As Susan Stanford Friedman puts it, juxtaposition as a strategy of comparison potentially "avoids the problems of epistemological hierarchy, instrumentalism, and stasis"[27] The result of Rihani's experiments with cultural juxtaposition is the creation of a uniquely hybrid romantic hero, Khalid. Khalid shares many of Rihani's own biographical details as well as anticipates many of Rihani's future endeavors. Through Khalid, Rihani explores the connection between Arab and American discourses on romantic identity formation to create a narrative of personal and political emancipation.

Rihani's *The Book of Khalid* offers a corrective to the narrative of Arab assimilation into an unhyphenated American culture that pervades earlier historical accounts of the *mahjar*. Whatever Rihani's eventual differences with intellectuals such as Mokarzel, the hero of his 1911 novel stands as a reminder of the coterie of Syrian intellectuals who sought to keep the Arab/Syrian/Lebanese heritage alive in their American identities. To revive Rihani's alternative story of Arab migration to the New World (and out of it) is to reconfigure the story of the Arab presence in America not as one of willing self-erasure and disappearance but rather as one of continuity. The struggle to reconcile sacred and secular rhetoric, Muslim and non-Muslim identity, American democracy and "Arab" tradition is at the heart of Khalid's story, just as it is at the heart of the Christian intellectual's effort to conceptualize an Arabness that encompasses multiple religions, ethnicities, and regional affiliations.[28] Khalid's ability to overcome these apparent oppositions by embracing pan-Arabism is the catalyst for his eventual apotheosis as prophet of modern Arab identity. In this sense, Rihani is the intellectual heir to the spirit of liberal reform initiated a generation earlier by the *nahda*. But whereas *nahda* reformers such as al-Tahtawi and al-Shidyaq were intellectual tourists who visited European countries to make observations that they would bring to bear on their birth countries, the *mahjar* reformer is a migrant who often moved permanently or semipermanently to a foreign country. A *mahjar* intellectual such as Rihani was far less interested in reforming his birth country, or even his host country, than he was in formulating the romantic idea of Arabia and Arabs. This romantic idea is produced by an arabesque form of translation, one that allows both Arab and American languages of identity to coexist as mirrored images of one another.

The Book of Khalid

The hero of *The Book of Khalid* has all the attributes of the typical Syrian migrant during the *mahjar* period. Born into a Maronite family, Khalid begins his life in Mount Lebanon before migrating with his friend and scribe Shakib across the Atlantic. Once in New York City, Khalid takes up pack-peddling. But it is Khalid's decision to successively abandon pack-peddling, capitalism, and eventually America that makes him unique among American literary immigrant heroes of the period:

> No, Shakib, it matters not how I travel, if I but get away from this pande-monium of Civilization. Even now, as I sit on this trunk waiting for the hour of departure, I have a foretaste of the joy of being away from the insid-ious cries of hawkers, the tormenting bells of the rag-man, the incessant howling of children, the rumbling of carts and wagons, the malicious whir of cable cars, the grum shrieks of ferry boats, and the thundering, rever-berating, smoking, choking, blinding abomination of an elevated railway. A musician might extract some harmony from this chaos of noises, this jumble of sounds. But I—extract me quickly from them! (*Khalid*, 136)

On the eve of his departure from turn-of-the-century Manhattan's "pan-demonium of Civilization," American literature's first Arab immigrant hero strikes a discordant note. He does not celebrate the United States as a land of monetary opportunity, nor does he marvel at the possibilities of American modernity and advanced technology. Khalid verbally gathers the rattle and hum of American progress, as well as the din of U.S. com-merce, into a cacophonic compendium of what is driving him not to the shores of the New World but away from them, back to his homeland in the Lebanese Mountains.

The symphonic promise contained in the melting pot theory of Ameri-canization breaks down in Khalid's account of New World noise. Instead of harmony, the sounds of Old World labor (hawkers, rag-men) compete with the noise of modern technology (cable cars, ferry boats, elevated rail-way). The howling demands of the next generation of "Americans" medi-ates the noise of the Old and New World modes of commerce. For the stereotypical immigrant to the United States in the 1880–1924 period, the still-infant generation was rhetorically positioned to reap the ben-efits of the outmoded labor of the pioneer generation. Yet it is precisely these future benefits that Khalid eschews by "silently stealing away" with

Shakib back to Lebanon. More than a hundred years prior to the publication of *The Book of Khalid*, James Leander Cathcart had written from the opposite side of the Atlantic, bemoaning the "pandemonium" that defined the multicultural cacophony of the Barbary Bagnio—a place he rhetorically positioned as the antithesis of enlightened American democracy. In the century that passed between the writing of Cathcart's Barbary captivity narrative and Rihani's novel, America had become exactly the heterogeneous society Cathcart had anxiously marked as incoherent. But Khalid reverses Cathcart's terms, complaining not about the pandemonium of Barbary but rather the "pandemonium of Civilization" that America represents. Rihani, in a move conversant with McKay's praise of barbaresques, has his hero reject Western civilization and its values in favor of a "primitive" return and primitivist aesthetics.

Foreshadowing Rihani's own later political efforts to link Lebanese identity to a larger Arab collective identity, Khalid does not remain in Lebanon long. Khalid's rejection of American civilization initiates a migration that will take him through Lebanon to Egypt and finally deposit him in the desert, where the tyro prophet ends the novel in search of his dream, "a great Arab Empire in the border-land of Orient and Occident, in the very heart of the world, this Arabia" (342). Situating this prospective Arab Empire symbolically at both center and fringe, at both the "very heart of the world" and "the border-land of Orient and Occident," Rihani suggests that conceptualizations of a greater Arabia must be figurative before they can be literal. But he also indicates that these conceptualizations of Arab identity must be translated across cultural memories in order to bring a real Arab Empire into existence. To achieve this "translation," Rihani plays with the trope of the primitive and wandering Arab, accounting for its presence in Western romantic narratives while simultaneously updating the figure with a modern purchase.

Khalid's desire to return East and leave the trappings of modernity behind is certainly in keeping with a romantic tradition in Western literature, as well as romantic notions of the desert prevalent in Arabian literature. Khalid's return to the "primitive" East is a return to the romantic space of mythmaking out of which influential philosophers of the state such as Johann Godfried Herder theorized collective national identity. Herder, a German writing before there was a Germany, used the figure of the Bedouin Arab to demonstrate cultural and linguistic continuity across time and space. "With his simple clothing, his maxims of life, his manners, and his character, are in unison," Herder writes of the Bedouin's natural nomadic independence, "and, after the lapse of thousands of years, his tent still preserves the wisdom of his forefathers."[29] Expanding out from the Bedouin to an assessment of Arabs in general, Herder continues in his *Reflections on the Philosophy of the History of Mankind*, "wherever the Arab is found, on the Nile or the Euphrates, on Libanus or in Senegal, nay even in Zanguebar or the islands of the Indian Ocean, if a foreign climate have not by length of time changed him into a colonist, he will display his original Arabian character."[30] Herder judges Arabness in relation to the archetype of the true Arab: the Bedouin. To be a colonist is to be removed from essential "Arab" qualities, that is, nomadism.[31] The Bedouin stands as an evocative example of *volk* identity in Herder's philosophy.

Khalid's motion toward the desert offers a revision of the myth of the primitive Arab that takes into account the way European philosophers of national identity formation had historically instrumentalized the Bedouin. Rihani posits Khalid not only as a Bedouin wanderer but also as a modern nation builder. "Now think what can be done in Arabia," Khalid announces; "think what the Arabs can accomplish, if American arms and an up-to-date Koran are broadcast among them" (303). By the novel's conclusion, the wandering Arab in the desert is not merely nomad; he is also a potential father of an Arab national homeland. Rihani translates the trope of rootless Bedouin wandering into a foundational figure. This translation not only resonates with Mokarzel's invocation of a pioneer Syrian peddler statue; it also mirrors Herder's own translation of Arab *volk* characteristics into European models of national identity.

In Rihani's "immigrant" novel, Khalid becomes Arab; he does not become American. But the path to Arab identity winds through America. Khalid's motion is not the unidirectional path of immigration but the multidirectional path of migration. Rather than exchanging Arabness for Americanness or whiteness or civilization, Khalid seeks to establish a home where Arab identity collects. He constructs this home not from one tradition or another but from the experience of the Arab exile in America. The experience of exile, Rihani suggests, produces a longing for a transhistorical concept with which the cultural outsider can identify. Yet the transhistorical concept Rihani latches onto, the wandering Arab, plays a significant role in both Western and Eastern theorizations of national identity. In juxtaposing the trope of the primitive and wandering Bedouin with the figure of the modern nation builder, Rihani is highlighting the cultural interpenetration that has been part and parcel of European national identity politics since the eighteenth century.

In *The Book of Khalid*, Rihani uses his hero's growing consciousness of an Arab identity that is opposed to the wholesale adoption of America's "modern" values to challenge a history of representation that borrows the figure of the Arab to create formulas for other national identities. Khalid's story is not a story of Protestant redemption, American assimilation, or the erasure of Arab identity. Instead Rihani plays off the story of the immigrant's Protestant reformation into an American citizen. Khalid ends the novel an advocate of reform, a reform led by the conservative and fundamentalist "Arabian Luther" Abd'ul Wahab, founder of Wahhabism.[32] Rihani takes the street Arab trope of American assimilation and transforms it into a *majazi* (figurative trope). This *majazi*, in turn, provides the grounding for a narrative of pan-Arab identity formation. Keeping the literal and the figurative Arab inextricably intertwined, Rihani insists on the importance of seizing the terms of representation as a form of political empowerment.

Rihani's message, however, was largely lost on mainstream American audiences. In his own era, Rihani endured multiple rejection letters from the editors of popular American magazines. "They are all too exotic for us," writes James Phillips, editor of the *American Magazine*, in a May 25, 1911, letter. "Perhaps I am mistaken as to the possibility of your writing appearing in a popular magazine."[33] "Once again we are afraid it would be a mistake for the Atlantic to allow itself to be carried so far afield," advises the editor of the *Atlantic Monthly* in a January 23, 1911, rejection letter. "After all, as you know, we Americans are of a conventionalized turn of mind in spite of everything we wish others to think of us."[34] The original *Book of Khalid* is filled with so many untranslated Arabic phrases, recondite English words, and Arabic-English neologisms that it was translated from English to English by Rihani's brother, Albert, in the 1940s. The "exoticism" and lack of conventionality that made Rihani unpublishable in popular American magazines are precisely what made him attractive to early twentieth-century modernist literary outlets. But it would be a mistake to dismiss Rihani as a merely part of a modernist fad for the exotic. Rihani's novel may have been of a "peculiar nature" and "unusual character," as it was described in a September 1911 review from the American magazine the *Bookman*, but the originality of *The Book of Khalid*'s narrative stands in stark contrast to its more popular contemporary, Khalil Gibran's *The Prophet*.[35] Gibran's *The Prophet*, published in 1923, is one of the most popular books ever to be put into print. Yet a reader would be hard-pressed to indicate what is Arab about *The Prophet*. What does the book tell the reader about Arab history, Arab culture, Arab food, Arab religions? Because the book traffics in vague Orientalist stereotypes, the answer is nothing. The most salient question to ask about *The Prophet* when comparing it to works in other ethnic American literary traditions is, What does it tell us about the Arab experience in America?

The Prophet does not explore a transition from religious to secular identity or from one cultural milieu to another, as is evident in many of the contemporary Jewish-immigrant narratives such as Abraham Cahan's *The Rise of David Levinsky*. "There is a streak of sadness in the blood of my race," the character David Levinsky announces in the first pages of Cahan's seminal novel of Jewish immigration to America; "very likely it is of Oriental origin."[36] *The Historical Dictionary of American Slang* gives this 1927 definition for Arab: "n. 1. Theat. A Jew.—used disparagingly."[37] Until the end of the 1920s, the word *Arab* was forbidden for many vaude-villians for the obvious reason that a good number of the players were Jewish—though many were performing in blackface.[38] Thanks largely to writers such as Cahan and those who followed him (but also thanks to these blackface performances), the figure of the American Jew transitioned out of the codes of "Oriental" identity and into a well-established ethnic American niche.[39] Just like Levinsky himself, by the close of the 1920s, the figure of the Jew had been assimilated into a hyphenated American culture and largely disassociated from Oriental association. Not so with representations of the Arab, a figure that still remains largely wedded to the Oriental codes of the nineteenth century.

Unlike Cahan's novel, *The Prophet* does not present a struggle with what it means to be "American" and not something other, something Old World. Gibran's book presents an abstracted Oriental identity largely shaped by Western readers' expectations. A book review from the *New York Times* on June 10, 1934, highlights Gibran's reception in the United States as an undifferentiated and conglomerate Oriental sage. "[Gibran evinces] an unworldliness reminding one of Guatama and the philosophers of the Upanishads; there is a lyric manner and picturesqueness that recalls the best of the old Hebrew prophets; . . . there is an epigrammatic pithiness of utterance that makes many of Gibran's sayings not unworthy to be placed side by side with those of older sages of the Orient."[40] Indian, Hebrew, Oriental—Gibran manages to be all these things at once to his reviewer. By offering a vapid repetition of the Oriental codes of nineteenth-century discourses on Eastern mysticism, *The Prophet* guaranteed itself a popular reception, but it also failed to provide any insight on the level of narrative content as to what it meant to be an Arab or a Syrian/Lebanese immigrant in America.

In contradiction to the claim made by the critic Geoffrey Nash that Rihani was *deracine* and that "in spite of the American framing of *The Book of Khalid*, Rihani's biculturality is not of the kind that can be considered ethnic American," I would argue that it is precisely by contextualizing Rihani's novel within a longer American discourse on Arab identity that its value to the canon of Arab American literature becomes apparent.[41] Whereas Gibran repeats the Orientalist codes of the nineteenth century, Rihani subtly challenges them. This difference, of course, largely accounts for the difference in the reception of their respective books. Gibran's *Prophet* is often evoked as an example of Arab American writing, and its popularity with American audiences continues unabated. *The Book of Khalid*, on the other hand, has traditionally been read as a problematic attempt at assimilation.[42] But recently, the critic Wail Hassan has revisited Rihani's 1911 novel and usefully placed it in a transnational context.[43] Hassan's analysis of Rihani's cultural translations reveals the novel to be part of a more complicated attempt to imagine transnational models of political citizenship. In *The Book of Khalid*, the figure of the Arab is neither a primitive nor an ethnic cipher. Instead, by the novel's conclusion, the hero conceptualizes a modern, sophisticated, and culturally cosmopolitan vision of Arabness. Rihani was thinking beyond the nation, but that does not obviate his importance to a tradition of Arab American writing. Contemporary Arab American writers are again thinking through their national identity by thinking through their multiple linguistic, ethnic, religious, and national affiliations—not in terms of either/ or but rather in terms of yes/ands.

To focus on *The Book of Khalid*, then, is to argue that it is Rihani, not the more recognizable and popular Gibran, who offers us the clearest way to see a continuum between current Arab American literature and a foundational moment of Arab migration to America. It is also to argue that it is not the canon of Arab American literature prior to 1967 that lacks cultural authority and ethnic authenticity but rather the way that canon has been approached. I return to Rihani's novel, then, with an eye toward revising its critical heritage by cultivating an appreciation for its subversion of the dominant American discourse on Arab identity. Rihani's novel presents identity as fluid, mutable, and multiple—a model that speaks saliently to the effort by current Arab American writers to claim multiple, often simultaneous, identities that fracture geographic and temporal continuities.

Masquerade as Arab Literary Form

A conscious attempt to amalgamate Eastern and Western literary styles, *The Book of Khalid* is arabesque in a number of senses that have to do with creating "fantastic mixtures." Conceived through the nesting-doll structure of *1,001 Nights*, *The Book of Khalid* repeatedly sheds its storyline to reveal another latent narrative trajectory. What appears to be an American immigrant narrative (Book 1: "In the Exchange") transforms into a Lebanese emigrant narrative (Book 2: "In the Temple"), both of which are finally displaced by a narrative of world migration and pan-Arab nation building (Book 3: "In Kulmakan"; everywhere). As Khalid passes through various phases of false consciousness and comes into realization of his destiny as a prophet of an Arab New Age, the focus of his concerns widens in scope to eventually encompass a global perspective. Stylistically the novel blends the conventions of the putatively teleological Western bildungsroman and the putatively circular Eastern romance to produce its vision of a modern Arab hero whose concerns are secular as well as sacred. Disguise thus operates in *The Book of Khalid* with a textual and metatextual register, indexing both the various roles Khalid will play within the book before realizing his prophetic mission and the novel's general thematic of revelation.

On the level of content, Rihani's novel is an extended masquerade dramatizing the dynamic relationship between authenticity and mimicry, reality and fiction, the Arab and the arabesque. The novel begins with a series of prefatory meditations on Khalid's authenticity from fictional editors who supposedly collected *The Book of Khalid* from manuscripts in Egyptian libraries and interviews with the tyro prophet's scribe, Shakib. But throughout the course of the book, the authority of the sources used to authenticate Khalid's story is constantly put under suspicion. An extended satire on identity construction, Rihani's novel uses humor, modernist narrative conceits, and familiar Orientalist archetypes to critique Western knowledge of the Arab as superficial. But *The Book of Khalid* also engages in its own identity politics by participating in the Orientalist discourse it sends up. The novel's hero becomes an Arab by inhabiting the figurative tropes of Arabness circulating in both Western and Eastern romantic traditions.

Looking at the dynamics of cultural exchange in one section in *The Book of Khalid*, a chapter entitled "With the Huris," allows us to explore Rihani's subversive treatment of Orientalist tropes. The chapter sets Khalid adrift in an American "Bohemia" where exoticism equals cultural cachet. Through Khalid's multiple female suitors, the chapter dramatizes the Arab immigrant's encounter with stereotypes of Arab identity. Khalid, a cultural naïf, responds to these stereotypes by playing the roles he is asked to perform. In an ironic twist on Orientalist fantasies of sexual plentitude that accumulated around the Islamic concept of the *huriyat* (virgins who await faithful Muslims in paradise), Rihani's "huris," who occupy the earthly "paradise" of Bohemia, are less concerned with spiritual than financial recompense and certainly are not virgins.[44]

Khalid's first Bohemian lover is the Medium. She tells Khalid, "Do you know, Child, I am destined to be a Beduin Queen. The throne of Zenobia is mine, and yours too, if you will be good. We shall resuscitate the glory of the kingdom of the desert" (86). Khalid's presence in the Medium's studio lends authenticity to her fantasy, and she plans to turn him into an exotic adornment that authorizes her own Arab playacting. The Medium earns her living by practicing "Tiptology," a theory of spirit rapping that purports to contact the Beyond. It is also a form of table-tipping opportunism. The Medium, in other words, is a fake, and when Khalid asks her to initiate him into the art of Tiptology, she refuses. This refusal is symptomatic of the white artist's relationship to the Oriental subject. Denying Khalid knowledge of Tiptology is tantamount to denying him access to a transcendent form of identification. While Tiptology allows the Medium to become Zenobia, she wants Khalid to remain fixed to his prescribed identity. To the white Medium, Khalid is cultural capital that she can appropriate. She is a Medium because she channels Khalid's authentic "Oriental" identity into her own fantasies and identity politics.

Zenobia was second only to Cleopatra in terms of the visibility of an Oriental woman in nineteenth-century American print culture. She appeared prominently in both historical romances such as William Ware's *Zenobia; or, The Fall of Palmyra* (1838) and popular romances such as Nathaniel Hawthorne's *The Blithedale Romance* (1852). In the preface to *The Blithedale Romance*, Hawthorne famously draws a bright line between fantasy and reality, marking them as distinct spheres that should be kept apart. Rihani's novel instead contaminates the two conditions and insinuates that fantasy can become reality, mimicry can become authenticity, and the roles we play are dress rehearsals for the people we will become. Khalid is the untutored, naïve parvenu in every American situation he encounters, and yet by the end of his experiences in these situations, he has been transformed into something new—a peddler, an anarchist, a politician, a Bohemian boy toy. Rihani embraces the arguably modern-ist blurred distinction between romantic representation and real life. Rihani's Zenobia brings attention to the tropic nature of Orientalist liter-ary representation not to critique it as much as to offer its logic as a way to think through the multiplying possibilities of identity formation.

Hawthorne's Zenobia "bruises herself against the narrow confines of her sex."[45] But whereas the trappings of Orientalist masquerade imprison Hawthorne's Zenobia, they liberate the New Woman "huris" of Rihani's Bohemia. Tossed about Don Juan–like in the free-love tides of early twentieth-century New York, Khalid is hardly a patriarchic presence. Fur-thermore, the feminized space of the "With the Huris" chapter owes less to male fantasies about the harem then to descriptions of harems as places of female privilege offered by writers such as the early eighteenth-century traveler and protofeminist Lady Mary Wortley Montagu. "'Tis also very pleasant to observe how tenderly he and all his brethren voyage-writers lament the miserable confinement of the Turkish ladies," Montagu com-ments about the harem and male misconceptions of its function. The harem women "are perhaps freer than any ladies in the universe, and are the only women in the world who lead a life of uninterrupted pleasure exempt from cares."[46] Montagu's categorization of the harem space as a place of uninterrupted pleasure, of course, is not devoid of its own Ori-entalist assumptions. Nevertheless, her willingness to afford Turkish ladies agency and make them authors of their own pleasure confronted many Orientalist assumptions about the role of the harem and the place of women in Oriental cultures. For Rihani, New York's Bohemia operates as a similar space of female agency, and the women Khalid encounters in it are New Woman agents of their own destiny.[47]

The Bohemian writer who seduces Khalid after the Medium does rein-forces the play between mimicry and authenticity. Ultimately she forces Khalid to blend Arab identity with arabesque performance. Dubbed the Enchantress, the writer quite literally uses her relationship with Khalid to create copy she can sell to contemporary magazines. The Enchantress "in a Japanese kimono receives [Khalid] somewhat orientally" (87) and "in an effort to seem Oriental, calls the Dervish 'My Syrian Rose,' 'My Desert Flower,' 'My Beduin Boy,' etcetera, always closing her message with either a strip of Syrian sky or a camel load of narcissus" (88–89). In response to the writer's Orientalist characterizations, Khalid decides to "adorn . . . her studio for a time" (89). The Enchantress, described to Khalid as "a hunt-ress of male curiosities, *originales*, whom she takes into her favor and ultimately surrenders to the reading public" (87), is a send-up of the aspiring New Woman journalists who populated turn-of-the-century New York City and wrote for periodicals such as the *Commercial Advertiser*. The joke of course is that nineteenth-century American writers, such as Hawthorne, used Oriental material, characters, and themes as marketable exotic adornments in much the same way as Rihani's Enchantress. The joke is reversed, however, by Khalid's willingness to become whatever it is his white Orientalist viewers want him to be.

The Medium and the Enchantress index the representation of the Orient, and in particular Oriental women, found in nineteenth-century American literature. As their capitalized names indicate, they are also typological caricatures of the white writers who produced exotic Oriental copy for their American audiences. But far from merely critiquing the appeal of authentic Orientalness to white artists in Bohemia, Rihani's "With the Huris" explores the complex play between white co-option of Arabness and Arab self-fashioning as a market strategy. Probing the possibilities of American Bohemia as a space of alternative enunciation and creation, Rihani demonstrates that cultural capital in modernist America is fluid and ultimately mutually created. If the Medium and the Enchantress present Arabness as a performance, Arabness, as represented by Khalid, is also a performance.

Khalid, a Syrian of Jesuit faith, comes to Bohemia professing to be a Muslim Sufi. "I am a Dervish at the door of Allah," Khalid announces, to which the Medium replies, "And I am a spirit in Allah's house" (83). The Oriental identities of the Medium *and* Khalid are mutually created fantasies—a kind of call and response of romantic formation. Khalid's ability to gain entrance to various homes and studios depends on him performing as a Sufi and responding to the title "Beduin Boy." Ironically Khalid's performance of Orientalist tropes reinforces the sense of his authentic Arabness for the reader. The narrator explains Khalid's sexual escapades with the women of Bohemia by averring, "And here, the hospitality of the Dervish does not belie his Arab blood. In Bohemia, the bonfire of his heart was never extinguished, and the wayfarers stopping before his tent . . . were welcome guests for at least three days and nights. And in this he follows the rule of hospitality of his people" (93). In this formulation, the Bedouin tradition of hospitality is used to authenticate the Orientalist trope of the Arab's sexual perversity and licentiousness. "Delicacy and intensity, effervescence and depth," the editor relates about Khalid's sexual proclivities, "these he would have in a woman, or a harem, as in anything else" (92). Khalid is passing in Bohemia by playing arabesque roles—as a Muslim, as a Sufi, as a Bedouin, as the patriarch of a harem.

In Rihani's hands, the conflict between a universalism that breaks down Orientalist differentiations and an essentialism that keeps the uniqueness of Arab identity intact instead becomes a question about authenticity and performance. The point of the quotation about Khalid following the rules of hospitality is not that Khalid is authentic but rather that he performs his role as an Arab expertly. The chapter's dramatization of questions of authenticity is part of the novel's overall approach to identity formation. "After all," exclaims the editorial voice upon discovering Khalid's manuscript in the Khedival Library in Cairo, "might it not be a literary hoax, we thought, and might not this Khalid be a myth" (7). Throughout Khalid's narrative, acts of authentication are constantly undercut by the commentary of an editorial voice that is piecing Khalid's story together for the reader from multiple, unreliable, sources.

The emphasis on performance evident in Rihani's novel has a legacy in Arab poetics. This legacy grows out of the difference that Arab linguistic scholars such as al-Jahiz (d. 869/255) mark between the performance of Bedouin poetry and post-Classical urban poetry. Discussing the implications of al-Jahiz's *Kitab al-Bayan w'al Tabyin* for the development of a sense of Arab identity, Adonis explains,

> This is what is embodied in the following characterization of eloquence (*fasaha*): "The pure bedouin Arabs are the essence of perfect eloquence," and in the characterization of naturalness (*badaha*) as "what differentiates the Arabs from other peoples in eloquent expression." It is the antithesis of an embellished style (*tahbir*), that is a style involving careful study and intellectual activity. *Tahbir* is an attribute of post-Classical poetry and urban culture, the product of self-conscious technique, while *badaha* and natural aptitude are properties of Bedouin poetry. (*Arab Poetics*, 29)

What makes Arabs a discrete and identifiable cultural entity, according to Adonis, is the eloquence of their language. This eloquence is associated with the *badaha* aesthetic of Bedouin poetry. Khalid, an autodidact with no system to his method of self-education, exemplifies the *badaha* aesthetic. "The air was his school; and everything that riots and rejoices in the open air, he loved," the editor explains in reference to Khalid's early years. "Bulbuls and beetles and butterflies, oxen and donkeys and mules,—these were his playmates and friends" (*Khalid*, 18). The *badaha* aesthetic, of course, is also a component of the classic nineteenth-century romantic hero that Carlyle had spoofed in *Sartor Resartus* and Rihani had revised in his own Carlyle-inspired *The Book of Khalid*. Khalid's innocence places him in both an Arab and a Western romantic tradition of "natural men."

Ultimately, it is not essences that are authentic or inauthentic but rather performances—the ability to intuitively play a role. Indeed, throughout the novel, Khalid continually changes masks, as though he were an actor playing various parts.[48] The stages for his roles include Tammany Hall politics, the Young Turks Revolution, the global mission of Baha'ism, and Arab Nationalism. Passing through an array of identities and co-opted by a multitude of American and transnational political and social movements, Khalid inhabits different temporary identities before finally ending the novel by disappearing into the desert—by, as it were, exiting the stage. The novel revolves around an interplay between Khalid's "authentic" identity and the various roles he inhabits which "authenticate" that identity, blurring the distinction between Arab and arabesque formations of self. "His first beau ideal was to own the best horse in Baalbek," the editor comments in recounting Khalid's youth in Lebanon, "and to be able to ride to the camp of the Arabs and be mistaken for one of them was his first great ambition" (*Khalid*, 23). In this formulation, the gap between the arabesque Khalid and the "Arab" becomes legible—Khalid wants to be "mistaken for one of them." But the gap quickly closes as Khalid's performance eventually gains him acceptance *as* "one of them."

To mark Khalid as an "authentic" Arab is a mistake, but it is also a mistake to consider him an imitation. It is more accurate to say that Khalid performs the archetypal elements of Arab behavior as codified in romantic literature. Wedding the imaginary and the real, the thing and its imitation, as well as the "authentic" Arab with the arabesque, Rihani uses the image of the Arab as a form of identification based on the transference principle of figurative language. It is in this final sense of a masquerade that I approach *The Book of Khalid* as an American arabesque. It is a consciously literary representation that obscures the distinction between the figurative and the literal Arab. The tropes that define Arabs in the Western literary canon, Rihani's novel suggests, provide the figurative tools necessary to create a very real Arab identity.

The Book of Khalid is humorous, experimental, unwieldy, and overwrought, but it is also a key work if the narrative about Arab American literature is going to be revised to account for the *mahjar* generation. Tongue in cheek, the book touches on themes that were essential topics of discussion for *mahjar* intellectuals—themes such as immigrant disenchantment with America, East-West amalgamation, prophetic apotheosis, and pan-Arab unity.[49] The last concern became one of Rihani's lifelong pursuits. *The Book of Khalid*'s exploration of the political potential of literary constructions of Arab identity presages Rihani's later, serious ruminations on Arab nation building and brings *American Arabesque*'s analysis of the figure of the Arab full circle. In Rihani's myriad writings, figurative constructions of Arabness ultimately underwrite his ability to translate Arab identity politics to his Western audiences. In the process, he transforms American idioms into arguments for Arab nationalism, demonstrating the multidirectionality of American arabesques.

The Literary Logic of Arab Independence

In 1939, Rihani, as part of a five-month-long lecture tour of the United States, stopped in San Francisco, California, lodging at the St. Francis Hotel in the affluent suburb of St. Francis Woods. Writing on the hotel's stationery, which featured an image of the hotel's adobe Spanish Revival façade, Rihani shared his impressions of the California mise-en-scène with a friend. "I have found in the architecture of the cottages in the district called St. Francis woods," mused Rihani, "much that recalls Andalusia and therefore the Moors or the Arabs." "Its fruits, its flowers and shall I say its flower-like women," he continued, "reminds me of Syria, my native land."[50] Moving easily from the vague to the specific ties that bind California to the Islamic Mediterranean, Rihani's initial references to Andalusia and Syria prepare his reader for the final, and most significant, connection that he wants to establish between America and the Arab world.

> But the Arabian origin in Spanish architecture is lost, alas, in St. Francis woods, and the memory of the Arabs like that of the Indians . . . is tucked away in the Sacramento Valley. Much like the Indians . . . the Arabs are still living and still striving to regain their place in the sun. They are today a people with a cause that is not unworthy of your interest. They are still struggling for freedom and independence as a people, as well as for unity and solidarity as a nation—; Northern Arabia [is today] under the gilded yoke of a mandate forged by the league of nations.[51]

By the end of Rihani's description of California, the personal has become political, and the romance of exoticism has transformed into a romantic quest for lost origins. Rihani connects American history and Arab history, as well as American national formation and potential Arab national formation, through the figure of the Indian. The transferences between the figure of the Bedouin and the figure of the Native Indian so prevalent in nineteenth-century American travel narratives returns here, as an argument for the establishment of an independent Arab nation. The model for this potential Arab nation, in Rihani's mind, was the United States of America. "I admit, however, that the complete success of Pan-Arabism—Arabia under one ruler—is not expected at the present or in the near future," Rihani explained in his standard 1920s and '30s public lecture on pan-Arabism. "But the success of an Arab confederation, following the pattern, more or less, of the United States of America, is not far off."[52]

Registering both the disappointment of the post–World War I mandate years and the optimism that Arabian independence was still achievable if only its cause could be translated into a language recognizable to the West, Rihani's St. Francis Woods letter resonates with the themes he had been sounding over the preceding two decades as a touring public intellectual. On and off over the course of the 1920s and '30s, Rihani lectured American audiences on Arabian culture, debated rabbis on the Israel-Palestine issue, and appeared at community venues in small towns from Barbourville, Kentucky, to Athens, West Virginia, to Upland, Indiana, as well as in big cities such as Boston, New York, and San Francisco. Though he insisted to Eleanor Roosevelt in a 1937 letter that he was not playing politics with the Arabs' cause but rather promoting "their cultural and racial resurgency," Rihani clearly had both political and personal motivations for doing these American lecture tours.[53] The metropolitan, cosmopolitan, transnational intellectual, Rihani, who was feted by kings in Iraq and Arabia, gave special attention to the small-town lecture circuits in the years between 1937 and 1939, the last he was to spend in America. His efforts were not lost on the Syrian community in America. As the editor and business manager of the Detroit-published *Phoenician Magazine* put it in a letter to Rihani, "We look to you as one of our world leaders, the intellectual sword of the Arabic-speaking world, our champion and our defender against the assaults of those who would disparage the Syrian and Arabian name."[54]

In 1924, the same year the Johnson Act restricted immigration in order, in the rhetoric of nativist literature, to "keep America for Americans," the Indian Citizenship Act was also passed, effectively Americanizing Native peoples by granting them citizenship. Tucked away in the folds of the American nation's memory, Rihani suggests in his 1939 letter, is an origin story latent with its own form of bedouinism—for Bedouins were conflated not only with Native Americans in American discourse but also with Biblical patriarchs. Capitalizing on the rhetorical purchase of the nomadic figure in narratives of nation formation, Rihani hopes to translate the Arab's claim to self-determination—to translate the American image of the Arab into Arab political representation. The key to this transfer is the linking power that figurative representations of the Arab have in American discourse.

Reliance on figurative representation not only helped Rihani translate Arab self-determination claims to Western audiences familiar with Arab tropes; it also allowed him to be supple in his composition of an Arabo-Islamic collective. In his 1930 Arabian travel narrative, titled *Arabian Peak and Desert* and published simultaneously in English and Arabic, Rihani describes his initial audience with Imam Yahya of Yemen. During this audience, the imam asks Rihani whether he is a Muslim. As Rihani lets the reader know, his life may hinge on the answer. In response to this schismatic either/or question about his identity, Rihani evokes *majaz*'s power to allow several, often competing, interpretations to exist simultaneously.

> Although a Syrian by birth, an American by naturalization, I am in my blood an Arab; and although Christianity is the religion of my inheritance, I am also of the faith of the great poets and philosophers—Al-Ghazzaly, Al-Farid and Abu'l-Ala—as well as the young Arabs of today who are working for union and independence, and seeking to reinvest their country with its former prestige and power. . . . "Who upholds Arabia, upholds Al-Islam."[55]

Rihani builds Arabo-Islamic identity through constellations, where constituent pieces orbit around one another rather than eclipse one another. This juxtaposed Arabo-Islamic identity is tangled, contaminated, and provisional, rather than pure and heterogeneous, largely because it owes its logic to figurative interpretation.

In al-Ghazali's twelfth-century treatise on the boundaries of theological tolerance in Islam, *Faysal al-Tafriqa Bayna al-Islam wa al-Zandaqa* (*The Decisive Criterion for Distinguishing Islam from Masked Infidelity*), he proposes applying what he calls the Rule of Figurative Interpretation (*Qanun al-ta'wil*) to decide whether an individual is an unbeliever. A prime example that al-Ghazali uses to prove the method's universal application is the fact that the founder of the most traditional school of Islamic jurisprudence (*fiqh*), Ahmad Ibn Hanbal, had occasion to resort to figurative interpretation in deciphering the meaning of three of the prophet's hadiths. One of these hadiths was Muhammad's statement, "Indeed, I find the breath of the All-Merciful coming from the direction of Yemen."[56] Because the content of the prophet's statement is logically impossible, al-Ghazali argues, and because the prophet never lies, we must accept a non-literal interpretation of his words—a figurative interpretation.

Though al-Ghazali certainly would not have accepted Rihani as a true Muslim, Rihani's invocation of his legacy in Islamic hermeneutics is calculated to impress Imam Yahya and to lay claim to a space of wiggle room in identifying himself. At this schismatic moment of either/or, Rihani insists on a continuum in identity, where one can be "Arab in blood," "American by naturalization," and "Syrian by birth." A capacious definition of Islamic identity was of course key to a Christian Lebanese intellectual exploring the possibility of forming a pan-Arab state with Muslim Arabian rulers. Islam and blood are both transformed into figurative associations by Rihani. These associations, in turn, create links between "Arabs." By responding to the imam's direct question with a figurative interpretation, Rihani places himself within a tradition of Arabo-Islamic hermeneutics that begins with al-Jurjani and travels through al-Ghazali all the way to the twentieth century. He also lays the groundwork for creating a category of Arab that is not limited by geography, ethnicity, or religion.

In a gesture of contestation and reconciliation intimately tied to the bond between the transnational politics of Arabism and the national politics of American immigration that found voice in the interwar period, the figurative bridge that Rihani constructs across potential boundaries of religious, ethnic, and national difference is his "blood." Rather than interpret this reference to "blood" strictly as an essentialist mode of identity politics born out of a particular post–Johnson-Reed immigration-quota historical moment, I want to suggest that Rihani offers us an opportunity to think about Arab American identity formation rhizomatically. Rihani, in this latter read, offers Arabness as a labile territorial assemblage, a form of becoming that allows us, in the words of Deleuze and Guattari, "to grasp the trace of creation in the created" nature of all self-identification.[57]

Rihani presents Arabness as a performative modality rather than as an essential identity. It is an act of self-interpretation. Arabness is for Rihani a matter not only of acting in the manner of the Arabians but also of using the romantic will to imagine pan-Arabia into existence.

Reencountering the Mahjar Legacy

The relationship between masquerade and authenticity broached in this final chapter is essential to an analysis of the relationship between a discourse of representation and a discourse of self-representation that informs the birth pangs of any ethnic literature. Yet the birth of Arab American literature might be said to be a special case, in large part because the question lingers whether such a tradition actually existed before 1967. If it did, the question still remains as to whether there is any connection between the writings of a few Christian Syrian immigrants at the beginning of the twentieth century and the writings of the American-born generations that appeared after World War II. This second question, the one about continuity, gets at the heart of the issue of assimilation and whether or not Syrian Americans did indeed "assimilate themselves out of existence" prior to 1967.

In the 1952 novel *Confessions of a Spent Youth*, Vance Bourjaily, himself the son of a Syrian/Lebanese immigrant to America, has his narrator, Quincy, also the son of a Syrian/Lebanese immigrant to America, confront the absence of Arab cultural heritage. Stationed in Baalbek during World War II, Quincy is situated in the same city that gave birth to Khalid, "a city that enticed and still entices the mighty of the earth" (*Khalid*, 14). There as a representative of a colonizing power (he is serving in the British army), Quincy ironically repeats the conquest and pillaging of Baalbek by "foreign" forces on which the fictional editors of *The Book of Khalid* comment: "The porphyry pillars, the statues, the tablets, the exquisite friezes, the palimpsests, the bas-reliefs,—Time and the Turks have spared a few of these. And when the German Emperor came, Abd'ul Hamid blinked, and the Berlin Museum is now richer for it" (*Khalid*, 14). The editors of Khalid's story impugn the usurper Turks, in the form of Abdul Hamid, for raiding Lebanese cultural heritage and shipping it out to German museums, but by the time Bourjaily was writing, those Turks had been usurped by European mandates. In this context, Quincy and his military buddies spend a night exploring a gravesite near Baalbek, searching for treasure and eventually dragging the bones of the dead (his own ancestors, Quincy comments sardonically) out of the crypt for potential keepsakes. It is a scene of ghoulish humor that announces nothing is sacred, as even the tokens of the connection between New World immigrants and their Old World families found in the crypt are mocked as "U.S. dime-store stuff" and thrown violently aside.[58]

What is striking in the second-generation Lebanese American's description of raiding the tombs of his own ancestry, however, is not his willingness to desecrate his cultural heritage but his lack of connection with it. "We climbed the hill, looking curiously at the Arabic inscriptions on the tumbled stones," Quincy explains. "We theorized of course" (*Confessions*, 229). Putting truth to the fear that first-generation Syrian-immigrant intellectuals expressed about the loss of heritage attendant on the next generation's inability to speak Arabic, Quincy must "theorize" about what is written on the gravestones. This theorization stands in for Quincy's larger relationship to an Arab cultural heritage that he was "brought up not so much to conceal as to ignore" (239). Quincy's ignorance of Lebanese culture, of Arab culture, of Arabic is a product of a childhood during which his father was "busy being an American" (239) and seems to support a narrative about the Syrians' rapid assimilation to an unhyphen-ated American identity. When Bourjaily was asked why Quincy was the only character in his fiction to whom he gave an Arab origin, he replied, "The felonious American immigrant novel would be my father's novel, not mine."[59] But even if the tensions between folkways and modern American life were absent in his own youth and that of his fictional stand-in Quincy, Bourjaily does have his only Arab American narrator register Arab cul-tural heritage in his past, if only as an absence.

When Quincy is in Egypt and then again when he is stationed in Tel Aviv, he, like Khalid before him, explores Arab identity through arabesque masquerades.[60] Quincy describes these performances as wearing an Arab face. The first performance is an extended masquerade as a beggar and ends humorously. "It was in Tel Aviv that I tried again to wear my Arab face," explains Quincy, "this time quite desperately" (*Confessions*, 248). After becoming entangled in a late-night tryst, Quincy and a female Jewish refu-gee find themselves in a tense situation in the Arab quarter of occupied Jaffa, being questioned by several men who Quincy fears might be Palestinian free-dom fighters. In an effort to ease the tension and pave a way for the two of them to escape unharmed, Quincy tells his interlocutor that he is an Amer-ican: "As a matter of fact . . . Lebanese" (256). In the swift back-and-forth of Arabic question and answer that follows, Quincy's Arab American cultural identity appears as a performative response to a historical lack of knowledge. Describing the interrogation that takes place, Quincy explains,

> He went through a roster of prominent Syrian-Americans, and Lebanese-Americans, and it occurred to me to be sorry, for the first time in my life, that we hadn't lived among them. But I hadn't much time to think this over; I had to formulate a personality now, in which to reply to the questions I didn't know the answers to. Should I be surly? Ingratiating? A little of both, I thought, suddenly remembering a cousin from Detroit, a boy my age named Saloom. . . . I tried to produce his voice, now, his diction. He was shorter than I, and I slumped a little. He scowled and smiled a lot, and I started doing so, too. (257)

Into the void of his Arab American cultural heritage, Quincy projects an Arab performance, one itself based on mimicry of an "authentic" Arab. Unlike Khalid, who performs Arabness for his white American audiences in Bohemia, Quincy performs Arabness for an Arab audience in occupied Palestine.

Connecting the "passing" performance of Khalid and that of Quincy points to two legacies in Arab American writing, one ignored and one institutionalized through most immigrant histories. The former is a legacy of inhabiting the image space of the Arab as a form of empowerment, and the latter is a legacy of passing out of Arab identity. This dual legacy is captured succinctly in a description that Bourjaily gives of his father's relationship to the editor of the *Syrian World*, Salloum Mokarzel. Mokarzel not only championed the peddler statue; he also championed Rihani's writings before the two of them ultimately came to their disagreements about the thrust of *mahjar* identity politics. "Mokarzel was a sophisticated man," Bourjaily explains, "with something of a magnetic personality that could draw back temporarily to the Lebanese community people like my father."[61] Perhaps this is the "Saloom" whom Bourjaily channels for Quincy, a man who represents a path not taken by his father and a legacy that is present as an absence for him. The response to that absence and lack of historical continuity lies in the retrieval of *mahjar* voices such as Mokarzel's and Rihani's, voices that insisted on retaining their Arab/Syrian/Lebanese identity in the face of the forces of American assimilation.

Afterword

Haunted Houses

مِرآةُ السيّافِ	*The Executioner's Mirror*
هل قلتَ إنَّكَ شاعرٌ؟-	Did you say that you are a poet?
. . . من أين جئتَ؟ أُحِسُّ جلدَكَ ناعماً	Where do you come from? I notice your skin is so smooth . . .
سيّاف تسمعُني؟	Executioner, do you hear me?
وهبتُكَ رأسَه،	I granted you his head,
خذهُ، وهاتِ الجلدَ واحذرْ أن يُمَسّ	Take it, but bring me the skin unharmed
. . . الجلدُ أشهى لي و أغلى	The skin is desirable to me and precious . . .
سيكون جلدك لي بساطاً	Your skin will be my carpet
سيكون أجمل مجملٍ،	It will be the beauty of beauties,
هل قلت إنك شاعر	Did you say that you are a poet?
	—Adonis[1]

Just outside Natchez, Mississippi, in a thicket of imposing live oaks, sits the main house of the Longwood Plantation. Described by its owner, Haller Nutt, as an "oriental remembrancer of times past," the octagonal structure stands six stories high and is capped by a large onion dome. Longwood was never meant to be a working plantation, and the main house was a place where Nutt's wife, Julia, planned on holding balls and social events. "It is creating much admiration," Nutt effused in a May 19, 1861, letter to his architect, Samuel Sloan. "I think after this the octagon will be the style."² Antebellum writers who wanted to critique the despotism, cruelty, and sexual licentiousness of slave owners often used Oriental imagery to describe the South. But Nutt, a slave owner, was only too happy to Orientalize himself and his summer home. Nutt's enthusiasm for the Arabo-Islamic "style," coupled with his musings on the Oriental house's "remembrancer" function, evidence a belief in taste as a form of possession. Through Longwood Nutt sought to control both time and space. The wealthy Louisiana plantation owner claims that Longwood allows him to dictate the meaning of the past, to architecturally write the history of what will be remembered. The aesthetic is rarely free from the political. By transplanting the exotic into the familiar geography of the antebellum American South, Nutt co-opted an Arabo-Islamic cultural referent as a sign of his wealth, power, and influence. But the history Nutt would have remembered through the Longwood structure was ultimately out of his control.

Nutt's architect, Sloan, lived in Philadelphia, as did the work crew he brought to Natchez. By 1861, Sloan and his men had erected the exterior structure of Longwood. The interior was never completed. The Philadelphia workers dropped their spades and picked up muskets. When they returned south, it was to fire those muskets at Confederate soldiers. Longwood remains to this day a ghostly skeleton. The house is an odd Oriental ruin of antebellum America's obsession with Arabo-Islamic forms, as well as a reminder of the role those forms played in conjuring transcendental and transhistorical fantasies of American identity. But Longwood is also a testament to how those Arabo-Islamic forms change meaning over time and why we should pay attention to the stories embedded within the American fantasies they shape.

As a façade without an interior, the Longwood mansion offers a visual analogue for the message of Adonis's "The Executioner's Mirror." The poem has three main players: a poet, a speaker, and an executioner who is doing the speaker's bidding. The speaker demands that the poet's head be discarded once he has been executed. He also demands that the poet's smooth skin be preserved as an exquisite adornment. The speaker wants the executioner to separate the poet's words from the poet so that he can co-opt them to perpetuate his own power and luxury. Adonis implicitly warns the reader to pay attention to what happens when a writer's words are taken from a writer, taken out of context, and translated into someone else's property. The reflected, refracted, and stolen subjectivity in Adonis's poem offers a working example of one way the arabesque as a literary

form operates: through linguistic and epistemic violence. But the Longwood mansion, itself a kind of detached skin, also offers a lesson on arabesque representation. For if Longwood is, in one regard, an antebellum
form hollowed of content, in another regard its haunted postbellum history accumulates in that hollow. The story Longwood tells is not an Oriental story but rather a very American story, a story of Civil War. *American
Arabesque* began with an anecdote about the interruptions of the American Civil War, and it ends with a return to those interruptions and the
competing fantasies of American identity they engender.

Prior to the Civil War, Haller Nutt's family had a tremendous influence on the cotton industry. His father, Rushworth Nutt, invented an
important appendage to the cotton gin that acted as a fan screen. He also
experimented with cotton cultivation. Eventually Rush Nutt created the
popular Petit Gulf blend by cross-breeding Mexican and Egyptian cotton. The Nutt family's material interest in the Arab world and particularly
Egyptian cotton had brought Rush and Haller's brother, Rittenhouse, to
Egypt in the 1830s. It may be the stories and mementos these two men
brought back with them that inspired Haller's own Oriental fantasy mansion.[3] Regardless, long before Nutt dreamed of building his aesthetic homage to the Orient, his family had reaped the material benefits of the literal
crossbreeding of Egypt and the American South. The Longwood octagon (the largest in America) not only marks a material linkage between
America and the Arabo-Islamic world; it also uses fantasy to make that
linkage visible to the naked eye. Nutt's personal fantasy soon turned to
personal tragedy, and before the Civil War ended, Haller had not only
lost almost all his property; he had also lost his life to pneumonia in 1864.
His gravesite occupies a small cemetery plot only steps from Longwood's
front door, a front door that itself opens onto the gravesite of the Nutts'
fortunes. The emptiness that Longwood encases, however, does serve as a
reminder of times past, as a historic relic not only of the antebellum South
but also of the complex stories hidden within seemingly binary oppositions such as Union and Confederacy, North and South, slave and free.

Only one of Longwood's six floors was completed, the basement. Originally meant to accommodate the thirty-two slaves working in the house,
the basement was instead occupied for the next one hundred years by
descendants of the Nutts. Haller himself was a Northern sympathizer,
and his support of Lincoln had putatively earned him exemption from
having his plantations burned and ransacked by Union forces.[4] These
exemptions were not honored, and the Nutts' Winter Quarters plantation

became Ulysses S. Grant's headquarters. Reportedly, one of Nutt's slaves told Grant where to cross the Mississippi at a key Port Gibson juncture in order to attack Vicksburg, a turning point in the war. When the Longwood mansion eventually passed out of the Nutt family's hands in 1968, there was an important provision added to the deed of sale. The house must remain in its unfinished state in perpetuity. Longwood remains as a Civil War cipher for a Southern, slave-owning family that supported the Union and came to live in its own slave quarters for the century that followed the war. Nutt's Oriental façade encases a Civil War history of fracture, miscommunication, and loss—reminding the visitor not so much of the comforts of plantation life as of the mutability of co-opted forms.

As this book goes to press, a series of civil wars and national conflicts are sweeping North Africa, the Near East, and the Arabian Peninsula. It is far too early to say what will become of the Arab Spring of 2011, but the amount of interest the events are garnering from American citizens and their government attests to the continued importance of the Arabo-Islamic world in the national imaginary. Controlling the meaning of these various Arab revolutions, if not always directly controlling their outcomes, has been a key component of President Barack Obama's foreign policy, as well as a lynchpin to how he rhetorically differentiates that foreign policy from his predecessor George W. Bush. In short, the Arab Spring has provided President Obama with a way to articulate the change in America's image he wants to express, both to the global community in general and to the Arab and Muslim world in particular. It has provided a pivot from the post-9/11 rhetoric of "with us or against us." But is the Arab Spring just a stolen skin for Obama, a way to use superficial images from the Arab world to articulate American identity politics?

Adonis wrote "The Executioner's Mirror," in part, as a response to a tradition in Arab poetry that stultified innovation and co-opted the artist's talent for the perpetuation of entrenched systems of power. The youth (*Al-Shabab*) at the vanguard of the Arab Spring have succeeded, to various degrees, in dislodging oppressive regimes and translating their message of freedom across cultural divides, into an idiom that resonates with American principles of government and justice. Whether their language and fine sentiments will be co-opted as adornments for Obama's vision of the nation's evolved global mandate and altered national identity politics remains to be seen. Whether this latest Arab Renaissance, which again seeks to blend Islamic principles with Western governmental forms and Arab cultural identity with the language of Western liberal values, will succeed where the previous one fell short also remains to be seen. What is clear, though, is that the exchanges between American culture and Arab culture that this book details haunt the current cultural exchanges between America and the Arab Spring. Exploring these nineteenth-century exchanges provides an opportunity to move beyond fetishistic, superficial, and co-opted representations of Arabo-Islamic culture and toward an appreciation of the deep interpenetration between American and Arab languages of national self. Indeed the very definition of democracy, as American citizens perceive it, will undoubtedly undergo significant changes if and/or when it is transplanted into Arab societies. The Arab Spring is something more than a chance for American politicians to articulate their view of American values against a global backdrop. The Arab Spring, whatever its final outcomes, is a political and social awakening that resonates directly with the mandates of U.S. citizenship and the history of individual American citizens' efforts to come to terms with what those mandates mean.

Notes

NOTES TO THE INTRODUCTION

1. For relevant discussion, see Edward Said, *Humanism and Democratic Criticism*, pp. 8–15. I use the terms *Western, Eastern*, and *Orient* with a full appreciation of the fact that they are imperfect constructions and unstable containers. To avoid distracting the reader, I have chosen not to encase them in scare quotes throughout the text. The analysis I provide of American Orientalism over the course of the book puts terms such as *Western, Eastern*, and *Orient* under enough duress to disturb any sense of their being transcendental markers of cultural identity or even of geography.

2. Albert Hourani, *Arabic Thought in the Liberal Age*, p. iv.

3. For the most recent work on transnational approaches to American literature, see Wai Chee Dimock and Lawrence Buell, eds., *Shades of the Planet: American Literature as World Literature*; and Caroline Levander and Robert S. Levine, eds., *Hemispheric American Studies*; and Malini Johar Schueller and Edward Watts, *Messy Beginnings: Postcoloniality and Early American Literature*.

4. Important work is being done in this direction by Anouar Majid. See *We Are All Moors: Ending Centuries of Crusades against Muslims and Other Minorities*.

5. Much has been written about the influence of Judeo-Christian ideologies on the discursive creation of the United States, and an understanding of the figure grounded in Judeo-Christian texts has informed many interpretations of American culture. See Sacvan Bercovitch, *The Puritan Origins of the American Self* and *The American Jeremiad*; Giles Gunn, *Interpretation of Otherness: Literature, Religion, and the American Imagination*; R. W. B. Lewis, *Trials of the Word: Essays in American Literature and the Humanistic Tradition*; F. O. Matthiessen, *The American Renaissance: Art and Expression in the Age of Emerson and Whitman*; Perry Miller, *Errand into the Wilderness*; Kenneth Murdock, *Literature and Theology in Colonial New England*; David S. Reynolds, *Faith in Fiction: The Emergence of Religious Literature in America*.

6. Lauren Berlant, *The Anatomy of National Fantasy: Hawthorne, Utopia, and Everyday Life*, p. 5.

7. Ibid., p. 7.

8. Wail Hassan, introduction to *Thou Shalt Not Speak My Language*, by Abdelfattah Kilito, p. x.

9. For the turn toward global approaches to American Studies, see Wai Chee Dimock, *Through Other Continents: American Literature across Deep Time*; and Dimock and Buell, *Shades of the Planet*.

10. Abdelfattah Kilito, *Thou Shalt Not Speak My Language*, p. 87.

11. This condition is attested to by the fact that both al-Jurjani and al-Ghazali were native Persian speakers but wrote their main works in Arabic.

12. For discussions of al-Jurjani's significance in regard to his categorization of figurative language, see Michiel Leezenberg, *Contexts of Metaphor*; and Kamal Abu Deeb, *Al-Jurjani's Theory of Poetic Imagery*. Also useful is the commentary in Adonis, *An Introduction to Arab Poetics*, especially chapter 2. For the text of *Asrar al-Balagha*, see the excerpt in Vincente Cantarino, *Arab Poetics in the Golden Age*, pp. 157–76, and the complete translation in Abd al-Qahir Al-Jurjani, *Kitab Asrar al-Balagha*, translated by Helmutt Ritter. For the original Arabic, see Abd al-Qahir al-Jurjani, *Asrar al-Balagha*, edited by Al Imam Al Sheikh Mohammad Abdo and Mohammad Rashid Ridah, or the version edited by Mohammad Abdul Mu'nem and Abdul Aziz Sharif (Beirut: Dar al Jeel, 1991).

13. Abu Deeb writes that "this fundamentally new concept of the relation of the image to poetic creation and composition is manifested in the fundamentally different approach to the analysis of the nature of the image adopted by al-Jurjani. Departing from the methods of the rhetoricians, he devotes his time and energy to trying to discover how an image operates in a poetic formulation, rather than producing logical or rhetorical definitions" (*Al-Jurjani's Theory of Poetic Imagery*, p. 66).

14. Al-Jurjani, *Asrar al-Balagha*, pp. 116, 118. Adonis, *Introduction to Arab Poetics*, p. 46.

15. See Baha' al-Din Khorramshahi, "Ta'wil"; and Maulana Syed Abu A'la Maududi, *The Meaning of the Qur'an*, pp. 14–15.

16. This translation is from Rashad Khalifa, *Qur'an: The Final Testament*. There are, of course, other translations which emphasize that only God knows the secret meaning of these verses, by marking a break after "only God knows the true meaning of these verses." Abdullah Yusuf Ali provides a good example of an alternative translation that changes the meaning of the passage: "He it is Who has sent down to thee the Book: In it are verses basic or fundamental (of established meaning); they are the foundation of the Book: others are allegorical. But those in whose hearts is perversity follow the part thereof that is allegorical, seeking discord, and searching for its hidden meanings, but no one knows its hidden meanings except Allah. And those who are firmly grounded in knowledge say: 'We believe in the Book; the whole of it is from our Lord: and none will grasp the Message except men of understanding." See Ali, *The Qur'an*, p. 29.

17. See Henry Corbin, *History of Islamic Philosophy*. Corbin quotes Ja'far Kashfi describing *taa'weel* as "to lead back or bring something back to its origins or archetype" (p. 93).

18. See Binyamin Abrahamov, *Islamic Theology: Traditionalism and Rationalism*.

19. I provide a thumb-nail sketch of these debates here and offer a bibliography of more extensive sources following. The *mutakallimun* (the practitioners of *kalam*) developed systematic and rational criteria for extracting religious and juridical doctrines from the Qur'an. They were opposed by the *muhaddithun* (the practitioners

of *hadith*), who favored a literal interpretation of the Qur'an and held that rational approaches to extracting meaning from dogma was borderline heretical. For the *muhaddithun*, the sayings of the prophet (*hadith*) and the Holy Qur'an itself were the only legitimate sources of religious doctrine. This latter group gave birth to one of the four major schools of Islamic juridical practice, the Hanbali school, named for Ibn Hanbal (d. 241/855). In the Abbasid Caliphate and especially under the Caliph Ma'mun (813–833 AD), a particular school of *kalam* known as the Mu'tazila gained prominence. The Mu'tazila rejected anthropomorphic interpretations of the Qur'an and held that the holy book was not coterminal with God but rather was created. Rational in outlook, Mu'tazila were strict adherents to the concept of *tawhid* (God's unity) but also held the belief that man has free will and can create. In time, another school of *kalam* arose to counter the doctrines of the Mu'tazila and reconcile them more closely with traditional positions held by *muhaddithun* and Ibn Hanbal. Named after their founder, Abu al-Hasan al-Ash'ari (d. 936 AD), the Ash'arites supported an Islamic occasionalist doctrine, while the Mu'tazilites supported an Islamic metaphysics which had much in common with Aristotelianism as well as Neoplatonism. Unlike the Mu'tazilites, the Ash'arites granted God some positive attributes which they claimed were distinct from his essence. They also held, in contrast to the Mu'tazilites, that because God has created everything, man cannot create but rather only imitate, discover, or acquire what has already been created. Though they applied rational methods, the Ash'arites held that there are limits to human reason, beyond which man should not ask questions. For more extensive discussion, see J. V. Ess, *The Flowering of Muslim Theology*; Andrew J. Lane, *A Traditional Mu'tazalite Qur'an Commentary: The Kashshaf of Jar Allah al-Zamakhshari*; R. C. Martin, M. R. Woodward, and D. S. Atmaja, *Defenders of Reason in Islam: Mu'tazilism from Medieval School to Modern Symbol*; Sayyed Hossein Nasr and Oliver Leahmen, eds., *History of Islamic Philosophy*.

20. See *Sura* 39.67: السَّمَوَٰتُ مَطْوِيَّتٌ بِيَمِينِه و/"and the heavens rolled up in His right hand."

21. There is, of course, a hermeneutic tradition in the West that also grows out of a concern with figurative language and exegesis. This tradition extends from Aristotle through Eric Auerbach, I. A. Richards, and T. S. Eliot and into the work of contemporary postcolonial critics such as Gayatri Spivak and Homi Bhabha. Auerbach argues in his seminal analysis of the *figura* that the figural approach is grounded in a fundamentally Judeo-Christian understanding of not only history but also language. The image of the Arab certainly has many attributes of Auerbach's *figura*. An approach to American figures of the Arab sensitive to Arab literary traditions, however, moves discussions of representation beyond Judeo-Christian hermeneutics and opens up the possibility for seeing a global network of influences at work in the production of American culture and identity.

22. This comparison, in turn, reveals the ultimate unity of creation. Discerning this unity through language, however, is a skill available only to the highly perceptive, and thus al-Jurjani calls the connection created by *majaaz* "*mulaahaZa*" (ملاحظة), from the verb *lahaZa* (لحظ), "to perceive."

23. See Richard Fox, "East of Said"; Lisa Lowe, *Critical Terrains: French and British Orientalisms*; Malini Johar Schueller, *U.S. Orientalisms: Race, Nation, and Gender in Literature, 1790–1890*; Timothy Marr, *The Cultural Roots of American Islamicism*; Scott Trafton, *Egypt Land: Race and Nineteenth Century Egyptomania*; and Hilton Obenzinger, *American Palestine: Melville, Twain, and the Holy Land Mania*.

24. Timothy Marr, *The Cultural Roots of American Islamicism*, p. 1.

25. The first four books all deal directly with the nineteenth century, but Edwards's *Morocco Bound* covers a different time period than this study does.

26. In the devastating aftermath of 9/11, the "Barbary analogy," as it came to be known, was invoked repeatedly as a historical precedent for waging war against stateless actors and the failed nation-states that give them refuge. Multiple writers, pundits, military analysts, and cultural critics posited a narrative of a historical continuum between Thomas Jefferson's refusal to pay tribute to Muslim pirates at the outset of the nineteenth century and George W. Bush's refusal to appease Islamic terrorists at the outset of the twenty-first century. For recent histories that endorse the "Barbary analogy," see Michael Oren, *Power, Faith, and Fantasy: America in the Middle East, 1776 to the Present*; and Frank Lambert, *The Barbary Wars: American Independence in the Atlantic World*. Two other works of history published in the wake of 9/11 that establish a continuum between the U.S. war on terror and the Barbary Wars by emphasizing the Manichean binaries I wish to avoid are Joseph Wheelan, *Jefferson's War: America's First War on Terror, 1801–1805*; and Joshua E. London, *Victory in Tripoli: How America's War with Barbary Established the U.S. Navy and Shaped a Nation*.

27. Berlant, *Anatomy of National Fantasy*, p. 5.

28. Eaton, explaining his decision to undertake the dangerous mission with Hamet, declares, "I would rather yield my person to the danger of war in almost any shape, than my pride to the humiliation of treating with a wretched pirate for the ransom of men who are the rightful heirs of freedom." From Charles Prentiss, *The Life of the Late General William Eaton; Principally Collected from His Correspondence and Other Manuscripts*, p. 267. Ultimately, "treat with a pirate" is exactly what the U.S. government did, much to Eaton's dismay.

29. In a letter dated February 16, 1806, Eaton discusses this "secret proviso" that the State Department diplomat Tobias Lear inserted into the treaty. "Mr. Lear observed, that it would be useless at present to send for Hamet's family; for that it was expected by the reigning Bashaw, they were not to be claimed until Hamet should be so withdrawn and so situated, as to remove all apprehension of his further attempting to regain his kingdom. This I understood to be a secret engagement on the part of our commissioner of peace." See U.S. Congress, Senate, Committee on Application of Hamet Bashaw, *Documents Respecting the Application of Hamet Caramanelli, Ex-Bashaw of Tripoli*.

30. Prentiss, *Life of the Late General William Eaton*, p. 356.

31. For more on the importance of manhood to the consolidation of U.S. national identity, see Dana D. Nelson's *National Manhood: Capitalist Citizenship and the Imagined Fraternity of White Men*.

32. Prentiss, *Life of the Late General William Eaton*, p. 364.

33. The Umayyad Caliphate lasted from 661 to 750 AD, when it was overthrown by the Abbasids. At the caliphate's greatest extent, the Umayyads controlled over five million square miles, making it one of the largest empires the world had ever seen. Named after Umayya Ibn Abd Shams, the Umayyads were originally from Mecca but made Damascus the capital of their caliphate. The Abbasids ruled the Islamic world from 750 to 1258 AD. They were named after Abbas Ibn Abd al-Muttalib and made Baghdad the capital of their caliphate. The Abbasids slowly lost power to the army it had created, the Mamelukes.

34. Unlike pre-Islamic dynasties, however, the Mameluke *mulk* was infused with a respect for the *Shari'a*, or the code of Islamic law.

35. J. M. Cowan, ed., *The Hans Wehr Dictionary of Modern Written Arabic*, p. 1081.

36. "The Tripolitan War Collection, 1804–5," Mss. Misc. Boxes T., American Antiquarian Society.

37. The relevant cases deciding Syrian ethnicity are *In re Najour*, 174 F. 735 (N.D. Ga. 1909), *In re Mudarri*, 176 F. 465 (C.C.D. Mass. 1910), *In re Ellis*, 179 F. 1002 (D. Or. 1910), *Ex parte Shahid*, 205 F. 812 (E.D. S.C. 1913), *In re Dow*, 213 F. 355 (E.D.S.C. 1914), *Ex parte Dow*, 211 F.486 (E.D.S.C. 1914), and the case referred to in the body of the introduction, *Dow v. United States*, 226 F. 145 (4th Circuit 1915). The rulings in these cases show that Syrian classification as white fluctuated until the *Dow v. United States* case. For more on these individual cases as they relate to other racial prerequisite cases in U.S. legal history, see Ian F. Haney López, *White by Law: The Legal Construction of Race*.

38. For more on the *Dow* case as it relates to Arab American conceptions of self-identity, see Alixa Naff's *Becoming American: The Early Arab Immigrant Experience*, p. 257. *Dow v. United States*, 226 F. 145.

39. See Frederic G. Cassidy, ed., *Dictionary of American Regional English*, p. 82; and Harold Wentworth and Stuart Berg Flexner, eds., *Dictionary of American Slang*, p. 8.

40. For the first systematic definition and historical analysis of the arabesque pattern, see Alois Riegl's *Problems of Style: Foundations for a History f Ornament*.

41. John D. Foss, *A Journal, of the Captivity and Sufferings of John Foss, Several Years a Prisoner in Algiers*, p. 92.

42. See Michel Foucault, *The Order of Things*. Arguing that "before the end of the 18th Century, man did not exist," Michel Foucault points out that the study of man and the tabulation of his relationships to the world was a phenomenon which appeared around the turn of the nineteenth century, a period coinciding with American captivity in Barbary and a formative moment of American national identity politics. This process of identifying man, in all his variations and connections, can plainly be witnessed in Foss's proto-ethnographic account of Barbary culture. "In the act of speaking, or rather . . . in the act of *naming*," Foucault asserts, "human nature—like the folding of representation back upon itself—transforms the linear sequence of thoughts into a constant table of partially different beings" (p. 309). Foss's act of *naming* these "partially different beings" offers not simply gradations of color, describing progressively darker peoples as he descends the social scale, but a hierarchy of level of civilization based on physical appearance. Foss's table is not

only linear, though; it also takes on depth and as a "constant table" eventually extends to include the kinds of man found in America as well as in Barbary. He begins with the group most akin to Americans (the Turks) in color of skin but also in "robust" stature, moves through the dark Moors, who most closely resemble "Indians," and finally to the darkest of the group and also the least in stature—the Arabs.

43. John Lloyd Stephens, *Incidents of Travel in Egypt, Arabia Petraea, and the Holy Land*, p. 234 (emphasis mine).

44. See David Kazanjian, *The Colonizing Trick: National Culture and Imperial Citizenship in Early America*. Also see Timothy Powell's *Ruthless Democracy: A Multicultural Interpretation of the American Renaissance*. Powell asserts that his book will attempt to answer a number of questions, among them, "Why has it been so difficult for the country to acknowledge and accept its historic multicultural character? What are the cultural origins of these destructive forces of psychological denial and nativist violence that seem to demand and effectively enforce a monocultural sense of national unity?" (p. 4). The captive, as necessarily disenfranchised from his culture though not his cultural identity, approaches this question of national unity from a unique angle and thus is forced to overcome the psychological denial of the existence of disenfranchised groups within the framework of American democracy, if only to grant his own appeal for justice authority. However, I am arguing not for a unified vision of what national identity claims in the Federal era looked like but rather for the specific version of national identity that white captives in North Africa struggled to establish, given their unique circumstance.

45. Kazanjian, in his book *The Colonizing Trick*, examines the homogenizing language of antebellum American democracy as it relates to the multicultural reality of the antebellum American nation. Kazanjian elaborates the claim that American tropes of imperial citizenship are indexed by articulate over inarticulate allegories that support the racial nationalism of a particular group of citizens, Anglos, even as these allegories posit that nationalism as universally applicable. But the language of democratic identity that emerges from the Barbary and Near Eastern zones of contact is not the recognizable racial nationalism of white male citizenship but rather a vernacular exploration of a national identity far less homogeneous and far more fluid. Through the screen of the Ottoman colonial milieu, the democratic imperatives of African slaves and Native Americans are provisionally wed with those of white, working-class sailors.

46. With regard to understanding Poe's arabesque aesthetic as providing a conduit between apparent opposites, Joan Dayan's work is key: "Standing decidedly in the realm of the relative, Poe defies the absolute, while using its trappings first to lure his reader (and tax himself) and then to expose its emptiness. His awareness of imperfection (our plot is not God's plot) results in the *convertibility* that I have identified as Poe's most original stylistic trait. . . . God's plot becomes the source of Poe's technique. And what most often strikes the reader as contradiction (or a one-way choice) in Poe's stories is his deliberate dramatization of contradiction—a ruse that leads to his disclosure of 'convertibility' between things that normally appear antithetical." Joan Dayan, *Fables*

of Mind: An Inquiry into Poe's Fiction, p. 15. While Dayan focuses on Poe's connection to eighteenth- and nineteenth-century philosophers such as Locke, Newton, and Jonathan Edwards, I am identifying resonances between Poe's literary aesthetic and Arabo-Islamic metaphysics.

47. Edgar Allan Poe, "The Philosophy of Furniture," *Burton's Gentleman's Magazine*, May 1840, p. 244.

48. William Carlos Williams, *In the American Grain*, p. 219.

49. In the ninth century, the *tawreeq* style that was developed under the Abbasid dynasty in the Arabian Peninsula distinguished itself more and more clearly from its possible Hellenistic and Sassnian sources by drawing on the ornamental motive of zigzag stripes and inner circles occasionally employed in Arabic folk art. The design achieved its definitive form in the eleventh century under the Seljuks, Fatimids, and Moors in the Levant and Maghreb. It reached Islamic Spain by the twelfth century, found its way to late fifteenth-century Europe with the name Moresque, and eventually became fashionable with Renaissance engravers and print makers. See Ernst Kuhnel, *Studies in Islamic Art and Architecture in Honor of K. R. C. Creswell*; and H. A. R. Gibb et al., eds., *The Encyclopedia of Islam*, p. 561.

50. Noble Drew Ali, *The Seven Circle Koran*, chap. 47, verses 2–3 (hereafter cited in the text as *Circle*).

51. Ameen Rihani, *The Book of Khalid*, p. v (hereafter cited in the text as *Khalid*).

NOTES TO CHAPTER 1

1. For more on captivity as a narrative genre in American culture, see Chris Castiglia, *Bound and Determined: Captivity, Culture-Crossing, and White Womanhood from Mary Rowlandson to Patty Hearst*.

2. For more on the English tradition of Barbary captivity narratives, see Nabil Matar's introduction to *Piracy, Slavery, and Redemption: Barbary Captivity Narratives from Early Modern England*.

3. Paul Baepler, introduction to *White Slaves, African Masters: An Anthology of American Barbary Captivity Narratives*, p. 24.

4. Rajagopalan Radhakrishnan, *Theory in an Uneven World*, p. 82.

5. Susan Stanford Friedman, "Why Not Compare?," p. 759.

6. Cathcart Family Papers, Box 1 (1787–1794), New York Public Library, Stephen A. Schwartzman Building (hereafter Cathcart Mss.).

7. John Quincy Adams to James Leander Cathcart (copy), March 25, 1822, Cathcart Mss.

8. James Leander Cathcart, *Tripoli: The First War with the U.S., an Inner History*, p. 88.

9. This term emerges out of a conversation I had with Roger D. Abrahams in March 2007. I thank Roger for helping me formulate a concept that captures the bottom-up, often vulgar cosmopolitanism of slave-diplomats such as Cathcart.

10. Of course slavery, dispossession, and exile can produce a "refined" language of cosmopolitanism as well. Prominent examples are Olaudah Equiano and Frederick Douglass.

11. For more on Cathcart's language and its relation to U.S. national identity politics, see Martha Elena Rojas, "'Insults Unpunished': Barbary Captives, American Slaves, and the Negotiation of Liberty."

12. James Leander Cathcart, *The Captives: Eleven Years a Prisoner in Algiers*, p. 87 (hereafter cited in the text).

13. Thomas Jefferson, *Notes on the State of Virginia*, p. 181.

14. Ibid., p. 91.

15. See Timothy Marr's "Imagining Ishmael: Introducing American Islamicism," in *The Cultural Roots of American Islamicism*.

16. Castiglia, *Bound and Determined*, p. 6.

17. Judah Paddock's 1818 account of Barbary captivity highlights the risks captives ran by acknowledging their fluency in Arabic and knowledge of Arabo-Islamic culture. After being taken by a band of "cruel Arabs" from the interior of Morocco subsequent to a shipwreck, Paddock describes a trio of white cabin boys (Laura, George, and Jack) whom he discovers as previous captives of the Moroccans.

> [Laura] understood about as much Arabic as George, but neither them as much as Jack. He, Jack (said the two other boys to me,) always joins with the Arabs in their prayers, and is more Arab than a Christian, and you must be guarded against him, for he is a little treacherous lying rascal, and ever prefers the company of these devils here to ours, and has made mischief among us, and if he and ourselves have a quarrel together, they always take Jack's part, and that makes him the more saucy.

The two cabin boys set up a dichotomy whereby they can be trusted and Jack cannot, based on proximity to Arab culture. In fact, Arab culture, in Paddock's narrative, is conflated with a religious identity that is directly opposed to Christianity. It is not just Jack's fluency in Arabic that makes him suspicious but also how that fluency is obtained—through intimacy with the Arabs and their customs. In the cabin boys' Manichean model of cultural identity, Jack has joined the dark side of the "devils." See Juddah Padock, *A Narrative of the Shipwreck of the Oswego*, p. 107.

18. Note, July 25, 1793, Cathcart Mss.

19. Interestingly enough, Cathcart has been published in Arabic.

20. See Jacob Rama Berman, "The Barbarous Voice of Democracy: American Captivity in Barbary and the Multicultural Specter."

21. I have in mind here Susan Buck-Morss's theorization of universal history found in *Hegel, Haiti, and Universal History*. Referring to the Haitian Revolution, Buck-Morss talks about the reaction of French soldiers in Saint Domingue to hearing slaves sing the French revolutionary anthem and wondering, in consequence, if they were fighting on the wrong side. "The moral universality to which such actions appeal is in the register of the negative—the conditions are not right when judged by the official values themselves—rather than imposing one's own morality on someone else," writes Buck Morss. "Such guilt has its source in the gap between reality and social fantasy, rather than between reality and individual fantasy" (p. 84). Though American captivity in Barbary and the

Haitian Revolution obviously occur in quite different contexts, to which I am attendant, the two historical phenomena occur contemporaneously and reflect on each other, as well as inflect each other, tangentially in fascinating ways. It is, I would argue, the experience of captivity in Africa that forces many white sailors (and their readers) to hear the claims of black slaves back in the United States with increased attention and sympathy and in turn to question the outcome of the Revolutionary War with renewed skepticism. The result is a similar recognition of the gap between reality and social fantasy that Buck-Morss argues can be productive of a sense of moral universality that outstrips its particularistic cultural and individual framework.

22. For a discussion of the American public sphere in relation to Barbary captivity during the Federal era, see Hester Blum, *The View from the Masthead: Maritime Imagination and Antebellum American Sea Narratives*, pp. 62–66.

23. Quoted in Baepler, introduction to *White Slaves, African Masters*, p. 19.

24. William Lloyd Garrison, preface to *Narrative of the Life of Frederick Douglass*, by Frederick Douglass, p. 7.

25. Charles Hansford Adams, "Introductory Details Respecting Robert Adams," p. 15.

26. Hugo Schuchardt, *Pidgin and Creole Languages: Selected Essays by Hugo Schuchardt*. See also Wai Chee Dimock's discussion of Schuchardt in "African, Caribbean, American: Black English as Creole Tongue."

27. For Enlightenment notions of patriotism, see Harvey Chisick, *Historical Dictionary of the Enlightenment*.

28. Walter Pritchard, Fred B. Kniffin, and Clair A. Brown, eds., *Southern Louisiana and Southern Alabama in 1819: The Journal of James Leander Cathcart*, reprinted in *Louisiana Historical Quarterly* 28, no. 3 (1945): p. 110 (hereafter cited in the text as *1819*).

29. *Oxford English Dictionary*, s.v. "patriot."

30. The story about Muhammad is retold by Sir Francis Bacon in his 1625 *Essays*, p. 45. It appears there in slightly different form: "Mahomet cald the Hill to come to him. And when the Hill stood still, he was neuer a whit abashed, but said; If the Hill will not come to Mahomet, Mahomet will go to the hill."

31. Uncle Sam is connected to Samuel Wilson, a meatpacker from Troy, New York, who supplied barrels of meat for the U.S. troops during the War of 1812. He stamped the meat "U.S.," and soldiers started calling it "Uncle Sam's." The name became official on September 7, 1813.

32. Al-Jabbarti wrote three versions of these events. The first, *Tarikh muddat al-Faransi bi Misr*, is the text I am working from and covers al-Jabbarti's highly impressionistic account of the first six months of the French occupation. The most famous of the three, *Aja'ib al-athar fil-tarajim wal-Akhbar*, covers Egyptian history from 1688 to 1821 and presents the French occupation in a dispassionate tone.

33. For a detailed account of this ambivalent relationship, see Hourani, *Arabic Thought in the Liberal Age*.

34. A watershed event in the history of both European Orientalism and Egyptian nationalism, the French occupation of Egypt had a direct influence on the rise to power

of the great Egyptian modernizer Muhammad Ali. Furthermore, the events which followed this occupation were a determining factor in the intellectual development of the man who first theorized modern Egyptian national identity, Rifa'a al-Tahtawi (1801–1873). Al-Tahtawi's contact with French Orientalists and French Egyptologists in the generation after Napoleon's exit from Egypt shaped his conception of Egyptian patriotism. As Albert Hourani puts it, al-Tahtawi's introduction to Egyptology filled his mind with "the idea of ancient Egypt . . . and was to contribute an important element to his thought" (*Arabic Thought in the Liberal Age*, p. 70).

35. Abd al-Rahman al-Jabbarti, *Tarikh muddat al-Faransi bi Misr*, p. 24 (hereafter cited in the text as *Chronicle*). See the French text of this proclamation in *Pièces diverses et correspondance relatives aux opérations de l'armée d'Orient en Égypte* (Paris: Messidor an ix, 1801), pp. 152–54.

36. Adonis, *An Introduction to Arab Poetics*, p. 22 (hereafter cited in the text as *Arab Poetics*).

37. For more on the development of the Greek notion of *polis*, see Harry Redner, *Ethical Life: The Past and Present of Ethical Cultures*.

38. Royall Tyler, *The Algerine Captive*, pp. 128–29.

39. Tyler's narrative exploits the fact that Christian slaves in Barbary could convert to Islam and shed their slave status. No such option was available to Africans in American slavery—a point driven home by a bathing scene in Frederick Douglass's *Narrative* when a young Douglass attempts to wash the skin off his body in the hopes that his transition from the plantation to the city will mean a transition in status. See Berman, "The Barbarous Voice of Democracy."

40. Eliza Bradley, *An Authentic Narrative of the Shipwreck and Suffering of Mrs. Eliza Bradley, the wife of Capt. James Bradley of Liverpool*, p. 255 (emphasis mine).

41. Allan D. Austin, *African Muslims in Antebellum America: Transatlantic Stories and Spiritual Struggles*, p. 11.

42. Sylviane A. Diouf, *Servants of Allah: African Muslims Enslaved in the Americas*, p. 100.

43. Ibid., p. 98; Austin, *African Muslims in Antebellum America*, pp. 473–74.

44. Gayatri Chakravorty Spivak, "Postcoloniality and Value." For a discussion of the catachrestic space and Spivak's formulation of it, see Homi Bhabha's *The Location of Culture*, pp. 171–97.

45. John Michael, "Beyond Us and Them: Identity and Terror from an Arab American's Perspective." "As figments of the Western imagination, the Arab's romantic identity has been and continues to be terribly useful for the maintenance of power" (p. 704).

46. Slavoj Žižek, *The Sublime Object of Ideology*, p. 109; discussed in Bhabha, *The Location of Culture*, pp. 184–85.

47. I am speaking here of President Obama's decision to have the United States participate in the military ouster of Mu'ammar Qaddafi, albeit largely through the auspices of the United Nations. I find it, at the very least, curious that Libya and not, at the point of this

writing, Yemen, Bahrain, Tunisia, Egypt, or Syria was chosen as an appropriate venue for the exercise of American military intervention in the name of humanitarian causes.

NOTES TO CHAPTER 2

1. Victor Wolfgang Von Hagen writes in his introduction to *Incidents of Travel in Egypt, Arabia Petraea, and the Holy Land*, "Within two years *Arabia Petraea* had sold 21,000 copies—this at a time when America's population was scarcely 20,000,000, of which only a fraction was literate as far as book reading was concerned" (p. xl). Harper and Brothers' sales records indicate that *Arabia Petraea* was in print up to 1882.

2. Edgar Allan Poe, "Review of Stephens' 'Arabia Petraea,'" in *Complete Tales and Poems*, p. 563. The review originally appeared in the *New York Review*, October 1837.

3. For a discussion of this passage, see Obenzinger, *American Palestine*, pp. 63–64.

4. John Lloyd Stephens, *Incidents of Travel in Egypt, Arabia Petraea, and the Holy Land*, p. 153 (hereafter cited in the text as *Incidents*).

5. The *Boston Daily Advertiser* is a particularly prominent example of the role newspapers played in advocating railways. It was owned by Nathan Hale, known as "The Father of the American Railroad."

6. See Richard Slotkin, *Regeneration through Violence: The Myth of the American Frontier, 1600–1860*.

7. Ibn Khaldun, *Muqaddimah: An Introduction to History*, p. 118 (hereafter cited in the text).

8. In Bruce Lawrence's words, "civilization [in Khaldun's theory] is everywhere marked by the fundamental difference between urban and primitive, producing a tension that is also an interplay between nomad and merchant, desert and city, orality and literacy." Bruce B. Lawrence, introduction to *Muqaddimah*, p. x.

9. For more on this subject, see Hourani, *Arabic Thought in the Liberal Age*, chapter 4.

10. Michael Rogin's *Fathers and Children: Andrew Jackson and the Subjugation of the American Indian* is still the best work on this subject in my opinion.

11. Mutability, not only of character but also of racial designation, over the course of generations is a consistent theme in Khaldun's *Muqaddimah*. To wit, in discussing race, Khaldun asserts, "Negroes from the south who settle in the temperate fourth zone or in seventh zone that tends toward whiteness, are found to produce descendants whose colour gradually turns white in the course of time" (p. 60). Khaldun, though he does generate some disturbingly racist opinions in the *Muqaddimah*, nevertheless attacks one of the basic tenets of nineteenth-century American racism—the idea that people with black-color skin were the descendants of Ham and thus cursed. "To generalize and say that the inhabitants of a specific geographical location in the south or in the north are the descendants of such-and-such a well-known person because they have a common colour, trait, or physical mark which their forefather had, is one of those errors caused by disregard, both of the true nature of created beings and of geographical facts" (pp. 61–62).

12. See Marshall G. S. Hodgson, *The Venture of Islam*; and Marshall G. S. Hodgson, "Hemispheric Inter-regional History as an Approach to World History," p. 717.

13. As Muhsin Mahdi explains, "It must be emphasized that Ibn Khaldun is devising and using technical terms to describe relationships among types of social phenomena which had been abstracted from the concrete data of history and made the objects of theoretical science." Muhsin Mahdi, *Ibn Khaldun's Philosophy of History: A Study in the Philosophic Foundation of the Science of Culture*, p. 194n. 7.

14. See Walter J. Fischel, *Ibn Khaldun and Tamerlane*.

15. Bhabha, *The Location of Culture*, p. 66.

16. Ibid., p. 67.

17. The model for my interpretation of *figura* comes from Erich Auerbach's seminal work on the subject in "The Figura" (translated by Ralph Manheim), in *Scenes from the Drama of European Literature*.

18. Ibid, p. 12.

19. Fascinating work has been done on the Argentine reformer contemporary with Stephens, Domingo Faustino Sarmiento, and his use of Orientalism as well as the figure of the Bedouin to establish Argentine national identity. Sarmiento describes Argentine gauchos as American Bedouins. See D. F. Sarmiento, *Life in the Argentine Republic in the Days of the Tyrants; or, Civilization and Barbarism*. For critical work on Sarmiento, see Mary Louise Pratt, *Imperial Eyes: Travel Writing and Transculturation*; and Christina Civantos, *Between Argentines and Arabs: Argentine Orientalism, Arab Immigrants, and the Writing of Identity*. The Iraqi traveler to South America Ilyas bin al-Qissas Hanna al-Mawsuli also compares Peruvian Indians to Arab Bedouins in his seventeenth-century account. See Ilyas Hanna al-Mawsuli, *Kitab Siryahat al-Khoury Ilyas bin al-Qissees Hanna al Mawsuli*.

20. John Lewis Burckhardt, *Notes on the Bedouins and Wahabys, Collected during His Travels in the East*, vol. 1, p. 32 (hereafter cited in the text as *Notes*).

21. For more on Twain's approach to the Holy Land in *Innocents Abroad*, see Obenzinger's *American Palestine*.

22. For an erudite analysis of the phenomenon of using the Near Eastern milieu to project narratives about American values across a global field in a slightly different context, see Timothy Marr's "Muslims, Millennialism, and Missionaries," in *The Cultural Roots of American Islamicism*.

23. Pratt, *Imperial Eyes*.

24. Sarah Rogers Haight, *Letters from the Old World*, vol. 2, p. 30 (hereafter cited in the text as *Letters*).

25. Arnold Krupat, *The Voice in the Margin: Native American Literature and the Canon*, pp. 149–50.

26. George Catlin, *North American Indians*, p. 2.

27. From the beginning, Catlin hoped ultimately to sell his "Indian Gallery" paintings to the U.S. government. His depictions of "primitive looks and customs" attempted to capitalize on the narrative of permanent destruction that he helped create both visually and

verbally. In a sense, Catlin manufactured exactly the "scarce" cultural capital he hoped to cash in on by producing stereotyped Indians for public consumption.

28. Mordecai Manuel Noah, *Discourse on the Evidences of the American Indians Being the Descendants of the Lost Tribes of Israel, Delivered before the Mercantile Library Association*, p. 28 (hereafter cited in text as *Evidences*).

29. John Winthrop, "A Modell of Christian Charity," p. 180.

30. The debate about Winthrop's intentions by using the term "city upon a hill"—whether it was invoked to create a sense of America as a potential world-redeeming beacon or invoked more anxiously as a caution against setting a bad example—goes back to Sacvan Bercovitch's engagement with Perry Miller's "errand in the wilderness" thesis that the "American character" was shaped by "the fact of the frontier." Bercovitch argues that we need not discount the validity of the frontier thesis to recognize that it does not explain the persistence of the Puritan jeremiad as a form of American literary expression. I am not so much concerned with Winthrop's intentions here as with a mode of viewing American space that connects Puritan colonial rhetoric and Jacksonian expansionist rhetoric through figures, figurations, and co-options of the Near East, as well as Near Eastern geographical names. See Bercovitch, *The American Jeremiad*; and Miller, *Errand into the Wilderness*.

31. Obenzinger, *American Palestine*, p. 5.

32. Ibn Battutah, *The Travels of Ibn Battutah*, p. 43.

33. Muhammad Ali himself was of Albanian heritage, not Turkish heritage. Nevertheless, he is consistently marked as a "Turk" by American travel writers. See note 35.

34. See Marr, "Islamicism and Counterdespotism in Early National Cultural Expression" in *The Cultural Roots of American Islamicism*.

35. Muhammad Ali, appointed viceroy of Egypt in 1805 following a power vacuum caused by the exit of the French and the fall of the Mamelukes, was born in what is present-day Greece (Kavala). Stephens and other Euro-American travelers refer to Ali as Turkish to indicate his association with the Ottoman Empire, but this designation also reflects the fact that in the Ottoman Empire the most important identity feature was one's religious affiliation. See Khaled Fahmy, "The Era of Muhammad 'Ali Pasha, 1805–1848."

36. Timothy Marr discusses the idealized imperialism modeled in American representations of the despotic Islamic Orient in his chapter "Islamicism and Counterdespotism," in *The Cultural Roots of American Islamicism*.

37. For an analysis of "sauntering" as it relates to the Holy Land travel narrative, via Henry David Thoreau's essay "Walking," see Brian Yothers, *Romance of the Holy Land in American Travel Writing, 1790–1876*, p. 6.

38. For the marking of West African Muslims as Arabs/Moors, see Berman, "The Barbarous Voice of Democracy." See also Diouf, *Servants of Allah*; and Austin, *African Muslims in Antebellum America*.

39. David F. Dorr, *A Colored Man round the World*, p. 11 (hereafter cited in the text as *CM*).

40. See Alex Lubin's fascinating work on this subject in his essay "The Black Middle East," in Evelyn Alsultaney and Ella Shohat's *The Cultural Politics of the Middle East in the*

Americas (forthcoming from University of Michigan Press). My discussion of Dorr has benefited a great deal from Lubin's work.

41. Trafton, *Egypt Land*, p. 16.

42. Randal W. MacGavock, *A Tennessean Abroad, or Letters from Europe, Africa and Asia*, p. 216.

43. Ibid., p. 217.

44. Martin Delany espoused a similar geography of freedom in describing the slave's passage through American space in his 1859 proto-black-nationalist novel of slave insurrection, *Blake; or, The Huts of America*. Henry, the novel's revolutionary-minded hero, explains to a group of runaway slaves the importance of an alternative geographical consciousness to their prospects of freedom. It is a geographical consciousness that contrasts natural markers with the unnatural manufacture of lines that divide the world into free and slave states. "When the North star cannot be seen you must depend alone upon nature as your guide," Henry insists. "Feel, in the dark, around the trunks or bodies of trees, especially oak, and whenever you feel moss on the bark, that side on which the moss grows is always to the north" (p. 153). Henry's alternative means of mapping American space through a geography of freedom resonates with Dorr's extranational mapping of American freedom through use of the Jordan.

45. Phillis Wheatley, "To Rev. Samson Occam, New London, Connecticut," p. 823.

46. Michael Gomez, *Black Crescent: The Experience and Legacy of African Muslims in the Americas*, p. 218.

47. *Blake* first appeared in serial form in 1859 issues of the *Weekly Anglo-African*.

48. Delany, *Blake*, p. 83 (hereafter cited in the text).

49. Martin R. Delany, *The Condition, Elevation, Emigration and Destiny of the Colored People of the United States*, p. 12.

50. Paul Gilroy, *The Black Atlantic: Modernity and Double Consciousness*, p. 23. Gilroy's first chapter contains an informative discussion of Delany's "Zionism."

51. For an analysis of Egypt's role in nineteenth-century American racial politics, see Trafton, *Egypt Land*.

52. Nathaniel Hawthorne, *The Blithedale Romance*, p. 180.

53. Though Petra was never actually lost from historical memory, its rediscovery is attributed to the Swiss adventurer-traveler John Lewis Burckhardt, who, disguised as a Muslim, convinced some Bedouins from a nearby village to guide him into Petra's environs in 1812. The story goes that Burckhardt only got a glimpse of Petra before his guides became suspicious, and he made a hasty exit after sacrificing a goat at the temple of Aaron (Haroun). Petra can more accurately be said to have been misplaced than lost by Islamic geographers in the interim between the fourth century and the nineteenth century. To wit, it appears on the famous Peutinger Table, a twelfth-century copy of a map of Roman period trade and population centers. For more on Petra, its myths, and its modern excavation, see Phillip C. Hammond, "Petra—Myth and Reality."

54. All of this Western "discovery" discourse ignored the fact that the site had existed uninterrupted in Bedouin historical consciousness, if not in Western historiography.

Usama ibn Munqidh's twelfth-century biography mentions a "cave of the seven sleepers" in the desert near Amman which can only be approached through a "narrow cleft." See Usama Ibn Munqidh, *The Book of Contemplation*, p. 23. The cave, or *khawf*, is mentioned in the Qur'an (18:9–26) but is not specifically located. Munqidh adds an interesting anecdote about how "no son of adultery" can pass through the cleft. Phillip Hitti creditably suggests in his translation of the Islamic courtier's text that Munqidh is referring to Petra. See Philip K. Hitti, *An Arab-Syrian Gentleman and Warrior in the Period of the Crusades: Memoirs of Usama ibn Munqidh*, p. 39.

55. Herman Melville, "Bartleby the Scrivener," p. 23 (emphasis mine).

56. For more on the plight of the clerk in nineteenth-century America in general and Bartleby in particular, see Thomas Augst, *The Clerk's Tale: Young Men and Moral Life in Nineteenth-Century America*.

57. See Donald Ringe, *The Pictorial Mode: Space and Time in the Art of Irving, Bryant, and Cooper*.

58. Herman Melville, *Redburn; His First Voyage*, p. 4 (emphasis mine).

59. Ibid., p. 4.

60. David Roberts (1796–1864), a Scottish topographical painter and illustrator, visited the site for five and a half days in March 1839. Ten years later, in 1849, he published twenty tinted lithograph views of Petra and its environs. See Katharine Sim, *David Roberts R.A. 1796–1864: A Biography*, pp. 63–181. The London-born Edward Lear, also a painter-illustrator, visited for one day in April 1858. He did not publish his narrative of the journey until 1897, but he did exhibit an easel painting entitled *Petra* at the Royal Academy in London in 1872. See Vivian Nokes, *Edward Lear, 1812–1888*, pp. 110–11. Gerald Carr speculates that Church may have been aware of Lear's painting because Church owned a copy of Lear's *Journals of a Landscape Painter in Albania, Illyria, &c.* (London: Richard Bentley, 1852), given to him by John McClure. See Gerald Carr, *Frederic Edwin Church: Catalogue Raisonne of Works of Art at Olana State Historic Site*, p. 387.

61. Carr, *Frederic Edwin Church*, p. 389.

62. I am indebted to Angela Miller for this reference. She writes, "The earliest cited example of the term 'imperial' given by the *Oxford English Dictionary* is from the October 1858 *Westminister Review*. Despite the general shift in meaning, it continued to serve as a term of opprobrium, particularly among Whig writers. In 'The President and His Administration,' *American Review*, n.s., 1 (May 1848): p. 439, the term is used to criticize the behavior of the Democratic administration in the Mexican-American War." Angela Miller, *The Empire of the Eye: Landscape Representation and American Cultural Politics, 1825–1875*, p. 39.

63. Carr, *Frederic Edwin Church*, p. 391.

64. The quotation is from M. Leon Laborde and L. M. A. Linant, *Journey through Arabia Petraea, to Mount Sinai, and the Excavated City of Petra, the Edom of Prophecies*, p. 175.

65. Carr opines about the association of Cole's *Desolation* and Church's *El Khasne'*, "Church's use of the word *desolation* conjures a comparison between Cat. No. 469 (*El Khasne*) and Thomas Cole's painting *Desolation* from *The Course of Empire*. The analogy

is tempting because in 1885 Church singled out the picture as his master's best and most moving work, and in 1888 he acquired a canvas by Cole of a related subject, *View of a Protestant Cemetery at Rome*" (*Frederic Edwin Church*, p. 323). The quotation about Cole's *Desolation* comes from Church's letter to John D. Champlin, Hudson, September 11, 1885, excerpted in Carr, *Frederic Edwin Church*.

66. Carr writes,

[Church] may well have conceived El Khasne Petra for himself and his family. He certainly retained it as a gift for his wife, as a striking memento of his expedition in the Near East in general, and an enhancement of the Near Eastern accent at Olana. He installed it above the fireplace on the north wall of the Sitting Room of Olana by the end of 1875. That he associated the room, the painting, and Mrs. Church is evident from his preliminary drawing for the fireplace of the Sitting Room, in which George A. Baker, Jr.'s portrait of Isabel Church appears over the gable of the fireplace. That association also reinforces the argument for a fundamentally optimistic interpretation of the painting. By 1880, the couple named their home Olana, after an ancient "fortress" and "treasure storehouse" in northern Persia, mentioned in Strabo's *Geography*. In that context, "El Khasne" became a synonym for Olana. (*Frederic Edwin Church*, p. 395)

67. Battutah, *The Travels of Ibn Battutah*, p. 25.

68. For an extended discussion of Bedouin tracking methods, see Wilfred Thessiger, *Arabian Sands*.

NOTES TO CHAPTER 3

1. William Carlos Williams, *Paterson*, p. 222.

2. M. Norton Wise, "What Can Local Circulation Explain? The Case of Helmholtz's Frog-Drawing Machine in Berlin," p. 20.

3. William Carlos Williams, *In the American Grain*, p. 221 (hereafter cited in the text as *AG*).

4. The tendency toward a dehistoricized reading of Poe's aesthetics continued through the twentieth century. For a succinct account of the different stages of Poe's critical reception that is implicitly critical of this dehistoricized tendency, see Donald Pease, "Poe and Historicity."

5. Talal Asad, *Formations of the Secular: Christianity, Islam, Modernism*, p. 52.

6. For more on the relation between Poe's criticism and his poetry, see Robert von Hallberg, "Edgar Allan Poe, Poet-Critic."

7. For the development of the cult of the genius in the eighteenth century, see Gloria Flaherty, *Shamanism and the Eighteenth Century*.

8. Asad, *Formations of the Secular*, p. 53.

9. Kilito, *Thou Shalt Not Speak My Language*, p. 9 (hereafter cited in the text as *ML*).

10. See G. R. Thompson's 1989 essay "Romantic Arabesque, Contemporary Theory, and Postmodernism: The Example of Poe's *Narrative*." Positing the arabesque as a "literary form or genre involving elaborately framed designs and ironic strategies that disturb illusion and narrative convention" (p. 219), Thompson argues that the design pattern provides a cipher for understanding Poe's version of romance. Thompson's understanding of the arabesque's formal qualities is grounded in German Romanticism and Friedrich Schlegel's theory of romantic irony. For Schlegel, the romantic arabesque laid bare the illusion of literature as such and promoted the formal ambiguity, ambivalence, and self-consciousness he admired, but it had little or no association with actual Arabians. For Thompson, the arabesque is a symbol through which to demonstrate a theory of influence almost entirely oriented to the West. When Thompson does acknowledge Arabic sources for Poe's own use of the arabesque, he refers to "the *Rubaiyat* of the Persian Omar Khayyam" (p. 201), the design patterns found in "Persian carpets," and the story cycle known as the *Arabian Nights*. The first two Persian sources are not actually Arab or the products of an Arabic-language culture but rather represent the conflation of one Islamic culture, Persian, into another, Arab. The final source, the *Arabian Nights*, is, arguably, as much an invention of Western imagination as it is of Arab culture. In reality, the *Nights* were translated into Arabic from ancient Persian (and perhaps had earlier sources in ancient Indian literature) and were not the product of popular Arab literature but rather a work that, in Dwight Reynolds's words, had existed in "its own cultural context in nearly complete obscurity." Dwight F. Reynolds, "The 1001 Nights: A History of the Text and Its Reception," pp. 270–91. As Reynolds points out, "only nine of the twenty-one stories in Galland's *Nights* are drawn from Arabic manuscripts of *Alf Layla wa-Layla*. Galland, however, never informed his readers that later volumes of his *Mill et une nuit . . .* were not drawn from Arabic manuscripts; in fact, he deliberately misled his audience by indirectly referring to the manuscripts in the introductions to the final volumes" (p. 279).

11. Hourani, *Arabic Thought in the Liberal Age*.

12. Al-Azhar, located in Cairo, is the most renowned center for Islamic studies in the world.

13. For more on al-Tahtawi and his significance, see Daniel L. Newman's introduction to *An Imam in Paris: Account of a Stay in France by an Egyptian Cleric (1826–1831)*.

14. Daniel L. Newman, "Myths and Realities in Muslim Alterist Discourse: Arab Travelers in Europe in the Age of the *Nahda* (19th C.)," p. 15.

15. For *waTin*, see Rifa'a Rafi' al-Tahtawi, *An Imam in Paris: Account of a Stay in France by an Egyptian Cleric (1826–1831)*, p. 145 (hereafter cited in the text as *Takhlis*). For *hurriyya*, see ibid., p. 196. Al-Tahtawi uses the word *hurriyya* in relation to personal freedom, in distinction from its traditional use in opposition to the word for enslaved.

16. Beyond providing access to European texts, al-Tahtawi's translation school also had another function: it Arabized Ottoman Egyptian thought by both replacing Ottoman translators (who were largely Turkic, Greek, or Armenian peoples) with Arabic-speaking Egyptians and changing the preferred language of translation from Ottoman Turkish to Arabic.

17. It would be almost impossible to overstate al-Tahtawi's significance to Arab reformism. A respected al-Azhar imam and a favorite of the Pasha Mohammad Ali, al-Tahtawi had immense influence in nineteenth-century Egypt and, especially, on Egyptian education. He literally rewrote the standard educational material for Egyptian primary schools, modeling his texts on French educational material. There is an excellent translation of al-Tahtawi's account of his stay in France (*Takhlis al-Ibriz fi Talkhis Bariz aw al-Diwan al-Nafis bi-wan Baris*), complete with an illuminating introduction, cited in note 14.

18. For more on this concept of constructing beginnings as opposed to finding origins, see Edward Said, *Beginnings: Intention and Method*.

19. Abu Nuwas, "Jinan," p. 206.

20. For more on the pre-Islamic ode, see Michael Sells's introduction to *Desert Tracings: Six Classic Arabian Odes*.

21. The traditional pre-Islamic Bedouin long poem, known as a *tawil*, is broken into three parts: an erotic ingress known as a *nasib*, a journey section, and the section where the poet delivers his final message.

22. Edgar Allan Poe, "Ligeia," in *Complete Tales and Poems of Edgar Allan Poe*, p. 657 (hereafter cited in the text as *CT*).

23. The name Rowena evokes Sir Walter Scott, but Poe, I would argue, uses the name to differentiate his conception of romance from the way Scott and other writers of his ilk understood the term. Poe, in other words, was consciously revising the romantic medievalism of Scott and his American counterpart Washington Irving, who like Poe, described his tales as arabesque. Poe's engagement with the term *arabesque* marks a shift in the meaning of the word *romance* in American literature. The emergence of a distinct sphere of "literary" narrative in American culture during the middle decades of the nineteenth century followed a transatlantic trend that had brought similar theorizations of the role of literature and the professional writer to England and Germany several decades earlier. In America, Poe, as both professional critic and professional writer, was at the vanguard of this movement, theorizing literature as a domain not guided by political, national, or generic concerns but rather by "the purest rules of Art" (quoted in Jonathan Arac, *The Emergence of American Literary Narrative, 1820–1860*, p. 66). Words such as "originality," "genius," and "imagination" defined his "elsewhere" of the purely "literary" sphere, as they had in England and Germany. The catchwords Poe preached were found in seminal nineteenth-century romantic texts such as Samuel Taylor Coleridge's *Biographia Literaria* (which Poe had enthusiastically reviewed). But they were also key elements of German romanticism's theorization of aesthetic modernity. "These Romantic premises," Jonathan Arac points out, "held that the traditional generic categories and divisions between high and low, serious and comic modes, no longer pertained and through a mixture of these levels or tones, the strongest, and most appropriately modern, effect could be achieved" (ibid., p. 69).

24. Edgar Allan Poe, "Review of Hawthorne—Twice-Told Tales," *Graham's Magazine*, May 1842, p. 299.

25. In the critical treatise "The Philosophy of Furniture," the arabesque pattern indexes the self-reflection the essay attempts to cultivate, mirroring the decorator's cultural

sophistication back to him through the vehicle of design. In Poe's tales, however, the narrative result of self-reflective encounters with one's own "arabesque" taste is invariably death for the individual and an Usher-esque collapse of the domestic sphere. The materiality of the medium of self-reflection remains invisible in these moments of confrontation with subjectivity. It would be impossible, for instance, to draw one of Poe's arabesques because nowhere in his tales does Poe detail their physical attributes. In Poe's criticism, the arabesque stands for rational order; in his tales, it violates that order through its unruly transformations.

26. For more on the tale "Ligeia" as it relates to the occult, see Dorothea von Mücke, *The Seduction of the Occult and the Rise of the Fantastic Tale*. Von Mücke posits that the arabesque, in this story, illustrates the imaginary materiality of the signifier: "the arabesque—situated at the threshold between the linearity of the two-dimensional composition of an image and the three-dimensional perspectival illusion of space—has been used to illustrate the imaginary materiality of the signifier" (p. 189). Von Mücke analyzes the three-dimensional vivification of the arabesque in "Ligeia" as a form of cultural anxiety. She claims that Poe was expressing his age's anxiety over print culture and the transformation of three-dimensional printing presses.

27. Poe, "The Philosophy of Furniture," pp. 243–44.

28. For more on Poe and race, see Toni Morrison, *Playing in the Dark: Whiteness and the Literary Imagination*; and J. Gerald Kennedy and Liliane Weissberg, eds., *Romancing the Shadow: Poe and Race*.

29. Walter Benjamin's analysis of the baroque German *Trauerspiel* is particularly helpful to understanding the dynamics of transference that takes place in Poe's own baroque short story. "Mourning is a state of mind in which feeling revives the empty world in the form of a mask," explains Benjamin, "and derives an enigmatic satisfaction in contemplating it." Benjamin, *The Origin of German Tragic Drama*, p. 138. In "Ligeia," the Lady Rowena is masked with the features of the mourned Ligeia.

30. Majnun Layla (Qays ibn al-Mulawahh) was a literal contemporary of the prophet Muhammad and the mythic originator of the love lyric in Arabic poetry, what came to be known as a *ghazel*. For more details on this story and its intercultural reinterpretations, see Maria Rosa Menocal, *Shards of Love: Exile and the Origins of the Lyric*.

31. Michael A. Sells, introduction to *Stations of Desire: Love Elegies from Ibn Arabi and New Poems*. p. 37.

32. R. W. J. Austin, "Introductory Note to Chapter II," in *Bezels of Wisdom*, by Ibn Arabi, p. 61.

33. Ibid.

34. See the somewhat outdated but still useful Duncan Black Macdonald, *The Development of Muslim Theology, Jurisprudence and Constitutional Theory*, pp. 215–42.

35. Mohammad al-Ghazali, *Al-Munqidh min al-Dalal* (hereafter cited in the text as *Munqidh*), p. 79. Al-Ghazali's invocation of the heuristic capacity of fear and especially of fear of the fire might be productively compared and contrasted to a strain of Puritan theology in American religious history, perhaps best represented by Jonathan Edwards's sermon "Sinners in the Hands of an Angry God." In this respect, see Miller, *Errand into the Wilderness*.

36. Mohammad al-Ghazali, *Ihya 'Ulum al-Din*, p. 36.

37. Al-Ghazali's approach to asceticism and the way in which it distinguishes the pleasures of this life from those of the hereafter is echoed by generations of Muslim writers. However, mid-nineteenth-century contact with European culture placed these Islamic meditations on materialism in the context of *nahda* debates about modernization and tradition. The nineteenth-century Moroccan envoy to France, Mohammad as-Saffar, provides a good example. After breathlessly narrating the wonders to be found in the French Jardin des Plantes, Bibliothèque National, and Royal Palace, as-Saffar assuages his Arabic readers' potential sense of inferiority by contrasting a vocabulary of materialism with a vocabulary of spiritualism. As-Saffar reminds his readers, "To some He gave a good life in this world, and for others He reserved the pleasures of the hereafter." Driving home the point, as-Saffar quotes the Qur'an: "Do not gaze longingly at what We have given some of them to enjoy, the finery of this present life: We test them through this (20:131)." See Kilito, *Thou Shalt Not Speak My Language*, p. 65.

38. Dayan, *Fables of Mind*, p. 185.

39. In the preface to *Alhambra*, Irving, as Poe had done in the preface to *Tales of the Grotesque and Arabesque*, describes his tales as "arabesque" (preface to *The Alhambra: A Series of Tales and Sketches*, p. 4), but the difference in their uses of the term is instructive. Irving emphasized verisimilitude in his "arabesque" sketches of Spain. Poe's "arabesque" tales sought not to depict real life on the page but rather to have the page come alive for the reader. For Irving, the arabesque is denotative; for Poe, it is connotative. Poe uses the term *arabesque* to indicate a psychological terror that does not rely on cultural difference for effect but rather embodies the self-sustaining power of affect. The narrator of "The Fall of the House of Usher" comments on Usher's appearance, "I could not, even with effort, connect its Arabesque expression with any idea of simple humanity." Edgar Allan Poe, "The Fall of the House of Usher," p. 234. The inimitable Usher, who models the fusion of reading with direct experience, stands as an "Arabesque expression." Here the term "expression" plays on the relationship between the physical body and the power of words. The "Arabesque" Usher conflates the difference between the two. The confrontation with the occult Usher is a confrontation with the abstracted terror of the sublime, not with the locatable "other" of contact narratives steeped in romantic medievalism. Usher is both medium and message.

40. Lois Ibn Faruqi, "Muwashshah: A Vocal Form in Islamic Culture."

41. Ernst Kuhnel, *Arabesque: Meaning and Transformation of an Ornament*, p. 8.

42. Ibn Arabi, *The Bezels of Wisdom*, p. 88 (hereafter cited in text as *Bezels*).

43. The intricacies of the doctrines of *tanzih* and *tashbih* are far too complex for discussion here, but this brief sketch allows us to grasp the sense of Arabi's poem and should suffice for the analysis which follows. For a more detailed discussion of these terms, especially in relation to Ibn Arabi, see Sachiko Murata and William C. Chittick, *The Vision of Islam*.

44. See William C. Chittick, *The Self-Disclosures of God: Ibn Arabi's Cosmology*; and William C. Chittick, *Imaginal Worlds: Ibn al-Arabi and the Problem of Religious Diversity*.

45. Though Ibn Arabi never used the phrase himself, the idea is implicit throughout his work. It was Ibn Tammiya who associated Ibn Arabi with the concept of *wahdat al wojud* and attacked him for it.

46. Riegl, *Historical Grammar of the Visual Arts*, p. 30.

47. Asad, *Formations of the Secular*, pp. 13–14.

48. For the presence of Oriental tales in leading mid-nineteenth-century American magazines, such as the *Democratic Review* and the *Knickerbocker*, see Dorothee Metlitzky Finkelstein, *Melville's Orienada*.

49. M. H. Abrams, *The Mirror and the Lamp: Romantic Theory and the Critical Condition*.

50. See Walt Whitman, *Specimen Days and Collect*, p. 157. "That figure of my lurid dream might stand for Edgar Poe, his spirit, his fortunes, and his poems—all lurid dreams."

51. M. H. Abrams, *Natural Supernaturalism: Tradition and Revolution in Romantic Literature*.

52. Austin, "Introductory Note to Chapter I," in *Bezels*, p. 48.

53. For more on Emerson and the political ramifications of his transparent vision, see Christopher Newfield, *The Emerson Effect: Individualism and Submission in America*; as well as Jay Grossman, *Reconstituting the American Renaissance: Emerson, Whitman, and the Politics of Representation*, particularly chapter 3.

54. I am referring to a concept coined by Wai Chee Dimock in her book *Through Other Continents: American Literature across Deep Time* and in particular her discussion of Hafiz and Emerson to be found in chapter 2, "World Religions: Emerson, Hafiz, Christianity, Islam." While I find Dimock's argument to be compelling and rendered with eloquence, I also feel as though there is an aspect of transnational exchange that reveals these cross-cultural influences to be more jagged, jarring, and at times, frankly, violent. This is especially so in Americans' (by which I mean both North and South Americans) use of the image of the Arab to structure nationalist sentiments that more often than not relied on models of exclusion.

NOTES TO CHAPTER 4

1. Claude McKay, *A Long Way from Home*, p. 338 (hereafter cited in the text).

2. Claude McKay, "Morocco," in *Complete Poems*, p. 234, l. 18. For a complete history of the publication of "Farewell to Morocco" and a copy of several different versions of the poem, see Claude McKay, *Complete Poems*, edited by William J. Maxwell, pp. 362–64. Maxwell comments that in *A Long Way from Home*, "McKay introduces the poem with a dose of appreciative Orientalism" (p. 364).

3. This document has been the source of much discussion and some controversy but can justifiably be called an ur-text of American Islamic literature. See Muhammad al-Ahari, *Five Classic Muslim Slave Narratives*; Ronald A. T. Judy, *(Dis)Forming the American Canon: African-Arabic Slave Narratives and the American Vernacular*; and Joseph

Progler, "Reading Early American Islamica: An Interpretive Translation of the Ben Ali Diary."

4. For biographical information on Timothy Drew, the best source is the suggestive information provided by Peter Lamborn Wilson, *Sacred Drift: Essays on the Margins of Islam.* See also Gomez, *Black Crescent;* and Sherman Jackson, *Islam and the Blackamerican: Looking toward the Third Resurrection.*

5. For more on black fraternal orders, see Maurice O. Wallace, *Constructing the Black Masculine: Identity and Ideality in African American Men's Literature and Culture, 1775–1995.*

6. For more on black Freemasons, see Alton G. Roundtree and Paul M. Bessel, *Out of the Shadows: The Emergence of Prince Hall Freemasonry in America.*

7. For more on the connection between African secret societies and African American fraternal organizations, see Michael Gomez, *Exchanging Our Country Marks: The Transformation of African Identities in the Colonial and Antebellum South.*

8. For speculations on W. D. Fard's identity and connection to Noble Drew Ali, see Michael Muhammad Knight, *Blue-Eyed Devil: A Road Odyssey through Islamic America.*

9. Wilson, *Sacred Drift,* pp. 13–50; Gomez, *Black Crescent,* pp. 203–75.

10. Ruben Johnson-Bey, who knew Noble Drew Ali firsthand, keeps this tradition alive and lives next door to the temple.

11. For this background information, see Gomez, *Black Crescent;* Wilson, *Sacred Drift.*

12. Quoted in Gomez, *Black Crescent,* p. 224, from materials found at the end of a 1996 reprint of *The Circle Seven Koran,* p. xvi.

13. Situated literally and figuratively between Europe and Africa, between whiteness and blackness, and between Christianity and Islam, the figure of the Moor opened up a space in transatlantic discourse where questions of individual and national identity had been negotiated for centuries. The term *Moor* predates Islam and has its etymological roots in a third-century BC Numidian kingdom in North Africa known as *Maure.* "They were called Maurisi by the Greeks," wrote Strabo, "and Mauri by the Romans" (Strabo, *Geographica,* 18.3.2, quoted in Rene Basset, *Moorish Literature,* p. iii). In the Classical Roman period, after the empire conquered a large swath of northern and western Africa known as Mauritania, the people inhabiting the region were referred to as *Mauri.* In the medieval period, when the Islamic caliphate stretched its sphere of influence into southern Spain, ruling it under the name of *al-Andalus,* Iberian Muslims were referred to as Moors. By the sixteenth century, European traders and travelers used the term *Mauri* to distinguish ethnic Berber and Arab peoples who spoke the Hasaniyya dialect of Arabic and lived in northern and western Africa. By the nineteenth century, the term *Moor* was used by Americans and Europeans in North Africa to refer to the Arabs and/or Berbers who lived in the city rather than in the desert or mountains. Joseph Dupuis, British vice consul at Mogadore, Morocco, at the beginning of the nineteenth century, described a particular group living in western Barbary as "the inhabitants of the cities or towns, who may be collectively known under the general denomination of Moor; although this name is only known to them

through the language of Europeans" (Robert Adams, *The Narrative of Robert Adams, a Barbary Captive*, p. 141). Consistently used since antiquity by people living north of the Mediterranean to refer to a range of darker "others," be they Berbers, Arabs, or Muslim Iberians, the term *Moor* has no ethnological value. Instead, it is a figural invention of European discourse, with no correspondent in either Berber or Arab histories of self-identification. The history of the term *Moor*'s Mediterranean exchanges, in turn, influenced its transatlantic passages. Just as it had been used in the Mediterranean context to organize the relation between race and religion, the term *Moor* came to have a similar function in American vernacular, often employed as a description of sub-Saharan Muslim slaves who had been transplanted to the Southern United States. As has been discussed already, marking a black African slave as a Moor usually remarked on his or her intelligence, regal carriage, and self-esteem, remaking him or her into an Arab African, though in point of fact they were not Arabs or Moors at all.

14. For references to this story, see Wilson, *Sacred Drift*, p. 18.

15. Edward Wilmot Blyden offers a model of earlier black nationalism that incorporated aspects of Islam but looked toward Ethiopia and Egypt, not North Africa. See Blyden, *Christianity, Islam and the Negro Race*.

16. Antar is Antarah ibn Shaddad al-Absi. Born a slave, Antar was the son of Shaddad, a well-respected member of the tribe Banu Abs, and Zaibabah, an Ethiopian whom Sheddad had enslaved in tribal warfare.

17. David Levering Lewis, *When Harlem Was in Vogue*, p. 115.

18. Ibid., p. 117

19. W. E. B. DuBois, *The Souls of Black Folk*, p. 221.

20. David Louis-Brown, *Waves of Decolonization: Discourses of Race and Hemispheric Citizenship in Cuba, Mexico, and the United States*, p. 1.

21. Ibid., p. 3.

22. Jason R. Young, "Between the Crescent and the Cross: W. E. B. DuBois on Christianity and Islam," p. 211.

23. W. E. B. DuBois, *The Negro*, pp. 16, 50.

24. DuBois, *The World and Africa: An Inquiry into the Part Which Africa Has Played in World History*, p. 183.

25. DuBois, *Black Folk Then and Now*, p. 53.

26. On Al Jolson and racial minstrelsy, see Michael Paul Rogin, *Black Face, White Noise: Jewish Immigrants and the Hollywood Melting Pot*.

27. For more on the connections between deracination and uplift discourse, see Kevin K. Gaines, *Uplifting the Race: Black Leadership, Politics, and Culture in the Twentieth Century*.

28. DuBois, *The World and Africa*, p. 185.

29. *Pittsburgh Courier*, October 5, 1929, p. 11.

30. Henry Louis Gates, Jr., marks the period between 1895 and the 1920s as the moment when an explosion of writings about the trope of the New Negro emerged. In these writings, the New Negro is distinguished from the compliant "Old Negro" familiar

from plantation stereotypes. See Henry Louis Gates, Jr., "The Trope of a New Negro and the Reconstruction of the Image of the Black."

31. Olaudah Equiano, *The Interesting Narrative and Other Writings*, pp. 43–44.

32. Vincent Carretta, editor's note, in ibid., p. 246n. 70; John Gill, *An Exposition of the Old Testament, in Which Are Recorded the Original of Mankind, of the Several Nations of the World, and of the Jewish Nation in Particular. . . .*

33. See Granville Sharp, *The Just Limitation of Slavery*; Thomas Clarkson, *Essay on the Slavery and Commerce of the Human Species*; and Ottobah Cugoano, *Thoughts and Sentiments on the Evil and Wicked Traffic of the Slavery and Commerce of the Human Species*.

34. The division of the races of humanity according to Biblical typology is quite evident, for instance, in Johann Friedrich's 1776 invention of the science of physiology (which eventually became physical anthropology) and Carolus Linnaeus's 1793 taxonomic invention of the order *Anthropomorpha*.

35. Louis-Brown, *Waves of Decolonization*, p. 234.

36. Eliot Weinberger, "The Falls," in *Karmic Traces*, p. 158.

37. William Brown Hodgson, *Notes on Northern Africa, the Sahara and Soudan, in Relation to the Ethnography, Languages, History, Political and Social Conditions of the Nations of Those Countries*, pp. 49–50.

38. Terry Alford, *A Prince among Slaves: The True Story of An African Prince Sold into Slavery in the American South*, p. 73.

39. Quoted in ibid., p. 107.

40. Gomez, *Black Crescent*, p. 178. See Paul Irwin, *Liptako Speaks: History from Oral Traditions in Africa*, pp. 46–77.

41. Gomez, *Black Crescent*, p. 180.

42. Ibid., p. 173.

43. For the Fulbes, see Paul Riesman, *Freedom in Fulani Social Life*; and Victor Azarya, *Aristocrats Facing Change: The Fulbe in Guinea, Nigeria, and Cameroon*.

44. Claude McKay, *Banjo*, pp. 282–83 (hereafter cited in the text).

45. W. E. B. DuBois, "Review of *Home to Harlem*," p. 359.

46. Brent Hayes Edwards, *The Practice of Diaspora: Literature, Translation, and the Rise of Black Internationalism*, p. 239.

47. Ibid.

48. Claude McKay, "Farewell to Morocco," in *Complete Poems*, p. 362, ll. 15–21.

49. Calvin Coolidge, "Address before the Pan-American Conference at Havana, Cuba," January 16, 1928, from the American Presidency Project, http://www.presidency.ucsb.edu/ws/index.php?pid=443#axzz1YjXOA2Yk.

50. Gomez, *Black Crescent*, p. ix.

51. Ibid., p. 12.

1. Frederic G. Cassidy, ed., *Dictionary of American Regional English*, p. 83, taken from H. L. Mencken's *The American Language: An Inquiry into the Development of English in the United States* (Supplement 2), p. 162.

2. Naff, *Becoming American*. For an alternative to Naff's analysis of the pioneer generation of Syrians in America, one that takes into account emigration as well as immigration, see Akram F. Khater, *Inventing Home: Emigration, Gender, and the Middle Class in Lebanon, 1870–1920*. For an account of Arab American presence in America that looks beyond the pioneer generation, see Gregory Orfalea, *The Arab Americans: A History*. For an analysis of Syrian immigration to South America during the same pioneer period 1880–1920, see Civantos, *Between Argentines and Arabs*; and John Tofik Karam, *Another Arabesque: Syrian-Lebanese Ethnicity in Neoliberal Brazil*. For earlier, informative edited collections of accounts of early Arab immigration to America, see Eric Hooglund, ed., *Crossing the Waters: Arabic-Speaking Immigrants to the United States before 1940*; Sameer Y. Abraham and Nabeel Abraham, eds., *Arabs in the New World: Studies in Arab American Communities*; Elaine C. Hagopian and Ann Paden, eds., *The Arab Americans: Studies in Assimilation*. For the seminal account of the Syrian presence in America, see H. L. Mencken's contemporary and friend Philip K. Hitti, *The Syrians in America*.

3. For the prevalence of this phrase in pioneer peddler jargon, see Naff, *Becoming American*. "'Those who had been here a month or two,' recalled Mary A., 'would teach them a few words they [the veterans] had already learned—to knock on a door and say "Buy sumthin', Maam"'" (p. 165).

4. The prevalence of this theory of rapid assimilation is evident in even a cursory look at the titles of many of the earlier accounts of Syrian and/or Arab immigration given in note 2 to this chapter—titles such as *Becoming American* and *The Arab Americans: Studies in Assimilation*. However, the assimilation argument is being challenged by more recent historians of Syrian migration to America, Khater prominent among them.

5. Hagopian and Paden, preface to *The Arab Americans*, p. v.

6. Abraham and Abraham, introduction to *Arabs in the New World*, p. 1.

7. Naff, *Becoming American*, p. 1. The question as to whether this narrative on immigrant assimilation does not create a self-fulfilling prophecy about the disappearance of Arabs from American ethnic consciousness is an important one. American citizens in the 1930s, well into the second generation for immigrant Syrian families, for instance, were aware of the Syrian presence in America. This awareness is evidenced in H. L. Mencken's discussion of "Proper Names in America" in his monumental book *The American Language*. Discussing the prevalence of Smith as a proper name, Mencken goes on to point out that fewer than half the proper names in America can trace their ancestry back to the British Isles, commenting that "the rest are German *Schmidts*, Scandinavian *Smeds*, Czech *Kovars*, Hungarian *Kovacs*, Syrian *Haddads* and Polish *Kowalczyks*, and Jews who have sought to escape from German and Slavic names" (p. 477). The prominent presence of Syrians in Mencken's catalogue of "other" Americans attests to the thriving state of

Syrian communities in America between the wars, a presence that Mencken elsewhere in the book estimates to be at "250,000 to 350,000," despite acknowledging that the 1930 U.S. Census put the population at closer to 150,000 (p. 683).

8. Naff, *Becoming American*, p. 330.

9. Horatio Alger, Jr., *Tattered Tom; or, The Story of a Street Arab*, p. 104.

10. For a fascinating look at parallel allegories of Arab conversion to whiteness in Israeli culture, see Ella Habiba Shohat's *Israeli Cinema: East/West and the Politics of Representation*.

11. Alger, *Tattered Tom*, p. 10.

12. Naff, *Becoming American*, p. 161.

13. For an insightful analysis of Riis and Protestantism as it relates to the Realist tradition of writing, see Gregory S. Jackson, *The Word and Its Witness: The Spiritualization of American Realism*.

14. The classic book on the American version of the jeremiad is Bercovitch, *The American Jeremiad*.

15. Jacob Riis, *How the Other Half Lives*, p. 68.

16. For an interesting discussion of photography as it relates to American immigration in general and Chinese immigration in particular, see Anna Pegler-Gordon, "Chinese Exclusion, Photography, and the Development of U.S. Immigration Policy."

17. Khater, *Inventing Home*, p. 15.

18. Ibid., p. 91.

19. Sarah M. A. Gualtieri, *Between Arab and White: Race and Ethnicity in the Early Syrian American Diaspora*, p. 99.

20. Naff, *Becoming American*, p. 265.

21. Greater Syria stretched across present-day Lebanon, Syria, and parts of Jordan and Israel.

22. Naff, *Becoming American*, p. 265. Naff and especially Khater have excellent source material on the active Syrian American press. By 1919, there were an estimated seventy thousand Syrian immigrants in America supporting nineteen Arabic-language newspapers.

23. Ameen Rihani frets in a 1930 *Syrian World* article that if Syrian Americans fail to embrace their own cultural heritage, "they will be lost in the great melting pot" of America, "and the loss will entail something of real value to the country of their adoption." "The Syrian in American Art," *Syrian World*, November 1930, p. 16, Ameen Rihani Papers, Box 5, Folder 3, Manuscript Division, Library of Congress. The idea that one can "lose" one's cultural identity, Walter Benn Michaels has argued, is the result of a shift that occurred in America's intertwined rhetoric of race and national identity during the 1920s. See Walter Benn Michaels, *Our America: Nativism, Modernism, and Pluralism*.

24. Naff writes, "Before World War I, Arabic press publications appeared and disappeared regularly. So keen was the Syrian penchant for publishing that between 1892 and 1907 (the lifetime of the first Arabic newspaper) twenty-one Arabic dailies, weeklies, and monthlies were published" (*Becoming American*, p. 319).

25. Lisa Suhair Majaj, "Arab-Americans and the Meaning of Race," p. 329.

26. For more on Salloum Mokarzel and the *Syrian World*'s influence on the Arab American community, see Michael W. Suleiman, "The Mokarzels' Contributions to the Arabic-Speaking Community in the United States—Naoum and Salloum Mokarzel, Publishers of Arabic-Language Newspapers in the United States."

27. Friedman, "Why Not Compare?," p. 759.

28. For more on the role of the Christian intellectual in Arab liberal thought, see Hourani, *Arabic Thought in the Liberal Age*.

29. Johann Gottfried Herder, *Reflections on the Philosophy of the History of Mankind*, p. 8.

30. Ibid., pp. 8–9.

31. For more on Herder and Bedouins, see Ian Almond, "Terrible Turks, Bedouin Poets and Prussian Prophets: The Shifting Place of Islam in Herder's Thought."

32. According to Ameen A. Rihani (in a letter to Geoffrey Nash), "One explanation for Rihani's support of political Wahhabism is perhaps his belief that this movement could end up, like Protestantism, by separating the state from the 'Moslem Church.' Wahhabism could have been a first step toward a secular state in Arabia." Geoffrey Nash, *The Arab Writer in English: Arab Themes in a Metropolitan Language, 1908–1958*, p. 148n. 11.

33. Letter from editor of the *American Magazine*, Ameen Rihani Papers, Box 1, Folder 8, Manuscripts Division, Library of Congress.

34. Letter from editor of the *Atlantic Monthly*, in ibid.

35. Nash, *The Arab Writer in English*, p. 25.

36. Abraham Cahan, *The Rise of David Levinsky*, p. 4.

37. J. E. Lighter, ed., *Random House Historical Dictionary of American Slang*, p. 32.

38. "Under the heading of Verbotens of 1929 . . . *Variety* once printed a list of words and phrases forbidden to vaudevillians in that year. It included . . . *Arab* (signifying Jew)." H. L. Mencken, *The American Language* (*Supplement 1*), p. 645.

39. For an account of Jewish-immigrant assimilation and the role of blackface in the transformation of Jews into whites, see Rogin, *Blackface, White Noise*.

40. Reprinted in Suheil Bushrui and John Munroe, eds., *Kahlil Gibran: Essays and Introductions*, p. 179.

41. Nash, *The Arab Writer in English*, p. 18.

42. The most salient example of this interpretation is Nash, *The Arab Writer in English*.

43. See Wail S. Hassan, "The Rise of Arab-American Literature: Orientalism and Cultural Translation in the Work of Ameen Rihani."

44. For a good analysis of the representation of women in Arabo-Islamic writing, see Fedwa Malti-Douglas, *Woman's Body, Woman's Word: Gender and Discourse in Arabo-Islamic Writing*.

45. Nathaniel Hawthorne, *Blithedale Romance*, pp. 2–3. In regard to the argument about Zenobia and patriarchy, see particularly the scene in which Coverdale discovers Hollingsworth, Zenobia, and Priscilla together after a masquerade ball. For a good analysis of Zenobia in an Orientalist context, see Luther Luedtke, *Nathaniel Hawthorne and the Romance of the Orient*. For a different take on Zenobia, see Russ Castronovo, *Necro*

Citizenship: Death, Eroticism, and the Public Sphere in the Nineteenth-Century United States.

46. Lady Mary Wortley Montagu, *Letters*, p. 168.

47. For more on New York's Bohemia and New Women, see Christine Stansell, *American Moderns: Bohemian New York and the Creation of a New Century.*

48. Rihani himself had run away from his uncle's dry-goods store to join a traveling theater group while still a teenager. The theater group ultimately ran out of money in the Midwest, and Rihani returned to New York City.

49. For more on these *mahjar* themes, see Khater, *Inventing Home*; Hassan, "The Rise of Arab-American Literature"; Nash, *The Arab Writer in English*; and Gualtieri, *Between Arab and White.*

50. Ameen Rihani, letter on St. Francis Hotel stationery, 1939, Ameen Rihani Papers, Box 1, Folder 5, Manuscript Division, Library of Congress.

51. Ibid.

52. Ameen Rihani, "Pan-Arab Lecture," Ameen Rihani Papers, Box 4, Folder 5, Manuscript Division, Library of Congress, p. 45.

53. Letters of Ameen Rihani, *Al-Kulliyal* 24 (Autumn 1949): p. 18.

54. Letter from the *Phoenician Magazine*, January 23, 1934, Ameen Rihani Papers, Box 3, Folder 6, Manuscript Division, Library of Congress.

55. Ameen Rihani, *Arabian Peak and Desert: Travels in Al-Yaman*, p. 95.

56. Mohammad al-Ghazali, *Faysal al-Tafriqa Bayna al-Islam wa al-Zandaqa*, p. 101.

57. Gilles Deleuze and Felix Guattari, *A Thousand Plateaus: Capitalism and Schizophrenia*, p. 337.

58. Vance Bourjaily, *Confessions of a Spent Youth*, p. 234 (hereafter cited in the text).

59. Quoted in Orfalea, *The Arab Americans*, p. 148.

60. For a different take on these performances, see Evelyn Shakir, "Pretending to Be an Arab: Role Playing in Vance Bourjaily's 'The Fractional Man.'"

61. Quoted in Orfalea, *The Arab Americans*, p. 149.

NOTES TO THE AFTERWORD

1. Adonis, "A Mirror for the Executioner," *Victims of a Map*, p. 88. Translation by Jacob Rama Berman.

2. Haller Nutt to Samuel Sloan, May 19, 1861 (nu. 310), Haller Nutt Papers, Huntington Library, Pasadena, California.

3. One story holds that a painting of an Oriental scene that the two men brought back with them from their journey east, and that still hangs in the house, inspired Haller.

4. See *Nutt v. United States*, 125 U.S. 650 (1888).

Bibliography

Abraham, Sameer Y., and Nabeel Abraham, eds. *Arabs in the New World*. Detroit: Wayne State University, 1985.

Abrahamov, Binyamin. *Islamic Theology: Traditionalism and Rationalism*. Edinburgh: Edinburgh University Press, 1998.

Abrams, M. H. *The Mirror and the Lamp: Romantic Theory and the Critical Tradition*. Oxford: Oxford University Press, 1953.

———. *Natural Supernaturalism: Tradition and Revolution in Romantic Literature*. New York: Norton, 1971.

Adams, Charles Hansford. "Introductory Details Respecting Robert Adams." In *The Narrative of Robert Adams, a Barbary Captive: A Critical Edition*, by Robert Adams, edited by Charles Hansford Adams. Cambridge: Cambridge University Press, 2005.

Adams, Robert. *The Narrative of Robert Adams, a Barbary Captive: A Critical Edition*. Edited by Charles Hansford Adams. Cambridge: Cambridge University Press, 2005.

Abu A'la Maududi, Maulana Syed. *The Meaning of the Qur'an*. Vol. 1. Translated by A. A. Kamal. Chicago: Kazi, 1999.

Abu Deeb, Kamal. *Al-Jurjani's Theory of Poetic Imagery*. London: Aris and Phillips, 1979.

Abu Nuwas. "Jinan." In *Classical Arabic Poetry: 162 Poems from Imrulkais to Ma'ari*, edited and translated by C. G. Tuetay. London: Kegan Paul, 1985.

Adonis. *An Introduction to Arab Poetics*. Translated by Catherine Cobham. London: Saqi Books, 1990.

———. "A Mirror for the Executioner." In *Victims of a Map: A Bilingual Anthology of Arab Poetry*. Edited and translated by Abdullah al-Udhari. London: Saqi Books, 2006.

Al-Ahari, Muhammad. *Five Classic Muslim Slave Narratives*. Chicago: Magribine, 2006.

Al-Dhahabi, Mubammad Husayn. *Al-Tafsir wa al-Mufassirun*. Cairo: Dar al-Kutub al-Hadithah, 1976.

Al-Ghazali, Mohammad. *Al-Munqidh min al-Dalal*. In *Deliverance from Error: Five Key Texts Including His Spiritual Autobiography, al-Munqidh min al-Dalal*. Translated by R. J. McCarthy. Louisville, KY: Fons Vitae, 1980.

———. *Ihya 'Ulum al-Din*. In *Deliverance from Error: Five Key Texts Including His Spiritual Autobiography al-Munqidh min al-Dalal*. Translated by R. J .McCarthy. Louisville, KY: Fons Vitae, 1980.

———. *Faysal al-Tafriqa Bayna al-Islam wa al-Zandaqa*. In *On the Boundaries of Theo-logical Tolerance in Islam: Abu Hamid al-Ghazali's Faysal al-Tafriqa Bayna al-Islam wa al-Zandaqa*. Translated by Sherman Jackson. Oxford: Oxford University Press, 2002.

Al-Jabbarti, Abd al-Rahman. *Tarikh muddat al-Faransi bi Misr*. In *Napoleon in Egypt: Al Jabbarti's Chronicle of the French Occupation, 1798*. Translated and edited by Shmuel Moreh. New York: Markus Wiener, 1993.

Al-Jurjani, Abd al-Qahir. *Asrar al-Balagha*. Edited by Al Imam Al Sheikh Mohammad Abdo and Mohammad Rashid Ridah. Cairo: Al Midan al Azhar, 1959.

———. *Kitab Asrar al-Balagha*. In *Arab Poetics in the Golden Age*, edited by Vincente Can-tarino and translated by Helmutt Ritter, 157–76. Leiden: Brill, 1975.

Al-Mawsuli, Ilyas Hanna. *Kitab Siryahat al-Khoury Ilyas bin al-Qissees Hanna al Mawsuli*. In *In the Lands of the Christians; Arabic Travel Writing in the Seventeenth Century*, edited and translated by Nabil Matar. New York and London: Routledge, 2003.

Al-Tahtawi, Rifa'a Rafi'. *An Imam in Paris: Account of a Stay in France by an Egyptian Cleric (1826–1831)* [*Takhlis al-Ibriz fi Talkhis Bariz aw al-Diwan al-Nafis bi-wan Baris*]. Translated by Daniel L. Newman. London: Saqi Books, 2004.

Alford, Terry. *A Prince among Slaves: The True Story of an African Prince Sold into Slavery in the American South*. Oxford: Oxford University Press, 1986.

Alger, Horatio, Jr. *Tattered Tom; or, The Story of a Street Arab*. Boston: Loring, 1871.

Ali, Abdullah Yusuf. *The Qur'an*. London: Wordsworth, 2001.

Ali, Noble Drew. *The Circle Seven Koran* (1927). In the Moorish Science Temple Papers, Schomburg Center for Research in Black Culture, New York.

Allen, Terry. *Five Essays on Islamic Art*. Sebastopol, CA: Solipsist, 1988.

Almond, Ian. "Terrible Turks, Bedouin Poets and Prussian Prophets: The Shifting Place of Islam in Herder's Thought." *PMLA* 123, no. 1 (January 2008): 57–75.

Arabi, Ibn. *The Bezels of Wisdom* [*Fusus al-hikam*]. Translated by R. W. J. Austin. Mah-wah, NJ: Paulist, 1980.

———. "Whoso Knoweth Himself . . ." In *Treatise on Being*. Translated by T. H. Weir. Gloucester, UK: Beshara, 1976.

Arac, Jonathan. *The Emergence of American Literary Narrative, 1820–1860*. Cambridge: Harvard University Press, 2005.

Asad, Talal. *Formations of the Secular: Christianity, Islam, Modernity*. Stanford: Stanford University Press, 2003.

Auerbach, Eric. "The Figura." In *Scenes from the Drama of European Literature*, translated by Ralph Mannheim. Minneapolis: University of Minnesota Press, 1984.

———. *Mimesis*. Translated by Willard Trask. Princeton: Princeton University Press, 1953.

Augst, Thomas. *The Clerk's Tale: Young Men and Moral Life in Nineteenth-Century Amer-ica*. Chicago: University of Chicago Press, 2003.

Austin, Allan D. *African Muslims in Antebellum America: Transatlantic Stories and Spiri-tual Struggles*. New York: Routledge, 1997.

Azarya, Victor. *Aristocrats Facing Change: The Fulbe in Guinea, Nigeria, and Cameroon*. Chicago: University of Chicago Press, 1978.

Bacon, Francis. *Bacon's Essays and Colours of Good and Evil.* Edited by W. Aldis Wright. Manchester, NH: Ayer, 1972.

Baepler, Paul, ed. *White Slaves, African Masters: An Anthology of American Barbary Captivity Narratives.* Chicago: University of Chicago Press, 1999.

Baker, Houston. *Modernism and the Harlem Renaissance.* Chicago: University of Chicago Press, 1989.

Barnby, H. G. *The Prisoners of Algiers: An Account of the Forgotten American-Algerian War, 1785–1797.* London: Oxford University Press, 1966.

Basset, Rene. *Moorish Literature.* New York: Collier, 1901.

Battutah, Ibn. *The Travels of Ibn Battutah [Rihla Ibn Battutah].* Edited by Tim Mackintosh Smith. Translated by Sir Hamilton Gibb and C. F. Beckingham. Oxford, UK: Picador, 2002.

Benjamin, Walter. *The Origin of German Tragic Drama.* Translated by John Osborne. London: Verso, 1998.

Bercovitch, Sacvan. *The American Jeremiad.* Madison: University of Wisconsin Press, 1978.

———. *The Puritan Origins of the American Self.* New Haven: Yale University Press, 1977.

Berlant, Lauren. *The Anatomy of National Fantasy: Hawthorne, Utopia, and Everyday Life.* Chicago: University of Chicago Press, 1991.

Berman, Jacob Rama. "The Barbarous Voice of Democracy: American Captivity in Barbary and the Multicultural Specter." *American Literature* 79, no. 1 (March 2007): 1–27.

Bernal, Martin. *Black Athena: The Afroasiatic Roots of Classical Civilization.* New Brunswick: Rutgers University Press, 1991.

Bhabha, Homi K. *The Location of Culture.* London: Routledge, 1994.

Blum, Hester. *The View from the Masthead: Maritime Imagination and Antebellum American Sea Narratives.* Chapel Hill: University of North Carolina Press, 2008.

Blyden, Edward Wilmot. *Christianity, Islam and the Negro Race.* 1887. Baltimore: Black Classics, 1994 (facsimile reprint).

Bourjaily, Vance. *Confessions of a Spent Youth.* 1952. New York: Arbor House, 1986.

Bowles, F. E. "Civilization in Africa at One Time Superior to Ours." *Chicago Defender,* October 11, 1924, A9.

Bradley, Eliza. *An Authentic Narrative of the Shipwreck and Suffering of Mrs. Eliza Bradley, the Wife of Capt. James Bradley of Liverpool* (1820). In *White Slaves, African Masters: An Anthology of American Barbary Captivity Narratives,* edited by Paul Baepler. Chicago: University of Chicago Press, 1999.

Buck-Morss, Susan. *Hegel, Haiti, and Universal History.* Pittsburgh: University of Pittsburgh Press, 2009.

Burckhardt, John Lewis. *Notes on the Bedouins and Wahabys, Collected during His Travels in the East.* 2 vols. London: Henry Colburn and Richard Bentley, 1831.

Bushrui, Suheil, and John Munroe, eds. *Kahlil Gibran: Essays and Introductions.* Beirut: Rihani House, 1970.

Cahan, Abraham. *The Rise of David Levinsky.* New York: Penguin, 1993.

Cantarino, Vincente. *Arab Poetics in the Golden Age.* Leiden: Brill, 1975.

Carlyle, Thomas. *Sartor Resartus.* New York: Oxford University Press, 2000.

Carr, Gerald. *Frederic Edwin Church: Catalogue Raisonne of Works of Art at Olana State Historic Site.* Cambridge: Cambridge Press, 1994.

Cassidy, Frederic G., ed. *Dictionary of American Regional English.* Vol. 1. Cambridge, MA: Belknap, 1985.

Castiglia, Chris. *Bound and Determined: Captivity, Culture-Crossing, and White Womanhood from Mary Rowlandson to Patty Hearst.* Chicago: University of Chicago Press, 1996.

———. *Interior States: Institutional Consciousness and the Inner Life of Democracy in the Antebellum United States.* Durham: Duke University Press, 2008.

Castronovo, Russ. *Necro Citizenship: Death, Eroticism, and the Public Sphere in the Nineteenth-Century United States.* Durham: Duke University Press, 2001.

Cathcart, James Leander. *The Captives: Eleven Years a Prisoner in Algiers.* La Porte, IN. Herald Print, 1899.

———. *Southern Louisiana and Southern Alabama in 1819: The Journal of James Leander Cathcart.* Edited by Walter Pritchard, Fred B. Kniffin, and Clair A. Brown. Reprinted in *Louisiana Historical Quarterly* 28, no. 3 (1945).

———. *Tripoli: The First War with the U.S., an Inner History.* La Porte, IN: J. B. Newkirk, 1901.

Catlin, George. *North American Indians.* New York: Penguin, 1989.

Chidsey, Donald Barr. *The Wars in Barbary: Arab Piracy and the Birth of the United States Navy.* New York: Crown, 1971.

Chisick, Harvey. *Historical Dictionary of the Enlightenment.* Lanham, MD: Scarecrow, 2005.

Chittick, William C. *Imaginal Worlds: Ibn al-Arabi and the Problem of Religious Diversity.* Albany: SUNY Press, 1994.

———. *The Self-Disclosures of God: Ibn Arabi's Cosmology.* Albany: SUNY Press, 1997.

Civantos, Christina. *Between Argentines and Arabs: Argentine Orientalism, Arab Immigrants, and the Writing of Identity.* Albany: SUNY, 2006.

Clarke, Lewis. *Narrative of the Sufferings of Lewis Clarke, during a Captivity of More than Twenty-Five Years, among the Algerines of Kentucky, One of the So Called Christian States of America.* Boston: D. H. Ela, 1845.

Clarkson, Thomas. *Essay on the Slavery and Commerce of the Human Species.* London, 1786.

Corbin, Henry. *Creative Imagination in the Sufism of Ibn Arabi.* Translated by Ralph Mannheim. Princeton: Princeton University Press, 1969.

———. *History of Islamic Philosophy.* Translated by Liadain Sherrard and Philip Sherrard. London: Kegan Paul in association with Islamic Publications for the Institute of Ismaili Studies, 1993.

Cowan, J. W., ed. *The Hans Wehr Dictionary of Modern Written Arabic.* 4th ed. Ithaca, NY: Spoken Languages Services, 1994.

Cugoano, Ottobah. *Thoughts and Sentiments on the Evil and Wicked Traffic of the Slavery and Commerce of the Human Species.* London, 1787.

Curtis, Edward E., IV. *Islam in Black America; Identity, Liberation, and Difference in African American Islamic Thought.* Albany: SUNY Press, 2002.

Davies, Robert C. *Christian Slaves, Muslim Masters: White Slavery in the Mediterranean, the Barbary Coast, and Italy 1500–1800.* London: Palgrave, 2003.

Davis, David Brion. *The Problem of Slavery in the Age of Revolution, 1770–1823.* Ithaca: Cornell University Press, 1975.

Dayan, Joan. *Fables of Mind: An Inquiry into Poe's Fiction.* New York: Oxford University Press, 1987.

De La Fuente, Ariel. *Children of Facundo: Caudillo and Gaucho Insurgency during the Argentine State-Formation (La Rioja, 1853–1870).* Durham: Duke University Press, 2000.

Delany, Martin R. *Blake; or, The Huts of America.* 1859. Boston: Beacon, 1993.

———. *The Condition, Elevation, Emigration and Destiny of the Colored People of the United States, Politically Considered.* 1852. Baltimore: Black Classics, 1993.

Deleuze, Giles, and Felix Guattari. *A Thousand Plateaus: Capitalism and Schizophrenia.* Translated by Brian Massumi. Minneapolis: University of Minnesota Press, 1987.

Dimock, Wai Chee. "African, Caribbean, American: Black English as Creole Tongue." In *Shades of the Planet: American Literature as World Literature,* edited by Wai Chee Dimock and Lawrence Buell, 274–300. Princeton: Princeton University Press, 2007.

———. *Through Other Continents: American Literature across Deep Time.* Princeton: Princeton University Press, 2006.

Dimock, Wai Chee, and Lawrence Buell, eds. *Shades of the Planet: American Literature as World Literature.* Princeton: Princeton University Press, 2007.

Diouf, Sylviane A. *Servants of Allah: African Muslims Enslaved in the Americas.* New York: NYU Press, 1998.

Dorr, David F. *A Colored Man round the World.* Edited by Malini Johar Schueller. 1858. Ann Arbor: University of Michigan Press, 1999.

Douglass, Frederick. *Narrative of the Life of Frederick Douglass.* 1845. Reprint, New York: Penguin, 1997.

DuBois, W. E. B. *Black Folk Then and Now.* 1939. Reprint, Millwood, NY: Thomson, 1975.

———. *The Dark Princess.* 1928. Reprint, Oxford: University Press of Mississippi, 1995.

———. *The Negro.* 1915. Reprint, Millwood, NY: Kraus-Thomson, 1975.

———. "Review of *Home to Harlem.*" In *Voices of a Black Nation: Political Journalism in the Harlem Renaissance,* edited by Theodore G. Vincent. San Francisco: Ramparts, 1973.

———. *The Souls of Black Folk.* 1903. In *Three Negro Classics,* edited by John Hope Franklin. New York: Avon, 1965.

———. *The World and Africa: An Inquiry into the Part Which Africa Has Played in World History.* 1946. New York: International Publishers, 1965.

Edwards, Brent Hayes. *The Practice of Diaspora: Literature, Translation, and the Rise of Black Internationalism.* Cambridge: Harvard University Press, 2003.

Edwards, Brian T. *Morocco Bound: Disorienting America's Maghreb, from Casablanca to the Marrakech Express.* Durham: Duke University Press, 2005.

Equiano, Olaudah. *The Interesting Narrative and Other Writings.* Edited by Vincent Carretta. New York: Penguin, 2003.

Ess, J. V. *The Flowering of Muslim Theology.* Cambridge: Harvard University Press, 2006.

Fahmy, Khaled. "The Era of Muhammad 'Ali Pasha, 1805–1848." In *The Cambridge History of Egypt: Modern Egypt, from 1517 to the End of the Twentieth Century,* vol. 2, edited by M. W. Daly, 139–79. Cambridge: Cambridge University Press, 1998.

Faruqi, Lois Ibn. "Muwashshah: A Vocal Form in Islamic Culture." *Ethnomusicology* 19 (January 1975): 1–29.

Finkelstein, Dorothee Metlitzky. *Melville's Orienada.* New Haven: Yale University Press, 1961.

Finnie, David H. *Pioneers East: The Early American Experience in the Middle East.* Cambridge: Harvard University Press, 1967.

Fischel, Walter J. *Ibn Khaldun and Tamerlane.* Berkeley: University of California Press, 1952.

Flaherty, Gloria. *Shamanism and the Eighteenth Century.* Princeton: Princeton University Press, 1992.

Foss, John D. *A Journal, of the Captivity and Sufferings of John Foss, Several Years a Prisoner in Algiers.* 1798. In *White Slaves, African Masters: An Anthology of American Barbary Captivity Narratives,* edited by Paul Baepler. Chicago: University of Chicago Press, 1999.

Fox, Richard. "East of Said." In *Edward Said: A Critical Reader,* edited by Michael Sprinker. Malden, MA: Blackwell, 1992.

Foucault, Michel. *The Order of Things.* New York: Vintage, 1970.

Friedman, Susan Stanford. "Why Not Compare?" *PMLA* 126, no. 3 (May 2011): 753–62.

Gaines, Kevin K. *Uplifting the Race: Black Leadership, Politics, and Culture in the Twentieth Century.* Chapel Hill: University of North Carolina Press, 1996.

Garrison, William Lloyd. Preface to *Narrative of the Life of Frederick Douglass,* by Frederick Douglass. 1845. New York: Penguin, 1997.

Gates, Henry Louis, Jr. "The Trope of a New Negro and the Reconstruction of the Image of the Black." In *The New American Studies,* edited by Phillip Fisher, 319–45. Berkeley: University of California Press, 1991.

Gibb, H. A. R., et al., eds. *The Encyclopedia of Islam.* Vol. 1. Leiden: Brill, 1986.

Gibran, Khalil. *The Prophet.* 1923. New York: Knopf, 1995.

Gill, John. *An Exposition of the Old Testament, in Which Are Recorded the Original of Mankind, of the Several Nations of the World, and of the Jewish Nation in Particular. . . .* London, 1788.

Gilroy, Paul. *The Black Atlantic: Modernity and Double Consciousness.* Cambridge: Harvard University Press, 1993.

Gomez, Michael. *Black Crescent: The Experience and Legacy of African Muslims in the Americas.* New York: Cambridge University Press, 2005.

——. *Exchanging Our Country Marks: The Transformation of African Identities in the Colonial and Antebellum South.* Chapel Hill: University of North Carolina Press, 1998.

Griffin, Cyrus. "Prince, the Moor." *Southern Galaxy*, May 29, June 5 and 12, and July 5, 1828.

Grossman, Jay. *Reconstituting the American Renaissance: Emerson, Whitman, and the Politics of Representation*. Durham: Duke University Press, 2003.

Gualtieri, Sarah M. A. *Between Arab and White: Race and Ethnicity in the Early Syrian American Diaspora*. Berkeley: University of California Press, 2009.

Gunn, Giles. *Interpretation of Otherness: Literature, Religion, and the American Imagination*. New York: Oxford University Press, 1979.

Hagopian, Elaine C., and Ann Paden. *The Arab Americans: Studies in Assimilation*. Wilmette, IL: Medina University Press, 1969.

Haight, Sarah Rogers. *Letters from the Old World*. 2 vols. New York: Harper and Bothers, 1840.

Hammond, Phillip C. "Petra—Myth and Reality." *Aramco World Magazine*, September–October 1991.

Harris, Joel Chandler. *The Story of Aaron (So Named), Son of Ben Ali; Told by Friends and Acquaintances*. Boston: Houghton Mifflin, 1896.

Harvey, Bruce. *American Geographics: U.S. National Narratives and Representations of the Non-European World, 1830–1865*. Stanford: Stanford University Press, 2002.

Hassan, Wail. Introduction to *Thou Shalt Not Speak My Language*, by Abdelfattah Kilito. Syracuse: Syracuse University Press, 2008.

———. "The Rise of Arab-American Literature: Orientalism and Cultural Translation in the Work of Ameen Rihani." *American Literary History* 20, nos. 1–2 (Spring–Summer 2008): 245–75.

Hawthorne, Nathaniel. *The Blithedale Romance*. 1852. Reprint, New York: Norton, 1978.

Hegel, G. W. F. *The Phenomenology of Spirit*. Translated by A. V. Miller. Oxford, UK: Clarendon, 1977.

Herder, Johann Gottfried. *Reflections on the Philosophy of the History of Mankind*. Translated by T. O. Churchill. 1800. Chicago: University of Chicago Press, 1968.

Hitti, Philip K. *An Arab-Syrian Gentleman and Warrior in the Period of the Crusades: Memoirs of Usama ibn Munqidh*. New York: Columbia University Press, 1929.

———. *The Syrians in America*. New York: George Doran, 1924.

Hodgson, Marshall G. S. "Hemispheric Inter-regional History as an Approach to World History." *Journal of World History* 1, no. 3 (1954): 715–23.

———. *The Venture of Islam*. 3 vols. Chicago: University of Chicago Press, 1977.

Hodgson, William Brown. *Notes on Northern Africa, the Sahara and Soudan, in Relation to the Ethnography, Languages, History, Political and Social Conditions of the Nations of Those Countries*. New York: Wiley and Putnam, 1844.

Hooglund, Eric, ed. *Crossing the Waters: Arabic-Speaking Immigrants to the United States before 1940*. Washington, DC: Smithsonian Institution Press, 1987.

Hourani, Albert. *Arabic Thought in the Liberal Age, 1798–1939*. London: Oxford University Press, 1967.

Huggins, Nathan. *Harlem Renaissance*. London: Oxford University Press, 1971.

Irving, Washington. *The Alhambra: A Series of Tales and Sketches*. Philadelphia: Carey and Lea, 1832.

Irwin, Paul. *Liptako Speaks: History from Oral Traditions in Africa*. Princeton: Princeton University Press, 1981.

Irwin, Ray W. *The Diplomatic Relations of the United States with the Barbary Powers, 1776–1816*. Chapel Hill: University of North Carolina Press, 1931.

Jackson, Gregory S. *The Word and Its Witness: The Spiritualization of American Realism*. Chicago: University of Chicago Press, 2009.

Jackson, Sherman. Introduction to *On the Boundaries of Theological Tolerance in Islam: Abu Hamid Al-Ghazali's Faysal al-Tafriqa Bayna al-Islam wa al-Zandaqa*. Oxford: Oxford University Press, 2002.

———. *Islam and the Blackamerican: Looking toward the Third Resurrection*. Oxford: Oxford University Press, 2005.

Jefferson, Thomas. *Notes on the State of Virginia*. 1785. New York: Penguin, 1999.

Jones, Dewey R. "Voodoo Rites of the Jungles in Odd Contrasts with Background of the City." *Chicago Defender*, December 10, 1932, 9.

Judy, Ronald A. T. *(Dis)Forming the American Canon: African-Arabic Slave Narratives and the American Vernacular*. Minneapolis: University of Minnesota Press, 1993.

Kaplan, Amy. *The Anarchy of Empire in the Making of U.S. Culture*. Cambridge: Harvard University Press, 2003.

Kaplan, Amy, and Donald Pease, eds. *Cultures of United States Imperialism*. Durham: Duke University Press, 1993.

Karam, John Tofik. *Another Arabesque: Syrian-Lebanese Ethnicity in Neoliberal Brazil*. Philadelphia: Temple University Press, 2007.

Kazanjian, David. *The Colonizing Trick: National Culture and Imperial Citizenship in Early America*. Minnesota: University of Minnesota Press, 2003.

Kennedy, J. Gerlad. *Poe, Death, and the Life of Writing*. New Haven: Yale University Press, 1987.

Kennedy, J. Gerlad, and Liliane Weissberg, eds. *Romancing the Shadow: Poe and Race*. Oxford: Oxford University Press, 2001.

Khaldun, Ibn. *Muqaddimah: An Introduction to History*. Translated by Franz Rosenthal. Princeton: Princeton University Press, 2005.

Khalifa, Rashad. *Qur'an: The Final Testament*. Capistrano Beach, CA: Islamic Productions, 2005.

Khater, Akram. *Inventing Home: Emigration, Gender, and the Middle Class in Lebanon, 1870–1920*. Berkeley: University of California Press, 2001.

Khorramshahi, Baha' al-Din. "Ta'wil." *Message of Thaqalayn: A Quarterly Journal of Islamic Studies* 3, no. 3 (Autumn 1997).

Kilito, Abdelfattah. *Thou Shalt Not Speak My Language*. Translated by Wail S. Hassan. Syracuse: Syracuse University Press, 2008.

Kitzen, Michael L. S. *Tripoli and the United States at War: A History of American Relation with the Barbary States, 1785–1805*. Jefferson, NC: McFarland, 1993.

Knight, Michael Muhammad. *Blue-Eyed Devil: A Road Odyssey through Islamic America*. New York: Autonomedia, 2007.

Krupat, Arnold. *The Voice in the Margin: Native American Literature and the Canon*. Berkeley: University of California Press, 1989.

Kuhnel, Ernst. *Arabesque: Meaning and Transformation of an Ornament*. Graz, Austria: Furlong von Sammler, 1977.

———. *Studies in Islamic Art and Architecture in Honor of K. R. C. Creswell*. Cairo, 1965.

Laborde, M. Leon, and L. M. A. Linant. *Journey through Arabia Petraea, to Mount Sinai, and the Excavated City of Petra, the Edom of Prophecies*. London: John Murray, 1838.

Lambert, Frank. *The Barbary Wars: American Independence in the Atlantic World*. New York: Hill and Wang, 2007.

Lane, Andrew J. *A Traditional Mu'tazalite Qur'an Commentary: The Kashshaf of Jar Allah al Zamakhshari*. Leiden: Brill, 2006.

Lawrence, Bruce. Introduction to *Muqaddimah: An Introduction to History*, by Ibn Khaldun. Princeton: Princeton University Press, 2005.

Leezenberg, Michiel. *Contexts of Metaphor*. London: Elsevier, 2001.

Levander, Caroline, and Robert S. Levine, eds. *Hemispheric American Studies*. New Brunswick: Rutgers University Press, 2007.

Lewis, David Levering. *When Harlem Was in Vogue*. New York: Penguin, 1997.

Lewis, R. W. B. *Trials of the Word: Essays in American Literature and the Humanistic Tradition*. New Haven: Yale University Press, 1966.

Lighter, J. E., ed. *Random House Historical Dictionary of American Slang*. Vol. 1. New York: Random House, 1994.

Linebaugh, Peter, and Marcus Rediker. *The Many-Headed Hydra: Sailors, Slaves, Commoners, and the Hidden History of the Revolutionary Atlantic*. Boston: Beacon, 2000.

London, Joshua E. *Victory in Tripoli: How America's War with Barbary Established the U.S. Navy and Shaped a Nation*. Hoboken, NJ: Wiley, 2005.

López, Ian F. Haney. *White by Law: The Legal Construction of Race*. New York: NYU Press, 1997.

Louis-Brown, David. *Waves of Decolonization: Discourses of Race and Hemispheric Citizenship in Cuba, Mexico, and the United States*. Durham: Duke University Press, 2008.

Lowe, Lisa. *Critical Terrains: French and British Orientalisms*. Ithaca: Cornell University Press, 1994.

Lubin, Alex. "The Black Middle East." In *The Cultural Politics of the Middle East in the Americas*, edited by Evelyn Alsultaney and Ella Shohat. Ann Arbor: University of Michigan Press, forthcoming.

Luedtke, Luther. *Nathaniel Hawthorne and the Romance of the Orient*. Bloomington: Indiana University Press, 1989.

MacDonald, Duncan Black. *The Development of Muslim Theology, Jurisprudence and Constitutional Theory*. New York: Scribner, 1903.

MacGavock, Randal W. *A Tennessean Abroad, or Letters from Europe, Africa and Asia*. New York: J. S. Redfield, 1854.

Mahdi, Muhsin. *Ibn Khaldun's Philosophy of History: A Study in the Philosophic Foundation of the Science of Culture.* Chicago: University of Chicago Press, 1971.

Majaj, Lisa Suhair. "Arab-Americans and the Meaning of Race." In *Postcolonial Theory
and the United States,* edited by Amritjit Singh and Peter Schmidt. Jackson: University
of Mississippi Press, 2000.

Majid, Anouar. *We Are All Moors: Ending Centuries of Crusades against Muslims and
Other Minorities.* Minneapolis: University of Minnesota Press, 2009.

Malti-Douglas, Fedwa. *Woman's Body, Woman's Word: Gender and Discourse in Arabo-
Islamic Writing.* Princeton: Princeton University Press, 1991.

Marr, Timothy. *The Cultural Roots of American Islamicism.* Cambridge: Cambridge University Press, 2006.

Martin, R. C., M. R. Woodward, and D. S. Atmaja. *Defenders of Reason in Islam:
Mu'tazilism from Medieval School to Modern Symbol.* Oxford, UK: Oneworld, 1997.

Marx, Karl. "On the Jewish Question." In *The Marx-Engels Reader,* edited by Robert C.
Tucker. New York: Norton, 1978.

Matar, Nabil. Introduction to *Piracy, Slavery, and Redemption: Barbary Captivity Narratives from Early Modern England,* edited by David J. Vitkus. New York: Columbia University Press, 2001.

Matthiessen, F. O. *The American Renaissance: Art and Expression in the Age of Emerson
and Whitman.* Oxford: Oxford University Press, 1968.

McKay, Claude. *Banjo: A Story without a Plot.* 1929. San Diego: Harcourt and Brace, 1957.

———. *Complete Poems.* Edited by William J. Maxwell. Urbana: University of Illinois
Press, 2004.

———. *A Long Way from Home.* New York: Lee Furman, 1937.

Melville, Herman. "Bartleby the Scrivener." In *Billy Budd and Other Stories.* New York:
Penguin, 1986.

———. *Redburn; His First Voyage, Being the Sailor-Boy, Confessions and Reminiscences of
the Son-of-a-Gentleman, in the Merchant Service.* New York: A. & C. Boni, 1924.

Mencken, H. L. *The American Language: An Inquiry into the Development of English in the
United States.* 4th ed. New York: Knopf, 1937.

Menocal, Maria Rosa. *Shards of Love: Exile and the Origins of the Lyric.* Durham: Duke
University Press, 1994.

Michael, John. "Beyond Us and Them: Identity and Terror from an Arab American's Perspective." *SAQ* 102, no. 4 (Fall 2003): 701–28.

Michaels, Walter Benn. *Our America: Nativism, Modernism, and Pluralism.* Durham:
Duke University Press, 1995.

Miller, Angela L. *The Empire of the Eye: Landscape Representation and American Cultural
Politics, 1825–1875.* Ithaca: Cornell University Press, 1996.

Miller, Perry. *Errand into the Wilderness.* Cambridge, MA: Belknap, 1956.

Montagu, Lady Mary Wortley. *Letters.* New York: Knopf, 1992.

Morrison, Toni. *Playing in the Dark: Whiteness and the Literary Imagination.* New York:
Vintage, 1993.

Munqidh, Usama Ibn. *The Book of Contemplation.* Translated by Paul M. Cobb. New York: Penguin, 2008.

Murata, Sachiko, and William C. Chittick. *The Vision of Islam.* New York: Paragon House, 1994.

Murdock, Kenneth. *Literature and Theology in Colonial New England.* Cambridge: Harvard University Press, 1949.

Naff, Alixa. *Becoming American: The Early Arab Immigrant Experience.* Carbondale: Southern Illinois Press, 1985.

Nash, Geoffrey. *The Arab Writer in English: Arab Themes in a Metropolitan Language, 1908–1958.* Brighton, UK: Sussex Academic Press, 1998.

Nasr, Sayyed Hossein, and Oliver Leahmen, eds. *History of Islamic Philosophy.* Vol. 1. London and New York: Routledge, 1996.

Nelson, Dana D. *National Manhood: Capitalist Citizenship and the Imagined Fraternity of White Men.* Durham: Duke University Press, 1998.

Newfield, Christopher. *The Emerson Effect: Individualism and Submission in America.* Chicago: University of Chicago Press, 1996.

Newman, Daniel L. Introduction to *An Imam in Paris: Account of a Stay in France by an Egyptian Cleric (1826–1831),* by Rifa'a Rafi' al-Tahtawi. London: Saqi Books, 2004.

———. "Myths and Realities in Muslim Alterist Discourse: Arab Travelers in Europe in the Age of the *Nahda* (19th C.)." *Chronos* 6 (2002): 7–76.

Noah, Mordecai Manuel. *Discourse on the Evidences of the American Indians Being the Descendants of the Lost Tribes of Israel, Delivered before the Mercantile Library Association.* New York: James Van Norden, 1837.

Nokes, Vivian. *Edward Lear, 1812–1888.* Exhibition catalogue. London: Royal Academy of Arts, 1985.

Obenzinger, Hilton. *American Palestine: Melville, Twain, and Holy Land Mania.* Princeton: Princeton University Press, 1999.

Oren, Michael. *Power, Faith, and Fantasy: America in the Middle East, 1776 to the Present.* New York: Norton, 2007.

Orfalea, Gregory. *The Arab Americans: A History.* Northampton, MA: Olive Branch, 2006.

Padock, Juddah. *A Narrative of the Shipwreck of the Oswego.* New York: Cap. James Riley, 1818.

Pease, Donald. "Poe and Historicity." *Emerson Society Quarterly* 35, nos. 3–4 (1989): 273–92.

———. *Visionary Compacts: American Renaissance Writings in Cultural Context.* Madison: University of Wisconsin Press, 1987.

Pegler-Gordon, Anna. "Chinese Exclusion, Photography, and the Development of U.S. Immigration Policy." *American Quarterly* 58, no. 1 (March 2006): 51–77.

Poe, Edgar Allan. *Complete Tales and Poems of Edgar Allan Poe.* New York: Vintage Books, 1975.

———. "The Fall of the House of Usher." In *Complete Tales and Poems of Edgar Allan Poe.*

———. "Ligeia." In *Complete Tales and Poems of Edgar Allan Poe.*

———. "The Masque of the Red Death." In *Complete Tales and Poems of Edgar Allan Poe.*

———. "The Philosophy of Furniture." *Burton's Gentleman's Magazine*, May 1840, 243–44.

———. "Review of Hawthorne—Twice-Told Tales." *Graham's Magazine*, May 1842, 298–300.

———. "Review of Stephens' 'Arabia Petraea.'" In *Complete Tales and Poems of Edgar Allan Poe*.

———. "The Tell-Tale Heart." In *Complete Tales and Poems of Edgar Allan Poe*.

Powell, Timothy. *Ruthless Democracy: A Multicultural Interpretation of the American Renaissance*. Princeton: Princeton University Press, 2000.

Pratt, Mary Louise. *Imperial Eyes: Travel Writing and Transculturation*. London: Routledge, 1992.

Prentiss, Charles. *The Life of the Late General William Eaton, Principally Collected from His Correspondence and Other Manuscripts*. Brookfield, MA: Ebenezer Merriam, 1813.

Progler, Joseph. "Reading Early American Islamica: An Interpretive Translation of the Ben Ali Diary." *Tawhid: Journal of Islamic Thought and Culture* 16, no. 3 (Autumn 2000): 3–43.

Radhakrishnan, Rajagopalan. *Theory in an Uneven World*. Oxford, UK: Blackwell, 2003.

Rampersad, Arnold. Introduction to *The New Negro: Voices of the Harlem Renaissance*, edited by Alain Locke. New York: Touchstone, 1997.

Ray, William. *The Horrors of Slavery; or, The American Tars in Tripoli*. Edited by Hester Blum. 1808. New Brunswick: Rutgers University Press, 2008.

Redner, Harry. *Ethical Life: The Past and Present of Ethical Cultures*. Lanham, MD: Rowman and Littlefield, 2001.

Reynolds, David S. *Beneath the American Renaissance: The Subversive Imagination in the Age of Emerson and Melville*. Cambridge: Harvard University Press, 1989.

———. *Faith in Fiction: The Emergence of Religious Literature in America*. Cambridge: Harvard University Press, 1981.

Reynolds, Dwight. "The 1001 Nights: A History of the Text and Its Reception." In *The Cambridge History of Arabic Literature*, vol. 6, *Arabic Literature in the Post-Classical Period*, edited by Roger Allen and D. S. Richards, 270–91. Cambridge: Cambridge University Press, 2006.

Riegl, Alois. *Historical Grammar of the Visual Arts*. Translated by Jacqueline E. Jung. New York: Zone Books, 2004.

———. *Problems of Style: Foundations for a History of Ornament*. Translated by Evelyn Kain. Princeton: Princeton University Press, 1992.

Riesman, Paul. *Freedom in Fulani Social Life*. Chicago: University of Chicago Press, 1977.

Rihani, Ameen. *Arabian Peak and Desert: Travels in Al-Yaman*. London: Constable, 1930.

———. *The Book of Khalid*. 1911. Beirut: Librarie du Liban, 2000.

Riis, Jacob. *How the Other Half Lives*. New York: Scribner, 1890.

Ringe, Donald. *The Pictorial Mode: Space and Time in the Art of Irving, Bryant, and Cooper*. Lexington: University of Kentucky Press, 1971.

Rogers, J. A. "Says Islam Faith Knows No Color Line." *Pittsburgh Courier*, June 25, 1927, A1.

———. "Words 'American Negro' Unknown to Arabs, Says J. A. Rogers." *Pittsburgh Courier*, April 16, 1927, 2.

Rogin, Michael Paul. *Black Face, White Noise: Jewish Immigrants and the Hollywood Melting Pot*. Berkeley: University of California Press, 1996.

———. *Fathers and Children: Andrew Jackson and the Subjugation of the American Indian*. New York: Knopf, 1975.

Rojas, Martha Elena. "'Insults Unpunished': Barbary Captives, American Slaves, and the Negotiation of Liberty." *Early American Studies: An Interdisciplinary Journal* 1, no. 2 (2003): 159–86.

Roundtree, Alton G., and Paul M. Bessel. *Out of the Shadows: The Emergence of Prince Hall Freemasonry in America*. Baltimore: KLR, 2006.

Said, Edward. *Beginnings: Intention and Method*. New York: Columbia University Press, 1975.

———. *Humanism and Democratic Criticism*. New York: Columbia University Press, 2004.

———. *Orientalism*. New York: Vintage, 1979.

Sarmiento, D. F. *Life in the Argentine Republic in the Days of the Tyrants; or, Civilization and Barbarism*. 1st American ed. of the 3rd Spanish ed. 1868. New York: Hafner, 1960.

Schuchardt, Hugo. *Pidgin and Creole Languages: Selected Essays by Hugo Schuchardt*. Translated by Glenn G. Gilbert. Cambridge: Cambridge University Press, 1980.

Schueller, Malini Johar. *U.S. Orientalisms: Race, Nation, and Gender in Literature, 1790–1890*. Ann Arbor: University of Michigan Press, 2001.

Schueller, Malini Johar, and Edward Watts. *Messy Beginnings: Postcoloniality and Early American Literature*. New Brunswick: Rutgers University Press, 2003.

Sells, Michael A., ed. *Desert Tracings: Six Classic Arabian Odes*. Middletown, CT: Wesleyan University Press, 1989.

———, ed. and trans. *Stations of Desire: Love Elegies from Ibn Arabi and New Poems*. Jerusalem: Ibis, 2000.

Sha'ban, Fuad. *Islam and Arabs in Early American Thought: The Roots of American Orientalism*. Durham, NC: Acorn, 1991.

Shakir, Evelyn. "Pretending to Be an Arab: Role Playing in Vance Bourjaily's 'The Fractional Man.'" *MELUS* 9 no. 1 (Spring 1982): 7–21.

Sharp, Granville. *The Just Limitation of Slavery*. London, 1776.

Shohat, Ella Habiba. *Israeli Cinema: East/West and the Politics of Representation*. Austin: University of Texas Press, 1989.

Silverman, Kenneth. *Edgar A. Poe: Mournful and Never-Ending Romance*. New York: HarperPerennial, 1992.

Sim, Katharine. *David Roberts R.A., 1796–1864: A Biography*. London: Quartet Books, 1984.

Slotkin, Richard. *Regeneration through Violence: The Mythology of the American Frontier, 1600–1860*. Middletown, CT: Wesleyan University Press, 1973.

Spivak, Gayatri Chakravorty. "Postcoloniality and Value." In *Literary Theory Today*, edited by Peter Collier and Helga Geyer-Ryan. New York: Routledge, 1997.

Stansell, Christine. *American Moderns: Bohemian New York and the Creation of a New Century*. New York: Holt, 2001.

Stephens, John Lloyd. *Incidents of Travel in Egypt, Arabia Petraea, and the Holy Land*. 1837. New York: Dover, 1996.

Streeby, Shelly. *American Sensations: Class, Empire, and the Production of Popular Culture*. Berkeley: University of California Press, 2003.

Suleiman, Michael W. "The Mokarzels' Contributions to the Arabic-Speaking Community in the United States—Naoum and Salloum Mokarzel, Publishers of Arabic-Language Newspapers in the United States." *Arab Studies Quarterly*, Spring 1999.

Thessiger, Wilfred. *Arabian Sands*. 1959. New York: Penguin, 2008.

Thompson, G. R. "Romantic Arabesque, Contemporary Theory, and Postmodernism: The Example of Poe's *Narrative*." *ESQ* 35, nos. 3–4 (1989): 163–272.

Trafton, Scott. *Egypt Land: Race and Nineteenth-Century Egyptomania*. Durham: Duke University Press, 2004.

Tuetay, C. G., ed. and trans. *Classical Arabic Poetry: 162 Poems from Imrulkais to Ma'ari*. London: Kegan Paul, 1985.

Turner, Frederic Jackson. *The Frontier in American History*. New York: Holt, 1920.

Turner, Richard Brent. *Islam and the African-American Experience*. Bloomington: Indiana University Press, 1997.

Tyler, Royall. *The Algerine Captive*. 1797. New York: Modern Library, 2002.

U.S. Congress, Senate, Committee on Application of Hamet Bashaw. *Documents Respecting the Application of Hamet Caramanelli, Ex-Bashaw of Tripoli*. Washington, DC: Duane and Son, 1806.

Vidler, Anthony. *The Architectural Uncanny: Essays in the Modern Unhomely*. Cambridge: MIT Press, 1994.

von Hagen, Victor Wolfgang. Introduction to *Incidents of Travel in Egypt, Arabia Petraea, and the Holy Land*, by John Lloyd Stephens. 1837. New York: Dover, 1996.

von Hallberg, Robert. "Edgar Allan Poe, Poet-Critic." In *Nineteenth-Century American Poetry*, edited by A. Robert Lee, 80–98. New York: Barnes and Noble, 1985.

von Mücke, Dorothea. *The Seduction of the Occult and the Rise of the Fantastic Tale*. Stanford: Stanford University Press, 2003.

Wallace, Maurice O. *Constructing the Black Masculine: Identity and Ideality in African American Men's Literature and Culture, 1775–1995*. Durham: Duke University Press, 2001.

Ware, William. *Zenobia; or, The Fall of Palmyra*. New York: Francis, 1838.

Weinberger, Eliot. *Karmic Traces*. New York: New Directions, 1993.

Wentworth, Harold, and Stuart Berg Flexner, eds. *Dictionary of American Slang*. New York: Crowell, 1960.

Wheatley, Phillis. "To Rev. Samson Occam, New London, Connecticut" (February 11, 1774). In *The Norton Anthology of American Literature*, vol. A, edited by Nina Baym. New York: Norton, 2003.

Wheelan, Joseph. *Jefferson's War: America's First War on Terror, 1801–1805*. New York: Carroll and Graf, 2003.

Wheeler, Roxann. *The Complexion of Race: Categories of Difference in Eighteenth-Century British Culture*. Philadelphia: University of Pennsylvania Press, 2000.

Whitman, Walt. *Specimen Days and Collect*. 1883. New York: Dover, 1995.

Williams, William Carlos. *In the American Grain*. 1925. Reprint, New York: New Directions, 1956.

———. *Paterson*. New York: New Directions, 1946.

Wilson, Peter Lamborn. *Sacred Drift: Essays on the Margins of Islam*. San Francisco: City Lights Books, 1993.

Winthrop, John. "A Modell of Christian Charity." In Winthrop Papers, edited by Alley Forbes et al., Massachusetts Historical Society, Boston.

Wise, M. Norton. "What Can Local Circulation Explain? The Case of Helmholtz's Frog-Drawing Machine in Berlin." *Journal of the History of the Science of Technology* 1 (Summer 2007): 15–73.

Wright, Louis B., and Julia Macleod. *The First Americans in North Africa*. Princeton: Princeton University Press, 1945.

Yothers, Brian. *The Romance of the Holy Land in American Travel Writing, 1790–1876*. Aldershot, UK: Scolar, 2007.

Young, Jason R. "Between the Crescent and the Cross: W. E. B. DuBois on Christianity and Islam." In *The Souls of W. E. B. DuBois: New Essays and Reflections*, edited by Edward J. Blum and Jason R. Young. Atlanta: Mercer University Press, 2009.

Žižek, Slavoj. *The Sublime Object of Ideology*. Lincoln: University of Nebraska Press, 1986.

Index

About the Author

Jacob Rama Berman is Assistant Professor of English Literature and Comparative Literature at Louisiana State University.